EMOTION, RESTRAINT, AND COMMUNITY IN ANCIENT ROME

CLASSICAL CULTURE AND SOCIETY

Series Editors
Joseph Farrell and Ian Morris

Emotion, Restraint, and Community in Ancient Rome
Robert A. Kaster

EMOTION, RESTRAINT, AND COMMUNITY IN ANCIENT ROME

Robert A. Kaster

OXFORD

UNIVERSITY PRESS

2005

OXFORD

UNIVERSITY PRESS

Oxford University Press, Inc., publishes works that further
Oxford University's objective of excellence
in research, scholarship, and education

Oxford   New York
Auckland   Cape Town   Dar es Salaam   Hong Kong   Karachi
Kuala Lumpur   Madrid   Melbourne   Mexico City   Nairobi
New Delhi   Shanghai   Taipei   Toronto

With offices in
Argentina   Austria   Brazil   Chile   Czech Republic   France   Greece
Guatemala   Hungary   Italy   Japan   Poland   Portugal   Singapore
South Korea   Switzerland   Thailand   Turkey   Ukraine   Vietnam

Copyright © 2005 by Oxford University Press, Inc.

Published by Oxford University Press, Inc.
198 Madison Avenue, New York, New York 10016

www.oup.com

Oxford is a registered trademark of Oxford University Press

Library of Congress Cataloging-in-Publication Data
Kaster, Robert A.
Emotion, restraint, and community in ancient Rome / Robert A. Kaster.
p.   cm. — (Classical culture and society)
Includes bibliographical references and index.
ISBN-13 978-0-19-514078-1
ISBN 0-19-514078-8
1. Latin literature—History and criticism.   2. Emotions in literature.   3. Literature and
society—Rome.   4. Ethics, Ancient, in literature.   5. Self-control in literature.   6. Upper
class in literature.   7. Community in literature.   8. Rome—In literature.   9. Upper class—
Rome.   I. Title.   II. Series.
PA6029.E56K37 2005
870.9'353—dc22   2004014386

Publication of this book was made possible in part by a grant from the Magie Fund
of the Department of Classics, Princeton University.

2 4 6 8 9 7 5 3 1
Printed in the United States of America
on acid-free paper

For Laura

PREFACE

"So what are you working on these days?"

"Oh, shame, disgust, envy, and regret."

"Ah, the story of my life."

In the course of writing this book, I heard that last comment so often that I appropriated it and made it part of my own reply ("Oh, shame, disgust, envy, and regret—you know, the story of my life"). None of this was meant very seriously, of course; yet I was clearly onto a topic that—unlike, say, the Roman grammarians of late antiquity—had some resonance with other people's experience. And, in fact, I had stumbled onto it as an offshoot of my own experience.

It was an experience that, all things considered, I would gladly have forgone, or so I felt at the time. In 1996, when I was president of the American Philological Association, it happened that some members of the Association, a faction, really, behaved in ways I thought shameful, and I wanted to acknowledge the fact in the presidential address that I was required to deliver at the year's end. Because I could not refer to the behavior directly, for a range of reasons, I hit upon the idea of talking about the Roman version of shame: I could thereby meet the obligations of the occasion—by custom, part scholarly lecture, part protreptic address—and at the same time allude to the events that had inspired me.[1] I thought that I succeeded, in so far as several people who had reason to know what I was talking about indicated that they knew what I was talking about; and in any case I came to see that the Roman versions of shame and some other familiar emotions opened a fascinating prospect for further investigation.

A fair amount of time has passed since then, not all of it spent in the pleasures of research. But that, as I've come to see, has been all to the good; for this has proved to be the sort of project that needed time, for my own thoughts to come into focus and for me to gain at least a working knowledge of contemporary approaches to the study of the emotions in other fields, where there has been an explosion of interest in the past twenty to thirty years. Within the field of Classics, too, there has been a serendipitous convergence of interests such that only a crystal ball could have foreseen in 1996: the major works on "ancient emotions" then available—I think primarily of Cairns 1993 (on *aidôs* in Greek thought and literature), Barton 1993 (on the place of "despair" and "envy" in Roman imperial culture), and Nussbaum 1994 (on the "therapy of desire" in Hellenistic philsophy)—have since been joined by the those of Cooper (1999), Sorabji (2000), Barton, Harris, Konstan, and Nussbaum (all 2001), Graver (2002), and Toohey (2004), to mention only book-length studies, as well as the collective volumes edited by Braund and Gill (1997), Sihvola and Engberg-Pedersen (1998), Konstan and Rutter (2003), and Braund and Most (2003). As a result, my initial study of "the shame of Romans," which I described at the time as "a very preliminary sort of sketch," has proved to be far more preliminary—not to say, inadequate—than I expected, as the project has taken me in rewarding directions I did not imagine when it began and taught me far more about emotions, and the relations between emotions and language, than I could have anticipated.

The book was begun at Chicago and completed at Princeton, the yin and yang of great universities: to have been associated with both seems more good fortune than any one person deserves. From the beginning to the end my work has been supported by several other splendid institutions: at Oriel College, Oxford, where I spent a term as a visiting fellow on leave from Princeton, in 1999, I first began to see the shape that the book would have to take, and it is a pleasure to thank once again the Provost and Fellows of the College, and especially Chris Kraus, for the privilege of being among them; then, in 2003–2004, another semester's leave from Princeton and a fellowship from the National Endowment for the Humanities allowed me to put the pieces together at the Institute for Advanced Study, where—thanks above all to Glen Bowersock and Heinrich von Staden—I enjoyed a sublimely intense year as a visitor. Less directly, the Packard Humanities Institute has also been responsible for making this book possible— or, at least, possible sooner—for without its CD-ROM #5.3 I would not have completed the basic research until I was far into my dotage. And once again, the good people at Oxford University Press—especially Elissa Morris and Keith Faivre—have provided all the support an author could want.

Earlier versions of chapters 4 and 5 were published, respectively, in *Envy, Spite, and Jealousy: The Rivalrous Emotions in Ancient Greece* (Edinburgh: University of Edinburgh Press, 2003) and *Transactions of the American Philological Association* 113 (2001): my thanks to David Konstan and Keith Rutter for organizing the conference that provoked the former and to Cynthia Damon for her exemplary work as editor in seeing the latter into print. Another stimulating conference on the emotions, organized by Ruth Caston at the University of California at Davis in May 2003, caused me to write the initial version of chapter 3; and all of the preceding, in various forms, together with early drafts of chapters 1 and 6, were tried out on audiences at Brown, Bryn Mawr, Chicago, Columbia, Cornell, CUNY, Fordham, Johns Hopkins, Penn, Oxford, and Yale: I'm grateful to colleagues on all these occasions for their conversation, correction, and encouragement. At different stages, Matt Roller and Jaap Wisse gave me helpful readings of chapter 5, as did Tony Long and Michael Nylan of chapter 6; and Rebecca Langlands kindly let me see some of her work on *pudicitia* in advance of publication. And I received much good advice—more, I know, than I took—from friendly critics who read all or most of a completed draft: Ruth Caston, Joy Connolly, Margaret Graver, Laura Kaster, David Konstan, Martha Nussbaum, and Peter White. Thanks to Peter's good sense, too, I also came to realize when it was time to stop.

Finally: this book is dedicated to Laura, my wife now of thirty-five years, for more reasons than I can say. But here are three: because she did not let me use a colon in the title; because she persuaded me some years ago to write as though I were talking with her—which is to say, with a generous, honest, and intelligent friend; and because—though I have been lucky enough to know many good people—she is the best.

Robert A. Kaster
Princeton, New Jersey
22 June 2004

CONTENTS

EMOTION, RESTRAINT, AND COMMUNITY IN ANCIENT ROME

INTRODUCTION

And so, in the time before we ourselves can recall, the way of our fathers on its own produced men of surpassing merit, and exceptional men held fast the ancient way and our ancestors' principles. . . . [But now] because of our faults . . . we maintain our community in name only, having lost it in fact long ago.

The race of Saturn was a just race, not because of coercion or laws but of its own accord, and it knew restraint from the ways of the ancient deity.

Not yet had human wickedness put Justice to flight (she was the last of The Ones Above to leave the earth), and in place of fear the very sense of shame kept the people in line, without force.

Nor was there need for rewards when honorable ends were by their very nature sought; and since people desired nothing contrary to established custom, they were forbidden nothing through fear of punishment. But after the principle of equality was stripped away, and ambition and force strode about in place of restraint and shame, forms of lordly power arose, and they remained, among many nations, forever.[1]

The ancients once knew paradise, and they threw it away for the sake of trash. Or so went the story the Romans told themselves, time and again, in various forms: how an easy and unforced virtue allowed a cooperative community of just, pious, and rugged equals to flourish, content with little, and how that community fell from virtue, as though from grace, to compete for dominion, to cultivate factions and division, and to need the curb of law.[2] Different versions of the story put the fall at different times and attribute it to different proximate causes, but on two key points they all agree. The flaw was not an appetite for too much knowledge, as it was in Eden, but an appetite for just too much—too much wealth, too much luxury, too much power, too much "me, ME, ME." And the source of the flaw lay not with a Tempter but in themselves.

3

Now, we can be pretty certain that these stories tell us less about some Edenic reality in the Roman past than they do about the values and yearnings of the story-tellers as they faced their grubby present. But the stories do raise an interesting question: what is the psychology of paradise? If people act rightly, in accordance with seemingly self-chosen norms, without the threat of force or law, why do they do that, and what is going on in their minds when they do? Put in the latter form especially, the question gains some historical traction, because it is plain that—like many if not most people today—many if not most Romans *did* behave that way at least a fair amount of the time. In that respect, the psychology of paradise does bear on human lives as they are lived in real time, and it has some bearing, too, on how we understand the Romans and their culture.

So this book is an expedition in cultural psychology: its primary goal, broadly stated, is to understand at least some of the interplay between the emotions and the ethics of the Roman upper classes (roughly, the male members of the senatorial and equestrian orders and their families) in the late Republic and early Empire. The focus falls on the often unreflecting and unarticulated ways in which people adopt norms as they grow up in a culture and the ways in which emotions, and talk about emotions, reinforce those norms. The more specific questions before us are these: how (in the Roman view) is virtuous behavior shaped by the emotions, especially those stirred by self-consciousness and the regard of (and for) others? how in particular do various Roman forms of fear, dismay, indignation, and revulsion support or constrain different sorts of ethically significant behavior? what are the specific domains of the several emotions on which we will concentrate, and how do they intersect, overlap, or complement one another? and how does their interaction create an economy of displeasure, a system that causes negative feelings to circulate in constructive ways?[3]

In short, our expedition has as its quarry a cluster of bad vibes, of a particular sort—not those that move me to lash out, to take vengeance by wounding or annihilating some offending other (feelings of "anger," "hatred," or the like), but those of a generally quieter, socially useful strain that, by exerting a normative pressure, aim to prevent or correct the offense: by giving off these vibes, or by turning them upon myself, I do my bit to realize the peaceful, unified, and righteous community of the folktale. In our search, we first examine two emotions that mobilize self-consciousness in ways that are closely related yet distinct: these are the emotions to which the labels *verecundia* and *pudor* (roughly, worried regard or respect and shame) are usually attached. We then consider the emotion usually labeled *paenitentia* (roughly, regret) that focuses displeasure on—among other things—my own shortcomings, followed by two emotions that focus displeasure on—among other things—the shortcomings of others, one of them a form of hostility, the other a form of revulsion (the emotions usually labeled *invidia* and *fastidium*, respectively). A brief epilogue then offers some reflections on what Romans of the elite meant when they spoke of being ethically whole (*integer*) or of possessing the virtue of ethical wholeness (*integritas*): as we will see, the virtue—though rather different from the modern virtue of integrity to which it gives a name—is not unrelated either to the emotions that are the book's main subject or to the paradise of a stable community.

Now, the questions noted here are certainly not the only questions that could be asked about the links between Roman emotions and Roman ethics, and the emotions we examine are certainly not the only sort that work to preserve community (various Roman forms of love and pity, to name only the most obvious, play a crucial role, as well);[4] but those questions, and the emotions tested by them, seemed sufficient for this one book. And, because the book asks such questions, it necessarily takes on board another large set of issues that provide a second major theme, involving questions of method. I hinted at these issues in speaking of "various Roman forms" of feelings to which we and the Romans customarily attach certain (different) labels: I intended there to suggest not only that Roman and English emotion-labels differ in their coverage and application but also that emotions and the labels that get attached to them are in important ways distinct. Let me bring these issues into focus now by way of two anecdotes.

Late in the pages of Apuleius's *Metamorphoses*, an upright young man finds himself in a terrible fix (10. 2–12). Having rejected the advances of his stepmother, a latter-day Phaedra, he is soon faced with a murder charge; for when the stepmother's biological son dies after intercepting a poisoned potion she intended for the stepson, the woman and a conniving slave frame the young man for the crime. On their telling of the story, it was the youth who made a pass at his stepmother and, angered by her response, took vengeance by poisoning the boy. This is the version that the slave perjuriously recounts in his testimony at the young man's trial, as the story builds to its climax (10. 7):

> Made indignant by his stepmother's *fastidium*, the young man had summoned [the slave] and, seeking vengeance for the insult (*iniuria*), had ordered him to murder her son, first offering a generous reward for his silence, then threatening him with death when he refused. The young man mixed the poison himself and gave it to [the slave] to administer; but when he came to suspect that [the slave] had neglected his office and had kept the cup as evidence for a criminal charge, he finally gave the boy the poison with his own hands.

The lying tale is awash in emotions, expressed and implied—the youth's indignation and desire for revenge, prompting his cajolements, angry threats, and fearful suspicions—but it starts from an emotion attributed to the stepmother, her *fastidium*: what, exactly, should the tale's audiences (we as read-

5

ers and, within the story, the jury) understand that she felt? How does that feeling fit into the transaction at the story's center? And how do we know?

Or, consider another story charged with strong feelings, this time an incident witnessed by the moralist Valerius Maximus on the island of Ceos while traveling with Sextus Pompeius, a governor of Asia under the emperor Tiberius in the first part of the first century CE.[5] In one of the island's towns, a very old and very distinguished lady had decided that it was time to die; following the local custom, she proposed to do so in public, by taking poison, having first given an account of her reasons to her fellow-citizens.[6] Because she "thought it very important that her death be made more distinguished by Pompeius's presence" ("mortem . . . suam Pompei praesentia clariorem fieri magni aestimaret"), she begged him to attend, and being a man of perfect *humanitas*, Pompeius did just that, first attempting to dissuade her from suicide, then respecting her resolve and allowing her to proceed. And so, arrayed in finery on a litter, she gratefully blessed Pompeius—"May the gods repay you because you did not feel *fastidium* at (the thought of) either urging me to live or watching me die" (". . . quod nec hortator vitae meae nec mortis spectator esse fastidisti")—then said her farewells to her family, took the poison with a steady hand, and reported its effects as it passed through her body, until her daughters performed the final duty of closing her eyes. Pompeius and Valerius left the scene stunned and deeply moved ("nostros [sc. oculos] . . . , tametsi novo spectaculo obstupefacti erant, suffusos tamen lacrimis dimisit"). But what, exactly, was the emotion—the *fastidium*—that the woman blessed Pompeius for *not* feeling? How (again) does that feeling fit into the transaction at the story's center? And how do we know?

I put the question concerning the *fastidium* common to these two stories—which (a dash of suspense now) we will revisit near the end of this book—as a way of posing a larger question: how can we understand, as fully and authentically as possible, the emotion-talk of another culture removed in time in a way that does not entail either simplification—by reducing the emotion to a convenient lexical package in our own language—or projection—by answering the question according to the emotion *we* might feel (whoever "we" might be) in the same circumstance? This question, of course, incorporates the question how one can appropriately translate a given emotion-term in a given setting ("scorn," for example, would be a reasonable, if oversimplifying, choice in both examples);[7] but it is broader than and distinct from just the concerns of lexical correspondence. Presenting one possible answer to this question is the second of this book's main goals.[8]

We can start from the fact that the Romans' language of emotions is not our own, that indeed no two emotion terms in either language map perfectly onto each other: their *amor* is not always and exactly our "love," their *odium* still less our "hate."[9] Of course, we can and must try to flesh out the lexical correspondences with appropriate supplements and nuances: we have only the

Romans' words (complemented occasionally by images), and the words must be our starting point. But an understanding that remained at the level of lexical correspondence would not be sufficient. Take the case of the emotion-term that figures in the examples, *fastidium,* the Latin word that most closely approximates the English term "disgust." In its most basic and straightforward application—for example, when used of creatures not burdened with self-awareness—the word denotes a feeling or reaction of aversion: so *fastidium cibi,* which can most aptly be translated as "aversion for food," is the expression used dozens of times by agricultural writers to describe the state or behavior of farm animals that go off their feed and by medical writers to describe the feeling of people who become ill and do not wish to eat.[10] "Aversion for food" is the first meaning that you will find given for the word in the *Oxford Latin Dictionary,* and that is right and fine as far as it goes. It does not, however, go very far, especially for the settings of greatest interest to most readers of classical Latin texts, where not only self-awareness but self-awareness deployed in personal and social interaction is crucial. Those are the contexts in which the dictionary's subentries branch out into disgust, contempt, fastidiousness, and a variety of other labels that all clearly converge on the idea of "aversion" but yet are significantly different from one another. How to understand that difference? And how to understand that that difference is a difference that exists only in English, because these meanings are all, in Latin, *fastidium?*[11]

We could, in effect, repeat the work of the lexica, reviewing the word's occurrences instance by instance—inquiring whether *fastidium* in a given case is disgust, or some milder form of aversion, or perhaps contempt, or scorn, and so on—in an attempt to devise criteria for making such distinctions. But the attempt (which I have made) would only lead us to realize that the process is, if not merely futile, then at least unsatisfactory. First, there is often little reason to think that one's own sorting would match that of other English-speakers (to say nothing of French-speakers, German-speakers, . . .), not just because there are very frequently insufficient clues in a given context to provide a sound basis for one's own sorting but especially because it is highly likely that no two English-speakers (et al.) will sort aversion vs. disgust vs. contempt vs. scorn in quite the same way. (Numerous conversations on the point leave me in no doubt of this.)[12] More important, such an approach only tends to replicate the impression conveyed by the lexica, that in any given place *fastidium* can mean only one of those sorted senses, that it just is disgust but not disdain or choosiness at the same time. (This is certainly false.)[13] Finally, and most important, the approach does not even touch the core problem: while my version of English might do its sorting this way and that, the Romans expressed no difference, no explicit sorting of any kind. It was all *fastidium* to them.

We can take this last fact, then, to suggest that the Romans mapped this corner of their emotional terrain differently, including under the single heading *fastidium* a cluster of affective experiences that we (English-speakers)

7

currently distinguish by a variety of terms, and the different sort of mapping that *fastidium* accomplishes will be a recurrent feature, in one way or another, of all the other emotion-talk that will engage us. (The divergent mappings of Latin and English are of course not limited to emotion terms.) To explore this fact, then, I propose that we suspend concern with lexical meaning or equivalence and instead think about all such talk just as the end-product of a process that engages body and mind together: any emotion-term is just the lexicalized residue of what happens when the data of life are processed in a particular way—through a sequence of perception (sensing, imagining), evaluation (believing, judging, desiring), and response (bodily, affective, pragmatic, expressive)—to produce a particular kind of emotionalized consciousness, a particular set of thoughts and feelings.[14]

Let me elaborate briefly some elements of this proposal with reference to the sort of experience central to this book: the conscious experience of an occurrent emotion.[15] By "lexicalized residue" I mean that if you are a Roman monitoring your emotions, you will register the playing out of this process by saying (for example) "*hui! fastidium!*" Typically, you will also link this registering closely with the last stage of the process, the response, and in particular a bodily response (say, gagging and/or nausea), or an affective response (say, upset and/or disdain), or a pragmatic response (say, an actual turning away), or some combination of these. The emotion properly understood, however, is the whole process and all its constituent elements, the little narrative or dramatic script that is acted out from the evaluative perception at its beginning to the various possible responses at the end. Subtract any element of the script, and the experience is fundamentally altered: without a response (even one instantly rejected or suppressed), there is only dispassionate evaluation of phenomena; without an evaluation (even one that does not register consciously), there is a mere seizure of mind and body that is *about* nothing at all.[16]

There are at least two advantages in approaching emotions in terms of narrative processes or scripts. First—and as others have seen before me—it allows us to think and talk about emotions in language that does not itself rely on emotion-talk: we can thus more directly get at what a given form of emotion is about without becoming embroiled in the tedious regress of defining emotion-terms via other emotion-terms that in turn need definition.[17] Second, the method is consistent with current thought on the nature of emotions, as it has developed over a range of disciplines in the past generation. In that time, cognition, the way we acquire knowledge and form judgments and beliefs based on our perceptions and memories, has been returned to a place in the spotlight—the place that it enjoyed in (for example) Stoic thought on emotions in antiquity—after it had been upstaged by evolutionary biology's concept of "hard-wired" emotions (innate responses acquired as genetically favored forms of adaptation) and by behavioral psychology's stress on the measurable elements of stimulus and response. (Cognitions cannot easily be quantified to produce data subject to a chi-square test.) Though there is still a range of opinion on the relation between, and the relative importance of, basic neurological structures and developmental biology (on the one hand) and the construction of emotions through education and socialization (on the other), it is uncontroversial that emotion's cognitive content is especially important in identifying the emotion that a person experiences, or is likely to experience, in a given setting, and in understanding why that emotion is matched with that setting.[18] Most important for the present project, returning the spotlight to cognition means that culture too—with its role in shaping judgments and beliefs and in giving us the emotion-talk by which we make our experiences intelligible—has regained a central place in the little drama that must be grasped as a whole.

This holistic approach, which conceives of any given emotion as "the unitary experience of the whole package deal"—from presentation of a phenomenon through evaluation to response—provides one of this book's cornerstones.[19] But—to return to the subject of emotion-talk—it is also true that "package deals" of somewhat different shapes and contents can have the same label attached to them, and in this respect many emotion-terms in both Latin and English behave alike. For example, the *amor* experienced by erotically engaged partners and the *amor* experienced by parents for children converged, for the Romans, on a cluster of responses (thoughts and feelings having to do with attachment, concern, and the like) that were sufficiently homogeneous to attract the the same label; similarly (but in English), my reaction to having a really great dinner and my reaction to having a good idea can comfortably accept the same emotional label—say, "joy" or "happiness"—because the experiences converge on a cluster of responses (thoughts and feelings having to do with contentment, satisfaction, and the like) that share a certain surface likeness.[20]

But, of course, erotic *amor* and parental *amor*, or the joy of good eating and the joy of good thinking, are not one and the same thing, either as psychophysical states or as scripts, the sequences of experience that include judgments, beliefs, and desires: the cluster of generally similar responses to which the label *amor* or "joy" gets attached is just the point on which the different scripts converge. The differences among the scripts can be variously drawn, and one of the most culturally interesting ways we can draw the differences is by considering how the relevant judgments, beliefs, and desires are constituted: what are their bases, aims, and implications, and how do they use some of the fundamental distinctions that we construct to make sense of the world—body vs. mind, or self vs. other, or right vs. wrong, or nature vs. culture?

Such questions are among the chief concerns of the book; but before we go on to pursue some answers, I should round off these introductory remarks by making plain what I think we can achieve through the approach sketched so far, what claims can fairly be made for it, and especially what limitations should be recognized. First, as already noted, this is a study above all of the social and cultural elite, from which emerged the people—for the most part male, wealthy, and "well-bred"—who wrote the texts on which we must rely: there is no obvious way to predict how (or whether) the emotional lives of nonelites were very different, and not much evidence that the elites themselves thought they were (save perhaps in thinking that a "sense of shame" was a luxury the poor could not afford),[21] but my references to "the Romans" necessarily do not embrace *all* the Romans. Similarly, and to a degree that is also unavoidable, this book is fundamentally about Romans *talking* about their emotional experience, or ascribing such experience to others, for the most part in the poised discourse of carefully crafted texts. We plainly cannot get at the unmediated character of the experience itself; equally plainly, not everyone who talks about experiencing a certain emotion can be taken actually to experience it, and still less can everyone to whom a certain emotion is ascribed be taken to feel it—to say nothing of fictional characters, to whom emotions are regularly ascribed though they have no actual capacity for feeling at all.

Fortunately, because of the stress placed here on emotions' cognitive content and the structures of thought that shape emotional scripts, such considerations do not raise serious obstacles. When I say to a friend, "Damn, Jack, I really envy that new car of yours!" or "You know, Jack, Jim is so envious of your promotion he's eating his heart out," Jim or I may or may not be experiencing the psychophysical effects associated with envy (if Jack is my friend, I'm probably not, but one never knows about Jim). The structure of the underlying thought, however, and the kind of evaluation it conveys are in each case same as they would be were Jim's or my feelings fully engaged: the statements are therefore intelligible, plausible, and accessible for analysis in a way that would not be true were I to say, "You know, Jack, Jim is so pink at your promotion he's eating his hair." For our purposes, it is the structure of the thought and the presumed evaluation that matter most.[22]

Relatedly, it is a kind of limitation that we are concerned almost exclusively with scenes of emotion where specific and explicit emotion-talk is used; for it is obviously not the case that texts (in any language) represent emotions only when emotion-terms are present, and neither is it the case that the emotion terms here considered are the only terms associated with the relevant scripts.[23] But for all that this is not a very short book, these are just the first steps that we are taking, and these steps can lead to broader views: when we understand the basic structures of thought and behavior that converge on a given emotion-term, and when we understand how those structures are related both to each other and to the structures associated with other terms, we can claim with greater confidence to understand—through Roman eyes, and not through the filter of our own sensibilities—scenes built upon the same structures, even when they happen to be devoid of emotion-talk.

A final important dimension of the book, and at least in a strict sense another limitation, is its chronological range. As remarked at the outset, we are concerned with the late Republic and early Empire—primarily, the first century BCE and first century CE, with excursions into the second centuries on either side. We will not extend our range much later, because the rise of Christianity surely reflects and produces changes in cultural psychology that deserve a book to themselves; nor will we directly take in the early and middle Republic, because we do not have the grounds on which to reconstruct the emotional experience of (say) the heroic general Quintus Fabius Maximus at the end of the third century BCE, much less of the semilegendary Camillus two centuries earlier. The evidence that we do have, of what their posterity assumed the emotional experience of such figures would be, is instead useful for understanding that posterity: when Livy (say) attributes an emotion to Maximus, with the structure of thought that the attribution implies, we are justified in assuming that the emotion and the thought made cultural sense to Livy and his contemporaries, whatever the ancient general himself would have thought and felt.

Finally, it is worth stressing that, for the period with which we are centrally concerned, the fundamental emotional scripts examined, as they are represented in the speech of the literate elite, do not (with one exception to be noted shortly) undergo significant change. Despite many profound alterations in social and political life, the basic structures abide: the "Roman revolution" did not entail a revolution in affect. This is, frankly, not a conclusion I quite anticipated, in so stark a form, when I began work on this book. But, as I learned more about the emotions as human phenomena, and about the specifically Roman versions of them in context, the deep conservatism of their structures made this outcome seem unsurprising, indeed expectable.

There are two reasons for this. First is the matter of time-scale. A man who as a youth had fought with the great Marius to turn back the Cimbri at Vercellae (101 BCE) might in old age have known a boy who would live to see the dread imperial minister Sejanus fall at Rome (31 CE); he, in turn, could have heard the schoolboy exercises of a poet who would later praise the reign of Trajan (98–117 CE). That significant affective change would sweep the elite of a profoundly traditional society in so short a time is improbable on its face. To consider the matter from another way around: in the nearly one hundred years since "the long nineteenth century" ended with the Armistice of November 1918, culture and society in North America (though of course not only North America) have seen—in communications, travel, warfare, commerce, education, health and human welfare, the structures of family and community, the arts and religion, and our conceptions of the self: in short, every consequential aspect of human life—upheaval and change that make the Romans' shift from Republic to Principate look like a placid sleeper's turn from side to side in the course of an afternoon's nap. Yet, in that time, while the prominence of (say) our shame or regret may have waxed or waned in the constellation of emotions, and while the actions or states of affairs that provoke these emotions may have shifted this way or that, as some new ones came into being while others passed away, the basic structures of thought that make shame and regret identifiable as such have remained the same. In much the same way, though the coming of the Principate no doubt introduced new occasions on which members of the elite might experience their versions of shame and regret, while older occasions passed away with the passing of the Republic, it was the circumstantial content of the behavior that changed, not the pertinent evaluations and feelings: as we shall see, for example, the younger Pliny expresses anxiety at the shame (*pudor*) he might experience should a protégé suffer electoral defeat (*repulsa*) because it will appear that he, Pliny, misled the emperor in making certain guarantees while pressing his patronage of the candidate; though this basis for concern would have had no very close counterpart in Cicero's day, we can be certain that *repulsa* was no less a cause of *pudor*—the pain experienced at seeing oneself seen as devalued—just as success was equally a cause of pleasure.[24]

Emotions, or anyway how we conceive and speak of them, do change, and some can even be said to come into being and pass away. *Acedia*—most familiar as Sloth, the misleading label that it wears among the Seven Deadly Sins—was a debilitating affective state, embracing not just idleness but despair and sadness as well, which seemed to come into being as a distinct emotion in late antiquity and to pass out of existence again with the waning of the Middle Ages, so that it can now be called "extinct."[25] But we do not put off and take on forms of emotion as we might doff last year's fashions in favor of the new: the shifts are very slow (think of the three centuries, and the cultural chasm, that separate Robert Burton's "melancholy" from that of George Norton),[26] and they often require jolts from outside the cultural context in which the emotions are embedded.

Which brings us to the other, still more important reason why we should not expect great change to be a feature of the story I am about to tell. For, in the history of Rome's empire—the seven centuries that followed Hannibal's defeat, let's say—the most profound and consequential change was not the emergence of the Principate, for all its importance, but the rise and spread of Christianity. Compared with the cultural changes that followed in the latter's wake, the Roman elite's accomodation of the Principate amounted to not much more than a rearranging of the mental furniture, an adjustment that could be made using the cultural and psychic materials at hand.[27] It is accordingly not surprising that the one notable change we will see—in the explicit conception of *paenitentia* as what we would call remorse—is precisely a product of Christianity.[28]

But even this change did not mean that other, older structures of thought were simply superseded. Rather, the new conception was just added as one more option to the emotional repertoire that interests us. Let's turn, then, to consider that repertoire, and to try to understand the first of its components.

1

Between Respect and Shame

Verecundia *and the Art of Social Worry*

The epitaph of the Republican poet Pacuvius (ca. 220–130 BCE) is preserved
by the scholar and littérateur Aulus Gellius, who presents it to us as "*verecundus*
and pure in the highest degree, and worthy of [the poet's] superbly discrimi-
nating dignity (*elegantissima gravitate*)":

> Young man, though you're in a hurry, this bit of stone
> asks you to look at it, and then to read what's written:
> here lie the bones of Marcus Pacuvius, poet.
> I didn't want you to be unaware of this. Fare well.[1]

Gellius was nothing if not keen for words, so it should be worthwhile to consider what makes him think this inscription—which is to say, the man for
whom it speaks—"*verecundus* in the highest degree." Pretty plainly, the trait
has to do with the way the poem negotiates what in other hands could be an
importunate request for attention: "Hey there, look at me!" I suggest that
three moves are crucial to the negotiation in this case. First, we see the restrained and unassertive terms used to refer to the self that is making the
request: initially, in a common conceit of epitaphs, the stone itself, here a
mere, diminutive *saxulum*, and then the poet, whose presence is marked in
seven simple words that state his identity in conventional terms without
trumpeting his achievement ("hic sunt poetae Pacuvi Marci sita / ossa")—
a reticence that contrasts strongly with the epitaph of another Republican
poet, Naevius, "full of Campanian arrogance," that Gellius quotes earlier in
the same chapter (1. 24. 2 *plenum superbiae Campanae*). Second, the speaking voice not only registers awareness of the addressee's circumstances—the
young passerby, caught up in a young man's haste—but also foregrounds that
awareness, suggesting that the other's circumstances are at least as important
as, and may well take precedence over, the interests of the person making the
request. Finally, that same concern for the other emerges at the inscription's
end, in the motive given for imposing on his attention: it was just an opportunity for the addressee to profit, by being relieved of some ignorance—"hoc
volebam, nescius ne esses."

It was this fine balance of self and other, I believe, that earned Gellius's approbation as *verecundissimum*, and it can be seen in many, many other texts. Here, briefly, are three other examples.

In narrating the end of Porsenna's attempt to restore the disgraced family of Tarquin the Proud to Rome (2. 15. 1–5), Livy tells us that a delegation sent by Porsenna to the senate received no reply; rather, that body hurriedly sent to Porsenna a delegation of its own, composed of all the most honored men from its midst (*missi confestim honoratissimus quisque ex patribus*). They did this (they explained to Porsenna when they arrived), not because they couldn't have just said to his ambassadors "What part of 'no' don't you understand?" but in order to put an end to the matter once and for all, lest in the midst of their mutually beneficial relations they be grievously upset by turns, Porsenna by requesting what the Romans could not grant, the Romans by having to say "no" to someone they wished to deny nothing. At that, Livy says, Porsenna was "vanquished by *verecundia*"—and in the transaction as it unfolded, that should be the Romans' *verecundia* no less than his own: for the Romans had scrupulously made plain their respect, both in selecting their noble delegates and in casting their refusal in terms that showed their sensitivity to Porsenna's own interests, thus allowing him to maintain face in relations generally marked more by cooperation than by confrontation; in response, Porsenna himself felt *verecundia*, which caused him to step back from pressing his point and to show respect to the Romans in his turn.[2]

Again from the early days of the Republic, Livy reports that, in 446, the consuls Titus Quinctius Capitolinus Barbatus and Agrippa Furius neither requested a triumph nor were offered one by the senate for their brilliant victory over the Volsci and Aequi. Because his sources gave no reason for this omission, Livy ventures a conjecture:

> because the senate [three years earlier, in 449] had denied a triumph to the consuls Valerius and Horatius, who had not only beat the Volsci and Aequi but also gained glory by ending the Sabine war, the [present] consuls felt *verecundia* (*verecundiae fuit . . . consulibus*) at requesting a triumph for half so great an accomplishment, lest the judgment appear to be personal rather than based on the merits of the case ("magis hominum ratio quam meritorum habita videretur"), even if their request were granted.[3]

In Livy's historical imagination, the consuls' *verecundia* must include two interlocking concerns: because any triumph they gained for themselves would appear to be less well deserved than the triumph that Valerius and Horatius were denied, their own honors would appear a bit lame at the same time that they compounded the insult already done to their predecessors by the senate's ad hominem snub—concerns that impel them to consider the others' position and, especially, to collaborate in maintaining the others' face, even at the price of forgoing what they themselves could rightfully claim. We can note, too, that by the time Livy makes his conjecture here, he has already characterized the senate's snubbing of Valerius and Horatius as malevolent (3. 63. 5 "maligne . . . decrevit"), has presented the two as being scrupulous in point of procedure (3. 63. 6–7), and has made plain both that they deserved to have a triumph decreed by the senate and that they were exemplary consuls in general, putting freedom (*libertas*) before their own material interests (*opes*: 3. 64. 3 ff.). In effect Livy has created for Valerius and Horatius the face that his conjecture allows Quinctius and Furius to save.

Third, and in contrast with public affairs of historical moment, a matter of domestic economy from the letters of the younger Pliny. It seems that Pliny's grandfather-in-law, Fabatus, at Ticinum, in northern Italy, wished formally to manumit some slaves, which he could do only before a magistrate. Not a problem, writes Pliny: if Fabatus will let Pliny intercede with his ancient and intimate friend Calestrius Tiro, he will arrange for Tiro to stop at Fabatus's place on his way to taking up a governorship in Spain.[4] Fabatus should just put aside his excessive *verecundia*, which in this case entails both thinking too much of the other's interests—in supposing it would be tiresome (*molestum*) for Tiro—and thinking too little of his own. Getting *verecundia* right means getting the balance of these interests right.

As the combined testimony of these texts suggests, *verecundia* animates the art of knowing your proper place in every social transaction and basing your behavior on that knowledge; by guiding behavior in this way, *verecundia* establishes or affirms the social bond between you and others, all of whom (ideally) play complementary roles. Most fully, this means that you will each gauge your standing relative to the others; you will each present yourself in a way that at least will not give offense—for example, by confrontation or importunity—and that preferably will signal your full awareness of the others' face, the character they wear in the transaction and the respect that that character is due; and you will stop short of overtly pressing your full claims, yet not be excessively self-effacing—not obliterate your own face, the character *you* are wearing and the respect that it is due.[5] This is the script, the sequence of interlocking motives and moves, that someone experiencing *verecundia*—a *verecundus* person—enacts; by enacting that script, the *verecundus* person draws a line for the self to observe, in settings where no such line is drawn by formal or external authority, where he or she must improvise a performance as a well-socialized person. Or so I argue in this chapter, in which we try to get a clear view of *verecundia*'s components and the cultural work that the emotion performs, before we move on in the next chapter to another, much more complex emotion of self-restraint and self-assessment, *pudor*. At the end of that chapter we will be in a position to consider the relation between the two.

Now, the anecdote from Pliny draws attention to and plays upon the ety-mological link between *verecundia* and the verb *vereri*, and so *verecundia*'s grounding in a kind of fear: to be *verecundus* is to feel, or to be disposed to feel, *vere-*, as being *iracundus* ("angry," "wrathful") is to feel, or to be disposed to feel, *ira*.[6] This fear is not dread or gut-wrenching anxiety, much less terror or panic. Rather, it is the fear suggested by the English words "wary" and "worry" (there is no etymological link among the three, *tant pis*): a mild and strategic sort of fear, which manifests itself above all in circumspection and the wish to avoid drawing attention to oneself in an improper way or to an improper de-gree.[7] As just indicated, this emotion can be experienced in two different forms, an "occurrent" form and a "dispositional" form; since this distinction will recur in all our discussions save one, it is worth pausing here a bit to clarify it.[8]

When I report that I am experiencing *verecundia* in its occurrent form, I mean to convey that I am experiencing a fully embodied worry about mishan-dling (in particular ways) a specific interpersonal transaction already in progress, a form of fearful self-consciousness that at least in some instances approximates our being and feeling flustered or embarrassed. By contrast, if I say that I am dispositionally a *verecundus* person (though, being such, I prob-ably would never say that), I mean that I tend as a general matter to be wary about mishandling (in particular ways) interpersonal transactions whenever they might occur: my self-description conveys that I am the sort of person much inclined to experience the occurrent form of *verecundia* and am habitually sen-sitive to contexts that arouse it. In this same way, *iracundia* (*iracundus*), in com-mon Latin usage, can convey either the disposition to feel *ira*—"irascibility," "wrathfulness"—or the occurrent emotion itself.

Now, though it is common to speak of an "emotional disposition" of a given sort or a "dispositional form" of a given emotion (as I do throughout), the dis-position itself is strictly just that, an inclination or tendency; it is not an expe-rience of the emotion—the sequence that runs from perception to reponse —and it has no particular feeling of its own. But such an inclination typically feeds, and is fed by, three other traits that do shape our experience of life in ways tied closely to feeling. Dispositionally fearful people (for example) are not only more inclined to experience occurrent fear than their bolder coun-terparts, they also are more inclined to imagine the potentially fearful aspects of life's circumstances; they more quickly imagine, too, the potential becom-ing actual, and they therefore more commonly feel a jolt of fear "as if" the potential were real, fear "at the very thought." (These traits together suggest why someone with no imagination would be unlikely to have any emotional dis-position at all.) And for the dispositionally joyful person, or the dispositionally *verecundus* person, exactly the same can be said, with only the appropriate changes in labels. Because the disposition so readily leads to an embodied ex-perience of the emotion proleptically, "at the very thought," the dispositionally *verecundus* person tends to live with the foretaste of this form of worry at the back of his throat, as the more generally fearful person chronically tastes a more generalized fear and as the dispositionally *iracundus* person lives with the fore-taste of anger: life habitually lived as one of these sorts of person (or as a sort that combines two or more of these sorts) simply "feels different" from a life lived as some other sort. It is such habituation, too, that causes emotional dispositions to be counted among the abiding ethical traits that we commonly call virtues and vices. That is one of the things meant by saying that the dispositional form of an emotion expresses what "sort of person" I am: it sorts me into an ethical category more reliably than any given occurrence of the fully embodied form that is prompted by a single judgment of one specific set of actual circumstances.[9]

However—and all that said—it is the structure of any given emotion's underlying thought that is our main concern here; because that structure is essentially the same in both the dispositional and the occurrent forms, the distinction between the two will not normally be at the center our discussion. So, to turn now to *verecundia* in action, we can say that the simplest social product of *verecundia* is what might be called "ignorability": not being invisible, quite, but being seen to claim the minimum amount of social space needed to carry out a given line of action.[10] This is a social virtue that most of us manage to practice most of the time—as when we amble down a city street without making a spectacle of ourselves or colliding with the odd passerby—and most of us acquire it early on—for example, when our parents teach us that speaking at top volume in an elevator is "not polite." In fact, as has often been observed, the modern elevator is a fine stage for observing this trait in action, as the occupants typically space themselves as far apart as possible, stand facing in the same direction to avoid eye contact, often break off conversations begun before entering the car, and generally mime a shared fascination with the display that marks the passing floors. Had the Romans known elevators, *verecundia* would surely have been mentioned in connection with their use.

Cultivating ignorability has two complementary aims that are also two of the basic effects of *verecundia*: avoiding offense to others, by avoiding improper assertion of the self. Were a fellow-passenger on our crowded elevator to extract a cell phone and begin a conversation in the braying tones that cell phones seem to require, I assume that the rest of us would consider him an offensive fool for claiming too much social space for himself while granting us too little: rather than being ignorable, he would force himself on our attention; rather than trying to minimize his own presence, he would treat us as though we were not there. Our estimation of him as a person—the minimal estimation, "competent adult," that we standardly grant strangers absent evidence to the contrary—accordingly would be lowered. These, too, are the concerns of *verecundia*, which monitors and restrains the self in order to avoid giving offense to others—and which by avoiding offense to others succeeds in protecting the self and its value. Cicero very helpfully makes these dynamics plain in his discussion of "appropriate actions," when he pairs *verecundia* with justice (*iustitia*) in discussing the respect—the *reverentia* (note here too the etymological link)—that should be paid to others and to their opinion of you: whereas it is the role of *iustitia* not to "violate" others—not to do them obvious, even violent, harm—it is the role of *verecundia* not to "offend" them.[11]

Implied here is that it fundamentally rests with the others to set the bounds of propriety and to define the degree to which, or the means by which, you can extend your self: you have offended me if *I* believe that you have offended me, and that means that you can never be completely sure before the fact—hence the wariness and the worry. This is one of the distinctions between *verecundia* and *iustitia*, insofar as the latter, concerned with *iniuria*, belongs more to the realm of objectively determinate violations and the workings of positive law. Not that *verecundia* is wholly indeterminate: if I go dancing naked through the forum just because I feel like it, I can be pretty certain that I will give offense and be considered *inverecundus* (and probably mad as well). But the boundaries of offensive behavior are much less clear than the boundaries of injustice and tend more to be established by the negotiation of each social transaction as it unfolds.

And so the wariness, the circumspection of *verecundia* must be constant and pervasive in all one's acts. Here is a *very* select catalog of behaviors—some obvious, others less so—in which a Roman speaker takes *verecundia* to play a role in restraining an agent from offensive self-assertion:

> —there is of course the *verecundia* displayed in not grabbing all the choicest morsels for yourself at the dinner table;[12]
> —but there is also the *verecundia* to be observed in using metaphors: you should be free of the extravagance that calls attention to itself and instead, like a person entering a "space that is not his own" (*alienus locus*), be conscious of being there on sufferance (*ut precario, non vi, venisse videatur*);[13]
> —there is the *verecundia* displayed in not blowing your own horn;[14]
> —and the *verecundia* displayed in not calling yourself a person's "friend" (thereby claiming equality) when you should properly say that you are his "client" (thereby acknowledging subordination);[15]
> —there is the *verecundia* displayed by nondogmatic skeptics, who stop short of claiming to know the truth;[16]
> —and there are the multiple forms of *verecundia* displayed in the courtroom, from not stalking about and invading the opponents' space to "bending over backwards," as we would say, to be fair when serving as a judge in a case where your own interests are at stake.[17]

Because the opportunities for offense are so rich and varied, the self-monitoring that *verecundia* entails is constant; because this constant monitoring makes it an emotion of self-attention and self-assessment—like our pride, shame, or embarassment—*verecundia* was understood by the Romans to differ from other forms of fear in the way it was embodied, being marked not by the pallor associated with *timor* or *metus* but by the blush associated with *pudor*.[18] But, having spoken so far in terms of "ignorability" and the avoidance of "offense," I should elaborate on the forms and consequences of this self-attention, lest I create the impression that *verecundia* was, and was regarded by the Romans as, an emotion confined to the realm of etiquette and mere politeness. That is far from being the case.

Social life, broadly understood, is the context in which *verecundia* operates: though there are many emotions that could readily be experienced by a lone castaway on a desert island—hope and fear most notably among them—he is not likely to experience *verecundia* unless some other poor devil is washed ashore with him. But, beyond being an emotion that social life prompts, *verecundia* itself is crucial to making social life possible. This role for the emotion was implied by Cicero's comments in *On Appropriate Actions* remarked earlier, and it is made explicit early in Book 2 of the same work: the gathering of humans in cities led to the creation of customs and formal law (*leges moresque constituti*), to equity and a fixed way of life (*iuris aequa discriptio certaque vivendi disciplina*); on these there followed the effects of what we call socialization—gentleness of spirit (*mansuetudo animorum*) and *verecundia*—and so the mutuality that makes life secure and supportable ("ut esset vita munitior atque ut dando et accipiendo mutandisque facultatibus et commodis nulla re egeremus").[19] The thought finds expression repeatedly, in one form or another, in Cicero's philosophical works, and it is a thought that shapes his practical advocacy as well, for example in his approach to attacking the reputation of an opponent in court. It is not something that he does readily, he says, but the circumstances require it, and so he will do it *verecunde modiceque*, with restraint and with proper regard for the face that both he and his opponent are wearing.[20] His own face is determined here by his relationship with his client, as a "loyal and reliable friend"; the attack he is about to deliver is both required by that relation and the means for making the relation plain in this context. His opponent's face, on the other hand, is determined by the relation he has to Cicero, as someone who has had no reason to judge Cicero a personal enemy before; the attack he is about to receive is both moderated by that relation and, in its moderation, intended to allow the relation to continue in its current mode. The mutuality of *verecundia*, the way that its wariness looks both to the self and to the other—to the extent of seeing the matter as the other sees it, as Cicero does here—is the essence of the emotion as a force of social cohesion. I cannot gauge where I stand relative to you unless I first consider where you stand; and while considering your standpoint does not strictly entail considering your viewpoint, it certainly exerts pressure in that direction.

The concern with face that we see here moving in both directions can have different emphases in different circumstances, being directed now more toward the self, now more toward the other. Sometimes the concern is predominantly with your own face, when what matters most is to avoid what a slightly archaic English turn of phrase calls "being out of countenance"—that is, having reason to be abashed. Quintilian illustrates this point when he connects *verecundia* with the job of advocates who find they must shade the truth in setting out and explaining the facts of a case in a way favorable to their side.[21] Some such "false expositions" rely on devices (*instrumenta*) external to the advocate's argument (for example, witnesses who provide a false alibi), while others rely solely on the wit (*ingenium*) of the advocate who makes up the story. That is where *verecundia* enters in: the crucial question is how big a whopper the advocate can tell without blushing—that is why (Quintilian adds in an etymological aside) this spinning of the facts is called a "color," because it can bring a blush to the cheeks. An advocate in that position, we can take it, could blush for one of two reasons, not mutually exclusive: becoming aware that others were looking at him (or anticipating that others would look at him) with frank disbelief, he would see himself being seen as a liar and so be unable to maintain the face of an honest man; or as the burden of falsehood became more than he himself could bear, he would see *himself* as a liar and so be unable to maintain the face of an honest man even in his own eyes.[22]

Let me give two other examples that involve similar dynamics, the first offered, again, by Quintilian. (That Quintilian, as a teacher of rhetoric, and the grammarian Servius are among the richest witnesses for understanding *verecundia* is not insignificant, given the role just such teachers played in socializing members of the elite in traditional virtue.)[23] When praising the vividness that Cicero lends his depiction of the corrupt governor Verres standing on the Sicilian shore—a disgraceful spectacle, "a praetor of the Roman people in sandals and a purple Greek cloak, his tunic extending down to his ankles, leaning on some bimbo" (*Verr.* 2. 5. 86)—Quintilian says that the depiction seems to make visible even details that it does not explicitly mention: certainly, Quintilian says, *I* seem to be able to make out the expression on the pair's faces, their looks, and their disgraceful endearments ("ego certe mihi cernere videor et vultum et oculos et deformes utriusque blanditias")—*and* not just that, but also the sentiments of those who were present to watch ("et eorum qui aderant tacitam aversationem ac timidam verecundiam").[24] The audience of the sordid scene is presumed by Quintilian to have felt—no doubt because he would have felt—revulsion (*aversatio*) and *verecundia*, a concern for their own face, which is affronted by being implicated in the scene at all. In essence, Verres' lack of *verecundia* causes the witnesses to experience *verecundia* of their own, as they see themselves being seen as the sort of people who could tolerate such a spectacle; seeing themselves being seen in this way endangers their face as decent people. But, because Verres was, after all, the praetor, actual confrontation is out of the question, and so their *aversatio* is silent (*tacita*), their *verecundia* timid (*timida*).

A second example, by contrast, expressly involves the threat to your face that results from failure to feel *verecundia* in the proper way. In one of his letters to Lucilius Seneca tells of riding in a rude country cart and blushing whenever he came upon an entourage with classier outfittings (*comitatus lautior*): in such circumstances, before such an audience, he became conscious of his face as a "gentleman," which he felt was under strain. The point of interest, however, is that to Seneca's Stoicizing mind it is the *wrong* face to begin with: as someone trying to make progress toward Stoic wisdom, he should not ascribe any value to externals—the rustic cart, the half-dead mules that pull it, or the muleteer's bare feet, all of which he catalogs—nor should he identify with them in any way. His blush is in this respect doubly motivated: the part of him that is not yet sufficiently Stoic feels distress because he is worried about maintaining the face of a conventional gentleman; by implication, the part of him that *wants* to be Stoic feels distress because he realizes that he is not maintaining the face of a sage, to whom the only important thing is the right action of his own mind. That is why Seneca here speaks of his sentiment as *perversa recti verecundia*, a "respect for what is right that has been turned on its head."[25]

But what of concern for the face of others? As I suggested earlier, in connection with Quintilian's response to Cicero's Verres, Quintilian imagines the onlookers' reaction by imagining how he himself would have felt had he been present to witness Verres' lack of *verecundia*: for that, in Quintilian's understanding, is the controlling element of the scene. Because Verres is incapable of feeling *verecundia*, he has no concern for his own face and so places no decent limits on his own behavior: he acts in a merely self-gratifying way, as gratification of the self happens to be defined at that moment. And, because he lacks concern for his own face, he has no concern for the face of others, either: were he aware of the onlookers as persons with their own claims to decency, he would not have made them witnesses to his behavior and in that respect implicated them in it. But, because the onlookers do (in Quintilian's imagination) possess this quality, *they* are more concerned with Verres' face than he is himself. They want to turn away, not only because they experience the feelings of decent people whose face has been implicated in disgrace but also because they experience the feeling that decent people have when confronted by another who is carelessly or willfully disgracing himself: the *verecundia* of "not knowing where to look," the form of the emotion comparable to our "being embarrassed for." As William Ian Miller remarks, "Our own embarrassment is often our best indication that we have judged others to be humiliating themselves": not looking such people in the face is the only means left to us for helping *them* save face—as we wish to do just because we are decent people—and so we avert our glance.[26]

We have seen concern for the position of others figure prominently in *verecundia* before, for example in Livy's account of the Romans' negotiations with

Porsenna. Here are two other examples from Livy, whose ear for this sensitivity was very well developed.[27] First, offering a mirror image to the dealings with Porsenna, there are the remarks Scipio Africanus is imagined making to Hannibal in their colloquy before the battle at Zama, when Scipio declares himself bound by no *verecundia* toward his opponent:[28] because Hannibal has not willingly sought peace, Scipio feels no need to avoid confrontation and no scruple in pressing his own interests to the full, and he has no concern for the interests and face of the other, as his peremptory tone by itself makes clear. The second, more elaborate example is drawn from Livy's vivid recreation of the debate, in 195 BCE, over legislation meant to curb spending on luxuries, when the women of Rome—against all custom—turned out en masse to protest in the forum and a shaken Cato the elder, as consul, had to make his way to the senate chamber through their midst. Having reached the safety of the curia, Cato has a few choice words to say about this "female upheaval" (*consternatio muliebris*), including remarks on the several ways in which it engaged his own *verecundia*. Having first reported that he could not pass through the forum in the midst of the massed array of women without blushing ("equidem non sine rubore quodam paulo ante per medium agmen mulierum in forum perveni"), he says that it was only the *verecundia* he felt before the dignity and decency of certain individual women—more than the *verecundia* he felt for the lot of them—that restrained him from rebuking them ("nisi me verecundia singularum magis maiestatis et pudoris quam universarum tenuisset, ne compellatae a consule viderentur"). And so he goes on to give them *in absentia* the scolding that his proper emotion kept him from giving them face to face.[29]

Cato's *verecundia* here is richly drawn and multidimensional. His own feeling, attested by his blush, is identical to the *verecundia* that Quintilian ascribed to the witnesses of Verres' unseemly display: by stepping beyond conventional restraints of decorum to gather in the forum, the women, like Verres, had shown no concern either for their own face as decent people or for the face of others; so Cato, like the onlookers, responds as someone who feels that his own face as a decent person has been put under strain. As in the case of Verres' audience, too, the self-regarding dimension of *verecundia* is paired with regard for the others, here explicitly: if Cato, as consul, *had* rebuked the women, their face would have been impaired, since they could not avoid seeing themselves being seen as what they would in fact have been—the sort of women whom a consul would rebuke. In this case, Cato seems to imply, his sensitivity toward the face of certain individuals overrode his responsibility as consul; in any event, his own sense of *verecundia* is presented as being fully active even when—or perhaps, especially when—the *verecundia* of the others was defective.[30]

So, in any given transaction where *verecundia* is in play, the explicit emphasis might fall more on the proper restraint of the self and the preservation of one's own face than on the proper attention to the other persons involved, or vice versa; but, standardly, both concerns are at least implied. In fact, the mutuality of the emotion, its two-way concern for face, is so pervasive that it occurs in contexts where we might not look for it, since our own cultural orientation is rather different.

Take nudity, for example. Romans of the elite long thought of themselves as being more reserved about nudity than Greeks, who they believed were ready to get naked on any pretext. In that regard, the Romans might seem very much like typical middle-class North Americans, whose anxiety at the thought of being seen naked in public shapes many a bad dream. But there is, I believe, a significant difference. My fear of being seen naked, as part of what we would call my "modesty," is above all self-protective: my anxiety over the impact your seeing me naked would have on me dwarfs any concern I might have for the ill effects that seeing me naked would have on *you*. In fact, there is often at least a tacit assumption that *you* would like nothing better than to see me naked (in dreams of being seen naked, the viewers are more or less explicitly figured as voyeurs). In that respect, the self-regarding character of our form of modesty has more than a touch of narcissism about it. Not so for the Romans, whose *verecundia* at the thought of nudity assumes that your seeing me naked would be as unpleasant and face-impairing for you as it would be for me. That is the assumption, for example, in the extended remarks on nudity that Cicero offers in *On Appropriate Actions*: in this connection (he says), human *verecundia* merely imitates the handiwork of *natura*, which has designed the human body in such a way that the parts that have an honorable appearance (*species honesta*) are put right where everyone can see them, while the parts that involve the necessities of nature, being ugly (*deformis*), are tucked away out of sight.[31] All the arguments in the passage, based as they are on a concern for decorum, approach the thought of nakedness from the point of view of the offended onlooker.[32] And Valerius Maximus, drawing on the same passage of Cicero, elaborates the thought.[33] Having just mentioned one form of *verecundia*—that felt by a wife for her husband's "greatness" (*maiestas*), a point to which we will return—he turns to another form—that which keeps adult male relatives from bathing in each others' presence—and he draws the moral: clearly the same profound scruple attaches to our relations by blood and marriage as attaches to our relations with the gods, for to expose yourself naked to either would entail the gravest disrespect.[34]

An emotion constructed in this way obviously is an important force of social control, regulating the behavior of free individuals in a civil community; and there are several components of the service *verecundia* performs in this regard that deserve emphasis, beginning with the words "free" and "civil." No slave is ever described as experiencing *verecundia*, presumably because slaves—at least according to the ideology of Roman slavery—have no autonomous volition, hence no actual self, hence no face to maintain or lose: there is, accordingly, no need for an emotion to draw a line that the nonexistent self ought not cross. Indeed, the one instance where *verecundia* is mentioned, prescriptively, in connection with slaves is the exception that proves the ideological rule: the jurist Ulpian (early third cent. CE) notes that though slaves are generally barred from bringing formal accusations against their masters, they can bring complaints before the praetor provided they do so under certain specific headings (of cruelty and the like), and provided they act with *verecundia* (*si verecunde expostulent*)—in a manner that shows that they know their place.[35] Similarly—and much more interestingly—soldiers experience *verecundia* not much much more frequently than do slaves. (By contrast, soldiers do very commonly experience *pudor*: we return to this contrast at the end of chapter 2.)[36] I take it that the lack of soldierly *verecundia* has less to do with the lack of a soldierly self than with the nature of the circumstances in which the self is active. *Verecundia* operates in circumstances where there is in principle a choice to be made as to whose interests will be put to the fore and whose will be restrained: as we have frequently seen, it implies a voluntary stepping back from pressing one's own interest (at a minimum) or a voluntary privileging of the interests of the other. For soldiers, however, issues of self-restraint, self-expression, and respect are not left to be sorted out by some haphazardly socialized emotion: the line that *verecundia* informally draws for us in civil society is more reliably drawn for the soldier by the chain of command and, ultimately, by the commander's *imperium*, his power to demand obedience (*obsequium*) on pain of death.

Slaves and soldiers aside, then, we are all called upon to exercise our *verecundia* to make our civil community a livable place. Even the emperor is expected to be *verecundus*, assuming he has any claim on being a "civil prince" (*princeps civilis*): as the younger Pliny tells Trajan again and again, his willingness to speak and walk with members of the senate, as merely one man among other men, is one of the traits that most distinguishes him from certain vile predecessors.[37] And, to the extent that the virtues of civil society are just the virtues of the household writ large, we can say that *verecundia* begins at home. It is certainly the case that the emotion is mentioned and discussed with special frequency in connection with those whose roles in the household are particularly important, though their capacities for self-control are thought to be underdeveloped relative to those of the adult male: I mean children and women.

The *verecundia* of the Roman child before the parent—and, above all, of the son before the father—is perhaps the archetypal case, always matching restraint of the self and concern for one's own face with concern for the interests and face of the other. This sort of *verecundia* begins to be represented with Plautus, and the representation extends the length and breadth of Roman literature:[38] the relationship is so common and familiar that just one example should suffice. In a letter to Minicius Fundanus, whose consulship he anticipated, Pliny promotes another friend's son, who would be a candidate for a quaestorship in the same year (*Ep.* 4. 15. 5–6): the son is a better man even than his father (*iuvenis . . . ipso patre melior*), Pliny thinks, and the father wants

Pliny both to think and to say that; but the son's own *verecundia* forbids such a thing ("nescio an dicam, quod me pater et sentire et dicere cupit, adulescentis verecundia vetat"). The son's willing subordination to the father, in the context of the letter of recommendation, adds one further guarantee that the man being commended is fundamentally the right sort of person; the fact that he is the right sort of person allows Pliny the conceit that he adopts, the suggestion that the father would be willing to have it said that his son outstrips him in excellence—which of course is the proper expression of paternal *verecundia* toward the son.[39]

The *verecundia* of women, by contrast, is somewhat more varied, but it is still largely confined to just three areas of behavior. Two of these we have already glimpsed. The first is the *verecundia* that restrained proper women from mixing themselves in the public concerns of men: it is not that Roman women were expected to keep themselves sequestered or behind the veil, but they were not supposed to involve themselves in business of the forum or the courtroom— and here the indignation that we heard Livy's Cato express earlier finds an echo not only in the moralizing of a Valerius Maximus but also, repeatedly, in the jurists of the *Digest*.[40] The second area in which a decent Roman woman experienced *verecundia* was in her relations with her husband, a point made with particular clarity in some remarks of Valerius Maximus at which we have already glanced.[41] When husbands and wives are at odds, Valerius tells us, they can go to the shrine of the goddess Viriplaca and take turns giving vent to all that's on their minds (*ibi inuicem locuti quae voluerant*); then they can return home from this therapy, in harmony (*concordes*) once again. Taking the goddess's name to be derived from "making husbands happy" (*a placandis viris*), Valerius makes plain what he means by "harmony" here. The spouses are *concordes* because each knows his or her proper place relative to the other: the wife pays *honos* to her husband, respecting his face as the greater party—that is, his *maiestas* (*virorum maiestati debitum a feminis . . . honorem*)—and the husband (it must be implied) respects his wife's face as the lesser party. In this way, they can remain "in affection's yoke on terms of parity" (*in pari iugo caritatis*)—the parity here being the complementarity of the arrangement, or perhaps its fairness in Valerius's eyes, obviously not its objective equality.

The third field of womanly *verecundia* was of course concerned with sexuality, where the emotion was allied to the chastity (*pudicitia*) that it served to protect; here again we are on very familiar ground.[42] A woman is expected to feel the restraint of *verecundia* whenever there is the prospect, or even mention, of sexual activity; if she does, she will remain *pudica*, a woman who engages only in licit forms of sex, in the appropriate circumstance, in appropriate ways, and with the appropriate person. That is why the *virgo*—the young woman of marriageable age who is not yet married—is closely associated with *verecundia*:[43] sex for her is a real possibility, as it is not for a mere child (*puella*), and still it is not yet permitted. That is also why a woman's nudity, when displayed anywhere to attract sexual attention, places a burden on *verecundia* over and above the queasiness already remarked of nudity in general: such a display threatens the *pudicitia*—their face as chaste persons—of both the woman being seen and the male who sees her.

As the *verecundia* of children and women suggests, the emotion often entails, and serves to reinforce, a hierarchical point of view: the self-restraint of the inferior parties, the respect they feel for their superiors, the virtue of knowing their place and keeping to it. And it is certainly true that many, probably most, instances of the emotion have what might be called a vertical orientation, as the person who experiences the emotion signals, by experiencing it, that he knows where he stands on the social pyramid: just some of the forms the emotion can take as a force of hierarchical ordering include the *verecundia* felt for the old by the young, for the *maiestas* of magistrates by private citizens, for literary authorities and other cultural *maximi viri* by people of ordinary attainments, for the rich by the poor, for the senate by the commons, for the gods by all right-thinking mortals.[44]

But, even where *verecundia* works to create hierarchy, it should not—in principle, as a matter of the sentiment's ideology—move in one direction only: the rich, for example, should respect the face of the poor and not simply oppress them (a moral taught with notable frequency in the declamatory themes of the rhetoric schools),[45] just as we've seen that *verecundia* works both ways in relations between father and son or husband and wife. Equally to the point, *verecundia* operates horizontally no less than vertically, since it is properly felt between people who are peers, or who are willing to behave as if they are. We have seen this in the *verecundia* that informs the pose of the *princeps civilis* as merely first among equals,[46] and we see it in the formula of politeness used when Cicero tells Brutus that if the essay on oratory that Brutus requested seems inadequate, it is perhaps because he, Cicero, imprudently took on too great a subject, out of the *verecundia* he felt at the thought of refusing (*verecundia negandi*)—for a refusal would have paid too little respect both to Brutus's face, as a friend entitled to make such a request, and to Cicero's own face, as an authoritative friend of whom such a request could be made.[47]

The *verecundia* between peers figures in less formulaic and more telling settings, too, as in the letter that Cicero wrote to Atticus in December of 61, when their relations were strained by the peevishness of Cicero's brother, Quintus, and his quarrels with his wife, Atticus's sister Pomponia.[48] After recounting to Atticus at some length how much he relies on his advice and conversation in all matters, Cicero adds that the *verecundia* of *both of them* has previously kept him from saying such things. Cicero does not elaborate, because of course one gentleman would know what another gentleman meant. I take it he means that speaking in such terms could betray a hint of condescension, framing Atticus in the role of mere adviser and supporter to the "great man" rather than his peer (earlier in the letter Cicero is at pains to stress, not really convincingly, that Atticus's choice of "tranquillity," *otium*, is honorable in a way parallel to his own "political striving," *ambitio*). But in the letter to which Cicero replies, Atticus, evidently provoked by Quintus's bad behavior, had catalogued the many services he had done for Cicero—something that (absent great provocation) *verecundia* would also normally keep a Roman gentleman from doing, out of concern for the beneficiary's face. And so Cicero feels that he must acknowledge all the benefits derived from his relations with Atticus, whatever the norms of gentlemanly restraint would usually enjoin.[49]

I hope now that I have made plausible my original claim, that *verecundia*, as an emotion, animates the art of knowing your proper place in every social transaction and binds the free members of a civil community, exerting its force both vertically, across the different ranks of society, and horizontally, among members of comparable status. It would be possible to elaborate the case at much greater length, of course—but to do that would risk ignoring the force of *verecundia* itself, insofar as I would claim more space for myself than I properly need and show too little concern for your interests as my reader. In doing that, I would respect neither my face as a responsible writer nor yours as an attentive audience, and I would reasonably expect to pay a price. In fact, if I had any decency at all, I should experience a good, strong seizure of our next chapter's subject, *pudor*. Probably best, then, to move along: we will return to *verecundia*, and its relation to *pudor*, after we have examined in detail just what *pudor*—a rather more complex entity—is about.

2

Fifty Ways to Feel Your *Pudor*

"Do you *see* the people *looking* at you? Do you *like* that?"

You will not find these questions, exactly, in any classical Latin text. I overheard them recently while waiting on line in Newark Airport, as they were addressed by a mother to her slightly bumptious three-year-old son. The mother's tone made it clear—as clear to the boy as it was to an eavesdropper—that the questions were not being put in the spirit of disinterested inquiry: as she bent to meet her son at eye level, the scolding in her voice conveyed that the only acceptable answers were "yes" and "no," in that order. Though the boy did not actually blush (so far as I recall), his downcast eyes and slightly protruding lower lip made two things plain: he felt his mother's displeasure and disapproval, and if he had not known the right answers to the questions before, he knew them now.

Watching this primal form of socialization so nakedly at work was exhilarating, if a bit queasy-making at the same time, rather like being witness to one's own birth. Certainly I could only admire the economy of the job, done in a mere dozen words. The mother's first question distilled—in "see" and "looking"—the double perception that gives rise to shame, your being aware of others being aware of you. Her second question condensed, in "like," various forms of evaluation, desire, and feeling, all at once. Because it linked self-attention and the attention of others to the embodied experiences of restraint, shame, and regret, the second question was much the more important one in terms of the cultural work it was doing.

That "no" was the only acceptable answer to the second question is eloquent of our uncomfortable relations with shame at this moment in Western history, when those who have good things to say about the emotion tend mostly to have in mind its use as an effective punishment (of scofflaws or the consumers of prostitution, for example), while others, especially in the therapeutic community, point mainly to its disfiguring effects on a private, privileged self.[1] This is not a way of looking at things to which members of the Roman elite would have subscribed, for all that they regarded their version of shame—*pudor*—as primarily a "negative" emotion, experienced as a form of fear and discomfort. (Though various Romans remark that *pudor* can be unpleasant or inconvenient, none speaks of it as a "pathology.") Being aware of others being aware of you, though certainly not the whole of life, was a desirable part of it; while it was understandably your goal to receive the largest possible share of creditable attention ("honor") and experience the least possible discomfort from discrediting attention ("shame"), honor and shame were experienced as complementary, rather than opposed.[2] Those who did not have what we would call (in a now slightly archaic turn of phrase) a "sense of shame" could not expect to gain much honor; those who valued honor most highly could expect to experience shame most intensely. Understanding the varieties of that experience is our aim in this chapter.

The variousness of *pudor* makes it a more complex emotion than the related but fairly straightforward affect of *verecundia*, considered in the preceding chapter, and this variousness requires a different, more complex approach. All experiences of *pudor* depend upon notions of personal worthiness (*dignitas*) and value (*existimatio*), which in turn derive from seeing my self being seen in creditable terms.[3] I experience *pudor* when I see my self being seen as *dis*credited, when the value that I or others grant that self is not what I would have it be. But though there are, accordingly, only two preconditions for my feeling *pudor*—that I have some sense of personal worthiness and value and that I see it being discounted—the ways in which I can see my value being discounted vary considerably, according to several different and fundamental criteria. For a coherent account of the emotion to be given, these ways and criteria must be brought into some sort of coherent relationship; but the simplest way of establishing such a relationship—through a straightforward narrative of linear "development"—is not available to us. While some experiences of *pudor* are more commonly spoken of than others, there is no historically recoverable reason to think that there was a single "original" or "authentic" or "real" form of the emotion from which the others emerged.

Furthermore, for the reasons already discussed in the introduction to this book, attempting to analyze the various forms of *pudor* simply by matching them up with lexical equivalents in English (or any other language) would beg a host of questions and doom the project from the outset. Instead, we can best understand and represent the multiple forms of experience that cluster under the label of *pudor* by thinking of a variety of "scripts," the little scenarios that we play out—as sequences of cause and effect, of perception, evaluation, and response—when we experience any emotion. Working with a complex of scripts, in this chapter and in each of the following, allows us to grasp the language of emotions in terms that are themselves emotion-neutral (and therefore not circular or otherwise problematic), by considering the emotions as they are defined in action and by examining, especially, the intentional states—the judgments, beliefs, and desires—that engage each of them. And, since stressing intentional states necessarily stresses the specifically cultural content of emotions, this approach most directly speaks to the concerns of this book.

So what script or scripts does a Roman who experiences *pudor* enact, what are the judgments and beliefs essential to the emotion, and what is their cultural content? To start to answer these questions, we can consider the partial taxonomy of *pudor*-scripts that appears as figure 2.1. I should stress that this taxonomy was not constructed a priori: I did not sit down and decide what a plausible taxonomy might look like, then try to sort the textual instances accordingly. The taxonomy was built inductively: these are just the consistent patterns that emerged from reading, at least two or three times each, every text in classical Latin in which *pudor* and its cognates occur and asking the question, What are the common threads in the stories that are told under the heading of *pudor*?[4] After examining the taxonomy closely, to see how it is put together, we will draw out at least a few of the important ways in which these scripts of *pudor* interact in different social contexts, and we will give some attention to the different forms of "seeing" that give the emotion its life, before rounding off the chapter by bringing *pudor* into relation with its close kin, *verecundia*.

Some Basic Structures

By representing the *pudor*-scripts that were simultaneously active in Roman life, figure 2.1 allows the eye and mind to take them in all together, the better to appreciate their symmetries and cultural complementarities. Of course, this synoptic convenience has a cost, since it allows us to represent only the gross anatomy of the emotion. The taxonomy is "partial" in the sense that its ramifications could be pursued downward in finer-grain analysis: for example, each of the scripts could be further divided to distinguish the occurrent forms of *pudor*—the fully embodied experience of the emotion (compare our "feeling ashamed")—from the dispositional forms—your habitual sensitivity to the emotion and your inclination to anticipate and avoid the circumstances in which you would experience its fully embodied form (compare our "sense of shame").[5] Because the basic structure of the underlying thought is the same in both forms, I have not represented the distinction, or others like it, though I will draw attention to them when they are relevant to the argument.[6]

With that qualification noted, we can go on to consider the taxonomy itself, which accounts for virtually all the evidence that offers a context sufficient to form a judgment and does not speak of *pudor* in unhelpfully general terms.[7] The only exceptions fall into two very limited and inconsequential categories, which I set to one side as negligible. First, there are the settings where for a posey and often fatuous effect—a reductio ad absurdum or mere claptrap, for example—a speaker declares, as though it were a controversial notion, that he does not (or never will) feel *pudor* for something that in fact would not be expected to cause anyone to feel it. So, for example, the narrator

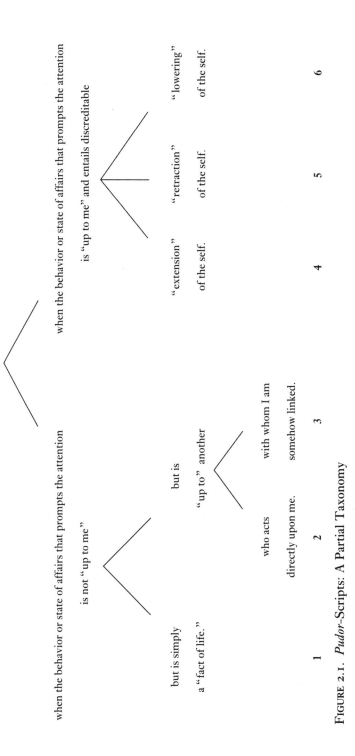

Upon (or at the prospect of) seeing myself being seen in discreditable terms,

I have an unpleasant psychophysical response,

when the behavior or state of affairs that prompts the attention is not "up to me"

but is simply a "fact of life."

1

but is "up to" another

who acts directly upon me.

2

with whom I am somehow linked.

3

when the behavior or state of affairs that prompts the attention is "up to me" and entails discreditable

"extension" of the self.

4

"retraction" of the self.

5

"lowering" of the self.

6

FIGURE 2.1. *Pudor*-Scripts: A Partial Taxonomy

in the historical epitome of Florus (who is rather prone to this sort of thing) exclaims, "Why marvel that the gods themselves again blocked Hannibal's path—yes, the gods, I say, nor shall I feel *pudor* to acknowledge it (*nec fateri pudebit*)!":[8] this is the Latin version of an anglophone "patriot"'s rounding off a denunciation of political dissent with the ringing—because hollow—declaration, "By God, I for one am not ashamed to say that *I* love my country!" The second, related category comprises contexts where the thought is otherwise merely eccentric or (occasionally) perverse. For example, when one old man remonstrating with another in a Plautine comedy sputters that "most people feel *pudor* when it's of no consequence but are deserted by *pudor* when *pudor* ought to be felt, when it's useful for them to feel *pudor*," we might doubt that the statement is a reliable proposition about the behavior of "most people" in actual life and suspect that it was framed as it was to allow the accumulated "*pud*- talk" to give emphatic color to the remonstrances.[9] Similarly, when the narrator of Lucan's *Civil War*—striving for pathos and achieving bathos— claims that it causes *pudor* to mourn the deaths of individuals when "the whole world" is perishing, we can recognize a thought that was as ethically empty in antiquity as it would be today, and as worthy of the adolescent poet as the dull and pornographic catalog of mutilations that follows.[10]

If we start at the "top" of the taxonomy, then, we find both the cognition that gives the emotion its distinctive content—the belief that I am being seen (or risk being seen) in terms that discredit me, that lower the value ascribed to me as a person (*existimatio*)—and the psychophysical response that the cognition evokes, experienced as a kind of displeasure. If I have dispositional *pudor*— the inclination to experience the occurrent form that gives me a "sense of shame"—then my sensitivity to being seen in such terms will commonly lead me, through my imagination and "the very thought" of such discreditng, to experience the displeasure in anticipation, "as if": a species of fear, not of physical punishment or the coercion of law but of a loss of worth that disfigures me in my own eyes or in the eyes of others (or both).[11] If my dispositional *pudor* and the thoughts to which it gives rise do not restrain me sufficiently, I am liable to lay myself open to the occurrent emotion, which responds to the self's disfigurement with (typically) a blush and some expressive use of the body, a posture or movement that signals a breaking off of contact with others: silence, downcast eyes, an averted glance, a turning away, or an actual withdrawal.[12]

At the next level of the taxonomy, we start to get at what the emotion is "about," the behaviors or states of affairs sufficient to prompt the processes of body and mind just described, and we find the question from which the rest of the analysis follows: is the relevant behavior or state of affairs "up to me"? Is the *pudor*-circumstance the outcome of an act that I chose to perform (or not) and therefore something for which I am at least causally responsible? Here the taxonomy divides according to whether or not the act (though not necessarily the outcome) was intentional, in the sense of being subject to my evaluations, judgments, and desires.

Now, it might seem odd that this distinction should enter into the discussion at all, much less play so pivotal a role, given, for example, that a prominent ancient "philosophical" definition in which *pudor* figures tells us that it is "a fear of just criticism."[13] If that is true, then surely I can experience *pudor* only in respect of things that are up me—for how can I be criticized justly for things that are *not* up to me? The simple fact, however, is that this definition is not adequate to describe the actual workings of *pudor* in the culture. Of course, it is not odd that philosophers (of any stripe or sect) would find the stipulation of "just criticism" useful when constructing an ethical system, since the definition, by excluding all forms of the emotion that involve things not up to me, excludes any considerations other than those of my personal virtue. As we shall see, however, it does not follow that differently oriented forms of the emotion are either rare or somehow illegitimate and irrational; it does suggest that any philosopher's definition of any emotion needs to be seen in context, doing the (often normative) work it does within the system of thought it is meant to serve, and should not be accepted at face value as the only form of the emotion available to a culture's participants. After all, *pudor* is first and foremost about perceptions—about seeing my self being seen as devalued— and it is just a fact of social life that not all the things that affect my self's perceived value are up to me—despite the best efforts of some ethical systems to combat just such conceptions of "value." It follows, then, that some forms of *pudor* I can experience will arise from actions or states of affairs not subject to my will, and given the rules of the social game I am playing, I will not be irrational in experiencing them.[14]

That said, let's start to work through the scripts themselves, starting with the left side of the taxonomy and the forms of the emotion based on conditions that are not "up to me."[15]

Script 1: Pudor *and the Way Things Happen to Be*

In 446 BCE, with Italian enemies knocking at the gates of Rome, the consul Titus Quinctius Capitolinus Barbatus called an assembly of the people and (according to Livy) began his address with these words (3. 67. 1–2):

> Although I am conscious of no wrongful act (*mihi nullius noxae conscius*), citizens, I nonetheless have come forth into your sight to address you with [feelings of] utmost *pudor*, [aware] that you know—and the knowledge will be handed down to posterity—that in the fourth consulship of Titus Quinctius the Aequi and the Volsci came with impunity to the walls of Rome under arms ("Aequos et Volscos . . . T. Quinctio quartum consule ad moenia urbis Romae impune armatos venisse"). Had I known

that this disgrace (*ignominia*) loomed over *this* year, I would have avoided this honorable office (*honos*) by exile or death, had no other escape been available.

By stressing that the present state of affairs is not his doing, the consul's opening words allude to a common expectation that *pudor* and causal responsibility go hand in hand; yet, he does not deny the feeling or immediately attempt (as a common impulse might prompt) to pin the responsibility on someone else.[16] This is just the way things are, and, because they are this way, he sees himself being seen as discredited and devalued, tarred with the brush of *ignominia*. And—in Roman terms—not unreasonably: because he is consul, this is "his" year, and it will be inscribed as such, under his name and the name of his colleague, on Rome's official calendar (*fasti*), along with such notable events as occurred in its course (indeed, the words "Aequos et Volscos . . . armatos venisse" look very much like such a calendric inscription). That is how the memory will be "handed down to posterity"; and so, though Quinctius believes that he is not causally responsible for the *ignominia*, he feels it as his own because it is "his" year, when all that happens—good or bad—will affect his *existimatio*, forever. So strongly is this felt (at least in Livy's rhetoric, which he presumably thought would be plausible to his readers) that Quinctius says he would have taken the most drastic steps, destroying himself as a person (by suicide) or as a citizen (by exile), had he known what was in store.

Quinctius here is enacting the first script of *pudor*, according to which I see myself being seen as devalued because of some state of affairs that, so far from being up to me, is the product of no personal agency at all, in any useful sense of the phrase: it is simply the way things have turned out to be. This is, by some distance, the most rarely expressed *pudor*-script, and in fact the case of Quinctius is, by some distance, the most culturally interesting instance of it. Otherwise, it seems to be found exclusively in connection with two external characteristics of a person: a place of birth viewed as provincial or otherwise disesteemed and (especially) a physical trait that is regarded as a defect—a disfigurement or debility brought on by age or disease or (in a woman) childbirth, or (perhaps) possession of a certain skin color.[17]

Because people would not all that rarely have found themselves in circumstances similar to Quinctius's, and in view of the ancient tendency to ascribe ethical weight to both birth and appearance—identifying the "ugly" with the "shameful" and the "fair" with the "fine"—it is mildly surprising that the script occurs so seldom. Perhaps it is the case that when people found themselves in circumstances like Quinctius's, there would typically have been others on hand to suggest that they really *were* causally responsible, through acts of omission if not of commission. And perhaps (with reference to the more common instances), it is simply that a people who delighted in giving each other nicknames like "Baldy" (Calvus), "Big-Nose" (Naso), "Flop-Ears" (Flaccus), and

"Squinty" (Strabo)—and who did not balk at adopting these nicknames as the *cognomina* to be worn by their posterity—were not much consumed by the angst of *pudor* where such traits were concerned: it is probably not coincidental that the real source of *pudor* in most of the instances noted seems to be less the disfigurement or weakness per se than the contrast with a former attractiveness or vigor, now lost. (Here "shame" shades off into "regret.") In any case, since this script does not figure much in the balance of the chapter, we can simply note it here and move on.

Script 2: Pudor and Iniuria

Where the preceding script was concerned (but not overly concerned) with *pudor* that might arise from my physical face—my pug-ugly physiognomy—the remaining scripts all have to do with my "face" in the metaphorical sense already met in chapter 1: the role I play in a given transaction, and the credit I can claim for playing it.[18] Central to this concept of face is my need to see you underwrite my positive view of myself—my estimation of my value—especially in the coin of respect. If your dealings with me show that you subscribe to that view and respect my face, I will see myself being seen in creditable terms, and my (dispositional) *pudor* will be unruffled. If, however, you threaten my face by showing that you deny my own estimate of my value—say, by subjecting me to gratuitous insults (if I am a decent man) or by making me the object of sexually appraising glances (if I am a decent woman)—I will typically regard your behavior as an *iniuria*, a wrongful act in which the notions of "injury" and "insult" mingle: I will then very likely enact some form of anger (unless I am a Stoic sage) and very possibly *pudor*, in the form of script 2.[19] The qualifications—"very likely," "very possibly"—are needed because neither anger nor, especially, shame is inevitable in this circumstance: the thought is available that *iniuria*, just because it is by definition a wrong and hence the work of a base person, cannot rightly affect your value and can even be despised.[20] Much would depend on the kind of *iniuria* involved and on the kind of person who offered it, and much would also depend on the kind of person I am: one of the important fault lines in Roman emotional culture, determined (we can suspect) as much by individual temperament as by anything else, distinguished those who had a "reflexive" sense of honor, demanding vengeance for even a mildly face-threatening slight, from those who did not. The evidence suggests that the number of those who did was not inconsiderable.[21] The following paragraphs, though far from an exhaustive catalog, should sufficiently convey the contours of the experience.

To draw out the relevant considerations, let us first take rape—in Roman terms, illicit sexual penetration inflicted by force (*stuprum per vim inlatum*)—as one paradigmatic subtype of this script.[22] Because it is one person's violent denial of another's face as a "chaste" person, the act is an *iniuria* that objectively puts the agent, not the sufferer, in the wrong. At the the same time, the act is commonly conceived by our sources (exclusively male) as causing raped persons (usually but not exclusively female) to experience *pudor* as a result of the rapists' actions, because they see themselves being devalued, and often even being regarded (against the facts) as in some sense blameworthy.

So when Ovid's fictional Rhea, after the river-god Anio's assault, says (*Am.* 3. 6. 77–78):

> "Why should I wait until I'm pointed out as an adulteress (*adultera*)
>   by the mob?
> Let there be no cheeks of mine for the *pudor* of disrepute to mark!"

she means that she will annihilate her physical face (by drowning herself) before it can reveal (by her blush) that she has lost her metaphorical face as a *virgo pudica*—that is, before she can suffer *pudor* by seeing herself being seen as an *adultera*. In saying that, she offers a take on her experience that needed no glossing or commentary to be intelligible to Ovid's patriarchal readers. Because a raped woman (*rapta*) was commonly seen as *vitiata* or the like—"damaged goods"—her value in others' eyes was diminished; whether or not she subscribed to that valuation in her own mind, its weight would inevitably be brought to bear upon her dispositional *pudor*, placing it under strain and causing a painful "wound."[23] Thus, another of Ovid's raped women—the nymph Callisto, companion of the virgin goddess, Diana—is described in these terms:

> How hard it is not to betray the misdeed (*crimen*) with a look!
> She scarce lifts her gaze from the ground, nor does she walk
> at the goddess's side, at the head of the troupe, as once she did,
> but in silence she signals, with a blush, the wound to her *pudor*.
> And were she not a maiden herself, Diana could have sensed,
> from a thousand signs, her flaw (*culpa*): the nymphs (it is said) did
>   sense it.[24]

Though the narrator has previously made it clear that Callisto resisted her attacker (Jupiter) to the limits of her strength,[25] the language of "fault" is twice used in the aftermath, the first time to give us the nymph's view (*crimen* is clearly focalized through Callisto), the second time (in *culpa*) to provide the "external" view of the narrator—and (reportedly) the other nymphs. Beset from both sides in this way, Callisto's dispositional *pudor*—her sensitivity to seeing herself being seen in such terms—becomes actual (occurrent) *pudor* under the force of the "wound": blood follows, in the form of a blush.[26] That *pudor*-responses of this sort are not limited to the raped women whom Ovid draws from mythology is made plain by his Lucretia (*Fasti* 2. 813–34), who first responds to her rape with fully embodied *pudor*—silently blushing, averting her gaze from husband and father, covering her head with her cloak—then refuses the "indulgence" offered to her because the act was not up to her (*dant veniam facto genitor coniunxque coactae*) and kills herself rather than speak of what she calls her "disgrace" (*dedecus*). And that such responses are not limited to Ovid's imagination is made stunningly plain by the very similar Lucretia of Cicero, "a noble woman possessing a strong sense of *pudor*," who "assessed herself the penalty of death (*sese ipsa morte multavisset*) on account of the wrong (*iniuria*)" *done to* her.[27]

In such cases, the person experiencing *pudor* is not only aware of the view that devalues them, and even casts them in the wrong, but also in some way subscribes to that view, though the actions were in no way up to them. This form of the script—which has the abused come to believe that they are somehow complicit in their abuse, so that their face as decent persons is marred or destroyed—is of course psychologically intelligible; indeed, the fact that something very much like it is clinically common in cases of rape today suggests that the Roman instances are not simply attributable to the ventriloquizing of a female subject by a male author but are symptomatic of patriarchy more generally.[28]

However, it is not the most common Roman form of this script: far more usually, when I find my face threatened by another's action, I am in my own eyes wholly the injured—and innocent—party, and the mere prospect that my value will be seen to be diminished is sufficient, at least, to place my dispositional *pudor* under strain.

The circumstances in which I can enact this form of the script are as various as the circumstances in which my value—often indistinguishable from my *amour propre*—seems to be at stake. Let me just quickly sketch a number of these, simply to indicate their range:

- being cuckolded, if I am married (Tac. *Ann.* 11. 35), or being subjected to a beating—treatment worthy of a slave—if I am freeborn (Val. Max. 9. 10 [ext.]. 2), or being killed—or, for that matter, saved—by a woman, if I am a hero ([Sen.] *Herc. Oet.* 1176–78, 1209, Val. Fl. 7. 479–82), or being turned into a pig, if I am human (Ov. *Met.* 14. 278–79);
- being rejected—or even appearing to others to be rejected—in any venue, whether amorous (Ov. *A. A.* 1. 625–26, Juv. 10. 326–29) or electoral (Plin. *Pan.* 91. 2);[29]
- being compelled to witness an outrageous spectacle (Suet. *Nero* 23. 3, cf. Sen. *Thy.* 1034–36), or being mocked by a deception (Ov. *F.* 3. 691–92), or being required to acknowledge publicly my dependence on another (Curt. Ruf. 8. 8. 9, cf. Sen. *Ben.* 2. 10. 4);
- being made the object of a shaming ritual or song (Tac. *Ann.* 14. 49, *Dig.* 47. 10. 1. 5 and 47. 10. 15. 27, cf. Mart.1. 4),[30] or being called into court by my freedman or child (*Dig.* 2. 4. 10. 12), or being involved in other legal procedures that bring my *existimatio* into question (*Dig.* 3. 3. 25. pr.).

37

The evidence ranges from the fanciful narratives of myth to the codified principles of law, and the consistency in point of view is enough to suggest that even the thought-world of the fanciful is in this matter closer to the law than might first be supposed.

Frequent in all these instances (which could be multiplied fivefold and more), besides the basic structure of the thought, are two other elements. First, there is the prickly imperative to protect my sense of *pudor*—my sensitivity to seeing myself being seen as devalued—by conspicuously rejecting the damaging view. The point is perhaps made most clearly by, precisely, someone whose *existimatio* has been brought into question by a legal procedure, the speaker in Apuleius's *Apologia*:

> Like a garment, a sense of *pudor* is treated all the more carelessly the more worn it is (*quanto obsoletior est, tanto incuriosius habetur*). And so I think it necessary, before addressing the substance of the charge, to keep my sense of *pudor* intact by refuting all the nasty charges that have been made against me, . . . lest I—who constantly strive to keep any hint of a blot or dishonor at a distance (*ne quid maculae aut inhonestamenti in me admittam*)—seem to anyone to have acknowledged, rather than despised, whatever bit of nonsense I leave unaddressed. For, I believe, it is proper to a mind that is sensitive to *pudor* and marked by *verecundia* (*est enim pudentis animi et verecundi*) to feel the oppressive weight even of false attacks (*vel falsas vitu<pe>rationes gravari*).[31]

Second, as the simile of the garment and the concern "to keep my sense of *pudor* intact" (*pro integritate pudoris*) here suggest, there is the palpability, the sheer physicality with which *pudor* is conceived in such cases. Especially in this script, my sense of *pudor*, as a disposition integrated with my self, is experienced as a three-dimensional extension or part of me: as such, it can be "burdened" or "bruised" or "pricked" or "wounded"—but also "unburdened" or "cleansed," if my temperament leads me to take the appropriate action.[32]

Script 3: Pudor by Association

The final script on this side of the taxonomy concerns the *pudor* that is prompted not by your own acts but by the behavior of one or more others with whom you are somehow linked. I will set to one side for now a closer definition of the "somehow"—the factors that make a given linkage matter for *pudor*—until the range of occasions has been surveyed. But you will probably draw some conclusions of your own if I organize the survey according the types of relationship that give this script its scope.

To start with the most intimate ties, there is the *pudor* that cognate kin— "blood relations," especially children and siblings—can reliably be expected to occasion. So when Demea, in Terence's *Brothers*, says "It causes me *pudor*: I don't know what to do or what to say" (485–86), he is referring to the discomfort entailed in seeing *himself* being seen in discreditable terms because of the apparent misdeeds of his permissive brother, Micio, and Micio's adoptive son (who is also Demea's biological son), Aeschinus. This form of the script—as common in antiquity, no doubt, as it is today—finds a slight but still completely recognizable variation in Cicero's correspondence, when—having evidently learned of the gluttony of his nephew, Quintus—he says "o gulam insulsam! pudet me patris" (*Att.* 13. 31. 4), which literally means something on the order of "Oh that idiot maw! I feel *pudor* (on account) of his father." Cicero does not mean that he feels (as we would say) "ashamed *of*" the boy's father, the elder Quintus (though the phrasing, with the genitive, could denote that form of *pudor*, too). Rather, he means that that he feels the *pudor* that attaches to the boy's father, in two subtly different senses at once: he feels the *pudor* that *he* would feel if *he* were young Quintus's father, experiencing the shame incurred by his son's disgraceful behavior as though it were his own, *and* he feels *pudor* as the elder Quintus's brother, experiencing his brother's shame as though it were his own.[33]

Moving to a more attenuated kind of relationship—agnate kin, or "in-laws"—we see, for example, that Ovid at several points in his poetry from exile assumes that one or another connection by marriage, starting with his wife, could experience *pudor* because of their ties to his disgrace.[34] Similar thoughts inform the advice offered in Horace's *Epistle* 1. 18, on the vetting of friends and protégés—

> Closely consider, again and again, the sort you'd commend, lest
> presently another's bad acts give you a good jolt of *pudor*—[35]

and they extend to the sensibilities engaged by other forms of association: between men of similar magisterial rank—for example, the *pudor* that one senator can feel at discreditable behavior of the senate as a whole; or between people who have some other valued status in common—for example, the *pudor* that one philosopher can feel at the foolish behavior of other philosophers; or between comrades-in-arms—for example, the *pudor* that Antony's partisans allegedly felt at his liaison with Cleopatra; or between countrymen more generally.[36]

Indeed, my ties to my "fatherland" or "civil community" (*patria, civitas*) can engage my *pudor* in a highly general way. So, when recalling the ascendancy of the freedman Pallas under Claudius, the younger Pliny exclaims, "How glad I am that I didn't happen to be born in those times, which cause me *pudor* just as though I lived through them!"[37] Here Pliny claims to feel *pudor* in response to a past state of affairs that he did not experience, much less cause, and for which he could not plausibly have been held responsible (by himself or another) even if he had experienced it: Pliny evidently feels *pudor* simply as a Roman *civis* in respect of behavior unworthy of the Roman *civitas*, much as citizens of a modern state might feel shame at some enormity (genocide, slavery) in their country's past. Much the same thought animates a recurrent gesture of Roman historians that might be called "the *pudor* of decent narration": when Florus in his epitome of Roman history reports that the Roman people "under Sempronius Gracchus's leadership dared to pursue [the Carthaginians] through Lucania and press them as they retreated, though it was then waging war—oh, the *pudor!*—with armed slaves," or when Tacitus turns from the deeds of great men to record the antics of a mere plebeian troublemaker and marks the transition with the phrase "it must cause *pudor* to mention . . . " (*pudendum dictu*), they both signal that the mere presence of such episodes in the annals of Rome must cause *pudor* to any decent Roman.[38] And the elder Pliny adopts this sort of gesture to his own ends when he repeatedly registers *pudor* at the degeneracy, not (certainly!) of his own behavior but of the sorry times in which he finds himself alive.[39]

If we return now to the question of the sorts of "linkage" on which this script depends, I imagine that you have concluded that the concept of "identification" is key; and with that I agree, if we understand the "identification" relevant to this script in two distinct but not mutually exclusive senses. There is, first, the highly internalized sort of identification, experienced as an affective and cognitive bond with another, that can cause me to regard the other's behavior as virtually my own: the bond is such that "the self [which experiences the emotion] is viewed as some kind of extension of the actual agent of the action."[40] Or to put it another way: when the mother in the airport was asking her son, "Do you *see* the people *looking* at you? Do you *like* that?," she was also, implicitly, saying, "Do you *see* the people *looking* at *me*? I don't *like* that!" At the same time, there is also the more externalized identification that we each have as social beings, according to the role that we are being seen to play at any given moment, such that our value is judged not only by how well or poorly we appear to play the role ourselves but also according to the value ascribed to others with whom the role identifies us, either because they play the same role (say, as one philosopher vis-à-vis another, or as a Roman vis-à-vis other Romans) or because they play a complementary role (say, as client vis-à-vis patron). In any relationship with another, I can experience one or the other form of identification, or both (or, of course, neither).

In both cases, my sense of how my value as a person is perceived—my *existimatio*—is at stake, but the *pudor* is likely to be rather differently nuanced and felt depending on which form of identification predominates. The more internalized and intensely felt the identification is, the more will concern for my *existimatio* tend to be overlaid with other judgments, desires, and feelings (in the case of a loved one, for example, sentiments that focus more on the other than on oneself, like anxiety over their well-being or disappointment at their failure); the more externalized the identification, the more will my *existimatio* tend to be my first, and perhaps my only, concern. So, in Cicero's letter about young Quintus, which I take to be largely an expression of affective identification, I should be surprised if thoughts of *existimatio* were close to the surface, in contrast, say, with the younger Pliny's indignant remarks about the honors done Pallas; in the case of the *pudor* that I would feel if you commit misdeeds after I've commended you, the form of identification that would be relevant— or, if both are relevant, their relative importance in constituting my emotion— would depend entirely on the nature of the preexisting relationship. Yet, we should not assume that relations of blood will necessarily guarantee a highly affective form of identification or a less emphatic and immediate concern with *existimatio*. When we read that Augustus, in the aftermath of his daughter Julia's disgrace, "long kept himself away from gatherings of men, out of *pudor*, and even considered suicide," we might doubt that he did so because the intimacy of their relations caused him to regard her misdeeds as in some sense his own; our doubt tends to be confirmed when we further read that—on learning of a freedwoman among Julia's sidekicks who had hanged herself after the disgrace—Augustus said that he would rather have been the ex-slave's father than Julia's.[41]

Now, perhaps you have noticed that I have so far said nothing about the actual *content* of the behaviors covered by this script, the sorts of things that my child or client can do to cause me *pudor*. That is because they are indistinguishable from the behaviors about to be considered on the right side of the taxonomy, concerned with actions that are "up to me": in effect, scripts 4–6 could be reproduced as a further level of analysis under script 3, to define the *pudor*-producing behaviors of those with whom I am identified. Or, to put it another way, if I experience the *pudor* of script 3, then the responsible persons damn well ought to be ashamed of themselves—though, alas, they too seldom are. As we will see, this is only one of the taxonomy's several symmetries.

When a philosopher defines (dispositional) *pudor* as "the fear of just criticism," or when a consul prefaces his expression of (occurrent) *pudor* by glancing at "consciousness of a wrongful act," each in his own way is referring to the conception of *pudor* that is integral to the scripts on the taxonomy's right side.[42] On this side, the defining thought is that the discrediting state of affairs is up to me, as the outcome of an act which I chose to perform (or culpably neglected to perform) and for which I am reasonably held responsible. The act, though not necessarily the outcome, was intentional, in the sense of being subject to my evaluations, judgments, and desires, even if those were distorted (by passion, say) at the time.[43] Though the three scripts surveyed on the other side of the taxonomy—especially the second and third—can hardly be said to be culturally eccentric, the scripts on this side are certainly more heavily represented when the Romans talk of *pudor*.

The three basic scripts that concern us here can be understood in terms of behavior demonstrating a discreditable "extension" of the self (beyond its proper boundaries), or a discreditable "retraction" of the self (shy of some spirited standard), or a discreditable "lowering" of the self (beneath an appropriate level of dignity).[44] I will explain and elaborate these metaphors as we examine each script in turn, and we can then consider the relations among them. But let me here anticipate two questions about the scheme's formal characteristics.

First (you might ask), if there is a script for discreditable "lowering" of the self, why is there no script for discreditable "elevation" of the self? To this I reply that there could be, but it would be a nearly empty category, since the data reveal very few acts regarded as *pudenda*, "shameful," that could be clearly distinguished under this heading—chiefly, boasting and related behavior (the dearth of data here seems culturally eloquent in itself). Rather than create an additional category for the sake of a finicky symmetry, I though it best simply to regard "self-elevating" behavior as a form of "self-extension": here it might be helpful to think of a balloon growing larger equally in all directions as it is inflated. Ah, then, in that case (the second question), why not similarly fold the category of "self-lowering" behavior into the script for discreditable "self-retraction," to simplify still further? To this I reply that the thought crossed my mind. But then I saw it would obscure the fact that behaviors that fall under the rubric of script 6 are not only numerous (certainly, and again perhaps interestingly, more numerous than discreditably "self-elevating" behaviors) and sufficient in themselves to cause occurrent *pudor* but also distinguishable from scripts 4 and 5 in other ways: for example, while the behaviors of scripts 4 and 5 tend to impact others directly—by being offensive or materially detrimental, respectively—script-6 behaviors tend to affect only the agents, by demeaning them.

In short, these are the metaphors that seem best to respond to the data in coherent and significant ways. In any case, they are only metaphors, not entities with an objective existence in nature, and as such are worth using (in any form) only to the extent that they illuminate the relations among the data. This is something I'm reasonably confident that they do. Let's turn, then, to the scripts themselves.

Script 4: Pudor *and Discreditable "Extension" of the Self*

Here it will be useful to introduce a nuance in our concept of "face," by distinguishing between "positive" face and "negative" face.[45] "Positive" face is really just the concept with which we have been working so far: it is my claim on the credit I believe I am due for playing the role I am playing in any given transaction, and I know that my positive face is being respected when my aims in playing the role are regarded as choiceworthy and when my playing of the role is valued. "Negative" face, by contrast, is in essence a close kin of "negative" liberty, the "freedom from": it is my claim, as a competent adult member of society, on having leave to pursue a chosen line of action unimpeded by others. In everyday terms, if you stop me as I walk down the street to ask me the time of day, you are threatening my negative face, albeit in a minimal and culturally acceptable way that generally requires no more compensation than a polite formula or two (if, however, you make the request by saying, "Hey, jackass, got a watch?," you are denying not only my negative face but my positive face, too). You are also threatening my negative face, in a more charged and vivid way, if you cut me off while I am driving down a highway at high speed (and if you offer me the *digitus impudicus* while cutting me off, you are threatening my positive face, too).[46]

To put the matter in more recognizably Roman terms: this *pudor*-script comprises any act that should cause me to see myself losing positive face (roughly, my *existimatio*) because I am regarded as arrogating to myself more negative face—more license for willful, unimpeded action, for doing what I damn well please—than is thought proper, especially if (though not only if) in so doing I appear to deny other people's face claims, whether intentionally or out of flagrant disregard (that is, by acting with what U.S. law calls "actual malice"). Under this script, suffering, or deserving to suffer, occurrent *pudor* means that, by refusing to yield any of my negative face, I have lost my claim to positive face; complementarily, acting in accord with my dispositional *pudor* requires that I willingly surrender some of my liberty. This is why, as the saying goes, "having (a sense of) *pudor* is a kind of slavery."[47] We will return to this notion.

Let me now survey the main forms of script-4 behavior in a very summary way, with only a few examples of each: because this is the most common single script, engrossing in one way or another more than half the Romans' *pudor*-talk, the evidence is far too abundant to review exhaustively. The cateegories of behavior will probably not surprise; nor should it surprise if the categories overlap to a degree, since they are merely convenient devices for sorting behaviors that derive from one impulse, to extend if not eradicate the limits placed on my actions and my wants.

Thrusting myself forward, especially in an importunate or precipitous manner: here I court occurrent *pudor* (and display too little dispositional *pudor*) if I inject myself into others' affairs against their will (Cic. *Div. Caec.* 20), or tell a *vir gravis* how to manage his affairs (Cic. *Fam.* 4. 5. 6 [Sulpicius], with *Phil.* 2. 23), or detract from another's honor by taking on a task beyond my own powers and failing to follow through (Hor. *Carm.* 1. 6. 9–12), or claim a privilege to which I am not entitled (Juv. 3. 153–55), or have no sense of when to end a conversation before it becomes tediously intrusive (Plin. *Pan.* 24. 3), or just barge in on my mistress when she is applying her makeup (Ov. *Rem.* 352).[48] We also obviously see the same concern expressed, in markedly gendered form, in the chief examples of female *pudor* not concerned with sexual license and chastity (*pudicitia*): for example, in criticism of a wife who is too bossy toward her husband (Plaut. *Men.* 793–96) or of a woman playing a warrior's role (Juv. 6. 252–53, on a *mulier galeata*, with Stat. *Theb.* 5. 354–56), or in praise of women who decently refrain from entering a gathering of men (Cic. *Verr.* 2. 1. 94) and whose *pudor* literally keeps them "in their place."[49]

Being physically or verbally aggressive: here my behavior might range from murder (though this actually is fairly rare)[50] or less spectacular crimes like venality, peculation, and the violent excesses of youth (Cic. *Flac.* 68, Caes. *BCiv.* 3. 60. 3, Tib. 1. 1. 74) to inappropriate physical contact—either sexually tinged (Ovid *Ars Am.* 1. 495–96, cf. *Am.* 3. 2. 21–24) or simply gross (Martial 7. 95. 9–18, on offering a snot-drenched kiss)—to farting (or worse) at the dinner table (Petron. *Sat.* 47. 3–4) or offensive physical display, whether of my nakedness (Sen. *Ben.* 7. 9. 5, *Ep.* 90. 20) or mere ugliness. When Martial tells an unattractive woman that a sense of *pudor* should compel her to wear her underwear over her head, it is not her ugliness as such that should arouse her *pudor* (that would be script 1) but her willingness to inflict it on others; when at the same time he compares her face unfavorably with her crotch, he trades on conventional feelings about genitals (male and female alike), the sight of which was regarded as repellent, not titillating.[51]

Similarly, the continuum of verbal aggression extends from harshest invective or actually defaming speech, of the sort just exemplified by Martial's poem,[52] to wounding witticisms (Sen. *Dial.* 5. 37. 1, cf. Anon. *Laus Pisonis* 106–7), to remarks that simply threaten to bruise the sensibilities and harm the positive face of listener and speaker alike (Plaut. *Bacch.* 481, Curt. Ruf. 4. 10. 32, [Quint.] *DMai.* 3. 6).[53] The latter form of the script inspires a variation on "the *pudor* of decent narration" already met under script 3: whereas there the narrative voice was moved to insert an aside—"It causes me *pudor* to say (*pudet dicere*)" or the like—to register dismay at a disgrace incurred through identification (as a Roman with Rome), here the sensitive speaker uses such signals to warn of, and excuse, a forthcoming statement that risks being received as the literary equivalent of a fart at the dinner table.[54]

Pursuing self-interested ends at the cost of social obligations: here the variations are as numerous as the varieties of selfish ends and the forms of social obligation. I can try to satisfy my appetites contrary to my city's "custom and law" (*mos atque lex*) and my father's wishes (Ter. *And.* 877–81, cf. *And.* 262–63, *Phorm.* 231–33), or desert a friend in need (Cic. *Fam.* 6. 6. 6, cf. *Fam.* 7. 3. 1, 11. 27. 4, all concerning his relations with Pompey), or refuse to demit a magistracy at the appropriate time (Livy 3. 7. 4, 9. 34. 22), or (as a military officer) defect and thereby undo the *pudor* of the rank and file (Tac. *Hist.* 3. 61, sim. *Ann.* 6. 44).[55] I can indulge my "swollen ego" with "self-seeking falsehood" (Apul. *Apol.* 92 *tumidus animus et ambitiosa mendacitas*)—that is to say, engage in "shameless" flattery or just plain lie, the form of this script that is (along with sexual license) the most common.[56] In much the same spirit, I can promote myself at the expense of another[57] and otherwise ignore their positive face claims,[58] or (conversely) I can make my own false or excessive claims on others' respect for my competence, achievements, or the like.[59] And, of course, I can simply seek more than my rightful share out of sheer greed, incurring the shame of "wanting everything."[60]

Finally, **giving free reign to appetites**: here the problem arises for one of two reasons (or, very easily, both at once). The appetites might, first, be discreditable per se, especially when sex or luxury (or luxurious sex) are involved:[61] women, whose dispositional *pudor* has chastity (*pudicitia*) as its most urgent concern, are thought to be particularly vulnerable to occurrent *pudor* when their *impatientia* in matters of passion—their lack of self-control—impels them to claim the same sexual liberty as men.[62] Alternatively, indulging the appetites can be problematic not only because of their inherent character but also because they lead to discreditable acts—like neglecting *fides* (the Dido of *Aeneid* 4 and *Heroides* 7 is paradigmatic) or rape (Sen. *Contr.* 7. 8. 2)—or to discreditable states like debt and bankruptcy.[63]

In general terms, then, I should enact this script of *pudor* when I have behaved (or am on the brink of behaving) as though I am the only one with claims that matter, or as though others are of no account, or both. We can be confident that we are in the textual presence of the script when epithets such as "reckless" (*audax*) and "treacherous" (*perfidus*) and "forward" (*procax*) or terms such as "license" (*licentia*) and "deceit" (*fraus*) are being bandied about (as we shall see, the other scripts on this side of the taxonomy have their own distinctive terms of abuse associated with them). Comparable pointers are provided by the epithet *pudens* ("characterized by dispositional *pudor*") and its opposite, *impudens* (*impudentia*), uses of which overwhelmingly cluster under this script when their specific content can be identified.[64] When an ancient taxonomist tells us that *pudor* (*tout court*) is a species of *temperantia*, this is the single script he has in mind.[65]

Passed in summary review like this, the *pudor*-occasions of script 4 seem to add up to little more than a tawdry catalog of sex, lies, and seedy mistakes. The script is of course more interesting and consequential than that, as we shall see when we have surveyed the two remaining scripts.

Script 5: Pudor *and Discreditable "Retraction" of the Self*

The previous script plays out a discreditable "extension" of the self and comprises any behavior through which I engage in willful, self-assertive action in a way that diminishes my *existimatio*. The present script, distinguished by the complementary metaphor of "retraction," comprises a complementary failure, the failure to extend myself as I should in vigorous action, especially when I am more protective of my self than is thought proper through acts of coward-ice, inconstancy, miserliness, laziness, or the like. If an act (or a failure to act) invites the label "pusillanimous" because it seems to show that I am unwilling to extend or expend myself in dealings with others or on others' behalf, we are pretty certainly in the presence of script-5 *pudor*. Where script-4 behaviors attracted pejorative epithets such as *audax, perfidus*, and the like, the epithets characteristic of this script run to terms denoting various degrees of timidity or inertia: *diffidens, iners, ignavus, instrenuus, parum patiens, segnis, socors*, or *timidus*. Where both men and women were eligible to experience the previous form of *pudor* (albeit often in gender-specific ways), this script is almost ex-clusively gendered male. In fact, we can summarize this form of *pudor* by say-ing that you should experience it when you have failed to play vigorously the role of an adult free man.[66]

This form of *pudor*, though far from insignificant, attaches to a narrower range of behaviors than the preceding, and so the survey in this case can be briefer. (There is an important reason why the range of behaviors in each of these scripts is so different, and we will return to it when it is time to elaborate the scripts' relations.) In social relations, I can avoid this form of *pudor* if I am willing to expend the *labor*—service and attendance strenuously performed—of the sort that commends me to a patron (Cic. *Fam.* 7. 7. 2), and if I am suf-ficiently large-spirited both to willingly "lose" a favor (*beneficium*) rather than seek its repayment (Sen. *Ben.* 5. 20. 7) and to refrain from refusing another his due honor out of sheer spite (*malignitas*: Livy 38. 50. 3).[67] If my sense of dis-positional *pudor* is fully engaged, I will avoid experiencing the bone-deep oc-current *pudor* that Cicero expresses, in writing to his wife from exile, because he has failed to meet his obligations to his family, not out of grasping self-interest (script 4) but from sheer lack of spirit:

> The fault is fully my own. It was my duty either to avoid the danger by accepting [an honorable alternative], or to resist it with the care and resources at my disposable, or to die bravely. No alternative was more wretched, more disgraceful, more unworthy than the present state of affairs. For that reason I am overcome by pain and especially by *pudor*. Indeed, it causes me *pudor* not to have displayed courage and care for my excellent wife and my sweet, sweet children. For the grief and mourning of all of you, and your own poor health, are before my eyes night and day.[68]

In political activity, I will display appropriate civic gumption by living the vigorous life of a *civis*, making contributions to the common good instead of burying myself away in "literature" (Cic. *Arch.* 12) and, if the need arises, stand-ing with the civil authorities in the face of sedition, when "hiding is as good as dying an utterly disgraceful death" (Cic. *Rab. Perd.* 24).

But though this script does important work in the civil community (*domi*), its heart is to be found on campaign and under arms (*militiae*).[69] Here my sense of *pudor* is put on trial when I quail at doing my duty, especially in the face of danger:[70] by hanging back (Curt. 9. 4. 32), by retreating (Hirt. *BGall*. 8. 28. 4), or by simply fleeing (Livy 39. 49. 2, Flor. 2. 13). I will be especially tested, under this script, when others have conspicuously pointed the right way by showing some backbone, even to the point of laying down their lives.[71] At the same time that it punishes defeat, this script promotes pleasure in being seen to be vigorous and brave; it thereby spurs the competition for glory.[72]

Because this *pudor*-script casts me in the forceful role of an adult free male, my failure to play it adequately is commonly conceived as behavior that turns the role on its head, so that I can deservedly be thought "childish" or "servile": in the latter respect, the *pudor* expressed by Cicero at the prospect of being a "slave" under Caesar is no different, in the structure of its thought, from either the *pudor* enacted by elegy's "slave" of love, lamenting his "passivity" (*patientia*), or the *pudor* felt by those who display an unbecoming dependency in accepting gestures of "mercy" (*clementia*) or "indulgence" (*venia*).[73] More commonly still, I will be said to be "womanish," lacking the self-mastery and vigor of spirit that makes a man; at my worst, I will see myself being seen as "servile" and "feminine" at one and the same time.[74]

Script 6: Pudor *and Discreditable "Lowering" of the Self*

The final script, marked by the metaphor of "lowering," comprises any behavior, or any state produced by my own behavior, that is regarded as merely humiliating in itself—as distinct, that is, from the humiliations consequent on the ethical failures covered by scripts 4 and 5. As in the case of those two scripts, the acts and states that distinguish this script attract their own distinctive terms of condemnation: "ugly" (*deformis*), "unworthy" (*indignus, dedignari*), "low" (*humilis*), "filthy" (*sordidus*). I will see myself being seen in these terms when I prove to be stupid if I fancy myself shrewd (Cic. *Dom.* 29),[75] or rustic if I am urbane,[76] or bestial if I am a human (Ov. *Met.* 5.460, 11. 180, cf. Sen. *Dial.* 4. 31. 6). More generally, I will experience this script if I behave in any of a thousand ways that are simply demeaning: for example, by doing deeds worthy of corporal punishment (a punishment that brushes up against the servile: Curt. 5. 5. 10), or by choosing to consort with persons *infra dignitatem*,[77] or by having to give my peers an account of my financial embarrassment (Suet. *Tib.* 47. 1), or by pursuing a discreditable livelihood (Livy 23. 3. 11), or by writing a poem in a "barbarian" language (Ov. *Pont.* 4. 13. 19), or by making myself ugly (Gell. 15. 17. 1), or by massaging a woman's genitalia during intercourse.[78]

Scripts 4–6 embrace potentially *pudor*-inducing behaviors of myriad sorts, and their very range appears to justify the metaphor of the "high-wire act" that has been used to express the risk of social disaster that animated the emotion: one slip—and there were slips of so many different kinds—and down you went, to disgrace and the discomfort of occurrent shame.[79] Yet, at the same time, the analysis implies that thoroughly well-socialized persons—whose "sense of shame" guarded against discreditable "extension," "retraction," and "lowering" of the self all at once—were also supported by scripts that had come to constitute a "second nature": like a gyroscope, the dispositional form of the emotion helped them to maintain their equilibrium, buoying them up to prevent their "lowering" and holding them in line, to avoid the pitch and yaw of erratic "extension" and "retraction." In short, the analysis so far suggests that the basic structures of the emotion were not static—mere categories into which different kinds of behavior could be sorted—but dynamic, organizing energy to accomplish different forms of psychological and ethical work in the culture. Now that we have a working familiarity with the scripts' contents, we can, in the next section, consider their dynamics more closely.

The Basic Structures in Action

The taxonomy just surveyed implies that any one of its basic scripts is sufficient to provoke *pudor*, whether it be dispositional *pudor*'s sensitivity to a potential slip or the occurrent *pudor* of an actual fall. But this does not mean that the scripts are mutually exclusive. It is generally characteristic of any emotion's scripts—in antiquity and today—that they can be experienced simultaneously, and that in two senses. First, it is obviously possible to experience different scripts of love (say) simultaneously toward different beings or states of affairs: I am certain that the love-scripts I enact in relation to my wife and my dog are (mostly) quite distinct, and certain, too, that each would be quite put out if that were not the case. But it is also plainly possible to enact different scripts of the same emotion simultaneously toward the same person or state of affairs: I am certain that my love for my wife is compounded of several different scripts all at once, each characterized by a distinct intentional state involving different sorts of judgment, evaluation, and desire, each sufficient in itself to constitute an experience that could plausibly be labeled "love"; I am certain, too, that this love has been variously compounded of different scripts at different stages of our nearly forty-year relationship. And what is true of modern (middle-class, North American) love is also plainly true of the Romans' *pudor*, as a couple of examples can demonstrate.

Consider, first, the following remarks by the younger Pliny, concerning his support for a protégé's political career:

> My friend Sextus Erucius is a candidate, and I'm really very worried.
> In fact, I feel much more anxiety and apprehension for my "second self"

(*pro me altero*) than I ever did on my own account. Besides, my *pudor*, my *existimatio*, and my *dignitas* are all at stake, for I was the one who persuaded the emperor to raise Sextus to senatorial rank by making him quaestor, and he's now running for the tribuneship on my nomination. If he's not elected by the Senate, I'm worried that I'll be seen to have deceived the emperor. It's therefore crucial that I get everyone to share the opinion of him that I caused the emperor to form.[80]

Pliny's dispositional *pudor*—his sensitivity to the state of his *existimatio* and *dignitas* (here helpfully made explicit)—is being tested by Erucius's candidacy, because he has given the emperor certain guarantees regarding Erucius's qualities: Pliny fears that if Erucius fails, he himself will seem—will see himself being seen—to have deceived Trajan regarding those qualities. By putting the matter in terms of his own *fides*, Pliny makes plain that he is concerned with a variety of *pudor* discussed earlier under script 4, concerned with satisfying one's own interests at the expense of obligations to others (in this case, making baseless claims on another's trust for the purposes of increasing one's own influence, *gratia*).[81] Yet, at the same time, he is plainly claiming to be animated by the sense of *pudor* that we have seen associated with script 3: his *pudor* is engaged, he says, not just because his own behavior is subject to scrutiny but also because he identifies with Erucius and his fortunes, whether because of an affective and cognitive bond that they share or because his own *existimatio* is implicated in Erucius's, or—as the strong phrase "for my 'second self'" seems here to imply—both. The force of the identification in such circumstances emerges no less clearly in another letter of the same sort, in which Pliny says, "I have undertaken to support the candidate, *and it is known that I have made this undertaking*. I am doing the canvassing, I am running the risk; in short, if [the candidate] gains what he seeks, the honor is his, but if he's denied, the defeat is mine" (*Epist.* 6. 6. 9). It is also worth noting that since Pliny wrote each letter to enlist the addressee's support for the candidate in question, he is performing a discreet and conventional sort of shaming ritual, using his own fairly intricate *pudor* (the dispositional *pudor* that he now claims to feel and the prospect of his occurrent *pudor* in the event of defeat, both compounded of at least two different scripts) to engage the *pudor* of his reader, whose refusal would damage Pliny's positive face.

For another example, more briefly, consider the reasons that Cicero gives to two intimates for his decision finally to follow Pompey in the civil war. Writing to Marcus Marius in spring of 46, he says:

You were worried both that I'd fail to do what I ought to do by staying in Italy and that I'd run a risk by setting off for war; at the same time you surely saw that I was so upset I couldn't work out what the best course was. Still, I preferred to put *pudor* and my reputation before considerations of my safety ("pudori tamen malui famaeque cedere quam salutis meae rationem ducere").

A few months later, he says to Aulus Caecina, in much the same vein:

> My *pudor* carried more weight with me than fear ("valuit apud me plus pudor meus quam timor"): I was worried lest I fail Pompey in his hour of need, since he, at times, had not failed me. And so—overcome by a sense of obligation, or by what patriots would say, or by *pudor* (*vel officio vel fama bonorum vel pudor victus*)—I set out, like Amphiaraus in the play, 'with foresight and full knowledge / to the doom that lay before me."[82]

Setting aside minor differences in nuance, we can see that the same central claim is made in both places. In choosing his course, Cicero overcame the fear of danger and concern for his own well-being in order to satisfy the demands of decent action, specifically the personal obligation that he felt toward Pompey: it is implied that this was the course enjoined by his dispositional sense of *pudor* and that he would have deserved to experience occurrent *pudor* had he not followed it. Conflict between satisfying your obligation to others and pursuing your own self-interests clearly brings us back to the dramas of script 4— but with a difference: for if dutiful behavior (*officium*) had been trod underfoot in this case, the cause would not have been mere untrammeled self-interest— the unlimited negative face of unimpeded action—but would have entailed a kind of cowardice too. In this way scripts 4 and 5 interpenetrate, too.

The scripts, then, are not mutually exclusive in any rigid, binary way— on/off, black/white, A/B—nor do they subject behaviors or states of affairs to a single evaluative grid so rigid that a given behavior or state of affairs ought always cause *pudor* for the same reason. Rather, the same behavior or state of affairs can be variously evaluated, according to its varying origins or motives, and cause *pudor* to be differently constituted (or, of course, not be constituted at all). Take poverty, for example. In *Epistle* 1. 18 Horace surveys a series of unfortunate types (21–25):

> The one whom ruinous lust strips bare, or reckless gambling,
> the one who dresses or scents beyond his means, ambitious for
>   distinction,
> the one whom hunger and thirst for cash hold fast, relentless,
> or *pudor* at his lack of means, and the effort to escape: the rich friend
> . . . loathes [them all] and is aghast.

We are to understand that—at least for the sake of the thought that Horace is developing here—"lack of means" is a cause of *pudor* and, further, that the sort of *pudor* it entails falls on the right side of our taxonomy: talk of "the effort to escape" (*fuga*) from poverty, implying an attempt to do something about it, also implies that something *can* be done and hence that persistence in poverty is "up to you," a state for which you are at least causally responsible. But what sort of *pudor* is that, exactly? The character types whom Horace has just described all embody the pursuit of "more, more, more" through forms of self-indulgence or greed: their *pudor*, if they felt it, would be shaped by script 4. *Paupertas* could cause *pudor* in that way too, but only if it were brought on by self-indulgent behavior, a taste for luxury (say) pursued to the point of bankruptcy; alternatively, it could be shameful because it betrayed *inertia* or *ignavia* on your part, a supine failure to extend yourself in a creditable way (script 5, cf. Tac. *Ann.* 2. 37), or just because it was regarded as something humiliating in itself (script 6). Or (we can think again of Pliny and Cicero) it could be all at once.

To take a more exquisite example, consider the following story:

> Euripides says that Vulcan was led by Minerva's beauty to seek her as his bride but did not gain his end, and that Minerva hid herself away. . . . They say that Vulcan followed her and tried to rape her: when, in the fullness of his desire, he pressed himself upon her and she pushed him away, he spilled his pleasure upon the ground. Deeply stirred by *pudor*, Minerva kicked dirt on it, and from this the serpent Erichthonius was born.[83]

Because the semen on the ground was plainly not Minerva's doing, we now find ourselves on the left side of the taxonomy in seeking to understand her *pudor* and the reason it moved her to cover the semen with dirt. Was it because, as a *virgo pudica*, she found the mere sight repulsive and sought to conceal it, like the Africans who (according to the elder Pliny) smear themselves with red pigment to conceal their black skin (script 1)? Or was it because, as a *virgo pudica*, she wished to avoid the suspicion that she was somehow involved in its spilling, fearing that it somehow would be identified with her willy-nilly (script 3)? Or was it because she found Vulcan's spilling of his seed in her presence a shaming action in itself, an *iniuria*, affronting her positive face as a *virgo pudica* and bruising her *pudor* as severely as if she actually had been raped (script 2)? Or was it—quite plausibly—all at once? The answer depends entirely on the cognitions involved, to which in this case (such are the ways of gods and mythographers) we have no access.

If the same behavior is open to different evaluations in this way, then it follows as a corollary that the same behavior can cause the parties involved in a transaction to experience different scripts of *pudor*, depending on their role or perspective. Take the story just considered: we've seen that the semen on the ground arouses Minerva's *pudor* for reasons that can plausibly be associated with any one of three scripts, or some combination of them; at the same time, the semen on the ground should have aroused *pudor*, for quite different reasons, in the one responsible for putting it there. And what is true of this story is true a fortiori of actual rape, any instance of which should, on the Roman view, be regarded as shameful from at two least complementary points of view, for at least two different reasons: from the point of view of the *raptor*, it should engage the *pudor* appropriate to someone whose desire for unimpeded action—his negative face—impels him to behave in a way that damages his (and another's) positive face—that is, script 4; from the point of view of the *rapta*, it should engage the *pudor* appropriate to someone whose positive face has been damaged by the *iniuria* of another—that is, script 2.[84] (And if the *rapta* has a father, his *pudor* will be engaged as well, by script 3.) To take quite the opposite case, impotence can be focalized in much the same way, as arousing one form of *pudor* in the man who sees himself devalued because he cannot sustain an erection and a very different kind of *pudor* in the woman who sees herself devalued because she cannot inspire one.[85] And, to turn our thoughts in still a different direction, when the elder Pliny grumbles (*HN* 2. 20–21) that "some people offer the gods no respect at all, others the sort that ought to arouse *pudor*" (*respectus . . . pudendus*), he primarily means that these people ought to feel the *pudor* properly aroused by actions that damage another's positive face (in this case, the gods'); from the gods' point of view, the same behavior could understandably arouse the *pudor*, and with it the *ira*, appropriate when one's positive face has been granted no due respect.

Cases such as these teach us that the scripts of *pudor*, where they concern relations between persons—or between persons and gods, which come to the same thing—are often complementary; in fact, the complementarity of the scripts, and the structural relations among them more generally, are their most culturally interesting features. (By the same token, the symmetries that we find also encourage me to think that our taxonomy describes a real and culturally coherent phenomenon.) We have already noted the structural relationship between the "*pudor* by association" of script 3 and the scripts for the *pudor* that is "up to me" (4–6), according to which any of the latter (on the right- side of the taxonomy) could appropriately be appended to continue the thought of script 3 (on the left).[86] We can now extend the thoughts prompted by the preceding paragraphs by considering the very consequential relations between scripts 2 and 4 and between both of them and script 5.

Let's start with script 4. Behavior that falls under this heading is not typically conceived as disfiguring the self directly and per se; quite the opposite, you as agent typically regard, or are imagined as regarding, the behavior as expedient, materially self-enhancing or self-satisfying, an expression of your freedom. Instead, the behavior damages the self to the extent that it offends others and thereby lowers their valuation of you. But, as we have seen repeatedly, behavior of this sort, by the nature of the offense it causes, commonly causes others *pudor* by denying their positive face and doing them an *iniuria* (script 2) at the same time that it should cause you *pudor* as the perpetrator. In this respect, scripts 2 and 4 are complementary, and this complementarity has an important extension: if I feel that my face-claims have been denied (script 2) because of your improperly "self-extending" behavior (script 4), and if I do not respond to the *iniuria* to reassert my face, then I risk being seen as improperly "self-retracting"—*diffidens* and pusillanimous. My script-2 *pudor* will then be compounded by the *pudor* of script 5.

We can thus say that discreditable "extension" of the self (script 4) entails a failure to act with creditable restraint, while in some circumstances attempts to act with creditable restraint can be interpreted as failures to act with creditable spirit, hence a discreditable "retraction" of the self (script 5). These are very much the thoughts that drive Cicero when, after his return from exile, he speaks about the destruction of his house in his absence by the tribune Clodius:

> Could I so harden my mind or look about me with such shamelessness (*impudentia*) that I—whom the senate judged, unanimously and repeatedly, the savior of the city—could bear to see my own home destroyed, not by a personal enemy but by the common enemy of us all, and to see the shrine that this same man has raised up and set before the eyes of the community, to ensure that real patriots would never lack cause for weeping?[87]

The destruction of his house represents the destruction of his standing in the community, his fall from being "savior of the city" (*servator urbis*) to being one whom Clodius—not a mere personal enemy (*inimicus*) but an actual public enemy (*hostis communis*)—could treat as of no account. Were Cicero able to look upon the site of his destroyed house with indifference, it would mean that he was bereft of (dispositional) *pudor*, that he was insensitive both to seeing himself being seen in such terms and to seeing himself in such terms: he would in fact be so pusillanimous that he would deserve to be seen in such terms. Though the disgrace done was not "up to him," his response to it is, and his response must not reveal an unworthy "self-retraction."[88] It seems to be the case that the more sensitive I am to *pudor* of this sort—the more dispositional script-5 *pudor* I have—the more sensitive I will be to *iniuria*-based *pudor* (script 2), as well. Furthermore, if I behave in such a way as to incur script-5 *pudor*— say, in suffering a defeat when victory was expected or within my grasp—I will typically behave as though script-2 (*iniuria*-based) shame has been inflicted *on* me: hence the common companionship of *pudor* and *ira*, in military and heroic settings especially.[89]

As these remarks suggest, scripts 4 and 5 are locked in a key structural relation, which is also a source of tension. Much of the tension derives from the fact that these scripts, broadly speaking, represent *pudor* "at home" and *pudor* "on campaign" (*domi militiaeque*): they describe the difference between the fierce manliness (*virtus*) of warriors who must commit and—much harder—face acts of sudden and savage violence when fear turns the bowels to water, and the restrained virtue of citizens. This difference is not (as one recent study suggests) the product of historical change, the result of a vivid and vigorous warrior-culture's *virtus* being supplanted by the mere "virtue" of humbled, "exsanguinated" souls.[90] It is the difference between the two spheres in which the Romans always saw themselves acting in alternation, the military and the civil: one script of *pudor* served to establish and maintain the community's boundaries against aggresssion from without and sedition from within, the other to make life within those boundaries livable once they were secured. Integrating and harmonizing the forms of excellence appropriate to the two spheres was no simple thing. Tensions could arise between them, and between the distinct but equally expedient scripts of *pudor* most typical of each, the one defined by your need to exert and extend yourself in conflict, the other defined by your need to restrain yourself from acts of unimpeded self-interest that violate the legitimate interests of others—or, to put it another way, the tension between acting as though you and your own wants are the only things that matter and acting as though you and your own wants matter hardly at all. In part, this meant that each person had to decide (as we have already seen) how much of his individual liberty he would sacrifice to gain the decent opinion of others: that, precisely, is why "having (a sense of) *pudor* is a kind of slavery."[91] But such is the price of having a communal existence. In this respect, we do better to conceive the Romans' emotional life as being concerned not with questions of high existential drama ("What did the Romans think was the core and definition of being? When everything solid melted into air, what would they cling to?")[92] but with the question "How can we live together well?," enjoying the sort of communal life worth living.

One answer to that question was conveyed by the folktale about human society's golden age with which we began this book: we can live together well if we act to meet the community's needs, not our individual wants, and if we live justly as equals, pious and content with little. This was in fact the salubrious vision of life that the *pudor* of scripts 4 and 5 tended to underwrite. Except . . . though there was surely no necessary conflict between the two scripts in the life of Rome—any more than (say) the life of scholarship entails conflict between vivid conceptual boldness and scrupulous fidelity in the treatment of evidence—it just happens that conflicts sometimes arise, and even in the absence of conflict certain tensions subsist. At Rome, the tension between the two scripts is epitomized—to take one example—by Cicero's desire to commend and embody the *pudor* of decent restraint (a desire documented by his frequent appearance in the footnotes to these first two chapters) and his contrasting, notorious penchant for self-praise: how, one might reasonably ask, can we take seriously his strictures against offensively self-enlarging behavior when he so frequently impersonates a whacking great blimp? As it happens, Cicero's own response to criticism for his boasting in effect acknowledged the tension betwee the two scripts by balancing them against each other, implicitly granting the basis of the criticism—that trumpeting one's own glory was inconsistent with a proper sense of shame—while arguing that the principle did not apply to his case: for extensively making plain the vigorous services he had done the commonwealth (thus acting the part of a free, adult male) was simply the line he had been compelled to take, the only way he could defend himself when attacked by his enemies (thus avoiding the shame of a discreditably wilting "self-retraction").[93] For another example of the same tension, consider the place of "recklessness" (*audacia*) in the common discourse of vice and virtue.[94] The many occasions on which Cicero (again) condemns opponents for *impudentia* readily convey the impression that *audacia* was *impudentia*'s even nastier twin, and unambiguously evil: denounced over and over again as the raw expression of individual will trampling on the claims of others and of the community, *audacia* is the antithesis of *pudor* in the civil sphere (script 4) and, evidently, the very lifeblood of "shamelessness."[95] And yet we know that was not exactly true: to be reckless was also a virtue in the military sphere, in fact one of the core components of *virtus* in the radical sense of being a real man. As such, it was a common spur to avoiding *pudor* (script 5).[96]

To the extent that the *pudor* of script 4 helped fence off civil life from the aggressiveness that the *pudor* of script 5 encouraged, the relation between the two scripts defines some of the tensions of *pudor*. One other source of tension, with which we can round off this section, is internal to script 4 itself. We saw that many of the behaviors this script aims to control entail my attempt, through aggression and self-assertion, to gain more of some good than others think is right—more money, more power, more regard, more sex, or more comfort—especially in a zero-sum setting where any more for me means less for you.[97] The unimpeded liberty that this form of *pudor* seeks to control is commonly, even typically, conceived as my desire not just to satisfy myself at others' expense but also to distinguish and separate myself from others, whose claims on me I can then ignore and—as important—whose equality with me I can deny.[98] Regarded in its most positive light, this form of *pudor* is a sentiment of parity and solidarity: it restrains me from gaining undue advantage over others, and (in partnership, as we shall see, with *invidia*) it tends to keep me alert to others' attempts to gain undue advantage over me. But if we go one step farther and ask, Parity and solidarity *with whom?*, we might be reminded that judging what constitutes undue advantage can be a slippery or tendentious business, especially if I think the advantage is being gained at my expense; and this brings us to the tension inherent in the script. At the same time that this form of *pudor* mobilizes the community's psychic energy to restrain the anarchic and solipsistic pursuit of more, MORE, MORE for me, ME, ME, it exposes to cries of "Shame!" *any* attempt to gain more, even on the part of those who have very little. This form of *pudor*, it is more than once observed, is a luxury for the afflicted; the sort of recklessness (*audacia*) decried as shameful keeps notably regular company in our sources with poverty (*egestas*).[99] Indeed, it is not too much to call this form of *pudor* an affect of the satisfied and complacent, those content enough with their own situation to afford the feeling and concerned chiefly to maintain the situation that leaves them content. As we shall see in later chapters, this form of *pudor* is not the only emotion useful in preserving the status quo for the benefit of those who find it comfortable.

Regarding Others

The most famous line in Ovid's *Art of Love*—on women who go to the games "to see, and to be seen themselves"—is followed immediately by a warning of the lurking risk to *pudor*, and no wonder.[100] As the tot in the airport with whom we began was learning, being seen is central to our notion of shame, and it was central to *pudor*, too. I have several times in this chapter already referred to "seeing yourself being seen," in discreditable terms or as devalued, and I use that slightly cumbersome turn of phrase for two main reasons.[101] First, the notion of "seeing yourself being seen" allows both for actual situations of being seen and for seeing yourself being seen with the mind's eye, using the ethical imagination that all adults—modern and Roman—are supposed have. Second, the phrase suggests the splitting of the self that occurs when *pudor* is at work, as I see my discredited self being discredited at the same time that I am that discredited self. This is the theatrical dimension of *pudor*, which involves my being both the protagonist in a play about virtue and the audience of that play at one and the same time. The forms that this drama can take and the relations between *pudor* and being seen, though not as diverse as the forms and occasions of *pudor* itself, are more varied and intricate than is often allowed.[102] In this section, I examine several of the most important of these before rounding the first two chapters off with an epilogue on the relation between *verecundia* and *pudor*.

For an evocation of "seeing oneself being seen" in the most direct and vivid sense, consider this tableau, which Tacitus paints in the fourth book of the *Histories*. Just before leading his troops to battle, the German rebel Julius Civilis "surrounds himself with the captured standards—so his own men would have their fresh triumphs before their eyes while the enemy was cowed by the memory of slaughter—and orders his own mother and sisters to stand behind him, together with the wives and small children of all the men, as an encouragement to victory and a (source of) *pudor* should they be driven back" (*Hist.* 4. 18). The wives and children are there as hostages of a sort, their lives hanging in the balance of the battle, to remind the men what is at stake, but they are also an audience before which the men will perform: seeing themselves being seen by this audience should bring their (dispositional) *pudor* into play and, by holding out the prospect of (occurrent) *pudor* if they are defeated, inspire them to exert themselves to avoid defeat.

This kind of example could be multiplied a hundredfold and more. For a less obvious but no less vivid case, consider the story that the elder Pliny tells about the cruel device used by king Tarquinius Priscus to "encourage" the reluctant Roman *plebs* to continue work on his great system of sewers. By crucifying and exposing the bodies of the wretches who had killed themselves rather than continue, he caused those still alive to keep plugging away, out of *pudor* at the thought of being treated the same way.[103] At some level, of course, the response is quite paradoxical, even irrational, a point Pliny too seems to appreciate: as Lucretius might have remarked, that the sight of another's exposed and outraged corpse should cause me *pudor* because I imagine—while yet alive—how *I* would "feel"—when dead—to "see" my own corpse being seen that way makes no more sense than it does for me to fear that my body will be burned or eaten by animals after my death (cf. Lucr. 3. 870 ff.). Yet, the sensitivity to seeing oneself being seen in such a state had so strong a hold on the imagination that it can be assumed to have caused the living to project themselves into the places of the dead.[104]

But the modalities of being seen—the relations between your worth and others' regard—are not all as straightforward as these example suggest: the formula "for the Romans, being was being seen" is unsatisfactory, not just because it reduces the complexities of Roman "being" but also because it reduces the complexities of "seeing."[105] To draw in at least some of these complexities, where *pudor* is concerned, we can start with two forms that invest great power in the literal regard of others, though in both forms the "seen self" and the "actual self" are quite distinct in the individual's own mind. Let's call these the case of Gyges' ring versus the artist's model.

The tale of Gyges' ring, used by Plato as a vehicle for moral inquiry in the *Republic* (2. 359D–360D), was taken up by Cicero for his discussion of "appropriate actions" and their relation to the "expedient" (*utile*) and the "honorable" (*honestum*: *Off.* 3. 37–39). In the story, Gyges the Lydian comes to possess a ring that makes its wearer invisible, free to commit, undetected, any act he might choose: the parable's point is to put the question, How then does the wearer choose to act, and on what grounds? Where the choice lies between right and wrong action, is it only the knowledge and disapproval of others that deters wrongdoing, or do we properly avoid the wrong and choose the right because of the very nature of the choice and its objects? Such questions obviously entail judgments of value, including the value of individuals, and so entail potential occasions of *pudor*: asking whether only the knowledge and disapproval of others deters wrongdoing amounts to asking whether *pudor* indeed derives its force only from the literal regard of actual others.[106]

In response to this question, there was, evidently, a substantial body of those inclined to answer "yes." This is made plain, for example, in the recurrent thought that the darkness of night dissolves *pudor*:[107] if no one can see me, I need feel no *pudor*, irrespective of my own knowledge. Common, too, is the related thought that writing (as opposed to talking) to another weakens *pudor*: if I do not need to speak with you face to face and look you in the eye while I speak, I feel freer to say expedient things—lies especially, but by no means only—that I might otherwise be deterred from saying.[108] And there are any number of comparable anecdotes—from reveling in an unbecoming lover to practicing the grossest vice or crime—that converge on the same point: *pudor* is absent while the secret is safe.[109] In such cases, it is understood that I, as agent, know what I am doing or have done, know what sort of person this shows me to be, have not beeen restrained by (dispositional) *pudor* from doing it, and in fact feel little or no (occurrent) *pudor* for having done it, so long as the deed is cloaked in actual or metaphorical darkness. The mode of "seeing" here entails a complete disjuncture between points of view, between my knowledge of the sort of person I am and the sort of person others credit me with being; it is assumed that this disjuncture, though not ethically admirable, is typical of the way many people in fact behave. With this mode of seeing compare now a second mode where a similar disjuncture is at work, but in exactly the opposite way.

Here we can start with another, less well-known parable.[110] After weeks of posing nude for the same male painter, a female model one day realizes that he is looking at her in a new way—not impersonally, as an artist solving a problem of planes and volumes, but as a man gazing with longing at a naked and available sexual object—and so, for the first time, she feels *pudor*. Why? She has done nothing different on this occasion, and nothing to invite this kind of attention: it is not "up to her." She does not identify with the artist's point of view—*she* does not think that she is a naked and available sexual object—she is merely aware that the artist sees her as such. But being seen as a naked and available sexual object—being seen as "that kind of woman"—is a position, she believes, in which no decent woman should find herself: it places self-respect under too much strain. And so she feels *pudor*, because she sees herself being seen in that way, because she deplores being seen that way, and because it is her *self* that is being seen that way—the kind of woman she is. If she is a Roman woman, she will very likely take this way of being seen as an *iniuria* per se.

In fact, we can glimpse (fully clothed) Roman women in comparable circumstances, with very much that response, in Suetonius's description of the emperor Caligula, who would invite ladies of distinguished station to dinner with their husbands "and regard them carefully and slowly as they walked past [his couch], in the manner of someone shopping for goods (*mercantium more*), and even raise a woman's face with his hand if she lowered her glance out of *pudor*" (*Cal.* 36. 2). A Roman *matrona*'s experience of *pudor* in such circumstances might be a complex thing, but a large role in provoking it would be played by the simple fact of seeing herself being seen in the discreditable terms that Suetonius helpfully supplies—as mere goods on offer—even when she rejected that ascription of *pudor*-worthy status. The response is not guided by the philosophically correct thought (also expressed by nonphilosophers) that when I know the ascription is wrong, I will not feel the *pudor*.[111] But that does not mean the response is either uncommon or irrational. It is exactly the response that informs an important type of script-2 *pudor*, aroused by acts of defamation or other types of *iniuria* that consist in the mere ascription of shameful behavior or status.[112] And, though my intentionality and agency are not involved, my positive face is in fact being treated with disrespect, and the judgment of my value (*existimatio*) is in fact at stake.

Both parables—of Gyges' ring and the artist's model—locate that value entirely in the judgment of others, who in each case get the judgment wrong, either by failing to see a fault that is actually in me (so that I escape *pudor*, rather than feel it) or by ascribing to me a fault that is not mine (so that I feel *pudor* for reasons that are not "up to me"). With these cases we can now contrast quite a different mode of seeing, which causes my alert dispositional *pudor* to be engaged in a fully internalized playing out of merely possible scenarios. These are cases that find my social identity under the stress of particularly close scrutiny, where the work of imagination gives the notion of "seeing myself being seen" a double sense: I see myself being seen literally, since I am indeed the center of others' attention—performing *an entirely creditable* act; but because that act involves the core of who I am as a social being, I see my worth being on the line as it seldom otherwise is, and I respond to the intensity of the *risk* as though I were responding to an experience that devalued me in fact.

These cases, it will not surprise, are highly gendered. For women, this mode of self-seeing is the source of the "maiden's blush": receiving a profession of love or proposal of marriage from a suitor, even if not *pudendum* in itself, will cause a woman to be "thrown into disarray by *pudor*, . . . [her] whole face flushed, [her] eyes fixed upon her lap," because she sees that her core "competence" in the culture—as a chaste yet desirable potential mate—is being tested or put on display.[113] Correspondingly, public speaking and giving testimony are the chief occasions where this mode of seeing is at work for a male. Arising to speak, a Roman man will commonly acknowledge experiencing *pudor*—in fact, acknowledge that *pudor* is properly felt—not because the act by its nature compels him to see himself being seen in discreditable terms but because the act by its nature causes him to see himself being seen conspicuously—stepping into the center of attention and claiming the authority to speak—in circumstances where it is all too easy, at the same time, for the mind's eye to see the many ways he can fail.[114] Providing testimony presents a similar opportunity. So in his defense of Lucius Flaccus, for example, Cicero describes the testimony given by several men hostile to Flaccus in terms that contrast "our" fine *mores* with stereotypical bad behavior of "the Greeks": if any of these witnesses had been *impudens* in the manner of a Greek, Cicero says, he would have spoken falsely to harm the person with whom he was angry, and he would have done so without blinking an eye, engaging in all manner of histrionics; but because each was an upright Roman, to whom *religio* and *fides*—the scruples involved in telling the truth—meant something ("our customs and training exert more force than a quarrelsome sense of grievance"), they all gave their testimony—even when it was harmless to the target of their anger—with the tremor of *pudor* and pallor of fear.[115] They did so because they realized that their worth as persons, so bound up with their *religio* and *fides*, was on the line. Were they to fall away from the standard of *religio* and *fides*, they could be exposed as liars and see themselves being viewed with contempt. In any case, they could not escape seeing themselves as liars.

And so we come to a form of "self-seeing" that looks very much like what we call conscience. In this mode, I risk or actually experience (occurrent) *pudor*, or I am restrained by (dispositional) *pudor*, with reference to no one's "seeing" other than my own: when I am conscious of making outrageous—but silent— requests of the gods; when, like Mezentius at the end of *Aeneid* 10, I realize I have harmed a loved one and give heartfelt expression to a *pudor* that has only my horse as its audience, or when, in the context of a private literary exercise, I see myself falling short of my model.[116] Indeed, it is not at all rare for me to see myself being seen in discreditable terms—by myself—even when that view is flatly contradicted by the way an actual audience expressly sees me. This is the *pudor* that moves Ovid's Philomela to see herself as her sister Procne's sexual rival (*paelex*) when she has been raped by Procne's husband, despite Procne's attempt to comfor her; it is the unconsolable *pudor* of defeated legionaries, crushed by their own awareness of disgrace (*conscientia flagitii*) despite the consolation and encouragement offered by other solders; it is the *pudor* that causes Terentius Varro, after he has rashly engaged battle in the disaster at Cannae, to refuse the office of dictator offered him by the whole senate and the people.[117] In this mode, we find the interiority of *pudor* most obviously at work: seeing the distance between his circumstances and what he expects of himself, the person open to *pudor* does not need to wait for others to call his attention to the gap. In fact, the gap might exist only in his own mind.[118]

It remains to stress that the various ways a Roman could "see himself being seen" cannot be reduced to a neatly linear tale of ethical "development," or anyway not a tale that the Romans themselves give us any warrant to tell.[119] We cannot take any one of *pudor*'s forms as a priori the "real" or "original" form on which the others are somehow "parasitic," nor can we describe an "evolution" (or, for that matter, a "decline") from a completely externalized sense of the self and its worth, embedded in the judgments of others, to a completely internalized sense of a self that exists independent of others. There is no such neatness in the evidence, and no reason to expect such neatness in life. These different modes of viewing and evaluating the self were all just available simultaneously to those living in the culture, as they continue to be today, their contrasts and their conflicts enriching the many-layered messiness of life.

Regard for Others: *verecundia* and *pudor*

Now it happens that the *pudor* of Terentius Varro, just remarked, serves as grist for the moralizing mill of Valerius Maximus, who retails it in a chapter devoted in general to—not *pudor*, but *verecundia*. The example reminds us, then, that we have some unfinished business, held in suspense since the end of the previous chapter: the need to sort out the relation between the two emotions that these terms name.

Let's start, then, with several obvious facts that highlight their similarity. Both emotions are experienced when attention is directed to an assessment of the self in a social setting, and they have in common certain visible symptoms, especially blushing and reticence.[120] That they are closely related did not escape the attention of the Romans themselves, who make this clear in several ways. For one thing, each of these emotion-labels is used by a careful writer of Latin as the equivalent of the Greek term *aischunê*—*verecundia* by Cicero, *pudor* by Gellius.[121] For another thing, the two terms are often used in ways that suggest they are synonymous. Thus, in speaking of his refusal to use "obscene" language, Quintilian says "Content with the habit of Roman *pudor*, . . . I shall by my silence champion the cause of *verecundia*" where such talk is concerned; the younger Seneca, while going on at some length about the vice of garrulity, says that "it can befall you only if you cease to have a sense of *pudor*. . . . It can't befall you, I say, as long as your *verecundia* is sound."[122] In both of these settings (and many others like them), the shift from one term to the other seems motivated by little more than a desire to avoid repetition. Indeed, it appears that one could simply interchange the terms without affecting the sense: when on another occasion, as a preface to citing a witty pun by his father, Quintilian says, "And why should *pudor* keep me from using a home-grown example?," it is not obvious that substituting *verecundia* for *pudor* would materially change the thought.[123]

Yet, it would surely be a mistake to jump to the conclusion that *verecundia* and *pudor*—the terms and the psychic states they denote—are simply identical. It is a readily observable fact of language that we often speak of closely cognate emotions in ways that treat emotion-terms as interchangeable. Probably no native speaker of English reading this sentence has not spoken of "envy" when a different state—the one commonly termed "jealousy"—was actually at issue, or of "regret" when "remorse" might better have conveyed the thought (or vice versa: we will consider the latter difference in the next chapter). I am still more confident that this is true of the distinct emotions of self-attention with which our labels "shame," "embarrassment," and "humiliation" are commonly (albeit with variable consistency) associated.[124] It may be that some such habit is at work in at least a few of the instances already remarked: we can observe, for example, that whereas Cicero seems to use the terms *pudor* and *verecundia* as though they were interchangeable in the passage of *On the Commonwealth* just noted, he elsewhere speaks of them as distinct, if closely related.[125]

And, in fact, some clear, substantive distinctions can be made. The feeling that the Romans speak of as *verecundia* always concerns my own behavior in a given transaction. Because it is the lens of wariness with which I as agent survey the scene in which I act, it concerns only things that are "up to me," and it is therefore reliably distinct from the scripts of *pudor* on the left side of our taxonomy. Similarly, *verecundia* restrains me from placing myself too much to the fore; it does not impel me to deeds requiring gumption. It is therefore distinct from the *pudor* of script 5, which urges (or punishes the absence of) creditably "self-extending" behavior, especially in settings of conflict: this, we can note, is yet another reason why *verecundia* is spoken of so rarely in military contexts.[126] Furthermore, since *verecundia* concerns my acting in relation to (and possibly offending) others, it is rather unlike the *pudor* of script 6, which concerns only actions by which I demean myself, by being stupid, rustic, or the like.

Nor, finally, does *verecundia* correspond to the occurrent version of script 4, as is evident from a "textbook" case of that form of *pudor* in action: Vergil's Dido in *Aeneid* 4. At the book's start, when her desire for Aeneas has begun to hurt, she famously addresses her *pudor*—her dispositional "sense of shame"—with a prayer that the earth might swallow her up or Jupiter obliterate her with a thunderbolt before she "violates" that disposition, bound up as it is with her promise to remain faithful to the memory of her husband, Sychaeus (*Aen.* 4. 24–27). In other words, she would sooner die than come to feel occurrent *pudor* by indulging these new appetites at the cost of her *fides* and her *pudicitia*, her sense of licit sexuality. But of course she does indulge her appetites, and so she does come to feel occurrent *pudor*. *Fides cineri promissa Sychaeo*—the loyalty promised to Sychaeus's ashes, now forfeit—are the last words of the speech in which she resolves on suicide (*Aen.* 4. 552): with her sense of herself deeply disfigured by the awareness of her failure, she obliterates herself in an agony of shame, after earth and Jupiter have failed to answer her prayer by obliterating her before she had reason to feel it. And this is exactly the difference between Dido's kind of occurrent *pudor* and *verecundia*. When I am gripped by that sort of *pudor*, I just do not want to be seen: I wish the earth could swallow me up (as Dido prays), and, in the extreme case (which Dido also enacts), my sense of a disfigured self can lead me to suicide, the most emphatic form of self-effacement. At a minimum, I will surely avert my glance from yours: I see you seeing me as discredited and ethically damaged, and I just cannot look you squarely in the eye. But, if I am experiencing *verecundia*, I avert my glance, not because I think you see me as ethically damaged but to avoid the ethically damaging misstep of being too self-assertive and aggressive. I do not want to efface a damaged self but am simply wary of thrusting too far forward a self that is not yet damaged; I do not want the earth to swallow me up but want merely to maintain face in the social transaction at hand.

By a process of elimination, then, we can see that *verecundia*'s resemblance to *pudor* is limited to the dispositional form of a single, very consequential script, the one that seeks to set limits on your own unimpeded action: script 4. I can also suggest that a significant distinction is at work within this similarity; so that my suggestion is not misunderstood, let me pause to make clear what I intend. The distinction I have in mind entails an empirical point, not a prescriptive or normative one. It is not that *verecundia* can be said to "properly mean" or "strictly mean" such-and-such while *pudor* "properly" or "strictly means" this-and-that (implying, among other things, that usages that depart from these meanings are "improper" or "loose"). It is rather that the "such-and-such" and the "this-and-that" I will describe are recognizably distinct affective states, each having a real existence independent of their association with any given lexical item; and it happens that, in classical Latin, one of them is more commonly and closely associated with *verecundia*, the other with *pudor*. In the same manner, my displeasure at appearing foolish because of a lapse that—though I'd avoid it if I could ("oh, Lord, I really must learn to check my fly before going to lecture")—leaves my overall sense of worth unimpaired is one plainly recognizable pyschic state, while my displeasure at seeing myself being seen as seriously devalued is another. Both states are distinct, and both exist independent of the language used to describe it: I could surely experience either one without being able to "name" it. It just happens that, in modern English, the former is more commonly associated with the lexical item "embarrassment," the latter with "shame."

I suggest, then, that the lexical items *verecundia* and *pudor* (in its dispositional script-4 guise) are commonly associated with emotional states of self-attention that, while similar, and even complementary, are nonetheless distinct. One of these states entails concern for where I stand relative to the other person in a transaction and what claim on my respect the other person has. The wariness or worry that I experience in this state is above all about process—about my handling of a transaction already or presently under way—and the question that it asks most pressingly is "How am I doing?" Further, the question and the attendant worry arise in part because I have regard for you and concern for your point of view, or at least your standing; and I commonly have this regard for you, not simply as a party who potentially will disapprove of me, but because of who you are in your own right and because of your integral role in the transaction: were I to ignore this aspect of you, the transaction would fall apart, or take on an entirely different character. In the other state, this sort of regard for the other, while certainly not alien or incompatible, is only contingent, not constitutive or essential. My concern in this state is first and foremost, and sometime exclusively, wrapped up with *me* and my potentially devalued self. If you figure in the emotion at all, it is as the judging witness of my behavior or as the person whom I am in danger of failing in respect of some obligation or decency; in either case, my anxious self-attention is oriented primarily toward a question that involves not process but outcome—"What if I fail?"—and the consequences of failure for the estimation of my worth. This latter state is the one most commonly associated with *pudor* of the dispositional script-4 variety: in fact it is just this *pudor*, for example, that Dido addresses at the start of *Aeneid* 4. The former state is the one most commonly associated with *verecundia*: its integral regard for the other is what causes *verecundia* to be linked with *iusititia*, as we saw in the previous chapter, as one of the cornerstones of civil society.

The similarity of the two states of course helps to explain why the terms associated with them might often be used with seeming indifference. (By the same token, instances of their seemingly indifferent use might take on a different appearance if considered in light of the distinctions just made.) The difference between the two states helps to explain, for example, why *verecundia* is spoken of only in relation to another, while dispositional *pudor*, as we have seen, can be felt by a man all alone, and even in contrast with others' judgments. The same difference explains why Cicero, writing to ask a favor of a friend, expresses the protocols of Roman reciprocity in these terms:

> If the dutiful actions (*officia*) I've performed for you, Curio, were as important as you yourself declare—which is certainly more important than I consider them to be—I'd press my case with greater *verecundia* when it came to making a big request. For it's no small thing for a person of dispositional *pudor* (*homo pudens*) to make a big request of someone he thinks he himself has well served.[127]

But, as it is (Cicero goes on to say), he is already so much in Curio's debt that he need not hesitate to run up the tab by candidly asking for something really big (*mihi omnium . . . maximum maximeque necessarium*). In this tactful dance, Cicero invokes *verecundia* to signal that he is conscious of where each party stands, aware of the claims that each could make, and respectful of the face that each will try to maintain; by including himself among the people dispositionally inclined to experience *pudor*, he demonstrates sensitivity to how his *existimatio* will be affected by the way he conducts the transaction. The *verecundia* is oriented more to the dynamics of the transaction and the relations of its participants; the *pudor* is oriented more to the valuation of the subject in light of his performance. The same difference (to give a final example) also explains why Cicero invokes, specifically, *pudor* of a dispositional variety to interpret Pompey's refusal to take any spoils from the temple precinct after capturing Jerusalem (*Flac.* 68):

> he did not want to give any scope to the gossip of detractors (*sermoni obtrectatorum*) in a city [sc. Rome] so given to suspicions and bad-mouthing. For I believe that so utterly distinguished a general was not restrained by any scruple felt toward people who were both Jews and public enemies, but was restrained by his own *pudor* ("non enim credo religionem et Iudaeorum et hostium impedimento praestantissimo imperatori, sed pudorem fuisse").

Where feelings of respect are explicitly denied and all weight is thrown on the subject's concern for his own good name, speaking of *verecundia* rather than *pudor* would not just change the sense; it would verge on nonsense.[128]

In these first two chapters, we have concentrated on the ways in which the Romans experienced and expressed emotional states that are about the worth of one's self, especially as that worth is tested and revealed in dealings with others. We have seen how thoughts of *verecundia* and *pudor* resemble, and yet are different from, each other, and we have seen, in the case of *pudor* especially, how it is useful to understand a complex ancient emotion in terms of the scripts that express it, how these scripts stand in relation to one another (our taxonomy), and how these relations entail dynamic symmetries of some cultural consequence. In the following chapters, we will be concerned especially with the scripts on the right side of *pudor*'s taxonomy, as we consider some other emotions that are called into play when dispositional *pudor* breaks down in matters that are "up to us." Our subjects will be, successively, the emotions that the Romans knew as *paenitentia, invidia*, and *fastidium*. Each has its own domain—its own "aboutness"—which we will try to understand in some detail; in each case, the domain includes interaction with behavior the Romans would call *pudendum*.

3

The Structure of *Paenitentia*
and the Egoism of Regret

Among hatred's first victims is a sense of humor. This regrettable truth is also a useful truth, at least for the limited purposes of the present chapter, for it provides a way into the story I want to tell concerning the way the Romans talked about regret. The sense of humor relevant to the story is first of all Cicero's, the hatred belongs to Asinius Gallus, and they converge on a text that provoked the only extant Roman discussion of *paenitentia* before the term and the idea were taken up and given a very consequential career by Christianity.

Gallus was a lesser son of a greater father, Asinius Pollio, the orator, general, and patron of the arts who prospered as a partisan of Mark Antony and lived on in ostentatious independence under Antony's victorious enemy, the emperor Augustus.[1] More to the point, Gallus seems to have been the sort of lesser son who revered his parent and resented anyone who cast a shadow upon him. That mindset—combined with the fact that Pollio himself had held Cicero in minimally high regard—would be enough to explain the one prose work for which Gallus was remembered, "books on the comparison of his father and Cicero" (*libri de comparatione patris et Ciceronis*). The work's hostility was enough to provoke a defense of Cicero—"quite learned," Suetonius judged—by no less a scholar than the future emperor Claudius. The comparison's captious character is suggested by the one fragment that survives, thanks to Aulus Gellius, concerning a passage in Cicero's defense of Marcus Caelius Rufus.

Early in that speech, while reviewing the aspersions cast on Caelius's character, Cicero has occasion to respond to slanders against Caelius's *pudicitia*, his propriety in the matter of sex: waving off the abuse that the prosecution has bruited about, Cicero drily remarks that Caelius will never be so pained by such gossip as to feel *paenitentia* because he was not born ugly.[2] Aha! WRONG!! Seeing his opening, Gallus pounces: "for" he says "we are accustomed to say [that something] *paenitere* when the things which we ourselves have done, or which have been done in accordance with our will and purpose (*de nostra voluntate nostroque consilio facta*), begin to be displeasing after the fact and we change our minds concerning them."[3] Obviously, since Caelius's looks, good or bad, were not his doing, Cicero had no business invoking *paenitentia* in that connection. Q.E.D. Gellius, in rebutting this criticism, in effect accepts its premise but says that Gallus missed Cicero's point: yes, Gellius says, the word is "properly used" only in connection with matters subject to our will, but Cicero used that proper sense as a jest, to suggest that it was as absurd for the prosecution to fault Caelius's chastity merely because of his good looks as it would be for Caelius to say *me paenitet* because of those same looks (17. 1. 9–11).

I believe that Gellius's interpretation happens to be along the right lines, and in any event his is certainly a plausible understanding of Cicero's intentions. But my real interest here lies with Gallus's premises, which are pretty clearly these: first, there is but one "proper," which is to say "real," meaning of *paenitentia*; second, this real meaning concerns only what we nowadays call agent-regret, entailing notions of personal agency and volition;[4] third, the situations to which this real meaning properly applies are experienced negatively, with some form of "displeasure"; finally, this displeasure is accompanied by what modern psychology would call an action-tendency, in this case an urge to undo the behavior or plan that led to the displeasure. To these premises the common response of modern scholarship has been "no," "no," "yes," and "sometimes." No, there cannot be just one proper meaning—and in fact it is child's play to find numerous examples that contradict Gallus's main contention (we examine some further on); by the same token, no, the range of *paenitere* is hardly confined to agent-regret. On the other hand, yes, *paenitere* denotes the psychophysical experience of "displeasure" or the like, but it is only sometimes that this "displeasure" is accompanied by the "wish to change" or, more precisely, the "wish to undo" that is central to our own conception of regret.[5]

Accordingly, modern scholars have constructed one or another narrative that runs roughly along these lines. The "original" or "early" sense of *paenitere*, visible in Plautus and Terence, simply concerned "displeasure" or "dissatisfaction" or "unhappiness," the feeling that we see, for example, when Anterastilis in the *Poenulus* declares how unhappy she is at the way she and Adelphasium are dressed or when Phaedria comments in the *Phormio* on the "innate" tendency of most people to be displeased with themselves.[6] Subsequently, it was only through a process of "development" or "evolution" that other, more complex notions became attached to the term, including notions of agency and action-tendency.[7] But, having considered several times over every passage in classical Latin in which *paenitere* and its cognates are found (there are just under 600 of these), I am persuaded that this modern view is only slightly less incorrect than Gallus's. And I am persuaded that it is incorrect because too much attention has been paid to the affective dimension of the emotion—the way it *feels* to be "displeased"—and not enough to the cognitive dimension, the judgments or evaluations that prompt it. If I am displeased or dissatisfied, I am typically displeased or dissatisfied *about* something: what is that something, and how does it work, in the case of *paenitentia*?

I propose in the following pages to suggest an answer, by considering first the basic structure of thought that shapes the emotion and then pointing to some of its complexity, before concluding with some remarks on its relation to the emotions of shame and remorse. As it happens, Gellius gives a starting point for thinking productively about the matter, in his slightly cryptic remark to the effect that "older [speakers and writers] used the word *paentitet* based on *paene* and *paenuria*" (17. 1. 9). This is Gellius's way of suggesting the etymology of *paenitere*, its derivation from thoughts of "almost" (*paene*) and "shortfall" (*paenuria*); and though the etymology cannot be considered certain (details of morphology remain unclear), it does seem to be the case that the emotion that the label names has at its core a concern with falling short, the sense of "almost—but not quite."[8] Thinking about the label in this way is useful, because it suggests a productive way of understanding the central judgment that serves to constitute the emotion.

There are two crucial points to be made in this connection. First, the feeling involved in the emotion is not some free-floating or absolute displeasure to which other thoughts—of responsibility, volition, or the like—come to adhere over time, to give it this or that specific shape. It is always a displeasure of a particular sort prompted by a particular kind of judgment, a *relative* judgment. Just as *paene*, "almost," is a relative notion, dependent on some conception of the whole or the sufficient—some *totum* or *satis*—so the displeasure of *paenitere* depends upon a relative assessment, the assessment of what *is* as opposed to what "should be" according some notional standard of wholeness or sufficiency: it is a displeasure that comes from perceiving a "shortfall," a "shortcoming," a "not measuring up." (In this respect, *paenitere* might have been exactly the verb that crossed Asinius Gallus's mind when he thought about himself relative to his father.) Second, and equally important, the feeling—the noncognitive part of the emotion—is not simple. If I say *me paenitet*, I mean that I feel not only a *displeasure* but also a *desire*, a more or less marked contrafactual urge: the thought is not simply "I am dissatisfied that X" but rather "I am dissatisfied that X rather than Y—and I would undo that state of affairs if only I could." Just because the emotion proceeds from a relative assessment, it always carries with it the awareness of—and the desire for—some preferred alternative: that is how *paenitet* differs from the simple displeasure of *non placet*. The desire is integral to the structure of the thought; to put it another way, if there were no desire, no wish to undo the gap between the "is" and the "should be," there would simply *be* no distress.

That is the basic structure of the thought, and I emphasize that it is present whenever *paenitet* and its cognates are present, from Plautus and Terence down through the full history of pre-Christian Latin. All else depends on the particular environments that give rise to the thought. These environments can, of course, be as varied as human life itself, but, before we consider some of the resulting complexities, it should be useful to examine a simplified taxonomy that organizes the main categories of circumstance in which the thought *me paenitet* can arise (figure 3.1). In a way similar to the taxonomy of *pudor* presented in the previous chapter, the scheme here comprises a range of scripts that a person experiencing *paenitentia* can be taken to enact. Central to the performance, and at the head of the taxonomy, is a displeasure joined with a wish—a painful desire, let's say—that I feel when I am faced with a fact (that X rather than Y) that I evaluate in a certain way (X—what is—falls short of Y—what should be). The next component of the script, and the next level down on the taxonomy, concerns the origin or cause of the state of affairs in question. Here—as Gellius's discussion anticipates (and as is the case in the taxonomy of *pudor*, too)—my own intentionality and agency are at issue: can the fact that-X-rather-than-Y be said to be "up to me," or is that fact generated externally, the result of others' actions or of nature or of chance or of general circumstances? Finally, there is the question, what really is at stake: is it a matter of *utilitas*, of my material or physical well-being as an individual? or is it a matter of ethical moment (*honestas*), concerning my reputational well-being as a social animal, my worth as a person (*existimatio*) in the eyes of some valued audience?[9]

As in the case of *pudor*, we can call these "scripts" of *paenitentia* because I will behave differently in each of the main cases: I will certainly have a different *persona* or sustain a different face, my expressive or effective actions will range from throwing up my hands to rolling up my sleeves, and I will have different psychophysical responses, too (as regret is compounded by rage or shame or frustration or . . .). My performance taken as a whole will vary.[10] To glance again at the examples from Plautus already noted,[11] we would say that the *senex* Nicobulus in the *Bacchides* is playing the role of the contented guest when he says that the way he has been entertained in no way causes him *paenitere*: faced with the externally generated circumstances of his reception, he registers no shortcoming relative to some notional standard, some *satis* (which he happens explicitly to invoke), and so he feels no painful desire to undo those circumstances. We would also say that the *senex* Philto in *Trinummus* is clearly enacting a role with different shading when he endorses the paradoxical maxim that the truly upright man is the one whose uprightness causes him *paenitere*: as he reflects upon his ethical worth—something regarded as "up to him"—such a man registers a shortcoming relative to some notional standard of virtue and so feels a painful desire to undo the present circumstances and make good the shortfall in excellence.

Let's survey, then, just a few examples of scripts from the left side of the taxonomy before concentrating on the right. Under the heading *utilitas*, consider first a passage from Cicero's defense of Aulus Cluentius in the year 66 (*Clu.* 80). After retailing at great length the furor that surrounded Cluentius's prosecution, eight years earlier, of his present accuser's father, Cicero says that it does not cause him *paenitere* to be defending Cluentius now rather than in

Upon seeing that (some actual) X falls short of (some notionally preferable) Y

I have an unpleasant psychophysical response comprising distress (e.g., *dolor*) and the desire to undo that-X-falls-short-of-Y,

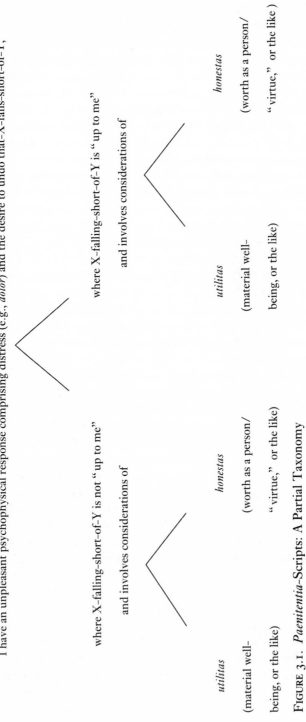

where X-falling-short-of-Y is not "up to me"
and involves considerations of

utilitas
(material well-
being, or the like)

honestas
(worth as a person/
"virtue," or the like)

where X-falling-short-of-Y is "up to me"
and involves considerations of

utilitas
(material well-
being, or the like)

honestas
(worth as a person/
"virtue," or the like)

FIGURE 3.1. *Paenitentia*-Scripts: A Partial Taxonomy

the former circumstances of "unfairness and ill-will" (*iniquitas atque invidia*): the present circumstances are not of Cicero's making but are simply the given, Cicero sees no shortcoming in those circumstances but rather finds them preferable to other circumstances he has in mind, and so he feels no distress and no desire to undo the fact that he is pleading the case now—all this conceived in terms of simple, material advantage. Or, consider that exemplar of self-absorption, Ovid's Paris, writing to Helen and complaining about having to watch "that bumpkin"—he means Menelaus—embrace his own wife (*Her.* 16. 215–22):

> What an outrage! That such an unworthy man holds you all night,
> night after night, and enjoys your embrace to the full! . . .
> I wish only on my enemies the sort of parties I enjoy
> (if that's the word) after the strong wine's been served!
> *paenitet hospitii*, when right before my eyes that bumpkin of yours
> drapes his arms around your neck.

Paris knows what satisfactory hospitality would look like, and this isn't it: E. J. Kenney's gloss on *paenitet hospitii*—"I wish I hadn't come"—captures the feeling exactly.[12]

Or, finally, a very different sort of text, and much more interesting: the point in *Scipio's Dream* at which Scipio Africanus, imagining himself standing amid the stars with his father, Aemilius Paullus, takes in the true scale of the universe and says that the earth seemed so small "ut me imperii nostri, quo quasi punctum eius attingimus, paeniteret" (Cic. *Rep.* 6. 16). A recent, excellent translation of the *Dream* gives Scipio's words an ethical sense: "earth itself now seemed so small to me that I was ashamed of our empire, which touches only a little speck of it."[13] But I do not think that that can be quite correct. I find it hard to imagine *puderet* replacing *paeniteret* here, and it is difficult to see exactly which script of shame would be involved, as we have seen the Romans construct the feeling, unless the phrase "me imperii nostri paeniteret" has an exceedingly pregnant sense, along the lines of "I felt *paenitere* at (having been so foolish and arrogant as to attribute real significance to) our empire."[14] Yet, at the same time, the thought does seem to have a poignancy and weight that a mere "I felt displeased" does not begin to touch. I suggest that the thought is this: Scipio, an exemplary Roman patriot, has always believed that *imperium nostrum* was great, and, indeed (as the preceding paragraphs emphasize), he would in the course of his career be responsible for making it far greater—yet now that he has been given a view of true greatness, he can evaluate *imperium nostrum* and see how far short it falls. The perception causes him to feel distress and the desire to undo not the *imperium* itself but its shortcoming. Yet, that is the source of the poignancy: the same vision that allows Scipio to perceive and regret the shortcoming makes it plain that the shortcoming is so vast it can never be undone ("earth itself now seemed so small to me that I was pained by the shortcoming of our empire, which touches only a little speck of it").

Now, it is in the nature of the case that, where the thought *me paenitet* arises from circumstances not of my own making, my ethical sense is not typically engaged, and my own honorable standing (*honestas*) is not at stake. But that is not inevitably true, as two quick examples can show. Take, first, another text from the *Heroides*, Ovid's imagining of Dido as she berates Aeneas (*Her.* 7. 129–32):

> Put down those gods and the sacred objects you pollute with your
>   touch!
> It's wrong that an impious hand pay cult to The Heavenly Ones.
> If you were destined to be the one to tend them once they'd escaped
>   the flames,
> It causes them *paenitentia* [= the painful desire to undo] that they
>   escaped.

In effect, the gods (in Dido's imagination) would rather not have escaped— would rather be "dead"—than be associated with Aeneas, and they have that preference not because it would be more advantageous for them in some material sense but precisely because they feel that their *existimatio* is at stake: they see their worth and stature diminished by their association with this terrible man. (It is not coincidental that similar thoughts will cause Dido herself to prefer death.)[15] We find a similar form of the feeling (in this case denied) when the elder Pliny, in the grip of his moralizing impulse, writes of the good old Roman practice of making images of the gods out of clay rather than gold or silver:[16] *he* does not (he says) feel *paenitentia* at—wish to undo his connection with, distance himself from—the good old Romans who worshipped such images (*nec paenitet nos illorum, qui tales eos coluere*), even though (it is implied) there are nowadays plenty of fastidious types around who would shudder at the thought of having such uncouth ancestors. Plainly, we cannot choose our ancestors, and so the connections that arouse regret in such people would not be up to them; equally plainly, such people would nonetheless squirm with discomfort, not at the thought of some material disadvantage, but at the thought that their own perceived worth was somehow bound up with *those* people. (This emotion has sometimes been observed by parents tactless enough to appear in public with their teenage children.) But, of course, Pliny is not such a person.[17]

So, yes, not only was Asinius Gallus certainly wrong, but also there is a fair amount of interesting material that involves this emotion even when a Roman's own *voluntas* and *consilium* do not create the circumstances that bring it about. Nonetheless, it is also certainly true that the left side of the taxonomy is very much the minority report, accomodating (roughly) only one occasion in every six of the Romans' talk about *paenitentia*. Agent-regret, for the Romans as for us, is much more the center of attention; since the phenomenon is certainly more familiar, I can offer a few brief examples of scripts from the right side of the taxonomy to round off this segment of my argument. From among the embarrassment of riches, let's consider just three texts from Cicero's correspondence.

The first of these comes from the letter to his friend Marcus Marius on the occasion of Pompey's great games in September 55. Here Cicero reminds Marius that he had asked for an account of the games and reminds him why he had made the request (*Fam.* 7. 1. 6 "quadam epistula subinvitaras, si memoria tenes, ut ad te aliquid eius modi scriberem quo minus te praetermisisse ludos paeniteret"): Marius had wanted assurance that missing the games need not cause him *paenitere*—that is, cause him to feel distress at and wish he could undo a decision that had come up short. The circumstances are presented as being up to Marius, and the ground for his potential distress is simply a matter of hedonistic advantage—the question whether his decision brought him more or less pleasure—with no plausible ethical content or bearing on estimations of Marius's worth or virtue. The second example runs along the sames lines, but in a more serious vein; it comes from Gaius Matius's famous letter defending his loyalty to Caesar's memory against the attacks of the so-called liberators, who were furious with him (among other reasons) for supporting a law hostile to their interests (*Fam.* 11. 28. 4). Why should they be angry, Matius asks, if he tries to make their deed *paenitere* them—if he tries to "make them sorry," make them feel distress at their deed and wish to undo it? He *wants* Caesar's death to be bitter to all. It is conceivable, I suppose, that Matius means he wants to compel them to experience ethically based *paenitentia*, by forcing them to take stock of what their deed says about their worth as persons or how it causes them to be seen by others. But that seems unlikely. Rather, he wants the outcome of their deed to be painful for them in a real, material way: he wants to make them *pay*. (Not unlike us, a Roman most often means just that when he says that he wants to "make someone sorry.")[18]

Contrast now with that text Cicero's letter to Atticus from November 48 (*Att.* 11. 6. 2). In speaking about his decision to leave the remnants of the Pompeian forces in the aftermath of the defeat at Pharsalia, Cicero is emphatic that this choice, his *voluntas*, has not and will never cause him *paenitere*, cause him to feel distress at his decision and wish to undo it (*me discessisse ab armis numquam paenituit*), and his reason is plain: the Pompeian faction had revealed its cruelty and barbarity, in which he would have been implicated had he stayed. The statement "leaving the conflict has caused me not a moment's *paenitere*" therefore implies the statement "remaining under arms would have caused me *pudor*": had he remained under arms, he would have had occasion to regret how that reflected on his worth as a person and so to feel *pudor* at how that caused him to see himself being seen. But notice the distinction that he immediately draws. Though he says, "I will never feel *paenitentia* at the choice

I made" (*voluntatis me meae numquam paenitebit*), denying honor-based *paenitentia* associated with his choice, he acknowledges that he *does* feel *paenitentia*—is distressed at and wishes he could undo—the practical plan (*consilium*) that he adopted to put his choice into effect. This *paenitentia*, by contrast, is predominantly prompted by considerations of material advantage: he sees now that the course he took in returning to Brundisium was inferior to the alternative of lying low in some hole-in-the-wall, because it has produced various undesirable, practical outcomes in his day-to-day life.

Now, there are two main reasons for favoring the distinction between the *utile* and the *honestum* as an important organizing device, as I have done in our taxonomy. One is that—unlike (for example) the distinction drawn in the *Thesaurus* between the "quantitative" and the "qualitative"—this distinction happens to work:[19] that is, it actually responds to an important fault line in the data, so that reading a given text in these terms helps to make clear and explicit what it is about. The second, more important reason is that the distinction reflects the categories in which the Romans themselves consciously thought when speaking of *paenitentia* and that they manipulated in their rhetoric, playing one category off against the other.

For an example of what I mean, consider Cicero's stout affirmation of his position at the end of the fourth *Oration against Catiline*, stressing that even the threat of death will not *paenitere* him, cause him to feel distress and wish to undo his deeds and his policy.[20] The *paenitentia* that he abjures would plainly be concerned only with outcomes inexpedient for his material well-being (ceasing to breathe, for example). Were Cicero to feel that sort of *paenitentia*, it would in itself reveal something ethically weak and unattractive about him (it would, for example, suggest that he was unworthy of the singular honors that had been decreed for him). And so, while that *paenitentia* would not be prompted by ethical judgment, it would itself be subject to ethical judgment. But, because he abjures it, we are to understand that he's a top guy, ethically speaking.

Cicero repeatedly uses this move to seize the ethical high ground by conveying that he (or someone he represents) will never feel *paenitentia* for serving the *res publica*, no matter what the cost to his personal, material well-being; and a notable range of other writers use the same basic move, not just in the arena of public action but also with reference to purely personal concerns.[21] So the passage in Horace's *Satire* 1. 6 where he reflects on his upbringing: after praising his father for instilling in him the virtue of moderation and contentment with his lot—indeed, he wouldn't have complained had he ended up following in his father's footsteps as a public auctioneer—he adds (*Serm.* 1. 6. 87–92),

But on this account, now,
I owe him even greater praise, and thanks.

> May having had this father never cause me *paenitere*, not while I'm
> sane;
> and so I'll not cop the plea that many do, saying it's not *their* fault
> that their folks weren't freeborn (*ingenuus*) and distinguished (*clarus*).

It might have been materially more expedient for Horace to have had a different father, one who stood higher on the social pyramid, as *ingenuus* and *clarus*,
and on that ground Horace might feel distress at and wish to undo the circumstances of his birth—a form of regret that stresses the mere advantage of making this or that kind of career. But, in fact, Horace does not feel such *paenitentia*
and prays that he never will—and (we're meant to think) good for him: such a
nice boy![22]

This move is also occasionally turned on its head, so that *paenitentia*
prompted by considerations of *honestas* is abjured on fundamentally utilitar-
ian grounds. This variant is understandably less common, but it occurs with
notable frequency in one particular connection, illustrated by Valerius Maximus's
comments on Tarquinius Priscus (3. 4. 2). Tarquinius, it is stressed, brought
several deeply discomforting liabilities to the kingship, since he was not only a
non-Roman but also (and worse) the son of a trader (*mercator*) and exile: the
Roman political community might well experience *paenitentia* for these reasons, and it would be a *paenitentia* motivated by considerations of its honor.
But the outcome of Tarquinius's reign brought so many material advantages
on so many fronts that the *civitas* was able to set aside this honor-based
squeamishness ("tam prosperum condicionis suae eventum industria sua pro
invidioso gloriosum reddidit: . . . praeclaris virtutibus effecit ne haec civitas
paenitentiam ageret"). And we find this same idea repeated in other historical
texts, when Livy writes about the introduction of various plebeian magistra-
cies, or when Sallust and Suetonius write about the rise of "new men" like
Marius and the Flavians.[23]

I have so far argued that the structure of *paenitentia* described by our taxonomy provides, in general, a productive way to think about the emotion. In
the balance of the chapter, we give our attention to two specific points. The
first concerns some complexities in the structure that I have not so far addressed. The second concerns the relation of this Roman version of regret to
notions of shame and remorse.

So first, to soften slightly the hard and clear lines of the picture I have
presented to this point, let's consider the fact that more than one script can be
enacted simultaneously, especially as concerns the distinction between the *utile*
and the *honestum* as the bases of the emotion. I have in mind here not instances
of incidental ambiguity—an opacity that could be clarified if only the text offered more data with greater precision—but cases of genuine multivalence,
in which there is no single, determinately correct analysis because the emotion is being shaped by more than one script at the same time. That *paenitentia*

behaves this way is only what we should expect, because it is in the nature of emotions that they can represent the simultaenous acting out of multiple scripts. So it was with *pudor*, so it will be with *invidia* and *fastidium*, and so it is too with *paenitentia*.[24]

To take an extreme example, consider Catullus's representation of Attis following his self-castration as an initiate in the rites of Cybele, the Great Mother of the Gods, when he has had time to consider the (let's call them) shortcomings of his new condition (63. 62–73). In his physical and psychic distress, he wishes he could undo what he has done, to regain his wholeness ("Now, now my deed causes me pain, / now, now it causes me *paenitentia*"), and it is plain that his *paenitentia* is based both on his physical well-being as an individual—the realization that he will have an undesirable life in the wilds, where once he had a comfortable life in the city ("Shall I inhabit the chill places cloaked / in the shows of green Ida? / Shall I spend my life / beneath the lofty pillars of Phrygia, / where the doe keeps to the wood, / where the boar roams the groves?")—and on estimations of his worth as a person, in his own and others' eyes: he reflects that he will be spoken of in a way that diminishes his worth ("Shall I now be called the hand*maid* of the gods / and the serving *girl* of Cybele?") and that he will in fact *have* less worth ("Shall I be a fragment of myself?"). This side of his *paenitentia* has a double edge of shame: he sees himself being seen in a discreditable way by others, and he sees himself the same way.

Very few have the chance to stand in Attis's shoes, but insofar as his experience is not structurally different from a case of what we would call "buyer's remorse," it bears comparison with a much more pedestrian example, the letter the younger Pliny wrote, as a friend of the prospective buyer to a friend of the would-be seller, to assist Suetonius in buying a small estate.[25] Pliny aims to insure that Suetonius pays a fair price, so that it will not come to seem a bad deal (*mala emptio*) and leave room for *paenitentia*, and Pliny's words make it tolerably clear that such *paenitentia* would follow from two different kinds of judgment: first, that the purchase had just not turned out well as a matter of simple material advantage; second, that the purchase appeared to expose and reprove the buyer's folly (*stultitia*)—"What a dunce to have paid that price!" Here Pliny ties into a very strong strand in the Roman discourse of regret: when any act can be attributed to folly (*stultitia*) or rashness (*temeritas*) or lack of foresight (*imprudentia*), those faults tend to give an ethicizing cast to any evaluation of the act itself. Just as practical shrewdness (*prudentia*) was a virtue and an index of character, failures of *prudentia* were vicious; their texts repeatedly make clear that the Romans took such failures to be blots upon their honor and as comments on their worth as persons.[26]

For a different kind of case, consider Livy's description of Quintus Fabius Maximus's tactics in the year 217 after taking over a badly shaken army. By conducting a series of small skirmishes in relative safety, Fabius hoped at last to accustom the solders to feeling less *paenitentia* for their courage (*virtus*) and luck (*fortuna*)—less distress and less desire to undo shortcomings in those areas (22. 12. 10). I take this to mean that Fabius was the adept psychologist that a good leader must be: realizing that as long as they brooded on the past, dwelling on what they took to be either bad luck (a state of affairs not up to them, just the way things happened to fall out) or deficits of courage (a state of affairs that was up to them, entailing judgments on their worth), they would not be worth much *now*. And so he set about restoring their confidence by turning their thoughts away from recriminations about their earlier failures.

Finally, we can look at the colorful account that Marcus Caelius Rufus gives Cicero of a forensic victory by the orator Hortensius, a victory so unexpected and outrageous that bribery was strongly suspected (*Fam.* 8. 2. 1). There was an immediate outburst in court against the judges, when the verdict was announced; when Hortensius entered the theater the next day—so that the crowd could share his joy (as Caelius drily puts it), which is to say, register its approval and support—he was thunderously hissed instead: special notice was taken of the fact that he had never been hissed before in his long life—but that day was enough to last anyone a lifetime, and to make Hortensius feel *paenitentia* for—distress at, and wish to undo—the fact that he had won. If Hortensius did in fact feel the *paenitentia* that Caelius confidently ascribes to him, it was surely of his own making, and it presumably was based both on considerations of practical advantage—for being hissed was neither pleasant in itself nor expedient for the accumulation of prestige—and on considerations of *honestas*, for the hissing was a shaming ritual, performed by the crowd with two ends in view, to send Hortensius the message that his *existimatio* had been badly damaged and to make it so clear to Hortensius how he was being seen—unfavorably—that he would virtually be compelled to see himself in the same way.[27]

This brings us to the final point I wish to develop, on the relation between *paenitentia* and two other emotions, shame and remorse. Two of *paenitentia*'s scripts have an obvious and strong connection to several scripts of occurrent *pudor* that we examined in chapter 2, insofar as both emotions clearly have to do with self-assessment, with the value set on your worth as a person. *Pudor*, as we explored it, is linked in a range of possible ways to seeing yourself being seen in a certain light, usually discreditable. *Paenitentia*, as I have been emphasizing all along, also has its origins in assessment, which often entails the judgment that what I am or have done falls short of some notional, superior alternative. Accordingly, when I feel distress that X falls short of Y and wish I could undo that shortfall in circumstances that involve considerations of my worth, it is not suprising that the thought *me pudet* will keep company with *me paenitet*.

Obviously, not all *paenitentia* entails *pudor*, especially where thoughts of material *utilitas* are to the fore; perhaps less obviously, not all *pudor* entails *paenitentia*. Consider the story that Curtius Rufus tells of one Dioxippus, falsely accused before Alexander of stealing a gold cup:

> Often a sense of shame (lit. "a blush," *rubor*) can muster less constancy
> than (awareness of) guilt (*culpa*): Dioxippus could not bear the glances
> that marked him out as a thief, and so he . . . wrote a letter to be given
> to the king and fell upon his sword. The king was deeply troubled
> by Dioxippus's death, judging it testimony to his righteous outrage
> (*indignatio*), not his *paenitentia*.[28]

No, certainly not *paenitentia*, in the sense of a painful desire to undo an action
that caused him to see himself being seen in a discreditable way. Rather,
Dioxippus rejected that way of being seen as incorrect, unjust, and unworthy
of himself (hence *indignatio*), and his suicide was (among other things) a way
of demonstrating that rejection; but that he felt *pudor* is also clear. In fact,
Dioxippus in this story is (*mutatis mutandis*) an exact counterpart of the naked
model who is made to feel shame by awareness of the artist's lustful gaze:[29]
she rejects the valuation that the gaze implies, and yet the fact of the valuation—seeing herself being seen in those terms—places a greater burden on her
sense of *pudor* than she can simply shrug off. It seems fair to suppose that most
such instances of *pudor*, provoked by another's act that amounts to an injury
or insult (the *pudor* of script 2, that is), are free of *paenitentia*.

We most often see *pudor* and *paenitentia* keeping company, then, in two
broad contexts: when the *pudor* is of the "*pudor* by association" variety (script
3), of which we have already seen a couple of examples in passing,[30] and when
the *pudor* is experienced in circumstances that are "up to me" (scripts 4–6). It
would be possible to illustrate the linkage by returning to some of the examples
that we have already inspected, to see how easy it would be for the verb *pudet*
to replace or supplement *paenitet* in those texts, but the material is so rich and
abundant that there is no need to recycle.

Consider, then, the speech that Livy puts in Scipio Africanus's mouth
in the year 206, when Scipio has reason to chew out his army at great and
elaborate length for mutinying when their pay has been delayed a few days
(28. 29. 2–7). Reaching his bottom line, he says that, aside from a few ring-
leaders, who will pay with their lives, the rest will pay only with the penalty
of their *paenitentia*, their distress at and wish to undo their error ("itaque
quod ad universos vos attinet, si erroris paenitet, satis superque poenarum
habeo"). The error, as the preceding sections make abundantly clear, is conceived in ethical terms, as a deed that reflects badly on their worth as persons, and it is Scipio's aim to make sure that they see themselves being seen
in those terms. In that respect, his point would remain quite intelligible were
the "penalty" of *pudor* to replace or supplement that of *paenitentia*; so would
Tacitus's point when he draws an unfavorable contrast between the Romans
about whom he is writing and their ancestors (*maiores*) by asserting that the
latter felt keener distress at and desire to undo their disgraceful acts (*flagitia*),
just as more vivid *gloria* attached to their *virtutes*.[31] Indeed, in the latter case,

pudor might even be more expectable than *paenitentia*, insofar as it is more nearly the opposite of *gloria*.

However, the fact that the point would be intelligible if *pudor* stood in for *paenitentia* in such cases—and there are hundreds—does not mean that the sense would be the same. Insofar as both sentiments involve self-assessment, they toil in the same corner of the psychological vineyard, but the jobs they do are distinct and, in fact, complementary. The way in which they are complementary is suggested by another general's shaming harangue in Livy, where both sentiments explicitly figure (27. 13. 1–6). Here the army has performed disgracefully, collapsing before an enemy that it had manhandled in the past and that it had prevented from even pitching camp not twenty-four hours earlier, before breaking off battle for the day. Setting aside past victories worthy of boasting, the general throws in the soldiers' faces the thing that really ought to cause them *pudere* and *paenitere*: the fact that they had broken off battle yesterday when the battle was even. In saying this, he does not mean that they should feel these emotions for having broken off the battle yesterday. Rather, he means that they should feel those emotions because what they did yesterday shows that there was simply no excuse for doing what they did today. They have just ceased to be themselves, and to be Roman soldiers: he is forcing them to see themselves being seen as unworthy of who they actually are, and at the same time he is providing the standard of sufficiency against which they can gauge their shortfall of today. Because they see themselves being seen in that way, it should *pudet* them, and that feeling, in turn, should *paenitet* them—cause them to feel the painful desire to make good the shortfall when they have seen themselves being seen as failing to measure up.

The relation between *pudet* and *paenitet*, we can say, is typically both complementary and sequential. Here are a few other brief but interesting examples:

- In the *Fasti*, Ovid suggests one possible reason why only six of the seven Pleiades are visible: all but Merope, who married Sisyphus, had a god as a consort, and so Merope, out of *paenitentia* and *pudor*, hides herself away (*Fast*. 4. 169–78). She sees herself being seen in a discreditable way as result of this connection and so feels the distressing desire to make up the shortfall relative to the standard set by the other Atlantids.
- Frontinus tells the story of the Persian general Datames who, when part of his cavalry deserted, took the rest of the force with him, caught up with the deserters, and, instead of punishing them, praised them for their eagerness in acting as an advance guard in pursuit of the enemy: as a result, "*pudor* brought *paenitentia* to the deserters" (*Strat*. 2. 7. 9). Here the force of *pudor* is different: it is not the occurrent emotion experienced at negative assessment but the dispositional form that makes you wish to avoid the occurrent feeling by avoiding negative assessments and seek-

ing positive ones. When Datames acted as though he assessed their behavior postively, despite their deserving condemnation, their sense of *pudor* kicked in and so brought about *paenitentia*—the desire to undo the behavior that had deserved condemnation and so to measure up to the positive assessment Datames had offered.

• Finally, according to Livy, king Perseus judged that having Antigonus as their king would in no way either *pudet* or *paenitet* the Macedonians, because of the recent glory of Antigonus's homonymous uncle. They would not experience *pudor*, because they would not see themselves being seen as ruled by a king unworthy of them (a form of *"pudor* by identification"); as a consequence, they would not experience *paenitentia*, because they would not feel a painful desire to undo that relationship as a result of the *pudor*.[32]

In all such cases, the central thought is this: the person's self-respect, his sense of worth as a person, has been placed under question, if not actually damaged; the question must be removed, the damage undone, so that the self can be seen as whole and fully valued again. It is the value of the self that is centrally at issue: that is why *pudet* and *paenitet*, like our shame and regret, are spoken of as emotions of self-assessment. It is also—to turn to our last concern—what makes them distinct from, in fact the mirror images of, the moral emotion we think of as remorse. For, where *pudet* or *paenitet* is fundamentally concerned with the worth of the person experiencing it and what perceived shortcomings say about that worth, the thought in remorse concentrates on the person's deed and, especially, on its impact upon others.[33]

Remorse, as it is generally understood in contemporary ethics and jurisprudence, has these five essential characteristics: (1) an acceptance of responsibilty for a bad act, a willingess to say that you chose to do as you did when you could, and should, have done differently; (2) an awareness of the harm that has been done to others as a result of your action, prompting both (3) a desire to repair the damage or provide compensation and (4) a feeling of sorrow, not for yourself but for the harm your action has done; and, finally, (5) a seeking of forgiveness, as a prelude to reintegration in a community. It is plain that whatever similarities there are to some scripts of *paenitentia* that we have surveyed, there is a fundamental difference in the essentially outward-looking character of remorse, the concern in the first instance for the impact on others. It is this difference of orientation that makes "self-regret"—regret directed at oneself—a perfectly transparent notion at the same time that it makes the idea of "self-remorse" unintelligible; it is the reason why remorse is *essentially* a "moral emotion," while regret is not.[34] It is also this orientation that allows a criminal's remorse to play a part in modern sentencing and parole procedures: a felon who expresses sorrow for his act and empathy for the pain he has caused presents a very different appearance not just from the "remorseless" criminal but also from one whose sorrow is limited to regret for the way the bad act has damaged his self-esteem. In this regard, modern penology owes much to the Jewish concept of *teshuvah* (atonement) and the Christian concept of penitence: for Tertullian, writing on the subject late in the second century of our era, it is *only* what we would call "remorse" that corresponds to true *paenitentia*, a change of heart that leads one to seek purgation and forgiveness for sins—for offenses against externally constituted moral obligations—just because they are such offenses, which above all offend against God as the form and source of all good.[35]

But, as Tertullian was pleased to point out, with complete accuracy if not perfect charity, that is not the *paenitentia* of pre-Christian Rome.[36] From among the hundreds and hundreds of texts that speak of one *paenitentia*-script or another, there are barely a dozen that I can even begin to persuade myself to read as, primarily, representations of remorse. Perhaps the most eloquent of these is a letter in which Pliny intercedes with a friend, Sabinianus, on behalf of a delinquent freedman:[37]

> The freedman of yours with whom you had said you were angry has been to me, groveling at my feet and clinging to me as if I were you. He begged my help with many tears, though there was long moments of silence too; in short, he convinced me of his genuine *paenitentia*. I believe he has reformed, because he realizes he did wrong. You are angry, I know, and I know too that your anger was deserved; but mercy wins most praise when anger was most justified.

This man, I take it, was not simply expressing a wish to undo seeing himself being seen in a discreditable light but was also—or primarily—expressing sorrow for his offense *just because* it was an offense against Sabinianus. I also take it that the great difference in status here, between the freedman and his *patronus*, as between the sinner and his God, bears a noncoincidental relationship to the nature of the sorrow experienced.

In the standard case of honor-based *paenitentia*, the shortcoming I wish to undo can of course have its impact on others, and reversing or compensating for that impact can be part of the wish to undo that is central to *paenitentia*. But the emphasis falls on my own sense of self that has been damaged, rather than on the damage done another: the first thought is "Look at me, what have *I* done!," not "Look what I've done to *you*!" Such other-directed concern as might occur is merely contingent on the circumstances, not essential to the emotion; even where such concern occurs, it is at base an expression of concern for the self: I undo the damage done to you *so that* I can undo the damage done to my self, *so that* I need no longer see myself being seen in a discreditable way, *so that* I can regain my self-regard and cease to feel distress at my short-coming. My compensation or undoing is instrumental, rather than an end in itself: it is part of the care of the self, and of the egoism of regret.

Now, it is not at all true that being Roman meant never having to say you're sorry, and I do not suggest that the Romans were innocent of what we think of as remorse. It is the case, however, that they almost never used the language of *paenitentia* to represent that experience. Rather, when they had occasion to express remorse, it tended to appear in the guise of shame. So, at the end of November in 58, when Cicero believed that he found himself in exile because of behavior that was variously foolish or spineless, he acknowledged the fault (*culpa*) as his own in writing to his wife, he identified the fault as a failure of duty (*officium*), to his family above all, and he spoke of the torment he felt at the thought of their consequent suffering ("for the grief and mourning of all of you, and your own poor health, are before my eyes night and day"). And all this is cast in terms that make the letter what I have already called the most complete and candid first-person expression of *pudor* outside imaginative literature.[38]

Of course, imaginative literature knows this emotional hybridization, too: let me draw your attention to just one example, which can also serve as a bridge to the next stage in our investigations. At the end of the *Aeneid*'s tenth book, after the wounded rogue-king Mezentius has withdrawn from battle under the cover provided by his son, Lausus, he soon sees the boy's companions come bearing his body, for Lausus has died in his father's stead. Even for a villain whom we have been taught to regard as impious cruelty incarnate, the sight is too much (*Aen.* 10. 844–56):

> Mezentius fouls his gray head with heaps of dirt,
> holds out both hands to heaven, clings to the boy's body.
> "Was I so much gripped by life's delight, my son,
> that in my place I let you face my enemy's weapon-hand,
> you whom I begat? Am I, your father, saved by these wounds of
>   yours,
> alive thanks to your death? Oh, . . . now the wound is driven deep!
> Yes, I am the one, too, who stained your name with crime,
> when I was driven from our fathers' royal throne on account of
>   *invidia*.
> Our homeland and my people's hatred rightly sought my
>   punishment:
> would that I myself had given up my guilty life in any and every kind
>   of death!
> Now I still live and do not yet leave behind the human world of
>   light.
> But leave it I shall."

The father here is battered by thoughts no father could bear: not just that his son has died in his place but also that he allowed the boy to die, that he allowed the boy to die out of his own craven longing for life, and that this was not the first time he had done the child an ugly wrong—for he had already involved him in his own dishonor when he fled from his kingdom rather than face the penalty that he justly owed his people.[39] He acknowledges and takes responsibility for the damage done to the boy, and because the damage is irreparable, he offers the only compensation he can, by giving up now the "guilty life" he should have surrendered long ago. So he mounts his horse and rides off to face Aeneas in a duel he cannot win.

Surely this is recognizable as remorse, if any scene in Roman literature is. But it is not *just* remorse, is it? If you assented to the phrase "ugly wrong," it is perhaps because you already recognized that Mezentius is speaking not only about the wrong his actions did to Lausus but also about the way his actions can be taken to look—ugly—and so about the way they can be taken to make *him* look. In fact, if you read Mezentius's words again, you will see that (in a way wholly faithful to the Latin text) "I" and "me" and "my" are rather more conspicuous than "you" and "your." Mezentius's grief and remorse are poured out lavishly for his son, and he will soon express great anger toward Aeneas. But, however much the emotional scripts he enacts are about Lausus or Aeneas, they are just as much—and perhaps a bit more—about himself, about his failings and the light in which those failings cause him to see himself: "Look at me, what have *I* done!" is a more prominent thought than "Look what I've done to *you*." It is in this respect fitting, then, that the narrator represents Mezentius's emotions, as he rides to meet Aeneas, in these terms: "there seethes vast / *pudor* in his heart, and also frenzy mixed with grief."[40]

Now, perhaps you also noticed that another emotion has a role to play in Mezentius's declaration of remorse and shame: the *invidia* that caused him to be driven from his kingdom. The emotion has a place near the beginning of the story that plays itself out in the passionate resolution we have just seen, and evidently the emotion has no small power, to achieve that effect. Understanding what that power is, how it is provoked, and how it interacts with the other passions that interest us is the work of the next chapter, to which we can now turn.

4

Invidia Is One Thing, *Invidia* Quite Another

Writing to his friend Atticus from Cilicia in September of 51 BCE, Cicero responds as follows to the news that an enemy of his, one Marcus Calidius, had recently met defeat in the consular elections:

> It is a great sign of affection to say that you are glad about the defeat of your sister's son's uncle's rival. Indeed, it prompts me to rejoice too— which hadn't occurred to me. You don't believe me? Just as you like; but frankly I do rejoice, since feeling *nemesis* is different from feeling *phthonos*.[1]

Cicero writes here in the relaxed and playful, even arch manner that he often adopts with Atticus. One token of the manner is the reference to Atticus's sister's son's uncle, who of course is Cicero himself: the periphrasis, probably first tossed off as a *jeu d'esprit* by Atticus, is here appreciatively lobbed back to its author. Another token is Cicero's semislipping into Greek when he speaks of *nemesis* and *phthonos* at the end, where he alludes to the sort of distinction that Aristotle draws between those emotions in the second book of his *Rhetoric*: the difference between feeling pain at another's undeserved success (*nemesis*) and feeling pain at another's success, not because the success is undeserved but because the other is your peer (*phthonos*).[2] This is the distinction approximated in Shackleton Bailey's translation of Cicero's semi-Greek, ". . . since malice is one thing, righteous indignation another": to be glad that Calidius failed just because he is Calidius would be malicious, a case of *phthonos*; to be glad that he failed because he did not deserve to succeed is a sign of healthy character.

The nod to Greek ethics is, as I said, part of Cicero's manner in the letter, both playful (Cicero demonstrates, tongue-in-cheek, that he is ethically "sound") and a reminder that their shared culture is one of the bonds between friends.[3] It is likely, however, that Cicero's use of the Greek terms here is not just mannered but a means of achieving clarity as well. For, if we ask how Cicero would have expressed the same idea using the most commonly deployed Latin terms that correspond to the Greek ethical concepts, the answer is clear—or, rather, not clear at all: for he would have said "plane gaudeo, quoniam invidia ab invidia interest"—"frankly, I do rejoice, since *invidia* is one thing, *invidia* quite another."

So much, at any rate, is the burden of my surface argument in this chapter: the Romans defined their emotional terrain in such a way that the one lexical label, *invidia*, did the work of two quite distinct labels in Greek. My more fundamental argument, however, is less concerned with the labels as such than with the main lines of thought developed in the preceding chapters: that the only sound way to understand the emotional language of any culture, especially (but not exclusively) one not our own, is in terms not of lexical labels but of "scripts," the narratives that we enact when we experience any emotion; that thinking in terms of scripts necessarily stresses the specifically cultural content of any given emotion, because it compels us to give due weight not only to the psychophysical feelings the emotion engenders or the responses to which it might lead—the usual centers of attention when talk turns to emotions—but also to the evaluations from which it proceeds; and that the ways in which a given culture's scripts interact reveal the structure and dynamics of its assumptions about emotion—how emotional energy is expressed, understood, and harnessed to do various kinds of cultural work.

Before I develop these contentions, some background first on the semantics of *invidia*, to make plain where my argument comes from. If you check *invidia* in the *Oxford Latin Dictionary*, you will find an account that rightly derives the word from the adjective *invidus*, which is in turn formed from the compound verb *invidere*, roughly "to look against":[4] that is, not just "to look at"—which would be the nonexistent compound **ad-videre*—but "to look at in a hostile manner or with hostile intent" (the difference is comparable, for example, to the distinction between *advehere* ~ "to carry to or toward" and *invehere* ~ "to carry against," that is, "attack"). In other words, we are in the territory of dark looks and the Evil Eye.[5] The *Dictionary* organizes this territory primarily according to an implied distinction between "active" *invidia*—the "ill will, spite, indignation, jealousy, [or] envy" that we feel toward some person or state of affairs—and "passive" *invidia*—the "odium" or "dislike" directed against us; what the *Dictionary* leaves implied is explicit in the very similar analysis of the *Thesaurus*.[6] (Both *Dictionary* and *Thesaurus* distinguish a third, more specialized sense of *invidia*—a "rhetorical" or "forensic" sense—used to describe the sentiment aroused against an opponent: for reasons that will become clear, I believe that it is historically misleading to regard this sense as a distinct aspect of the term, but the point does not matter to my argument.)[7]

Now, in general, I think that both lexica are doing the job that lexica are supposed to do, and I have no serious quarrel with them. In distinguishing the so-called passive and active senses, they reflect the Romans' understanding of one feature of the word's usage, a feature that even led to the coinage of the term *invidentia* to express the "active" feeling, so that the ambiguity could be avoided.[8] And the lexica provide a decent range of glosses, in the sense (for example) that most occurrences of the Latin label *invidia* can be intelligibly translated by one or another of the English labels that the *Dictionary* offers.

But a label is not a meaning, and a lexicon is not the language. A lexicon's approach to the language of emotions generally, and inevitably, leaves unanswered a host of crucial questions; and what is true of emotion terms overall is certainly true of *invidia*. For example, what exactly is the relation between labels such as "dislike" and "envy" and "spite"? Is it merely contingent? Is it just the case that if you "envy" people (as we would put it) you will probably "dislike" them, too, or that if you "dislike" people you will probably be inclined to "spite" them, too?[9] But what causes us to feel any of these things to begin with? *Why* do you "look against" this person or thing and not another? What range of persons or things can provoke that look? And why are all these English labels bundled together under the single Latin label *invidia*?

We can answer these questions only if we consider the different intentional states of the people who are said to experience *invidia* (or, for that matter, "envy" and "spite")—their different judgments, beliefs, and desires—which are in turn embedded in the narratives—the sequences of cause and effect, of perception, evaluation, and response—that we have been calling "scripts." We have already seen the fairly complex sets of scripts variously enacted by people in the grip of *pudor* and *paenitentia*, and we have examined the evaluations essential to the emotions and something of their cultural content. Now we can consider the comparable taxonomy of *invidia*-scripts that appears as figure 4.1, which weaves together the common threads in all the stories the Romans tell under the cover of *invidia*.

At the most general level, all the stories share a perception—that another person is enjoying some good—and an unpleasant psychophysical response, some sensation of pain or sickening (*dolor*, *aegritudo*, or the like): these traits are not surprising, because they are the very traits that the Romans themselves picked out when they defined or otherwise reflected on the emotion.[10] At the next level, however, the most important narrative distinction is not the ancient distinction between "active" and "passive" that we find repeated in the lexica— between feeling *invidia* and being the object of it—but whether or not the story must be told with reference to some principle of right or fairness or the like: in short, whether or not it is a story with a "moral."[11]

So, on the left side of the taxonomy (scripts 1 and 2), I feel *invidia*—I have an unpleasant psychophysical response to seeing your good—not with reference to some principle of justice but just because it is a *good* ("Ah, the laughter of happy children at play—I'll put a stop to *that!*") or just because it is *your* good ("Such a big shot, you with your promotion: I hope you choke on it!"). As the parenthetical sentiments here suggest, these scripts are not exactly foreign to our own thought-world: it is such thoughts that earned *invidia* a place among the Seven Deadly Sins, and they explain why (among the Romans, and,

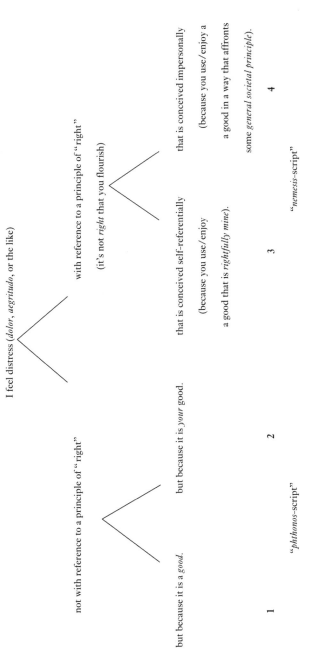

Upon contemplating your good (*commoda, res secundae, felicitas,* or the like),

I feel distress (*dolor, aegritudo,* or the like)

not with reference to a principle of "right"

with reference to a principle of "right"

(it's not *right* that you flourish)

but because it is a *good.*

but because it is *your* good.

that is conceived self-referentially

(because you use/enjoy

a good that is *rightfully mine*).

that is conceived impersonally

(because you use/enjoy a

a good in a way that affronts

some *general societal principle*).

1

invidia
invidere
invidus

2

invidia
invidiosus
invidere
invidus

3

invidia
invidiosus
invidere
invidus

4

invidia
invidiosus
invidere

"*phthonos*-script"

"*nemesis*-script"

FIGURE 4.1. *Invidia*-Scripts: A Partial Taxonomy

I suspect, among us, too) these scripts are far more often discovered in the behavior of others than acknowledged in oneself.[12] The first is much like the sheer malice aroused in Melville's John Claggart by the goodness of Billy Budd or that directed by Iago at Desdemona's goodness, just because it *is* goodness ("So will I turn her virtue into pitch"). The second is the "core" envy—the envy of mere differential status—that Iago feels for Othello's happiness, just because it is Othello's ("Oh, you are well tuned now, but I'll set down the pegs that make this music").[13]

In Roman terms, too, these scripts will look familiar, and so they probably need no elaborate illustration. Scripts 1 and 2, for example, both shape Ovid's extended and brilliantly detailed personification of Invidia (*Met.* 2. 760–832), who "is not glad to see men prosper but withers at the sight" and "tramples down the flowers in her path," just because they are flowers.[14] The scripts are similarly implicated in two of the most frequently uttered commonplaces about *invidia*, the related notions that *invidia* loves to target *virtus* (thus explaining why bad things happen to good Romans) and that *invidia*, like lightning, strikes the "peaks"—of achievement, fame, and so on—just because they are the peaks.[15] One or the other of the scripts is active, too, in a pair of passages from *Aeneid* 4 that we can consider briefly to bring the scripts into focus.

As he sends Mercury to give Aeneas the order to sail from Carthage, Jupiter expresses his general displeasure at the hero's failure to keep his shoulder to the wheel (227–31):

> "Not that sort did his fair, fair mother tell us he was,
> and on strength of that twice snatch him from Greek arms;
> no, he'd be the sort to rule Italy (she said), a land pregnant
> with power, rumbling with war, and bring forth a line
> from Teucer's lofty blood, and make all the world submit to law."

The father of gods and men then caps his complaint with the question (232–34):

> "If glory bought by such great deeds does not kindle him,
> and if he sets no massive toil in train for his own name's sake,
> does he as father feel *invidia* against Ascanius over Rome's citadels?"

"Does he as father 'look against' *Ascanius* with respect to the citadels of Rome?"—which is to say "Does the father feel *dolor* at the thought of his *son's* good?" The question presumes that the father does not want the good for himself, for he has abandoned "glory bought by such great deeds." No, he merely begrudges his son that good, as we would say, just because it is a good, or just because it would be Ascanius's good, or conceivably both. In any case, such feelings would of course be wicked, and that is why Jupiter says what he says: he wants to put Aeneas in the wrong, and so he casts him in a role that has no ethical basis.

It is with some irony, then—for, of course, Aeneas does not hear Jupiter's reproach—that Aeneas takes precisely the same tack barely 100 lines later, in the speech that finds him at his rhetorical low ebb in the poem, as he tries to cast Dido in a similarly wicked role (347–50):

> "If the heights of Carthage and the sights
> of a Libyan settlement keep you, a Phoenician, rapt here,
> why in the world is it a matter of *invidia* that Trojans settle
> in the Land of the West? It's fair that we, too, seek alien realms."

The form of the expression here is slightly different, but the thought is the same. Dido (Aeneas alleges) wants to deny the Trojans the good in question, yet she has no interest in it herself—in fact, she already has a good of her own very much like it. She can therefore have no defensible reason for feeling *invidia* for the Trojans: she must want to deny them the good just because it is a good, or just because it would be theirs, or conceivably both. In any case—acting out either script—she would be acting without reference to any principle of fairness.

On the right side of the taxonomy, by contrast, I feel *invidia* at your good only with reference to some sense of "right": here such criteria as "deservingness," "fittingness," and "fairness" become relevant, as we pass from the forms of *invidia* that resemble the *phthonos* of the Greeks to the "righteous *invidia*" that corresponds more closely to *nemesis*.[16] In one of its manifestations, it may be a sense of right that is self-regarding (and therefore potentially self-serving): here the controlling thought is that the good *you* enjoy is *rightfully mine* (script 3). This is the script that Al Gore is uniquely eligible to enact in contemplating the "election" in 2000 of George W. Bush (to the rest of us, only script 4 is available: see below); and—since no man is wholly a villain in his own eyes—it is the script that Iago acts out in relation to Cassio and the preferment he receives ("I know my price. I am worth no worse a place"). It is also the script that Vergil invokes—only to elide it—at the resolution of the archery contest in the funeral games for Anchises (*Aeneid* 5. 485–542). Aeneas, recall, has tethered a bird to a mast and promised top prize to the archer who strikes the fluttering creature. First, one archer's arrow hits the mast, then another's severs the tether, then Eurytion's brings the bird to earth—but still king Acestes shoots, and his arrow, miraculously catching fire in midair, is consumed. Recognizing a portent when he sees one, Aeneas awards top prize to Acestes, and the narrator adds (541–42):

> Nor did good Eurytion feel *invidia* at the "preferred honor,"
> though he alone had brought the bird down from lofty heaven.

Good Eurytion did not feel *invidia* at the *praelatus honos*—a Vergilian way of saying that he did not feel *invidia* against Acestes, who had been *praelatus*, given precedence, in honor. The comment is added because, in other circumstances (had Acestes been *praelatus* by a politically interested Supreme Court, say), Eurytion *would* have felt *invidia* and indeed would have been quite justified in that feeling, for a prize that was rightfully his by the rules of the game had been given to another: that is the point of the final clause. But Eurytion is "good" here precisely because he can see these circumstances for what they are and so willingly forgo his right.

In script 4, by contrast, the relevant sense of right has no explicit reference to myself at all. My *dolor* derives from seeing you gain or use some good—wealth, prestige, authority, office, or the like—in a way that affronts some general societal principle: in your public or interpersonal dealings you have behaved highhandedly, cruelly, self-indulgently, or against the common good, and you damn well ought be ashamed of yourself.[17] That, at any rate, is the burden of my argument in the rest of this chapter. Whereas people who enact scripts 1 and 2 typically have the flavor of their lives tinged both by the gall proper to those forms of *invidia* and by hatred and a desire to annihilate, too, those who enact scripts 3 and 4 savor the harsh but heady tang of indignation, blended with anger and the desire to punish and shame. This is "righteous *invidia*"; the *invidia* of script 4 in particular—the script that most clearly distinguishes *invidia* from both Greek *phthonos* and English "envy"—is intimately connected to the emotion of shame. In this manifestation—and it is in fact the manifestation of *invidia* most often on the Romans' lips, by some distance—*invidia* bears the same relation to *pudor* that *nemesis* does to *aidôs* in Greek. Before I develop that argument, however, let me first briefly round off my discussion of the basic taxonomy by noting a few other general aspects of it that seem to me important.

First, as in the case of *pudor* and *paenitentia* in the earlier chapters, the taxonomy of *invidia* offered in figure 4.1 is only partial, in the sense that it could be extended downward in further ramifications, here omitted because they are not relevant to my main argument. For example, in the case of script 2, if I feel *dolor* at seeing a good because it is *your* good, I can feel that way because it is *your* good, period, or I can feel that way because it is *your* good *and not mine* (i.e., a distinction between a merely begrudging thought, as we might put it in English, and a thought that is begrudging and covetous at the same time).[18] For another example, each of these scripts can be enacted either "in fact" or, so to speak, "proleptically": in the case of script 1, for instance, I can feel *dolor* at, and so begrudge you, a good that you in fact already possess, just because it is a good (I can want to wipe that smile off your face, just because it is a smile), or I can feel *dolor* at, and so begrudge you, a good that you might come to possess (I can deny you a drink of water when you are thirsty, just because it would quench your thirst).[19]

We should note, too, that, as in the case of *pudor* and *paenitentia*, the taxonomy's constitutive scripts are not mutually exclusive, and that in two senses. First, it is obviously possible to experience different *invidia* scripts simultaneously toward different persons or states of affairs. (Iago does this very conspicuously, and it is the multifariousness of his emotion, as it engenders and elaborates the elements of the plot, that makes him the brilliant creation he is.) But it is also possible to experience different *invidia* scripts simultaneously toward the same person or state of affairs, a point I can illustrate with "the case of the negligent colleague." (Fellow academics will recognize that this case is of course purely hypothetical.) Professor X habitually shirks administrative jobs so that he will have more time to write, publish, and feed his scholarly reputation. Worse, he even tells his graduate students his little secret: the first time you are given a committee assignment or the like, just foul it up—there will be no real penalty, and you will never be asked again. Now, you know all this about X, you feel *dolor* at what you are sure is an intentional, highhanded, and self-interested use of his position that is damaging to your department's common purpose and communal ethos, and you think that he should be ashamed of himself. At the same time, you are aware of the advantage that this behavior brings him, and you feel *dolor* because his taking this advantage puts you at a disadvantage in a zero-sum game: it is just not *fair* that he gets to spend more time on his research while you have less time because you have to pick up some of the slack. You are acting out versions of scripts 3 and 4 at once, in other words. *And*, if you happen to be a less-than-perfect human, you will perhaps at some level simultaneously feel *dolor* accompanied by the thought "To hell with fairness: I just wish I could get away with the same deal, instead of him." Welcome to a form of script 2. We could say in this case that your *invidia* is richly experienced, many-sided, and overdetermined.

As a final fact about the taxonomy I note a curiosity that deserves mention, though I am not able to explain it: the relevant Latin lexical items—the cognates *invidere* / *invidus* / *invidia* / *invidiosus*—are not distributed evenly among the scripts. The verb *invidere* and the adjective *invidus* (the Latin words that correspond most directly to Gk. *phthonein* and *phthoneros*) cluster very densely on the left side of the taxonomy: while they very occasionally appear in contexts where script 3 is being acted out, *invidere* rarely appears in connection with script 4, and *invidus* never so appears. Conversely, occurrences of the adjective *invidiosus*, derived from the noun *invidia*, are concentrated on the right side of the taxonomy, though it sometimes appears in connection with script 2, especially where what we would call "covetous thoughts" are involved. Only *invidia* appears at all commonly across the whole range of scripts. But its most common setting, as I have already mentioned, is the little drama of script 4: that is where it appears about two times in every three, to do the work done in Greek by the idea of *nemesis*. Hence my original contention that Cicero slipped into Greek to make plain a distinction that ordinary Latin would have left unclear, when he wanted to express the idea that the shameful Calidius deserved to be the object of "righteous indignation"; hence my contention that the right side of the taxonomy, and script 4 above all, provide Latin's *nemesis*-script.

Now, when I make that claim I have something quite specific in mind: the behavior and concept of *nemesis* in early Greek that has been described in very similar terms by James Redfield, Douglas Cairns, and Bernard Williams.[20] On this view, *nemesis* stands in a precise and special relationship with *aidôs*: together they form what Redfield calls a "reflexive pair." If you have a proper sense of *aidôs*, you know your standing relative to others in any circumstance, you know what obligations (including obligations of respect) that standing imposes on you, and you know what obligations (including obligations of respect) that standing imposes on others relative to you. If your behavior fails to meet those obligations, you should feel *aidôs* (which for present purposes we can call "shame"), and in fact you *will* feel *aidôs*, unless you are what we would call "shameless." But whether or not you feel *aidôs*, others will certainly feel *nemesis*, a reaction "ranging from shock, contempt, and malice to righteous rage and indignation."[21] By feeling and expressing this emotion, they show that *they* have a proper sense of *aidôs*, and they try to jump-start your own sense, if it has shown itself deficient. The two emotions are thus the "inner and outer aspects of the same thing," as failures of *aidôs* provoke the *nemesis* of others and "the *nemesis* of others evokes *aidos* in oneself":[22] so the princess Nausikaa, a young woman with a proper sense of *aidôs*, says that she fears the reproaches that would be spoken against her if she were seen walking with Odysseus, then adds, "And I would feel *nemesis* for any other girl who would do such a thing" (*Od.* 6. 286). The most common script of *invidia* in Latin forms with *pudor* a very similar reflexive pair.[23]

Take the following passage from one of Suetonius's lives of ancient teachers—an example of which I am particularly fond because I see only now that I did not fully understand the passage when I edited and translated the text several years ago. Suetonius is talking about Albucius Silus, a distinguished rhetorician and declaimer of the Augustan era, who combined with his teaching a very choice practice at the bar. Here is what Suetonius says, in my published translation:

> He also argued cases in court, but that quite rarely, since he sought only the most substantial cases, and even then would take on no part of a case save the conclusion. He later withdrew from the forum, partly out of shame and partly out of fear (*renuntiavit foro partim pudore, partim*

metu). For on the occasion of a suit before the centumviral court, when he was attacking his opponent for impiety towards his parents, he offered the man the opportunity to swear an oath—"Swear," he said, "by the ashes of your father and mother, which lie unburied!," with some other remarks along these lines, intending none of them to be taken literally—whereupon the man took him up on the offer and the judges allowed it, so that *he made a botch of his case, incurring substantial ill will in the process (non sine magna sua invidia negotium adflixit)*. And on another occasion he was defending a man on trial for murder before the proconsul Lucius Piso at Mediolanum: as the lictors sought to quiet the excessive cries of his admirers, he flew into such a rage that—having lamented the condition of Italy, which he claimed was being reduced once again to the status of a mere province—he topped things off by invoking Marcus Brutus, whose statue was in sight of the courtroom, as the source and defender of laws and liberty, and he very nearly paid the penalty.[24]

The general point and structure are clear. As an advocate, Albucius was a prima donna who not only wished to perform the most desirable role (the role of summation) in the most desirable cases but also was given to untimely and self-indulgent displays, with lamentable results: he withdrew from the forum partly out of shame (*pudor*) and partly out of fear (*metus*), Suetonius says, and then he cites two anecdotes to bear out his assertion.

The second anecdote obviously has to do with *metus*: what Suetonius depicts as Albucius's brush with death when he threw a tantrum and called upon the memory of Caesar's murderer in a courtroom ultimately under the authority of Caesar's heir. The first anecdote has to do with *pudor*—and with *invidia*; it turns on a technical point of civil law.[25] Seeking to bring the opprobrium of impiety upon his opponent, Albucius called on the man to swear an oath by his parents' allegedly unburied ashes (that is, allegedly left unburied by the man's callous negligence). But, whereas that sort of florid gesture might be just the thing in a purely academic declamation, Albucius failed to reflect that under the rules of civil procedure the party offered the oath could win the case merely by swearing the oath in the form offered. So Albucius made a mess of the case and incurred great *invidia* in the process. Here the translator's choice of "ill will," while perhaps intelligible, is rather lame and insipid. It scarcely approaches the real thought behind *invidia* in this little drama, which I take to be something like this: viewing the wreckage of the case, an onlooker would be inclined to think, "Well, now, look at Mister Big-Shot Professor, with his big reputation and his pick of juicy cases—he's so wrapped up in himself and his tricks, he screws up big time by making a schoolboy mistake: he oughta be ashamed of himself!" (In fact, the satirist Persius expresses a view very much like that regarding an advocate more concerned with praise for his style than with actually defending his client.)[26] And so, Suetonius assures us, ashamed is what he was.

This is *nemesis-invidia* at work, and its link with shameful behavior is strong and clear as far back as we can trace the concept *invidia*. Let me offer just a few more illustrations, starting with our earliest example of continuous Latin prose, the preface to Cato's *On Agriculture*, in which he famously compares farming with trade and money lending:

> Granted, it's sometimes preferable to seek wealth through trade—save that it's so risky (*periculosum*)—and similarly by putting money out at interest—if it could be as honorable (*honestum*). Here's what our ancestors thought, and established in law: that a thief is fined two-fold, but a money lender fourfold. . . . Now a trader I judge to be a vigorous sort and dead keen on making money, but, as I said, vulnerable to risk and liable to disaster. But it's from amongst farmers that the bravest men and most vigorous soldiers arise and the most righteous and reliable income (*maxime . . . pius quaestus stabilissimusque*) derives, and the sort least liable to *invidia* (*minime . . . invidiosus*), and the people engaged in this pursuit are least of all given to wicked scheming.[27]

The problem with trade, he says, is that it is insufficiently secure, while the problem with money lending is that it is insufficiently honorable. Farming, by contrast, is the way of making a living that avoids the insecurity inherent in trade and the *invidia* that clings to money-lending—the feeling that those who engage in it are in fact worse than thieves, that, like thieves, they are violating a social norm and should be ashamed of themselves.

This script of *invidia* responds to the gaining or use of an advantage in a way deemed socially destructive and discreditable; accordingly, the script appears in contexts as varied as the forms of socially destructive and discreditable behavior itself. Some other examples, very briefly:

- Defending Caelius, Cicero says (*Cael.* 30) that he will not ask that the indulgence owed to youth be extended to his client: no, no, it may be that *other* members of the *jeunesse dorée* lead lives of self-indulgence, going into debt, surrendering to coarse and licentious impulses, and thereby incurring the *magna invidia* owed to vice (*vitia*) and sin (*peccata*)—but *not* his blameless client!
- Speaking of himself, Cicero returns repeatedly during the last twenty years of his life to the *invidia* directed at him as a result of his role in suppressing Catiline's conspiracy, a role in which—on the view of those feeling the *invidia*—he exercised his authority highhandedly and against the interest of the *res publica*.[28]

- In a structurally identical circumstance, the dictator Cornelius Cossus suffers *invidia* for imprisoning the seditious Manlius Capitolinus in 385 BCE: as Livy tells the story (6. 16. 5), the triumph over the Volsci that Cossus celebrated at the same time as Manlius's imprisonment was read by much of the plebs as symbolic not of his glorious victory over a foreign enemy but of his arrogant and shameful abuse of power in dealing with a fellow citizen.

- Then there is Mezentius's speech of shamed self-awareness at the end of *Aeneid* 10, which we considered from a different angle at the end of the preceding chapter.[29] As we saw, Mezentius berates himself not only for allowing his son to die in his stead but also for having in the first place "stained" the boy's name, his honor, by his own bad acts, "driven from [their] fathers' royal throne on account of *invidia*"—the *invidia* in question being that felt by the subjects whom he cruelly abused. Had his subjects' *invidia* caused Mezentius to feel then the shame that he feels now, he would not now have to feel the shame he feels. But, of course, had Mezentius then been capable of feeling such shame, he would have been less likely to behave in a way that provoked his subjects' *invidia*.[30]

- Or take the humiliating charade in which Agricola, according to Tacitus, was forced to perform (*Agr.* 42. 1–2): when the tyrant Domitian's agents made it plain that it was not prudent for him to seek the proconsulship of Africa or Asia that he deserved, he first had to beg to be "excused"—and then had to thank the emperor for the "favor." Domitian's role in the charade, and the hollow *beneficium* he extended, was shameful and so, appropriately, the object of *invidia*: but of course the shameless Domitian did not blush (*nec erubuit beneficii invidia*).

- And, as a final example, consider an epigram of Martial: a slave who had been branded on the forehead as a punishment saved his master's life during the proscriptions—a gift, in the event, not of *vita* but of *invidia*. The thought is that only a cruel and abusive master could mistreat so obviously loyal a slave, and so, in Shackleton Bailey's translation, "This was not saving his master's life but putting him to shame."[31]

Now the slave in this tale, I take it, did not *intend* to put his master to shame. That is rather the unintended consequence of his action, as it is interpreted by a notional set of onlookers: placing the action in a larger, implied narrative of past actions (the master's, the slave's), the onlookers construct and act out an emotional script that then connects them to that larger narrative. This is the way our emotional scripts tie us to the narratives of each other's lives. In the case of *invidia*, an "onlooker" is always at least implied, just because it is *invidia*, linked by etymology and actuality to "seeing"; this essential link to seeing explains the intimate connection of *invidia* with shame, which depends on (among other things) the sense of seeing yourself being seen under some discreditable description.[32]

So all of *nemesis-invidia* implies a performance observed and judged. Furthermore, much of *nemesis-invidia*—and I think the most interesting part—is the result of *managed* performances, the more or less stylized and ritualized forms of behavior by which one person seeks to arouse shaming *invidia* against another. Consider the following tabulation:

Arousing invidia *in "formal" settings*

In speeches to the people in assembly (*contiones*): Cic. *Verr.* 1. 1. 1–2, *Clu.* 93 (cf. 95), *Mil.* 12, Ascon. *Mil.* pp. 28, 32, 45 C., *Att.* 1. 16. 1, Val. Max. 5. 7. 2, cf. Cic. *Verr.* 2. 2. 72–74, *Nat. D.* 3. 3, *Luc.* 144, *Off.* 3. 79, Livy 3. 11. 10, 4. 40. 5, Plin. *Ep.* 9. 13. 4;

In the senate: Ateius Capito *iurisprud.* frag. 4 (on Caesar and Cato, cf. Plut. *Cat. min.* 33. 1–2), Livy 26. 32. 5, Suet. *Aug.* 43. 1–2, cf. Tac. *Hist.* 4. 41, *Ann.* 2. 37–38;[33]

In appeals to the onlookers (*corona*) in a trial: Cic. *Flac.* 66, 69;

In military settings: Tac. *Hist.* 1. 82, *Ann.* 1. 23, Suet. *Cal.* 9. 1.

Arousing invidia *in "informal" settings*

Through forms of public, more or less plangent dunning (*flagitatio*): Cic. *Verr.* 2. 4. 41, Quint. *DMin.* 279. 16, 316. 4, 11, 318. 4, [Quint.] *DMai.* 9. 18, 18. 9, Tac. *Ann.* 11. 34, 16. 10, cf. Petron. *Sat.* 14. 6–7, 101. 3, 107. 10, DServ. ad *Aen.* 2. 124 (glossing the verb *flagitat*: "that is, 'demands in a way that arouses *invidia*,' whence that which deservedly suffers *flagitatio* is called a *flagitium* [= outrage]": "id est 'invidiose poscit,' unde et quod flagitatione dignum est 'flagitium' dicitur");

By carrying (or the like) the emperor's image "to arouse *invidia* against another" (*in invidiam alterius*): Tac. *Ann.* 3. 36, *Dig.* 47. 10. 38. pr., 48. 19. 28. 7 (cf. 28. 5. 92. pr.), cf. Ov. *Met.* 13. 408–14;

Through physical displays (e.g, showing scars, dressing in mourning): Livy. 2. 23. 1–7, 3. 58. 8, Sen. *Contr.* 10. 1. 9 (on dressing in mourning; cf. Stat. *Theb.* 6. 41–44) with *Dig.* 47. 10. 15. 27 (cf. ibid. 6), Plin. *HN* 28. 148;

Through suicide: Sen. *Contr.* 7. 3. 4, 10. 3. 15, Quint. *Inst.* 9. 2. 85–86, Quint. *DMin.* 337. 1–2 (cf. 317. 13, [Quint.] *DMai.* 17. 4), Tac. *Ann.* 3. 16, 6. 29, 12. 8, cf. Suet. *Cal.* 56. 1, Serv. ad *Ecl.* 8. 60;

Through other dramatic shaming-gestures: Livy 37. 57. 15 (withdrawal from competition for *honos*), Ov. *Met.* 8. 142–44, Sen. *Contr.* 10. 1. 1 (throwing oneself at another's knees), Frontin. *Strateg.* 4. 5. 1 (Pompey flings down his *fasces*), Quint. *DMin.* 283. 2 (a Cynic son "shames" his father by begging for food), 294. 8, [Quint.] *DMai.* 19. 4 (a mother's mourning arouses pity, *miseratio*, for herself and *invidia* against her husband), 19. 9

(a father tortures his son to shame an entire *populus*), Apul. *Apol.* 25 (reading a letter aloud in the forum);

Through more subtle shaming-gestures, especially to arouse *invidia* against highhanded displays of *potentia*: Decimus Brutus in Cic. *Fam.* 11. 1. 6 (cf. Vell. Pat. 2. 62. 3), Ascon. *Mil.* 31 C. (on Milo and Pompey), Quint. *Inst.* 6. 2. 15–16 (behaving submissively to highlight another's oppression, cf. 9. 2. 8), Quint. *DMin.* 301. 13 (self-humiliation), [Quint.] *DMai.* 1. 16 (bringing *invidia* against a step-mother's *odium*), 5. 21 (a son's denying nourishment to his father, cf. also 16. 5–6), Sen. *Dial.* 6. 14. 2 (on Bibulus's "seclusion," cf. Vell. Pat. 2. 44. 5; cf. also Suet. *Nero* 34. 1, Nero "burdens" his mother with *invidia* by threatening to withdraw to Rhodes), Sen. *Contr.* 9. 5. 9 (a grandfather's visit to his ailing grandsons brings *invidia* on the father, cf. ibid. 11), Tac. *Ann.* 13. 15 (the song of Britannicus, "whence arose more palpable pity [for his lot]. . . . Nero, perceiving the *invidia*, intensified his *odium*": "unde orta miseratio manifestior. . . . Nero intellecta invidia odium intendit").

Merely skimming this catalog is enough to show that these performances are both very common and very rich in their diversity. But there is one thought common to them all: I feel *invidia* toward this person because he (overwhelmingly, he) is shamefully abusing his favorable circumstance, and I am going to make you feel the same thing—or, in the idiom that occurs scores of times, I am going to *invidiam facere*, create this *invidia* in you against the other.[34] The emotion and the performances that it inspires thus produce a type of social glue, reinforcing certain kinds of judgment and unifying a group against a renegade. Let's just glance briefly at some of these performances, which (for the sake of convenience only) are sorted in the catalog just presented according to the "formality" and "informality" of their setting—roughly, the degree of their institutionalization.

So, for example, there is the highly structured setting of the *contio*, the address to a gathering of the people that could be convened only by a magistrate or priest. The *contio* is *the* formal space for creating *nemesis-invidia* under the Republic, when the *contio* is to *invidia* what the *iudicium* is to *poena*: the *contio* aims to create a consensus that I have done something for which I should be ashamed; the *iudicium* creates the formal judgment that I have done something for which I should be punished.[35] But the *contio* is only a highly regulated instance of the sort of performance that filled the open spaces of public life every day, as the streets and marketplaces of great cities and small towns witnessed a lively theater of indignation and shame. The *flagitatio*—a raucous, public dunning—and similar forms of semiritualized behavior provide a cluster of examples. Cicero, for example, vividly evokes such a performance in his indictment of Verres, imagining one of the reprobate's victims returning from the dead for the purpose (*Verr.* 2. 1. 94):

What are you waiting for? For Malleolus to rise up from the infernal spirits and demand (*flagitet*) of you the duties [you owed his son]? Very well then, here he is: "You utterly greedy and filthy fellow, give your comrade's son his goods back" (*homo avarissime et spurcissime, redde bona sodalis filio*).

And we hear exactly the same rhythms a generation later, when Catullus marshalls his personified invective verses to pursue a (presumably, former) girlfriend and demand back some drafts of his poetry (42. 6, 10–12):

> Let's follow her and demand them back (*reflagitemus*). . . .
> Surround her now and demand them back:
> "You stinking whore, give my writing tablets back to me (*moecha putida, redde codicillos*);
> Give them, you stinking whore, back to me."[36]

Following someone about and proclaiming that person's malfeasance or abuse was obviously intended to achieve your purpose not only by encouraging your abuser to reflect on the error of his ways but especially by making him feel the *invidia* of others—by bringing to bear against him the gaze of witnesses who would see him for the highhanded or abusive person that he was and all but compel him, by the force of those gazes, to see himself in the same terms. That was the aim, too, of the hissing that the orator Hortensius had to endure when he entered the theater the day after winning a transparently corrupt verdict,[37] and a similar "theatrical" coup is brilliantly evoked by Apuleius in his *Apology* (25), where he recounts how his main persecutor came into the forum of Oea, breathless and distraught, and read out to the gathered crowd part of a letter by Apuleius's wife, Pudentilla, in which her "enchantment" was supposedly revealed.

The performance, however, could be no less effective for being wordless. Following someone around town dressed in mourning is a way of creating *invidia* that appears not only in the semifictional world of declamations (Sen. *Contr.* 10. 1. 9) but in the *Digest*, where it is expressly forbidden (47. 10. 15. 27, cf. ibid. 6); similarly forbidden is any use of the emperor's image with a view to expressing or creating *invidia* against someone (*in invidiam alterius*) by, say, carrying the image to invoke the emperor's protection against an overbearing other (*Dig.* 47. 10. 38. pr., 48. 19. 28. 7, cf. 28. 5. 92. pr.). In all such performances, the crucial move is to cast yourself in the role of the disadvantaged, the victim. That is what you do when you publicly throw yourself at the knees of another, not only to arouse his pity but to threaten him with others' shaming *invidia* if he spurns your plea. It is what Bibulus did when he withdrew to his house during his consulship, to bring *invidia* against the highhandedness of his colleague, Caesar (Sen. *Dial.* 6. 14. 2, cf. Vell. Pat. 2. 44. 5). According to Tacitus (*Ann.* 3. 16), it is what Tiberius complained the elder Piso had done in committing suicide, and it is what Caligula did when he brought "great *invidia*" upon a group of senators suspected of conspiring against him by (in effect) taking himself hostage (Suet. *Cal.* 56. 1): drawing his sword, he offered to kill himself right there if they judged he deserved it. (One tries to imagine the senators' mixed emotions here, while suppressing thoughts of Cleavon Little's Sheriff Bart taking himself hostage in *Blazing Saddles*.) And it is what poor Britannicus did in the game that ensured his death (Tac. *Ann.* 13. 15): called on to sing a song at a celebration of the Saturnalia, he chose lyrics that alluded to the denial of his patrimony—a choice that aroused pity for him and *invidia* for Nero. But, perverse creature that Nero was, he did not feel the shame that such *invidia* should have aroused but only heightened hatred (*odium*).

All these performances attempt to marshall emotion against someone judged guilty of misusing an advantage or a position of superiority. It is structurally fitting, therefore, to find almost identical performances mounted in relations with the divine, to arouse *invidia* against the gods when they have let us mortals down.[38] Not surprisingly, death provides the most common context: the high emotional energy of mourning is conceived as expressing not only the mourners' own pain and loss, and not only their attachment to the deceased, but also their outrage toward the gods for having caused or allowed such a thing. When mourners weep and cry out, tear their clothing or their hair, they are among other things trying to shame the gods, a point made helpfully explicit in the *Song of Mourning for Drusus*:

> The gods stay hidden in their precincts and do not show their faces
> at the cruel funeral, they do not demand an offering of incense at the
>   pyre:
> their shrines keep them out of sight, (the thought of) looking their
>   worshippers
> in the face causes them *pudor*, for fear of the *invidia* that they have
>   deserved.[39]

But *any* situation in which the gods let us down—and the possibilities are beyond number—is a suitable occasion to *invidiam facere* against them. So Juvenal imagines that the inhabitants of Egyptian Memphis might turn to cannibalism (the theme of satire 15) to create *invidia* against the Nile if it refused to rise (122–23): that is, they would act out as vividly as possible the desperate disadvantage at which the Nile's outrageous and shameful refusal had placed them.

I hope that I have given reason enough to link this script of *invidia* with the shaming impulse present in the Greeks' *nemesis* and to bring it into relation with the scripts of *pudor* examined earlier in this book. I round off the chapter now by offering some observations on the relation of this script to the other forms of *invidia* that in general are comparable to the Greeks' *phthonos*: my argument here is that "*nemesis-invidia*" commonly functions in Roman social and emotional life as the rhetorically useful complement of "*phthonos-invidia*."

Consider, first, one feature of the practice just described, that of creating *invidia* against the gods. In all these cases, it is obvious that creating *invidia* against the gods entails ascribing *invidia*—of a different sort—to the gods. The aggrieved party is trying to arouse *nemesis-invidia* against them by accusing them of *phthonos*-style feelings: if your child or spouse dies or the Nile refuses to rise, it is not (of course) because you or your loved ones have deserved it, or because the gods or fate or the Nile were just having a bad day; it is because the gods or fate or the Nile were feeling the sort of *invidia* that has no moral basis—they were, as we would put it, intentionally and maliciously begrudging you the good that you desired. And that is in fact exactly how the "envy of the gods" (*invidia deorum*) is most commonly conceived in Latin, and how the Roman conception differs from the "envy of the gods" (*phthonos tôn theôn*) of late archaic and classical Greece. The gods of Aeschylus, Pindar, and Herodotus are said to feel *phthonos* for an Eastern potentate or a Greek tyrant because he seeks or threatens to surpass the lot of the merely mortal and rival the gods themselves.[40] But, while there are traces of this conception in Roman thought as well (with reference to Hannibal or Alexander, for example),[41] the *invidia* that our texts most often ascribe to the gods is the feeling that motivates you to deprive another of a good just because it is a good, or just because you do not want the other to have it.[42] That the gods are so commonly taken to act out *phthonos-invidia* makes them plausible targets of *nemesis-invidia*.

What is true of the gods is true of the human overclass, too, as we see, for example, in the conception of the *invidia* that members of the nobility are so commonly said to feel for "new men" in the late Republic. Take the following remarks (Sall. *Cat.* 23. 5–6):

> These circumstances above all fired people's eagerness to entrust the consulship to Marcus Tullius Cicero. For previously most of the notables had been seething with *invidia* and thought the consulship was being (so to speak) polluted (*quasi pollui*) were a new man to gain it, however distinguished he might be. But with danger present, *invidia* and arrogance (*superbia*) took a back seat.

To those unsympathetic to the *nobiles'* view—Sallust speaking here of Cicero, say, or Cicero speaking repeatedly of himself—this is basest *phthonos-invidia*.[43] From this perspective, the notables wish to deny the new man a good, not with reference to some principle of fairness (indeed, their arrogant begrudgement is the very opposite of *aequitas*) but because they just do not want the new man to have it, or because they want it for themselves, or both. And, as in the case of the gods, so in the case of the *nobiles* the two main styles of *invidia* are complementary: attributing *phthonos-invidia* to the notables is a move in creating *nemesis-invidia* against them.

But these two styles of *invidia* are complementary in a second and perhaps more interesting way. When Sallust, for example, glosses the notables' *invidia* by saying that they "thought the consulship was being, so to speak, polluted" by the likes of Cicero, he purports to give us their take on the matter. He ascribes the emotion to the *nobiles*, adds a dash of hyperbolic metaphor ("polluted"), and then uses the ascribed hyperbole as a stick with which to thrash them. Their haughty fastidiousness only compounds their *phthonos*, and so we are all the more right to feel *nemesis-invidia* toward them: these arrogant *nobiles*, they ought to be ashamed of themselves! But now strip away the hyberbole and the metaphor while retaining the basic thought of the ascribed emotion: it is not implausible that at least some *nobiles* did in fact feel *invidia*— and, from their perspective, with complete justification, as *nemesis-invidia* of their own. The "new man" audaciously thrusting himself forward, pressing his own interests without regard for tradition or the support of family and experience, *was* an outrageous disruption of the accepted order and the common good, which it was the notables' proper place to define and defend: these *novi homines*, they ought to be ashamed of themselves![44] And so the complementary scripts of *invidia* confront each other as adversaries: "You're just feeling *invidia*," I say, to which you reply, "Damn right I do—and any decent person would feel the same."[45]

The complementary relation of *invidia*-scripts thus means that we commonly find the emotion pitted against itself, explicitly or by implication, in the texts that represent it. I close the chapter by offering three examples of increasing richness to show how this is so; the examples could easily be multiplied fiftyfold and more.

In the first, rather transparent example, the elder Pliny relates how the freedman Gaius Furius Cresimus enjoyed much greater yields on his small plot of land than his neighbors did on their much larger holdings; and so he came to be *in magna invidia*—he became the object of great *invidia*—as though he had magically charmed his neighbors' crops onto his own land (*ceu fruges alienas perliceret veneficiis*: *HN* 18. 41). Expressly, the *invidia* seems to be focalized through the neighbors, giving their point of view: *they* could quite properly feel *nemesis-invidia*, because using magic to "seduce" the crops of others meant gaining an advantage in a highhanded, outrageous, and shameful way—in fact, the practice was expressly forbidden in Romans' first code of laws, the Twelve Tables.[46] But, from a more disinterested perspective, the *magna invidia* in question just as clearly follows the *phthonos*-script: the charge of magic is obviously a way for the neighbors to put a decent face on their own naked envy, as they measure Cresimus's crops against their own and find the assessment painful.[47] From this point of view, the anecdote reminds us that slander is the tribute that malice pays to shame.

My second example shows us Cicero deploying the dynamics of *invidia*, with the polemical mastery we would expect, in his campaign against his enemy Gabinius (*Sest.* 93). As governor of Syria, we are told, Gabinius drained that rich land's vast wealth to build a villa so magnificent that it made the grand villa of Lucius Lucullus look like a hovel by comparison—the very same villa of Lucullus that Gabinius himself, in his character as a "pure and unselfish" tribune (*castus ac non cupidus*), had assailed as outrageously luxurious in public assemblies not a dozen years earlier, to bring *invidia* upon its owner. There are at least three layers of *invidia* here. First, a tribune who was in fact "pure and unselfish" could credibly condemn the luxury and self-indulgence of a magnate and use the *contio* to cry "Shame!": as we have seen, arousing *nemesis-invidia* was one of the important purposes a *contio* could serve, and such self-indulgence would offer a fat target, falling squarely under the most common script of *pudor*, provoked by "discreditable self-extension" (script 4). But, of course, the phrase "pure and unselfish" is sarcastic, and we know that Cicero's Gabinius was not that sort of tribune. Rather, we are to understand that he was a rank hypocrite: while seeking to arouse *nemesis-invidia* against the wealthy, he was himself seething with *phthonos-invidia*, coveting the very thing that he was decrying. And, now that Gabinius has achieved more-than-Lucullan luxury, Cicero himself, of course, uses the episode to arouse *nemesis-invidia* against the man—one of his chief occupations in the years 57–56.

My last example comes from—how to put it?—a pen less subtle than Cicero's, that of Valerius Maximus, but it nonetheless has intriguing layers of its own. In his chapter "On humankindness and mercy" (*De humanitate et clementia*), Valerius tells us of Caesar's respectful treatment, first of Pompey's severed head, then of the younger Cato's estate, after both his enemies were dead; and he relates how Caesar remarked, on hearing of Cato's suicide, that each felt *invidia* for the other's glory.[48] Valerius's report virtually compels us to focalize the *invidia* three different ways. For Valerius himself, *invidere* almost certainly has the watered-down sense that it often does, similar to the English idiom that allows one friend to say to another, "Oh, I envy you that vacation," expressing the covetous judgment of envy without engaging the psychophysical responses that give the emotion its force and flavor: that is, Cato and Caesar would each simply have been glad to have the other's *gloria*. This is entirely consistent with Valerius's overall historical sensibility, sentimental and soaked in kitsch as it is, which probably pictured Cato and Caesar letting bygones be bygones in the afterlife, downing a few pints together and shaking their heads over old times.[49]

As for Caesar, it is I suppose conceivable that he meant something of the sort that Valerius intended. But Caesar was, after all, also the author of the *Anticato*, a vicious posthumous polemic, and he is unlikely to have said that he coveted Cato's *gloria*. Far likelier, instead, that he had a more realistic and hard-nosed understanding of the emotion, as entailing sheer begrudgement: he and Cato each felt pain at the other's glory just because it *was* the other's glory.[50]

And what of Cato's *invidia*? Well of course, as a good Stoic, Cato should have felt no *invidia*—nor any other passion—at all. Still, if we imagine for a moment that Cato was human, we might suppose that he, like Caesar, did feel the begrudgement of *phthonos-invidia*. But we also remember that suicide—the one act for which Cato was most renowned and revered—was among the performances by which you could express *and* create *nemesis-invidia* against someone whose advantage was gained or used in ways that were highhanded, outrageous, and shameful—adjectives that surely capture Cato's view of Caesar's *gloria*. We might then imagine his agreement with Cicero that "*to nemesân* interest *tou phthonein*": *invidia* is one thing, *invidia* quite another.

Unlike *verecundia, pudor,* and *paenitentia,* all of them emotions of self-attention and self-assessment, *invidia* is primarily directed outward, taking shape and gathering force in an unadmiring view of some other person or group. How that view expresses itself, and the aim that it has, will depend on the script or scripts being enacted. If one or more of the *phthonos*-scripts are at work, it may lead to the divisions and discord that malice and envy produce, setting one person or faction against another in, especially, competition over contested goods. If *nemesis-invidia* is at work, it will attempt not to divide but to create an ethical consensus, unifying a group of "right-thinkers" who can also see themselves as "right-feelers," mobilized to isolate and bring shame upon a highhanded renegade and thereby reaffirm the values of equity and community (*invidia* can also, as we have seen, do all of the above at once). The final Roman feelings that we will examine are also primarily directed outward; to be more precise, they are feelings that are aroused by looking outward at some person or thing but that recoil from the sight in one or another form of revulsion. These are the feelings that cluster under the label *fastidium.* As we shall see, they too, like *invidia,* work either to divide or to unify, if in rather different ways.

5

The Dynamics of *Fastidium* and the Ideology of Disgust

At the very start of our investigations, we encountered two scenes of high emotion—the trial of an innocent young man framed for murder (Apul. *Met.* 10. 2–12) and the suicide of a *grande dame* who had decided it just was time to die (Val. Max. 2. 6. 8)—in which feelings of *fastidium* played a pivotal role. Though those feelings provided a point of departure for discussing this book's general concerns and methods, we never did get around to answering, in the introduction, the question with which we began: what is this *fastidium* all about? Now is the time to attempt some answers; to that end, I propose that we approach *fastidium* along lines similar to those we have followed while tracing the workings of *pudor, paenitentia,* and *invidia.*

Like these other items of emotion-talk, *fastidium* is, on the one hand, a label given to a cluster of thoughts and feelings that share a certain surface likeness, which in the case of *fastidium* has to do with aversion: "This person / object / state of affairs is repellent—he/she/it makes me want to turn away—I *will* turn away"—an evaluative belief or judgment that yields an intention, accompanied by some psychophysical agitation. On the other hand—as in the case of "joy" and "happiness" or *pudor* and *invidia*—the processes of judgment and belief that converge on "aversion" are constituted and experienced differently in different cases. How, then, are such processes represented, when the Romans speak of *fastidium*? What different processes constitute the experience that a Roman would denote as *fastidium*, and what different scripts do they enact?[1]

Here the answer, while a bit more complex than in the case of *verecundia,* is a bit less complex than in the case of *pudor, paenitentia,* or *invidia*: in general, only two kinds of process, two basic scripts, are needed to account for the production and representation of *fastidium.*[2] One of these scripts can for the sake of convenience be labeled a "per se reflex" ("absolute and autonomic" would do as well). This is the *fastidium*-reaction that sick people have to food: it is not this kind (quality, quantity) of food as opposed to that kind (quality, quantity) for which they feel an aversion but food per se, and the aversion seems to arise autonomically, as something independent of will and choice—it is simply there, willy-nilly and "naturally." But it is also the *fastidium*-reaction that, for example, the elder Pliny registers in response to bedbugs (*HN* 29. 61) or to the thought of eating a green lizard for medicinal purposes (*HN* 30. 90): it is not this bedbug (lizard) as opposed to that bedbug (lizard) that causes the reaction; it is bedbugs (lizards) as such, and Pliny makes it quite clear that the response does not proceed from any sort of conscious deliberation—it is visceral and seemingly reflexive, it is just the way these things make him feel (*BAD*). And it is also quite clear that this reaction occurs (to the Roman mind) in response not only to things but to people or situations, too, including ethical situations: we will have a chance to consider examples later.

On the other hand, there is the pattern of engagement that might be labeled "deliberative and ranking." This is the *fastidium*-reaction that people experience when they have considered at some level of consciousness the relative value or status of two or more things (or people)—including, very often, their own value or status relative to some thing (or person)—and have decided to rank one of those things (or people) so low as to have an aversion to it (or him). This is the *fastidium* that a connoisseur might feel toward this example of poetry (music, food) as opposed to that, or that a person of a certain social status might feel toward being offered this particular honor (gift, friendship) as opposed to that: it implies an act of choice and will and proceeds by tacit or explicit evaluation relative to some standard. In the case of both reactions, what counts for our understanding of *fastidium* is how the process and its outcome are perceived and represented (something for which our texts give much evidence), not how the process "actually" unfolded in a subject's mind (something for which there is no evidence).[3]

In the several sections of this chapter I try to sustain these claims and to elaborate the processes and scripts of *fastidium*. The first three sections give a sampling of the evidence on which the claims are based.[4] The final section then draws out a few of the implications that bring *fastidium* into connection with the other emotions we have pondered and with our broader understanding of Roman mentality and culture.

The Dynamics of *Fastidium* (I): "Per Se Reflex"

We can start with the kinds of aversion that concern basic animal drives. Foremost among these is the drive for food, and the blocking of this drive by sickness, which turns natural appetence into aversion, is one of the most common types of reflexive *fastidium*; it is also a type of *fastidium* that can be manipulated by human beings, for example in the aversive conditioning that keeps birds from eating a planter's grapes.[5] The sex drive, too, can become pathologically blocked, as when a stallion experiences *fastidium* at mounting a mare: we could safely assume that this *fastidium* was not the expression of deliberative connoisseurship on the stallion's part even if the cure for the problem (touching his nostrils with a squill that has been wiped on the genitals of a mare in season) did not appeal to the horse's autonomic responses.[6] On the other hand, some kinds of sexual aversion in animals are entirely "natural": so the elder Pliny tells us that "it is natural for the ram to feel *fastidium* for lambs and to make for old sheep."[7] It happens that Martial notes a similar preference in a certain Bassus, who "get[s] it up for the old ladies but feel[s] *fastidium* for the young," only to point out, in effect, that what is "natural" in a ram is not in a man: Martial's dig at Bassus frames the matter not as a deliberative preference but as an overpowering reaction, the "mad" response of Bassus's "wacky dick."[8]

Less colorfully, humans experience the same *fastidium* for food known to animals as a consequence of illness, and the feelings of *fastidium* associated with pregnancy, including the queasiness and nausea (our "morning sickness") that are among the early signs of conception.[9] Humans also know the aversion to food associated with what we would call depression, the condition unmistakably described by Ovid writing from Tomis (*Pont.* 1. 10. 5–8):

I feel no pain, nor am I parched by fevers that leave me
gasping; my pulse is steady as ever it was.
But my palate is dulled, the courses laid before me stir up *fastidia*,
and I lament when the hated dinner-hour has arrived.

This absolute aversion to food as such is figured as a "dead weight upon the stomach":[10] as we shall see, the description is typical of the way in which *fastidium* of the "per se reflex," specifically, is represented as being embodied.

Maladies of body and mind aside, one of the most common kinds of reflex *fastidium* is the aversion that results from a feeling of satiety, or the closely related feeling of monotony: in short, the feeling that you have "had it up to here" and cannot take it any more, like the priest's slave (in a simile of Horace) who simply could not stand to look at one more sacrificial cake.[11] Animals can experience this form of *fastidium*, for example, from the force-feeding used to fatten fowl or from a simple lack of variety in their diet.[12] But the human form of this aversion is more commonly encountered and is certainly more varied, capable of being elicited by just about any common presentation to the senses, including those that are not initially perceived as at all repellent. Since this type of *fastidium* is obviously represented as reflexive—a matter not of deliberative choice but of spontaneous reaction to "the last straw"—it should be sufficient to give only a few examples.[13]

Even the most pleasant or rewarding sensations or states can arouse this *fastidium*. Cicero notes the apparent paradox when he says that "it is difficult to explain why the things that especially stir our senses with pleasure at their first appearance should most quickly affect us with a certain *fastidium* and satiety and cause us to turn away," and the same thought is turned to advantage in both the moralizing of Seneca and the natural science of the elder

Pliny.[14] Similarly, it pleases a declaimer to suggest that success, when it continues too long, can cause the fortunate man *fastidium*,[15] and Livy makes the great general Quintus Fabius Maximus argue that glory itself can have the same effect (28. 40. 6–9):

> In dissenting from that hasty crossing to Africa, I know full well that I must face two charges: first, of an innate tendency to delay . . . ; second, of desire, born of *invidia*, to detract from [Scipio's] fame as it grows day by day (*obtrectationis atque invidiae adversus crescentem in dies gloriam*). But if my former life and character do not free me from such suspicion, together with the dictatorship and five consulships I've held, and so much glory won in war and peace that I am closer to feeling *fastidium* for it than yearning (*desiderium*), then at least my age should acquit me: for what rivalry could exist between me and a man who is not even my son's age?

As with sensations and states, so with persons and their activities in the public eye. Speaking of the face-to-face relations of Republican politics, Cicero notes the difficulty of balancing the advantage and influence (*gratia*) derived from being in the people's sight against the *fastidium* and *satietas* one might arouse by being constantly in their sight—and on into the Principate it is just this risk that is mentioned as a possible reason for Tiberius's notorious retirement to Rhodes.[16] In a different sphere of endeavor, the elder Pliny is repeatedly (and no doubt justifiably) worried that he will arouse *fastidium* in the reader of his *Natural History*, whether by treating again material that is all too familiar, or by reeling off long lists of names, or just by telling his readers more than they really want to know.[17] And, as a teacher, Quintilian is similarly concerned, first to vary the student's lessons at the earliest stage (by alternating reading and writing) so that "he will be refreshed by the change, just as a variety of food restores the digestion and provides a wider range of nourishment with less *fastidium*," and later to make certain that the would-be orator knows the pitfalls of creating *fastidium* through one monotonous habit or another.[18] When orators use the same ploys in case after case, he says, they stir up *fastidium* like a serving of cold leftovers (2. 4. 29 "fastidium moveant velut frigidi et repositi cibi").

For the most part, the *fastidium* of satiety and monotony is caused by objects or activities that are not ordinarily repellent but become repellent through excessive repetition or glut: while cabbage once is at least tolerable, leftover cabbage—the *crambe repetita* of Roman proverb—is a different matter. But with Quintilian's simile of (specifically) *cold* leftovers, we edge closer to the last major type of per se and reflexive *fastidium*: the aversion to things that are perceived as distasteful and noisome per se, the *fastidium* of "thick, greasy life."[19]

To answer the question "How do you make a Roman retch?," let us count a very few of the ways, beginning with the most intimate involvement of the senses and moving on to less body-based causes. For taste and smell, the elder Pliny is a particularly fecund source. Olives grown in a damp climate, or excessively sweet substances, or potions made of goat's urine are all, on his telling, the sort of thing to arouse *fastidium*;[20] so similarly the smell of asses' urine in a cure for thinning hair, or of a particular kind of wood, or of impure euphorbea when it is burned.[21] Among the other senses, sound (interestingly) seems hardly implicated in this sort of *fastidium*, and the same is true (more interestingly still) of touch,[22] but sight is very much involved. So, when Horace, for example, remarks "the great feelings of *fastidium* [that are stirred up] in the stomach, if the slaveboy has pawed the winecup with greasy hands while stealing a sip, or if a noisome deposit has stuck to the old mixing bowl," he evokes a feeling of repugnance that is not aroused by unmediated taste, touch, or smell.[23] Similarly, Martial's advice on the preparation of cabbage—"Lest the pallid leaves stir feelings of *fastidium* in you, let the cabbage be made green with a solution of potash" (or some other alkali)[24]—seems to be motivated in the first instance by considerations of appearance: the difference between cabbage leaves that are repellent because they *look* "dead" (*pallens* as an adjective associated with sickness or death) and those that are enticing because they *look* "fresh and alive" (*viridis* as an adjective associated with the color of growing vegetation).[25]

These examples concern, specifically, the connection between sight and ingestion, a connection that seems generally to be present in cases of reflexive sight-*fastidium* (at least when the object is not another person: more on that later). Moreover, it appears to be the case that *fastidium* can be aroused by the mere thought of ingesting something noisome. Consider Pliny on the medicinal use of green lizards: remove the heads and feet, he says, and add seasoning to "wipe away" *fastidium*.[26] What, exactly, is the purpose of these *condimenta*, and what, exactly, is the cause of *fastidium* here? It is plainly not the *fastidium* of satiety or the *fastidium* for food induced by illness: it is an aversion to eating something that you would not ordinarily eat and that you find difficult to eat when you must (when it is "good for you"). Further, the seasonings do not appear to be needed to conceal a disagreeable taste (the honey-on-the-cup-of-bitter-medicine ploy): there is no indication that green lizards actually taste bad, and in any case the *fastidium* (in Pliny's representation) already exists, it is "there" as a thing to be "wiped away," prior to the tasting. It appears that the seasonings are needed as a source of appetence, to overcome an a priori aversion to putting in your mouth something that you think is repugnant: the seasonings are just meant to keep you from gagging as the lizard crosses the hedge of your teeth.[27]

Certainly, Pliny elsewhere gives clear testimony to the power of mere thought to arouse this type of *fastidium*, even when it is not a question of eating the object in question. So we can almost see him writhe when he must talk about bedbugs and a certain kind of beetle:

Some things, though one ought to feel *pudor* to talk about them (*pudenda dictu*), are recommended so insistently by our authorities that it would be just wrong to pass them by (*ut praeterire fas non sit*) . . . : so, for instance, the nature of bedbugs—utterly foul creatures, one ought to feel *fastidium* at the very mention of them (*animalis foedissimi et dictu quoque fastidiendi*)—is said to be effective against snake-bites, especially that of the asp, and likewise against all other poisons. . . . (*HN* 29. 61)

A third kind [of beetle]—loathesome because of its unbearable odor (*odoris taedio invisum*) and having a pointed tail—is said to heal otherwise incurable ulcerations, swollen glands, and abscesses when applied with pisselaeum for twenty-one days, and puncture wounds, bruises, malignancies, eczema, and boils when the feet and wings have been removed. I feel *fastidium* even hearing about these things (*nos haec etiam audita fastidimus*); but, my God, Diodorus says that he has prescribed [the beetles] with resin and honey even in cases of jaundice and orthopnoea. So powerful is the craft [of medicine] when it comes to prescribing whatever it wishes as a treatment! (*HN* 29. 141–42)

Even mentioning the "utterly foul creature" ought to be a cause of *fastidium*, here overcome only out of respect for the authority of his sources and his obligation as a purveyor of beneficial information: indeed, the opening reference to some things "one ought to feel *pudor* to talk about" suggests that, at some level in Pliny's mind, the *fastidium* that he feels has a positive ethical coloration—that where *pudor* and this kind of *fastidium* intersect, it is not only normal but even decent to feel as he does.[28] The case of the foul-smelling beetle is more vivid still. After cataloging the remedies in which it can be used (with or without legs and wings), Pliny says, "I feel *fastidium* even hearing about these things." The source of the repugnance is of course all in his mind: he has not, at the present moment, smelled (seen, touched, tasted) the beetle, or the remedies made from it, or the bloody, ulcerous, scabby, and pustular surfaces to which the remedies are customarily applied. But what *are* "these things" to which he refers as the source of his repugnance? Having started (in his mind) with the *fastidium*-elicitor of smell, does Pliny retain that as the dominant stimulus? Does he modulate from the thought of the beetle's smell to the thought of applying the smelly substance to the various conditions, some of which are surely smelly themselves, as well as visually repugnant? Does the thought of the conditions themselves, which receive more words, at some point come to dominate? What role might the thought of handling the beetles (and the sores) play? All of the above?[29] We can best say that Pliny's *fastidium* here has more than one sufficient cause.

But bedbugs, beetles, and the like have no monopoly on the *fastidium* of the noisome. Humans can evoke the same reaction, most commonly through odor and sight:[30] a woman's cloak that might retain the odor of her nether parts; one's own body odor, or the smell of one's own crapulent breath; and the combined sensory assault of the hag who reeks of sweat while her makeup—a combination of chalk and crocodile dung—runs in a smeared stream across her face.[31] For sheer memorability, however, there is nothing like the *fastidium* caused by the prospect of eating human flesh: "All my legatees besides my freedmen will receive their bequests," says the testator in the *Satyricon*, as he sets his brilliantly grisly terms,

> "only on the condition that they butcher my body and eat it before the people in assembly. . . . I'm not worried that your stomach will rebel (*de stomachi tui recusatione non habeo quod timeam*): it will follow orders as long as you promise it a rich reward in return for but one hour's *fastidium* ("sequetur imperium, si promiseris illi pro unius horae fastidio multorum bonorum pensationem"). Just close your eyes and make believe that you're eating, not human flesh, but [a great pile of cash]."[32]

But (you might say) there must be more at stake in this last tableau than in the physical noxiousness of body odor or the nauseating prospect of eating a lizard whole: the thought of eating a lizard, repugnant though it might be, is ethically neutral; the thought of eating your neighbor is not. Indeed, and so the subject of cannibalism brings fully to the fore a matter that was raised glancingly by Pliny's reaction to creepy-crawlies: the reflexive *fastidium* caused by things or acts that are ethically noisome, that in fact amount to "taboos." Cannibalism is one such taboo. Defecation and cowardice are two others, nicely linked in a story told by Valerius Maximus:[33]

> Gnaeus Carbo, too, causes the annals of Rome great *verecundia* (*magnae verecundiae est Latinis annalibus*). Having been led off to execution in Sicily at Pompey's orders [82 BCE] . . . , he begged the soldiers abjectly and tearfully to be allowed to relieve himself before dying, that he might prolong the wretched light of life, and he drew the business out so long that they cut off his head while he sat in the place of filth. As I relate such a disgrace (*flagitium*) my very words are conflicted: they find silence uncongenial, because the tale should not be covered up, yet they do not feel at home with the telling, because one ought to feel *fastidium* at saying such things (*quia dictu fastidienda sunt*).

That mere longing for life (*cupiditas vitae*, Valerius's theme here) should cause a notable man to die this way, clinging cravenly to breath while (or: *by*) emptying his bowels, is an embarrassment to the history of Rome, one that leaves Valerius's words and his impulses at war with one another, as his sense of responsibility to his authorial task is pitted against his sense that such things are just not decent to talk about. The conflict is framed in terms almost identical to those used by Pliny when he talks about bedbugs and beetles;[34] though in both cases the writer's "sense of responsibility" wins out, he must make the gesture of registering his *fastidium* at using the words needed to record an indecent subject.[35]

Yet another instance of *fastidium*-as-ethical-reflex concerns incest—for it is here, I suggest, that we can best understand Apuleius's story of the upright young man and his petulant stepmother that provided a point of entry for our investigations.[36] Recall the perjurious tale that is told against the young man as he is on trial for his life: "Made indignant by his stepmother's *fastidium*, the young man had summoned [the slave] and, seeking vengeance for the insult (*iniuria*), had ordered him to achieve her son's murder."[37] Though the *fastidium* ascribed to the stepmother here is a lie within a lie, as part of a lie it should signify something useful to the liars: what sort of *fastidium* would that be? It plainly cannot be any sort of *fastidium* due to "ranking." On no construction of the story could the stepmother's aversion be thought to be based on some ordinal judgment such as "Sorry, dear, you're just not X enough" (where X is some adjective implying value: "tall," "dark," or "handsome"). The aversion must be absolute, just because of what the youth is (her stepson), and the whatness of the youth is itself not relevantly defined in terms of hierarchical status relative to the person experiencing the aversion. (The category "stepson" is not inferior to the category "stepmother" according to any ranking criterion relevant to the transaction, as, for example, the category "slave" would be relative to the category "master" or "freeborn man.") Furthermore, what the youth is is hedged about by known and absolute ethical notions: simply, it is always wrong for a stepmother to have sex with a stepson. Nor can the stepmother plausibly (for the purposes of the story) be thought to have deliberated, even fractionally, in her response to the stepson's supposed approach. The response must be thought to have been reflexive and even visceral, the equivalent of finding a cockroach instead of dinner on your dinner plate: in reacting, you do not rank this cockroach relative to some other (e.g., taller, darker, more handsome) cockroach, nor is your reaction shaped by a desire to maintain or establish some hierarchical status relative to cockroaches, singly or as a group; in fact, you do not *do* anything but recoil, turning away or closing your eyes immediately and without hesitation, so that you will no longer see the cockroach. In short, the stepmother's response must be (imagined to be) a reaction of ethically reflexive *fastidium*. That the *iuvenis* would nonetheless be "indignant" at such a reaction and regard it as an insult calling for revenge not only provides him with a motive for murder, according to the lie, but also effectively blackens his character still further: it shows him to be, in fact, some very large variety of ethical cockroach.[38]

Cannibalism, defecation, and incest are all subject to "big" taboos, matters of intense and deep-seated aversion in most human cultures: it is not surprising to see them appear among the Roman responses of per se *fastidium*. But we do, perhaps, learn a bit more about the specifically Roman character of this response when we find their company shared by cowardice, or by another taboo deeply rooted in Roman social and political culture: the taboo against boasting.[39] So Quintilian's reminder on this subject: hearing someone's boasting, and especially hearing an orator boast about his eloquence, not only makes the audience feel like turning away but often makes them hostile, too—it is apt to elicit not just aversion (*fastidium*) but even aggression (*odium*).[40] The hostile reaction, being more vigorous and pointed, is no doubt more undesirable when it occurs, but what one can always expect (Quintilian implies) is the absolute aversion of ethical *fastidium*. And, as Quintilian goes on to explain, boasting has these effects because the listeners see themselves being devalued by someone playing ranking games: "for the human mind by its nature has something lofty about it and noble and unable to endure a superior. . . . But the person who elevates himself inordinately is taken to be oppressive and contemptuous, not so much making himself greater but making all others less."[41] In the dynamics of the transaction, we might say that boasting is tantamount to defecating in public, while having to bear the brunt of a boast is comparable to being shat upon.

The manifestations of *fastidium* considered so far—whether elicited by maladies, by satiety, or by physical and ethical presentations perceived as noisome in themselves—all share the same dynamic, as products of a per se and reflexive response. Not surprisingly, they are all also conceived as being embodied in the same way: they are centered in the stomach, especially, where they are experienced as a "dead weight" or a form of upset,[42] or in the eyes, when the object of *fastidium* is visual, prompting the urge to turn away from a repellent sight.[43] The recurrent metaphors applied to the feeling figure it as a physical presence that is "moved" or "stirred up" at its inception and that can be removed by being "wiped away"; at other times, it is spoken of as something that "befalls" or "oppresses" a person, as though from the outside and beyond voluntary control.[44] In its etiology, dynamics, and representation, the *fastidium* of absolute and autonomic aversion is distinct from the other type of *fastidium*-response, to which we can now turn.

The Dynamics of *Fastidium* (II): "Deliberative Ranking"

The response considered in the preceding section did not entail considerations of rank or status, self-awareness or self-concern (beyond, perhaps, a concern to avoid a noisome presentation), or the conscious exercise of thought and will. The type of *fastidium*-reaction about to be considered typically comprises all these elements. At the same time, the *fastidium* of absolute and autonomic response was correlated not only with a fairly wide range of objects but also with several different states, and there were some specific linkages between states and objects: the *fastidium* associated with being ill resulted from presentations (typically, food or sex) that in most other circumstances would arouse not aversion but appetence, while the *fastidium* associated with satiety and monotony was evoked by some phenomena (for example, certain repetitive sounds) that would hold no particular repugnance for sick people as such. The *fastidium* of deliberative ranking, by contrast, seems to involve but a single disposition and a single impulse, and it certainly involves a narrower range of objects. Accordingly, although this form of the feeling is more commonly the subject of *fastidium*-talk (by a ratio of roughly 3:2), it does not require a lengthier discussion than its counterpart.

This is the *fastidium* of aversive connoisseurship: it typically entails a judgment, represented as "refined," made on objects—predominantly items of daily intimate use (food, clothing, furnishings), or products of the literary culture, or people—when consuming those objects has significance for the consumer's status, affirming that status (when the aversion is registered) or questioning it (when it is not).[45] In the area of quotidian consumables, it is the *fastidium* of diners who would refuse the upper part of any bird—save the fig-pecker—and the lower part, too, unless it is stuffed, and who might sooner go hungry than eat anything but exquisite delicacies; in Horace's fable, it is the *fastidium* felt by the town mouse, with his "proud tooth," for his country cousin's table.[46] But the response is not confined to the elite (human or murine): the standard of judgment moves along a sliding social scale, as Juvenal suggests when he speaks of the vegetables once taken as a sufficient meal by the ascetic hero Curius, now subjected to the *fastidium* of a filthy ditchdigger, who remembers the greater delights of a cheap delicatessen.[47] And, because the standards of judgment, and so the judgments themselves, are cultural constructs at any social level, they are likely to be represented as deviations from or corruptions of "natural" appetite. That sort of deviance is the target of Horace's imperatives in one of his *Satires* (2. 2. 14–16):

> When toil has pounded the *fastidia* out of you, when you're thirsty
> and empty, go on and spurn cheap grub, don't drink anything but
>   honey
> of Hymettus thinned by Falernian wine. . . .

And what the Epicurean Horace only implies, the Stoicizing Seneca drives home again and again.[48] It is a point to which we will return.

The pathologies of consumption associated with this form of *fastidium* are not the concern only of moralists informed by philosophical doctrine: hence the popular verses aimed (Suetonius reports) at the emperor Tiberius (*Tib.* 59. 1):

The bastard feels *fastidium* for wine, because now he thirsts for
  blood:
this he drinks as greedily as he used to drink wine unmixed with
  water.

As the second line shows, Tiberius's *fastidium* for wine is figured not as a
per se reaction to something that he would normally ("naturally") be averse
to consuming but as an aversive dispreference, a ranking, and subject to
change over time: the pathology consists in the fact that the preference for
wine has been displaced by a preference for blood, a drink that *should* cause
per se *fastidium*.

The representation of such *fastidium* itself obviously implies a point of
view, a judgment conveyed by a selective framing of the data: it implies, in
fact, a point of view shaped by *fastidium*. Consider how Valerius Maximus
frames the story of the consul Sextus Aelius Catus, who sent a delegation of
Aetolians packing when they offered gifts of silver vessels to replace the poor
pottery objects (*fictilia*) they had noticed on his table (4. 3. 7):

> When he had warned them against supposing that his self-control (*con-
> tinentia*) required the sort of subvention owed to poverty, he ordered
> them to leave with their baggage. How well had he done in preferring
> domestic to Aetolian goods, if only this later age would have wished to
> follow his frugal example! But now where have we come to? You can
> scarcely get slaves to overcome their *fastidium* for the sort of household
> wares that a consul did not blush to use ("a servis impetrari vix potest
> ne eam supellectilem fastidiant, qua tunc consul uti non erubuit").

As represented by Valerius, Tubero himself was plainly engaged in an a game
of ranking, judging goods of material value against goods with ethical significance, and in his priggish admonition of the legates he could with no dis-
tortion be described (by a neutral observer, or by the legates themselves) as
fastidiosus, conveying that he found their impertinence and luxury so far inferior to his own honest poverty that he felt aversion for them.[49] Yet, his (virtuous) part in the game is characterized in terms of a mere "preference"
(*praetulerat*), while, in the moral that Valerius draws, the uppity latter-day
slaves are taxed with a pretentious *fastidium*—even as they are made the object of Valerius's own tacit *fastidium*.[50] There is a game-within-the-game implied in Valerius's account, as the *fastidiosi* being represented are made objects
of *fastidium*. (We will see this reversal frequently in the following few paragraphs and return to it at chapter's end.) The same game appears on the surface early in the *Satyricon*, when our heroes, believing that they have lost a
cloak with a wallet of money sewn inside, see it turn up in the hands of a
peasant (13. 1–2):

What a lucky break! The bumpkin had not yet put his prying hands to the seam, but was even offering the thing up for sale *fastidiose*, as though it had been ripped off a beggar's back (*tamquam mendici spolium*). When Ascyltos saw that the stash was undisturbed, and saw too the despicable character of the peddlar (*personam vendentis contemptam*), he led me a little way from the crowd and said, "Brother, do you realize that the treasure I was just now mourning has returned to us? . . . What do we do now? How do we lay our rightful claim to the thing?"

The scene is filtered through at least two different layers of perception, both informed by a deliberative, ranking *fastidium*. Unaware of the concealed windfall, the *rusticus* flogs the tunic with an expression of *fastidium*, as though it belonged to a person even lower than himself on the social ladder (Heseltine's "with a condescending air," for *fastidose*, conveys the idea nicely in the Loeb edition), whereas Ascyltus regards the peasant as a "persona contempta"—that is to say, regards him *fastidiose*. As we shall see in greater detail, such a regression is in principle open-ended, from the bottom to the top of the social pyramid: the "beggar's" cloak is regarded with *fastidium* by the *rusticus*, who in turn is regarded with *fastidium* by Ascyltus, who in turn could be regarded . . .

The dynamics of deliberative and ranking *fastidium* in respect of ordinary items of consumption scarcely differ from *fastidium* expressed toward products of the literary culture. To experience this type of *fastidium* toward one's own productions is unproblematic, even commendable, as Cicero implies when he tells Atticus that he would not have dared send along one of his compositions if he had not vetted it "slowly and with *fastidium*";[51] but those who express *fastidium* toward Latin literature in general, avoiding it because they rate it low relative to Greek, receive very different treatment at Cicero's hands.[52] The ranking game comprises both substance and style. Listen to the elder Pliny as he speaks about the "level" of subject matter he is about to address at *Natural History* 11. 4:

But we marvel at elephants' shoulders, carrying towers of war, the necks of bulls and the fierce tossings [of their heads] high in the air, the predation of tigers and the manes of lions, although nature is nowhere more wholly herself than in her smallest creatures. Accordingly, I ask my readers—seeing that they despise many of these creatures—not to condemn with *fastidium* my account of them as well ("ne legentes, quoniam ex his spernunt multa, etiam relata fastidio damnent"), for in the contemplation of nature nothing can appear superfluous.

Because the subject is insects, Pliny fears that he will lose readers who think insects insignificant and superfluous (*supervacuum*) compared to elephants and bulls and tigers and lions. He therefore seeks to restrain the readers' ranking impulse by telling them that it literally runs contrary to Nature, an argument he later repeats in even more forceful terms in a similar context, when the authority of Nature, now supplemented by that of Vergil and Homer, is again mobilized to beat back the forces of ranking *fastidium*.[53]

Such literary *fastidium*, when directed to matters of style and diction,[54] is perhaps most vividly and instructively captured by the younger Pliny when he recounts his little fit of outrage (*indignatiuncula*) at the behavior of certain men at a recital:[55]

The work being read was highly finished in every way, but two or three clever persons—or so they seemed to themselves and a few others—listened to it like deaf mutes. They never opened their lips, nor stirred a hand, nor even rose to their feet if only as a change from sitting still. What is the point of all this dignity and learning, or rather this laziness and conceit, this want of tact or even good sense, which makes you spend a whole day giving offense and leaving an enemy in the man you came to hear as your dearest friend? Are you cleverer than he is? All the more reason not to feel *invidia* at his success, for *invidia* is a sign of inferiority (*tanto magis ne invideris; nam qui invidet minor est*). . . . Personally, I always respect and admire anyone who achieves something in literature: for it's a demanding business, difficult and lofty, *fastidiosa*, and apt to despise those by whom it is despised ("est enim res difficilis ardua fastidiosa, et quae eos a quibus contemnitur invicem contemnat").

The offenders were (on Pliny's interpretation) putting on airs, spurning the presentation offered to them because they wished to appear "learned" and "wise," superior in judgment to both the reciter and the rest of the audience: they behaved, in a word, *fastidiose*. But Pliny does not apply that word to them, instead reading their posture in terms of *invidia*, which in this case amounted to an unintended betrayal of inferiority by a pose of superiority.[56] Rather, Pliny applies the word to the idea of literary activity itself, as a "a demanding business, difficult and lofty, *fastidiosa*," and he thereby achieves a kind of one-upmanship in the game-within-the-game. For the exact modality of the relevant *fastidium* is picked out by the clause that follows: literary activity is "apt to despise those by whom it is despised." Who "those" are in this case of dueling *fastidium* is clear: the offenders are put in their (proper, lowly) place before the *res difficilis ardua fastidiosa*, as the epithet *ardua* (both "steep" and "challenging") not only reinforces the preceding *difficilis* (as a near-synonym) but also anticipates *fastidiosa*, suggesting that literary activity sits enthroned upon a high and sheer pinnacle, where it has the superior vantage point from which to render its ranking judgment, *de haut en bas*.

The behavior of the *fastidiosi* in this episode had social consequences beyond offending Pliny. They left as an enemy the man (the reciter) whom they had visited as a dear friend, primarily because they had violated the presumption or pose of equality that was central to the ethos of *amicitia*: they had committed the cardinal social sin of "showing *fastidium* toward equals and peers" (*in aequos et pares fastidiosus*).[57] It was improper to have that feeling toward peers precisely because the feeling powerfully underlined the fact of differential status, drawing persons and classes apart and ensuring that they stayed apart. Like any powerful force, it required proper calibration and precise distribution by the right people. Far more often than not, according to our texts, this was treatment it did not receive.

We caught a glimpse of *fastidium*'s part in this social dynamic earlier, in Petronius's tale of the peasant and the cloak. The same dynamic was active from the base to the pinnacle of the social pyramid. Slaves, it goes without saying, were the object of this *fastidium*, being ranked below everyone else. This is obvious to Seneca, for example, when he considers categories of persons against whom we refrain from expressing anger:

> Different considerations should deter us in different cases: fear in some, respect in others, *fastidium* in others again. It would really be a great accomplishment, wouldn't it, to toss some paltry, wretched slave in the workhouse![58]

The argument, in the case of the slave, is based not on his person (which is, in effect, beneath contempt) but on the person of the master, according to the criterion of what constitutes a significant action for him to perform (*magnam rem facere*).[59]

Slaves arouse an easy and almost offhand *fastidium* just because their abasement was a matter of consensus. The feeling is more intense in the case of that ambiguous figure, the freedman. Here is Velleius Paterculus on Menas and Menecrates, freedmen of Pompey the Great in the service of his son Sextus (2. 77. 3):

> [The pact of Misenum] restored to the state, among other highly distinguished men, Claudius Nero and Marcus Silanus, Sentius Saturninus and Arruntius and Titius. But as for Staius Murcus, who had doubled Pompey's forces when he arrived with his very large fleet [cf. 2. 72. 4]— Pompey had had him killed in Sicily, after he was covertly attacked with false allegations, because Menas and Menecrates had conceived a feeling of *fastidium* (*fastidierant*) at having such a man as their colleague.

The verb here, *fastidierant*, is caustic: the thought is that Staius Murcus, a man of praetorian rank and an *imperator* (2. 69. 2), would have been far more justified in feeling *fastidium* for the freedmen than the freedmen were in feeling *fastidium* for him.[60] In general, Velleius is highly critical of Sextus's use of slaves and freedmen to achieve his ends, and Menas and Menecrates are among the foremost symbols of that use: his bitter ascription of *fastidium* to the pair not only characterizes their impropriety toward Staius but also constitutes the expression of his own implied *fastidium* toward them.

We have seen this kind of reversal before, and we see it again when the younger Pliny vents his indignation (lively even at half a century's remove!) at the praetorian *ornamenta* and other honors awarded to the emperor Claudius's freedman Pallas (*Ep.* 8. 6. 14):[61]

> It was resolved that all the honors of this profoundly fastidious chattel (*fastidiosissimum mancipium*) be inscribed on bronze, both those that he had refused and those that he had taken up. . . . Upon our immortal public monuments were incised and engraved the praetorian insignia of Pallas—yes, just like ancient treaties, just like sacred laws!

Among the many galling aspects of this transaction, as Pliny represents it, is Pallas's own exercise of deliberative *fastidium*, accepting some honors, ranking others too low to be worth taking up: the point of the oxymoronic phrase *fastidiosissimum mancipium* is that Pallas, as mere "chattel," was himself a deserving object of the sort of *fastidium* he displayed.[62] And, at the same time that Pliny is outraged by the *fastidium* of a freedman toward honors he did not deserve, he is no less outraged at the *fastidium* that emperors showed toward senators before Trajan's happy rule (*Pan.* 24. 5):

> Previous emperors had lost the use of their own feet, out of *fastidium* for us (*fastidio nostri*) and a certain dread of equality. Accordingly, they were borne along above our heads on the shoulders and necks of slaves; but *you* are borne aloft, above the emperors themselves, by your fame and glory, by the devotion (*pietas*) of the citizenry, by freedom; *you* are raised to the stars by that ground that you share [sc. with us], by the princely footsteps mingled [sc. with our own] ("te ad sidera tollit humus ista communis et confusa principis vestigia").

Pallas's *fastidium* expressed his refusal to accept his proper, subordinate station, while the emperors' *fastidium* for senators, expressed by being carried on litters in their midst, acted out their refusal to accept the founding myth of the Principate, that the *princeps* was only "first among equals": in both cases, at opposite ends of the social spectrum, the expression of *fastidium* was a grievous failure to experience the wary social emotion with which we began this study, *verecundia*.[63] In their deliberative rankings, the freedman and the emperors all got the deliberations wrong and so claimed a rank that was not theirs, in a misguided celebration of self. In that respect, the behavior of the emperors was as gross as that of Caligula, who at a dinner party expressed his *fastidium* by loudly observing to an *amicus*, the consular Valerius Asiaticus—a fierce character, and touchy about his honor—that Valerius's wife wasn't very good in bed.[64]

It is in the context created by this form of *fastidium*, as an often-abused force in the definition of hierarchy, that we must understand the other text that introduced the themes of this book, Valerius Maximus's tale of Sextus Pompeius and the *grande dame* of Ceos.[65] As Valerius tells the story, it is not only drenched in emotion but also informed, in detail after detail, by a concern with rank and status: the lady was herself of highest standing (*summa dignitas*), the couch on which she lay was spread in an exceptionally fine way (*lectulo cotidiana consuetudine cultius strato*), and she judged it worth a lot (*magni aestimaret*) that her death be made still more distinguished (*mortem . . . clariorem*). But, however grand the lady was, Pompeius as consular and governor was vastly grander. His higher status is the reason the lady wished him to attend her death, to add to its luster, and his higher status is the reason that the lady blessed him in the terms that she did, "because [he] did not feel *fastidium* at (the thought of) either urging [her] to live or watching [her] die" ("quod nec hortator vitae meae nec mortis spectator esse fastidisti"). One so grand *would* be expected to feel and show *fastidium* at such an occasion, regarding it as beneath his dignity, but Pompeius did the unexpected. Because of his *virtus* and *humanitas* (on Valerius's telling), he showed himself to be free of *fastidium* and, with it, of the self-regard that enlivens this form of the feeling.[66]

Ranking *fastidium* implies an instrumental view of its objects: the persons and things subjected to it, and the very transactions that arouse it, are simply the means for the *fastidiosus* to act out his *amour propre* or achieve self-satisfaction. It matters little what the objects are. They might be gifts that you do not think worth taking up, or cases at the bar that you refuse because they are beneath you or will detract from your reputation.[67] They might be the unfortunate, whose appearance merely prompts complacent thoughts about your own fortunes.[68] They might be persons who provide an opportunity to aestheticize virtue, allowing you to judge what is good by the standard of what you find comely and pleasing.[69] They might be—and often are—those who seek your affections, for this self-concern is not least evident in the *fastidium* of love. The would-be beloved quails before the *elegantia* of the other, fearing that it will produce *fastidium* and the judgment "Nope, not good enough for me."[70] When it does, we have Corydon's lament in Vergil's second *Eclogue*, an extended meditation on the *fastidium* of love from the object's point of view,[71] or Ovid's shrewd characterization of the feeling from the perspective of the self-absorbed *fastidiens*, in the utterly fitting person of Paris (*Her.* 16. 95–100):

> Not only did the daughters of kings and generals set their sights
>   on me,
> but nymphs too felt the pang of love for me.
> Whose lovely face should I admire beyond Oenone's? In all the world
> there's not another—after you—worthier of being Priam's daughter-
>   in-law.
> But feelings of *fastidium* for all of them come upon me, now that
> there's hope, Tyndaris, of marriage with you.[72]

Princesses and nymphs? Not nearly good enough, once something better—more satisfying to the subject—has come along. In fact, where *fastidium* guides *amor*, only one happy outcome seems possible: a love that results from recip-rocal ranking games, when *both* parties assume the role of *fastidium*'s object (Petron. *Sat.* 127. 1–3):

> In her delight she smiled so alluringly that I thought a full moon had
> shown its face from behind a cloud. Presently . . . she said, "If you do
> not feel *fastidium* for a woman well turned out, one who has known a man
> for the first time this year, then I give you, dear young man, a sister.[73]
> Indeed you do have a brother (nor was I loath to inquire on this point),
> but what keeps you from adopting a sister, as well? I come to you in the
> same degree of relation. Only may you deign to acknowledge, when it
> pleases you, my kiss as well" (*tu tantum dignare et meum osculum . . .*
> *agnoscere*). "Oh no," said I, "rather do I beg you by your beauty not to
> feel *fastidium* at admitting a foreigner among your worshippers. You will
> find me scrupulous in my observances, if you shall allow yourself to be
> venerated" ("*te rogo ne fastidias hominem peregrinum inter cultores*
> *admittere. invenies religiosum, si te adorari permiseris*").

Each would-be lover asks the other not to look down on her or him, not to feel and express *fastidium*. At the same time, in a conciliatory gesture, each assumes a submissive posture that preempts the other's deliberation by making plain the ranking that exists in the speaker's mind: she asks him to "deign" to ac-cept her kiss; he presents himself as her "worshiper." The happy result (here, at least) is *gratia conciliata* and *concordia* (ibid. 5).

The differences between this form of *fastidium* and the per se sort are consid-ered in detail in the chapter's final section; here I can note one contrast that concerns their style of representation. As you recall, per se *fastidium* is associ-ated with a set of metaphors that consistently suggests its physicality, and it is repeatedly represented as being embodied in the eyes and, especially, the stom-ach. The *fastidium* of deliberative ranking, by contrast, is not much spoken of in ways that suggest its physicality—perhaps precisely because it was experienced predominantly as deliberative, or perhaps (more important) because those who speak of it are most often not representing an experience of their own at all but are ascribing the experience to another (we will return to this point). Further, when its physical embodiment is touched upon, it is associated with different parts of the body: the lips and, especially, the nose, rather than the eyes and the stomach. Quintilian says that "we express almost nothing in a becoming manner by using the nose and lips, although derision (*derisus*), contempt (*contemptus*), and *fastidium* are usually signified in this way."[74] The association with derision and contempt suggests that Quintilian has in mind the sort of *fastidium* with which we have just been concerned, and the suggestion is corroborated by a couple of Pomponius Porphyrio's comments on Horace. When Horace, stressing what Maecenas does *not* do, uses the phrase "naso suspendis" (lit. "you suspend [strangers] from your nose," *Serm.* 1. 6. 5), Porphyrio glosses it by saying "as the common expression has it, 'you nose [them] off,' that is, you express derision through a kind of *fastidium,*" where the nose, derision, and *fastidium* are linked as they are by Quintilian.[75] More evocative still is a comment in which Porphyrio gets Horace wrong, but in a revealing way: "DVCI VENTRE LEVEM, NASVM. 'nasum' pro 'derisore' posuit, 'nidorem' pro 'risu,' a quo verb<um> fit 'renideo'. SVPINO. 'fastidio'" (i.e., Horace here used the word *nasum* / "nose" to mean *derisor* / "one who mocks," *nidor* / "aroma," from which the verb *renideo* / "I grin" is [supposedly] derived, to mean *risus* / "smile, grin," and *supino* / "I tilt or incline backward" to mean "I feel *fastidium*"). The phrase in question (only partly represented in Porphyrio's notes) occurs at *Satires* 2. 7. 37–38:

"etenim fateor me" dixerit ille
"duci ventre levem, nasum nidore supinor. . . ."

Horace's speaker, a professional hanger-on (*parasitus*), "confess[es that he is] fickle, led about by [his] belly, tilting back [his] nose to catch the aroma" of a free meal, like an animal testing the wind. Porphyrio, however, is bent on associating this nasal imagery again with "derision" and *fastidium*, and, in so doing, he nicely shows that the *fastidium* of deliberative ranking is thought to reside not merely in the nose but specifically in the *upturned* nose. Porphyrio's error suggests that this *fastidium* is first cousin to that wonderfully evocative English derivative from "snout": "snootiness."

The Dynamics of *Fastidium* (III): Ambiguity and the Scripts at Play

The affects described and analyzed in sections I and II, though both labeled *fastidium*, are represented as being produced by two distinct ways of engaging experience, two scripts constituted by cognitive processes that are

complementary: the "absolute" or "per se" element of one has as its counterpart the "ranking" (ordinal, relational, selective) element of the other; the "reflex" component of one is the opposite of the "deliberative" component of the
other. In purely formal terms, then, it is not implausible that the two complementary reactions together could be more or less comprehensive in explaining
how *fastidium* is produced in the Roman mind as a single end-product.[76] This
is not to say that there are no ambiguous instances: *fastidium* as we are able to
know it is only a discursive gesture made in natural language, and no natural
language is wholly free of ambiguity. It is the case, however, that some kinds
of ambiguity are more instructive than others.

In a few instances, the context simply gives too little information for reliable judgment: when the elder Pliny tells us only that Sicilians feel no *fastidium*
toward the artichokes native to their island, we cannot know whether he means
that they do not find artichokes absolutely repellent or that they do not rank
them so low, relative to other artichokes or to other foods in general, as to have
an aversion to them.[77] In some other instances, the *fastidium* represented in
the text seems overdetermined: it not only *can* be understood as a product of
either reaction but probably *should* be understood as a product of both—an
aspect of emotion-scripts that we have seen repeatedly before.[78] For example,
when Juvenal urges trade as a profitable alternative to the toil and terror of
military service, he gives this advice (14. 200–205):

> Buy what you can sell
> for half as much again: don't let feelings of *fastidium*
> come over you for wares that must be banished beyond the Tiber,
> and don't believe that some distinction must be drawn between
> fine perfumes and tanning: profit smells good, no matter what
> its source.

Tanning was one of the smelly and polluting industries relegated to the far
bank of the Tiber across from the city center, and it is the absolutely repellent
stench of the trade that Juvenal clearly invokes in the last two clauses.[79] Yet,
tanning (like most trades) was also less socially respectable than soldiering, the
alternative source of income just discarded, and so was a possible cause of "ranking" *fastidium*, too: Juvenal is probably playing on both nuances of the feeling
at once.[80]

More revealing for the dynamics of *fastidium*, however, are three other sorts
of ambiguity associated with responses that can be labeled "focalized," "piggy-
back," and "perverse." It is worth considering each of these in some detail.
"Focalized" ambiguity, as we have seen before, results from the fact that the
same presentation can be perceived and evaluated differently by the different
people involved in any given transaction.[81] For example, when speaking about
the rhythms to be used in speech, Quintilian remarks that the ears respond to

("judge") both good and bad effects, including "excessive and extravagant" effects that produce *fastidium*:

> On that topic an excellent judgment can be formed by the ears, which perceive effects that are properly filled out and feel the lack when they are not, which approve effects that move surely and regularly and catch out those that limp, and which feel *fastidium* at superfluity and excess. And so, while the learned (*docti*) grasp the principles of proper composition (*ratio componendi*), the ignorant (*indocti*) too grasp the pleasing effect (*voluptas*).[82]

The final sentence suggests that, whereas a given effect will produce the same basic response—pleasure or displeasure, attraction or aversion—regardless of the audience's sophistication, the response will be differently constituted—will follow from different modes of evaluation—according to individuals' differing degrees of learning: though the ignorant, not having access to the relevant *ratio*, have not learned how to refer the effects they hear to a standard of judgment in an informed and systematic way, they can nonetheless have an immediate, in fact "natural" and "instinctive," reaction to the sensation itself; by contrast, the learned can presumably both enjoy this "natural" response and, thanks to their informed judgment, identify "superfluity and excess" as such and rank them aversively relative to some standard of "appropriateness and sufficiency."

There are also instances to remind us that *fastidium*, when it has another person as its object, is a form of social relations and that its understanding is therefore likely to be a relative matter. Consider, for example, the following passage from Ovid's *Love-Cures*, recommending a strategy for getting over the "malady" of an affair (537–42):

> Go ahead, enjoy your girlfriend to the full—let no one stop you—
> Let her account for all your nights and all your days.
> Try to feel that you've had it up to here with your woe (*taedia quaere mali*): such feelings too bring an end (*faciunt et taedia finem*).
> Presently, even when you think you can do without her, keep at it,
> Until you've glutted yourself, until overabundance destroys your passion,
> Until there's no pleasure in being at her house, which has become an object of *fastidium* (*et fastidita non iuvet esse domo*).

The "teacher" is plainly recommending a form of aversive conditioning: in similar terms, you can cure an unhealthy craving for bonbons by eating them until you are sick of them—for the next time someone offers you a bonbon, you are likely (at a minimum) to say "Uff! bonbons—no, thanks, couldn't touch another one!" If we then ask what sort of cognitive process results in the *fastidium* here—in the girl's *domus* becoming an object of *fastidium* in the lover's eyes—the answer also seems plain enough: having had it "up to here" with the girl, the lover feels an absolute and autonomic aversion to any further contact. But, if we think a bit further about the process—if we bear in mind that the reaction it represents involves two parties and that the *domus* here is merely an objectifying metonymy for the *puella* herself—we might see that the process has a different appearance according to the party through whom it is focalized. For the recipient of the advice, who is "in on" the strategy, the *fastidium* in question is indeed the product of an absolute and autonomic response, the sort usually associated with mere satiety:[83] he has simply had enough, the response is now beyond his choice and will, and the *fastidium* (as far as he is concerned) carries no ethical charge. If, however, we read against the grain for a moment, we can imagine that to the *puella*—now suddenly home alone, and presumably not at all pleased to be home alone—it will no doubt appear that she has been dumped, whether in favor of another to whom she has been found inferior or simply, disdainfully dumped, as unworthy of the lover: *she* is likely to conclude that she has been subjected to *fastidium* of the deliberative, ranking variety and draw quite different ethical conclusions about the lover's conduct.[84]

In other instances involving the perceptions, evaluations, and responses of a single individual, it appears that one type of *fastidium*-reaction depends on another and rides piggy-back upon it. Here is Seneca in two passages from *De clementia*:[85]

You should deal with citizens, with the obscure and lowly, all the more moderately the less you have to gain from afflicting them. Some you should spare gladly, others you should feel *fastidium* to chastise, just as the hand must be drawn back from small creatures that dirty you if you crush them ("a quibusdam te vindicare fastidias et non aliter quam <ab> animalibus parvis sed opterentem inquinantibus reducenda manus est"); but you should use the opportunity for clemency toward those whose preservation or punishment will be a subject of talk in the town.

All the other things that I wish those who feel pity to do [the merciful man] will do gladly and magnanimously: he will bring succor to another's tears, not join in them; he will give a hand to the shipwrecked, shelter to the exile, a coin to the needy—not the insulting sort of offering that most of those who want to appear compassionate just toss away, feeling *fastidium* for those they help and afraid of being touched by them, but a coin given by one human being to another from a common fund ("non hanc contumeliosam, quam pars maior horum, qui misericordes videri volunt, abicit et fastidit quos adiuvat contingique ab iis timet, sed ut homo homini ex communi dabit"). . . .

In both cases, it seems clear that the *fastidium*-response is figured as an absolute and autonomic reaction: in the first passage, a reflexive drawing back from crushing a small creature—a bug, say—that would dirty your hand; in the second, a reflexive shuddering at the thought of contact with (as the contrasting injunction "but . . . by one human being to another . . . " implies) something not quite human. Yet, in both cases, it is equally clear that the object of *fastidium* is *not* a bug or some other subhuman creature: the object is a person who must first be classified—that is, deliberatively ranked—as no better than a bug as a precondition for the response to occur. This is a familiar pattern of prejudice-formation: having ranked X as so far inferior a specimen as to be deemed worthy of aversion, you then feel a visceral and reflexive aversion at the sight, smell, touch, or even thought of X. (Once the prejudice has taken hold, of course, you might at future encounters move directly to reflexive aversion, drawing back from the bug that you now "know" X to be.)

The *fastidium* that Seneca represents is in fact fundamentally indistinguishable from the visceral aversion that George Orwell recalled feeling for lower-class army recruits as a result of his "lower-upper-middle-class" background:[86]

> When I was not much past twenty I was attached for a short time to a British regiment. Of course I admired and liked the private soldiers. . . . And yet, after all, they faintly repelled me; they were common people and I did not care to be too close to them. In the hot mornings when the company marched down the road, myself in the rear . . . , the steam of those hundred sweating bodies in front made my stomach turn. And this, you observe, was pure prejudice. For a soldier is probably as inoffensive, physically, as it is possible for a male white person to be. . . . But I could not see it like that. All I knew was that it was *lower-class* sweat that I was smelling, and the thought of it made me sick.

The "Whites Only" drinking fountains of the old, segregated American South can be understood in terms of the same sequence of *fastidium*, and you will probably think of other prejudices that can be similarly understood.

In other cases it is the *fastidium* of deliberative ranking that rides piggyback upon the *fastidium* of absolute and autonomic aversion. In a discussion of suicide, Seneca finds occasion to retail how a gladiator—which is to say, a slave—was able to liberate himself by taking his own life (*Ep.* 70. 20):

> Just recently, in a training school for beast-fighters, one of the Germans went off to relieve himself when he was being got ready for the morning show—only this was he allowed to do all by himself, without a guard. There he took a stick with a sponge attached to it for cleaning off the filth, and he stuffed the whole thing down his throat and choked himself

to death. That's what I call slapping death in the face (*hoc fuit morti contumeliam facere*).

And Seneca rounds the lesson off by anticipating a possible response: "Oh, yes, absolutely," he says, "that wasn't a very elegant or very comely way to die (*ita prorsus, parum munde et parum decenter*): what is stupider than feeling *fastidium* about your way of dying (*quid est stultius quam fastidiose mori*)?" The stupid objection of those who would prefer to die with a display of *fastidium* is incongruously and mockingly cast as a matter of deliberative ranking, insofar as the repeated adverb *parum*, "too little," implies a standard—a "sufficiency," *satis*—to which judgment in such matters could be referred. But, of course, the precondition for such an effetely aestheticized and distancing response is a different sort of *fastidium*, an absolute and reflexive horror at the thought of shoving a shit-stained sponge down your own throat.

Lucan trades on a cognate horror when he describes the aftermath of the battle at Pharsalia (7. 838–46):

Often, above the victor's upturned face and impious standards,
gore or rotting flesh splashed down from high heaven,
and the carrion birds let drop limbs from claws grown weary.
So the entire host was not reduced to bones, was not
torn apart to become beast-fodder; the greedy birds
do not bother with the inmost tissue or suck all the marrow:
they browse on joints. The greatest part of the Latin throng
lies subject to *fastidium* (*fastidita*): sun and rain and time's
long passing made it mingle with the fields of Macedon.

The scene is no doubt calculated to induce *fastidium* per se—to make the reader's gorge rise—as a rain of clotted blood, decaying tissue, and even whole limbs is let loose upon the victors by the birds who have feasted upon the dead. But the aversion represented within the passage—the "greatest part of the Latin throng" lying *fastidita*, unburied and yet uneaten as the object of the scavengers' *fastidium*—is of a different and slightly more complex sort. It is again fundamentally a reflexive *fastidium*—here, the *fastidium* of satiety—that follows from there being simply too many corpses for the scavengers to consume. But this satiety has a secondary effect. The creatures do not bother (*non . . . curant*) go after the internal organs and the marrow but merely "browse on"—taste and sample (*degustant*)—the exposed flesh. They behave in the manner of languid connoisseurs—the archetypes of deliberative *fastidium*—exercising a choosiness at once dainty and grisly.[87]

In Lucan's imagination, an obscene abundance produces in the scavengers a kind of behavior that is perverse, even unnatural: that is just not the way scavengers normally act. Such a deviation from the "normal" brings us to the last and most consequential type of ambiguity, involving situations in which human tastes and behavior are figured as being similarly transformed. It is the type especially beloved of moralists. To understand it, we can begin by thinking about chickens.

There is this type of hen from Africa (a speaker in Varro's dialogue on husbandry tells us), large and multicolored and hump-backed, which has very recently been introduced to the banquet-menu because of people's *fastidium*: the birds are pricey because they're rare.[88] The last detail suggests that this is primarily the *fastidium* of connoisseurship, of deliberative ranking: these are now regarded as the really choice hens, and people are willing to pay a lot of money to acquire them. It is certainly not the case prima facie that an absolute and autonomous aversion to this variety of hen has kept them from being served until very recently. Nor does it seem that their recent introduction is due to an absolute aversion to eating ordinary kinds of hen—such hens could generate no sort of per se revulsion that any normal person would feel.

But were the people who paid high prices for African hens "normal"? A Roman moralist (the guise in which for the moment Varro speaks) would have his doubts. Luxury—conceived as a reaction against sameness, familiarity, and monotony, leading to a search for novelty underwritten by wealth—made people strange. For such people, the threshold of "monotony" or "sameness" came to be so low, the experience of the quotidian so aversive per se, and the index of self-concern and self-satisfaction so high, that they could express, and perhaps even feel, a kind of per se reaction comparable to "satiety" or the "food-*fastidium*" response of the ill: "Oh, no," we might imagine someone of this sort thinking, "I simply could *not* eat another of those common *gallinae*." Hence the search for the new hen, at great cost; and the new hen, when purchased at great cost, will not surprisingly be thought to taste better, thereby "justifying" the preference for it. (It might even taste better in fact, but that is not likely to account for its first being sought out.)

In fact, Varro knew such people, as his story of Marcius Philippus shows. When the guest of a certain Ummidius at Casinum, Philippus was served a common wolf-fish, and a fine figure of a fish it was (*lupum piscem formosum*); but, having taken a bite, he immediately spat it out, declaring, "I'll be damned if I didn't think it was a *fish!*" (*peream, ni piscem putavi esse!*). Here's this nice piece of fish, and he reacts that way—I ask you (Varro's tone implies), is that normal? Varro did not think so when he told the story to condemn the *luxuria* of his age, nor did Columella, when he retold the story about a century later to condemn both the *fastidium* of Philippus and the lesson that it taught in making men's palates "learned and cultivated."[89] Unnaturally cultivated, we would say—and so Seneca suggests, in a similar jeremiad on the subject of fish (*QNat*. 3. 18. 2–3). People, he says, are nowadays subject to such *fastidium* (*tantum illis inesse fastidium*) that they won't touch a fish unless it was caught that very day and had, preferably, flopped and shuddered out its life before their eyes: for these people, a fish already dead is as good as rotten (*iam pro putrido his est piscis occisus*). To react to a perfectly good piece of fish as though it were rotten is just crazy (Seneca further says): it's a kind of madness that despises the customary usages of life (*furor usitata contemnens*). Such people's thresholds of repugnance have been brought so pathologically low that they treat as "naturally" (absolutely) repellent what is simply ordinary.

The repugnance of the ordinary is a recurrent motif in moralizing invective against luxury.[90] It is a symptom of a mind steeped in luxury (*luxus animi*), Gellius says, to feel *fastidium* for things readily at hand (*parata atque facilia*) because of an abnormal and wicked feeling of satiety.[91] We bring all manner of difficulty upon ourselves, Seneca says in much the same terms, because of an unnatural *fastidium* for consumables that are easily obtained.[92] And he returns to the thought again and again, to speak of the *animus* that has become used to feeling *fastidium* for the customary and to regarding the usual as "filthy."[93] But, because such a mind soon finds even the unusual ordinary, it finally leaves no room for novelty: feelings of satiety and monotony overwhelm it, until the thought "How long the same old thing?" inspires *fastidium* for life and the world.[94] The feeling in question is perhaps best understood as a perverse hybrid, combining the toxic level of self-concern typical of deliberative, ranking *fastidium* and a warped version of the normal, reflexive response to satiety.

This is the *fastidium* that Tacitus, for example, ascribes to the empress Messalina to explain her turn from "ordinary" adultery to unheard-of lust.[95] Feeling *fastidium* for adulterous affairs could in another woman be a positive quality—a form of reflexive ethical revulsion, like aversion to incest, discussed in the first section of this chapter—but it is in this case made a vice by Messalina's perversity. Indeed, in this sphere of activity her threshold of satiety was so low and her perception of monotony so reflexive that (as Tacitus soon tells us) she summoned a handsome Roman knight to her bed and kicked him out the same night, "with a wanton fickleness in her desires and in her feelings of *fastidium* alike."[96] It is also the *fastidium* of Horace's "lord of the land" (*Carm.* 3. 1. 36–37 *dominus terrae fastidiosus*), who builds his palace out over the sea because he feels an aversion for the earth itself (though that will not save him from Fear and Dread). The notion upon which Horace only touches is developed by a younger contemporary, the philosophizing declaimer Papirius Fabianus, who exploits it to contrast the unrecognized good of poverty with the rich man's paltry wits:[97]

> Poverty, how little known a good are you! [Rich] men even ape mountains and woods in their rotting houses, green fields, seas and rivers amid the gloom and smoke. I can scarcely believe any of these people have seen forests, or green, grassy plains . . . ; or even seen from a cliff the

seas either sluggish or, when winds stir them to their depths, stormy. For who could delight his mind with such debased imitations if he knew the reality? . . . Small minds have no room for great things. So they pile up masses of masonry even on the seashore, stop up bays by heaping earth in the depths of the ocean. Others let the sea into the land by means of ditches. For truly they do not know how to enjoy anything real, but in their sickness they need unnatural fakes of sea or land out of their proper places to delight them. Do you still wonder that, in their *fastidium rerum naturae*, they now don't even like children—except those of others?

The exorbitant building projects of the wealthy, through which they variously try to imitate or overcome nature, merely reveal their inability to grasp and take pleasure in real things: they are sick, and their falsified delights show that their sickness is constituted by an aversion to the very way things are, a *fastidium rerum naturae*. Drawing out the "unnatural" *fastidium* of the wealthy, the passage goes to the core of this perversely ambiguous form of the feeling.[98] These wicked rich folk, we are given to understand, really are not like you and me.

The Ideology of Disgust

There is a straightforward philological gain in regarding the *fastidium*-family from the perspective of "process," a gain in understanding what the words signify in their cultural context: attending to the dynamics of *fastidium*, rather than one or another lexical "equivalent," can yield a richer and more nuanced way of reading, if only because one must pause to consider exactly what kind of human response the text is attempting to represent. It is clear that some English lexical items (like "satiety" and "contempt") align themselves more or less predictably with one process or the other, while others (like "disgust" and "scorn") are a good deal less predictable in this regard. The point, however, is that there is less need to fret about the denotation of the English terms and how one sorts them (or how they would be sorted if someone else were doing the sorting): the English labels are not the concern, and the focus on process is more flexible, more multivalent, and truer to the ancient mind for which the Latin speaks. But there is more than a philological lesson to be learned from this analysis, for a cultural dynamic of some interest emerges as well, in a way that draws together several major themes of this book.

Consider the following set of oppositions entailed in the two processes, picked out and assembled here from the traits already noticed in the analyses above:

Per Se Reflex	*Deliberative Ranking*
natural	cultural
involuntary	intentional
self not at stake	self to the fore
object-centered	subject-centered
universalizing	individuating
centripetal	centrifugal

Implied in these oppositions is an inchoate Roman theory of disgust, a structure of ideas useful for organizing and interpreting the facts of aversive behavior. The *fastidium* represented as absolute and autonomic is an apparently immediate ("instinctive," "natural") reaction, of the sort that any "normal" person would have if placed in the same circumstances and faced with the same presentation. The response, seemingly, is not learned, nor is it a product of any script involving conscious choice or will: it is, by definition, just not "up to you" as you experience it. In part because of its involuntary character, it need imply no valuation of your self, beyond the valuation implied in being "normal"; in fact, because of its involuntary character, it cannot be something that you identify with—something that you choose as your own—and so it cannot be something that identifies *you*, as a person distinct from others. Nor do you aim at any purpose through the response beyond that of putting some distance between yourself and the *fastidium*-inducing object. That object is therefore the center of attention in the transaction, and the center of power: *it* has the upper hand over *you*, and you can only react. Furthermore, just because it is "normal," the response is something that you can be presumed to share with all other "normal" people, as a token of your common human makeup: at the same time that it distances you from the object, it unifies you with all other subjects who are in the same boat when it comes to body odor, bedbugs, or lizards—and to defecation, incest, or boasting, too.

Deliberative, ranking aversion is in every respect the other side of the coin. This is the *fastidium* that creates differentials of status and invokes standards of judgment that are all cultural constructs. The response is therefore part of a symbolic structure far larger than itself; at the same time, the center of the structure—the point about which all else for a moment revolves—is your own act of volition. The response is by definition entirely up to you, as a certainly intentional and probably calculated expression of your will, and the point of expressing your will in just this way has entirely to do with your self-conception: the conception of where you stand relative to others, what you deserve as a result of that standing, or what will prove most satisfying to you, aesthetically or otherwise. Because the response is in this sense self-centered, you as subject are more important than, and have power over, the object of the response: the *fastidium* itself is the expression of that power, treating the object as a means of satisfaction or a gauge to measure your higher value.

Furthermore, and accordingly, your response is the result not just of your volition but of a second-order volition: you not only wish to do or have (or not do or have) some thing (or another), but you also wish such wishes to become effective (or not), having weighed them on some scale of value or applied some other standard of judgment.[99] By willing a desire to be effective, you make it specifically your own, as a thing that you identify with—that you cannot disown or claim "just came over you"—and that therefore identifies *you*: the act of volition mediating between perception and response must express something central about your self. And because the response is thus highly personalized and individuating, it registers what distinguishes you from others, not what you share with them. It is in this respect a form of boasting: an enactment of your higher rank or value and of your "*fastidium* for the shared way of life."[100]

It is plain, however, that each side of this opposition not only represents and interprets the way things are but also says something about the way things ought to be: each form of *fastidium* has ethical implications, and the theory of behavior that they together signify is a normative theory, which we might as well call an ideology. This ideology is expressed in our texts by the way in which persons who experience *fastidium* are represented in a good, bad, or indifferent ethical light, prompting the reader to think well or poorly of them or to draw no ethical conclusions at all; and the pattern of these representations is absolutely clear. In more than 90 percent of the relevant texts, reflexively registering aversion in circumstances where any "normal" person would do the same is no worse than ethically neutral, and it is sometimes ethically positive, as when the aversion is the correct response to some taboo, mingling *fastidium* and proper *pudor*: even when another person is made the object of aversion—whether because of smell, sight, or mere satiety—the reader is at least left room to think, "Of course, I understand: I'd feel the same way in those circumstances."[101] By contrast, and with even greater frequency, deliberatively registering aversion as a way of asserting your higher status—especially when another person is the object of aversion—is represented as just wrong, whether because it is so strong an assertion of self, or because it treats its objects instrumentally, or because it deviates from what is "natural," or because the deliberation is unjust, or for all these reasons.[102] Experiencing this form of *fastidium*, which expresses too expansive a sense of self, is the polar opposite of *verecundia* and so should engage the appropriate form of *pudor* (script 4). But, because it typically does not, it is an appropriate target of the "righteous *invidia*" (script 4) that aims to punish offenses against "the shared way of life" and its underlying principles. What those underlying principles are is clear: taken together, the two conceptions of *fastidium* underwrite a normative state in which shared experience is preferable to distinction, wealth is not used to "unnatural" ends, zero-sum games of ranking—like explicit boasting—are deplored, and the dynamics of social distance are not distorted or placed under strain. That is to say, your inferiors regard themselves as no better than they are, your peers seek no advantage over you, and your superiors pretend they are your peers.[103] It is an ideology that bears a strong family resemblance to the folktale with which this book began, of the just community of equals who lapsed from the spontaneous exercise of virtue because of their desire for too much.

That, at any rate, appears to be what is happening on the surface. There is, however, a final facet of deliberative, ranking *fastidium* that muddies the surface a bit. Whereas the per se reaction is either expressed by the voice in the text or ascribed by that voice to another—with no different implications in either case—the *fastidium* of deliberative ranking is very rarely expressed but almost always ascribed: like the scripts of *invidia* that appeal to no principle of "right," it is what someone else feels, not what you feel yourself.[104] Further, unlike a third-party ascription of per se and reflexive aversion, which can be a factual report based only on observable physical signs (the symptomology of illness, satiety, revulsion), the ascription of deliberative *fastidium*—absent some report by the subject—must be an interpretation, entailing inferences about intention, disposition, and other invisible processes or states. And, as we saw time and again in the survey of deliberative *fastidium*, not only is that interpretation usually unfriendly, aiming in effect to cry "Shame!" upon the *fastidiosi*, it also frequently serves the interests of the interpreter, as a move in the game-within-the-game that the text enacts. The snarky or sniffy voice deploring the other's feeling can itself reasonably be said to express the feeling that it deplores: attributing deliberative *fastidium* is commonly a way of displaying deliberative *fastidium*. As such, it offers a way to stake out the ethical high ground, and so claim superiority, without actually being seen to engage in boasting (*iactatio*). (Perhaps this is why the maneuver is so beloved of moralists.) If the *fastidium* of deliberative ranking amounts to an elevation of the self over others, and thus a kind of *iactatio*, then ascribing that *fastidium* to a deplorable other often amounts to *iactatio* carried on by other means: less directly but no less effectively, it makes the speaker greater by making the other less.[105] In this way, the surface ideology of *fastidium* is undercut, to a degree, by the manner of its representation; in this way, too, we glimpse one of the impulses that made the paradise of equality only a myth.

We have now examined in some detail the constellation of emotions that cluster under five different labels—*verecundia, pudor, paenitentia, invidia,* and *fastidium*—and have taken them apart to see how they work, especially through the scripts that give each form of the emotion its distinctive shape and feel in the emotion-talk of the Roman elite of the late Republic and the early Empire. Each of the scripts that converge upon a given label has its own domain, as a way of processing experience that engages body and mind together; at the same time, many of the scripts intersect, overlap, or complement each other in systematic ways that are both psychologically and ethically consistent. In some cases—most notably, the relation between one script of *pudor* and the wary state to which which the label *verecundia* is usually attached—the the scripts are so thoroughly integrated that they can hardly be spoken of separately (indeed, their integration is such that the relevant labels are sometimes used interchangeably). More commonly, the relation is complementary: so some forms of *pudor* (but only some forms) stand in relation to some forms of *paenitentia* (but only some forms) as cause to effect, while some failures of *verecundia* and *pudor* can be ascribed to a certain form of *fastidium*, and that form of *fastidium*, together with still other failures of *verecundia* and *pudor*, can be expected to provoke some forms of *invidia*. In all such cases when the emotional scripts overlap or interact, they exert a normative pressure, encouraging certain styles of self-expression and certain modes of dealing with others—whether other individuals or the community at large—and at the same time discouraging other styles and modes. In this way, emotions underwrite ethics, in the service of answering the question "How can we live together well?"

Now, it should in principle be possible to continue along these lines, to trace the distinct workings and the systematic interactions of all possible emotion-scripts, with their attendant labels, in the universe of elite Roman affect, including the "positive" emotions, too: it would be nice to leaven *fastidium* with a little *gaudium*. We would then have a synoptic view of Roman emotional "wholeness." But such a project probably exceeds the limits of any one study; in any case, it plainly exceeds the limits of the present study. So, to close this book with a kind of epilogue (certainly not a "conclusion"), we will consider "wholeness" of a different kind, one to which emotions and emotion-talk are relevant but that is itself not an emotion. Rather, it is a state of being: the state of being "wholly" Roman.

6

Epilogue

Being "Wholly" Roman

It was the spring of 50 BCE, and Cicero keenly wanted the honor of a triumph. As governor of Cilicia, he had received the salutation "Imperator!" from the soldiers under his command after leading them on some successful, if rather modest, skirmishes near the province's border with Syria, where the threat of the Parthians could still be heard rumbling off to the east, and he had lobbied members of the senate to approve a *supplicatio*, the decree of thanksgiving to the gods, issued in the victorious general's name, that was often the prelude to a full triumph. His substantive claim to a triumph was, we can say, a bit thin. Yet, that honor had of late been awarded for little more—and, besides, didn't he deserve it as a kind of lifetime achievement award, to recognize all he had done for the Republic? Viewing the matter in light of one of our latter-day triumphal institutions—Hollywood's Motion Picture Academy Awards—we might think of Cicero as, say, Spencer Tracy, and of his Cilician command as *Guess Who's Coming to Dinner.*[1]

Cato, however, was having none of it: though Cicero had sought his backing, he refused to support the motion for the *supplicatio* and then wrote to Cicero to explain his action. Cato's pinch-spirited, disingenuous apologia and Cicero's dignified, ironic reply are among the gems of the correspondence, and corrective reading for anyone who believes Cato's character obviously superior to Cicero's. Though the decree of thanksgiving was approved, and though Cicero could in the aftermath express a generous equanimity regarding Cato's role, the episode evidently left him simmering;[2] we soon see him explode with anger in a letter to Atticus. "Cato has in fact been disgracefully mean-spirited toward me," he complains, then elaborates on Cato's behavior in the senate, as reported by other friends:

> He offered a testimonial to my integrity, justice, clemency, and good faith—something I wasn't looking for; what I *did* request, he refused. And so Caesar, in the letter of congratulations and limitless promises that he sent—he was practically beside himself with satisfaction over the insult done me by that "utter ingrate"! And yet this same Cato sup-

ported a *supplicatio* of 20 days for Bibulus! Forgive me: I cannot put up with this, and I will *not* put up with it.[3]

The sources of Cicero's anger here are rich and varied. Cato had not only refused a favor that Cicero thought he had a right to claim—an insult (*iniuria*) in itself—but had done so in the most public way, thereby compounding the insult and detracting from Cicero's honor.[4] In the course of doing so, he had offered—with what ponderous condescension his letter allows us to infer—praise of Cicero's qualities as governor—his *integritas, iustitia, clementia,* and *fides*—that all present would have recognized as conventional, and that Cicero must have so recognized, having used the conventional language often enough himself.[5] And—now the last straw—Cato had done all this despite the fact that he supported the same sort of honor for Marcus Calpurnius Bibulus, a limp reed who happened to be his own son-in-law. In short, while praising Cicero's *integritas,* Cato had extravagantly demonstrated his own lack of integrity.

Or had he? In that last remark there is a glide from *integritas* to "integrity" that is perhaps too easy. The glide is, of course, a product of our borrowing from the Latin: indeed, "integrity"—the name and the notion—is one of the very few important ethical concepts that descend to us wholly and uniquely from the Romans (there certainly is no counterpart in the lexicon of earlier Greek ethics). Yet, it is an open question whether such a glide is justified.

Our conception of "integrity" derives, on the one hand, from a highly individualized sense of the self as the repository of normative principles: as such, it runs heavily to notions of inwardness, autonomy, and authenticity.[6] On the other hand, this deeply interiorized quality rooted in the core of our self-conception makes its presence felt only in visible and exteriorized ways, through our actions, especially in adversity. In this sense, integrity is what connects our identity, especially our moral identity, as we conceive it with the behavior by which we make our selves known in the world: integrity provides this connection by making our behavior conform to and express an inner or true self constituted by a set of principles to which we are strongly committed. For this self to have a consistent shape and "wholeness," and for the life-narratives constructed by our actions to be coherent and "whole," these principles must be coherently conceived and consistently acted upon. If you are a "person of integrity," your unconditional commitments cannot conflict and your conditional commitments must be intelligibly ranked; you must do the right thing, as your principles define it, for the right reason; you must not deceive yourself or others as to what those principles are or how your actions flow from them; and if you change those principle, the changes must be based not on expedience or caprice but on thoughtful reassessment. To achieve this sort of coherence, then, you must make your principles the object of some reflection and choice (your actions will not likely be consistently principled if you behave in merely spontaneous or intuitive ways), and this reflection will have at least two important consequences beyond grounding and harmonizing your commitments. You will come to some conscious conception of the sort of person you are, and this reflective self-conception will underwrite your adherence to your principles with a particular kind of self-consciousness: "Given the sort of person I am," you will be able to reflect, "I must in these circumstances do X, because in these circumstances X is what that sort of person would do." And you *will* do X, even in the face of external pressures or inducements to the contrary, for were you to do otherwise, the narrative of your life would cease to make sense and you would cease being fully, wholly yourself in your own eyes. A "person of integrity" can say, "When push comes to shove, I am wholly my own person, and no one or nothing has a piece of me": such a person is an actor in an ethical world that overlaps only partly with the external world of society and politics.[7]

It is, however, far from clear that the Romans meant anything along these lines when they spoke approvingly of a person as possessing *integritas* or as being *integer*.[8] In fact, before I began my inquiry, I had no very clear idea just what— exactly and substantively—the Romans meant by approving a person in that way. That sort of approval and other references to the virtue conceived to underlie it are exceedingly common, appearing hundreds of times in our texts. Yet, no Roman, so far as we know, examined the content of the idea or even so much as defined it. It was evidently the sort of ethical understanding that is acquired insensibly and exercised intuitively in (I assume) all cultures: in the manner of Justice Potter Stewart on hard-core pornography, you were supposed to know it when you saw it. But an observer viewing the culture from the outside is left to ask: what was *it*? What sort of ethical "wholeness" did *integritas* comprise—and what did it not comprise?

To begin, then, here are a few general and unproblematic observations on the basic semantics of the terms involved, the epithet *integer* and the abstract noun derived from it, *integritas*, the state of being *integer*. The derivation of the epithet is clear: it is the privative prefix *in-* ("un-" / "not") combined with the root **tag-*, the same root from which the verb *tangere* ("touch") is derived. Etymologically, in other words, *integer* is barely distinguishable from *intactus* ("untouched"/"intact"), with which we find it coupled by Livy and several other writers.[9] The coupling itself might suggest that these native speakers were not aware they were using, in effect, one and the same word and in any case did not feel that they conveyed exactly the same thought; rather, the words apparently were taken to converge on the same idea, like other couplings in which *integer* commonly figures—for example, *integer et incorruptus* (". . . and uncorrupted / unspoiled"), *integer et inlibatus* (". . . and undiminished"), *integer et inviolatus* (". . . and inviolate").[10]

Be that as it may, the core notion of *integer*—"not touched"—was deployed in several perfectly familiar and understandable ways. There is, for example, the whole peppercorn (*piper integer*) that is the indispensible ingredient in many recipes found in the cookbook of Apicius, or the *cibi integri*, the pieces of food that (Columella tells us) flat-fish have to gobble whole because they lack teeth, or any number of other physical objects that are said to be *integer* in virtue of the fact that they retain their original dimensions, mass, or volume without being crushed, sliced, diced, or otherwise diminished.[11] On the other hand, in usages that correspond to a slightly different semantic field in English, there are the liquids—blood or spring water or wine—that remain (as we would put it) "fresh" or "pure" or "unspoiled";[12] or the *virgines integrae*, young women of marriageable age who are "intact" (are "virgins" in our sense, that is) and, accordingly, are "pure";[13] or the sort of beauty (*pulchritudo*) that reaches the eyes of men "fresh and unsullied" (*recens atque integra*: Cic. *Verr*. 2. 4. 64); or the *vires*, the physical powers of soldiers and others, that are *integrae*, "fresh," before being put under strain.[14]

Plainly, a very wide range of physical entities and their attributes could all be placed under the same description (and the examples I've offered only suggest that range): we should be able to infer from this range something fundamental about the descriptive term. I take it to be equally evident that though this fundamental something can be expressed in English through words that belong to two distinct semantic fields—one centered on the idea of "wholeness," the other centered on the idea of "purity" or "freshness"—this does not indicate that one of these fields corresponds to the "real" meaning of *integer*, the other to an extension of that meaning. Rather, this is simply another one of those instances where Latin and English organize meaning a bit differently, so that Latin uses a single term to convey an idea that English normally assigns to two or more terms.

In the case of *integer*, I suggest that the core idea runs along these lines: a physical entity is *integer* when it retains the characteristics that make it essentially and entirely what it is, with nothing added (to spoil its "purity," for example) or subtracted (to diminish its "wholeness").[15] The idea is perhaps best captured in all its dimensions by the way the Romans understood the motion of some rivers. The Rhône, according to Pomponius Mela, or the Tigris, in Seneca, or the river Jordan, in Tacitus's account, all remain *integer* even while passing through lakes or vanishing underground entirely:[16] none, that is, suffers either loss of volume (its "wholeness") or contamination (its "purity"). After seeming to be engulfed, they all re-emerge unaltered, as essentially what they are.

So much for the physical sense of *integer*: let's try now to apply thoughts along these same lines to exploring its behavior as a term of ethical assessment. The person who was *integer* in an ethical sense was, we might suppose, conceived as passing through life like a great river, "whole" and "pure," retaining all the essential qualities that made him what and who he was no matter the circumstances in which he was engulfed. That is a suggestive notion, perhaps, but still rather vague: what *were* those essential qualities? To develop an answer to that question, we can consider a typical way in which the notion of *integritas* was deployed for rhetorical effect. There is nothing more common than to find a person characterized as "a man *integer* and X" or "a man of highest *integritas* and X," where X is another epithet or noun denoting an ethical trait. For example:

- "We will not have this man available to serve as a judge after January 1, nor will we have Quintus Manlius and Quintus Cornificius, two judges of utter strictness and *integritas* (*duo severissimi atque integerrimi iudices*), because they will then be tribunes of the plebs; and Publius Sulpicius, a stern and *integer* judge (*iudex tristis et integer*), must enter his magistracy on December 5 . . . " (Cic. *Verr.* 1. 1. 30);
- "He informed him that a certain Philodamus was . . . easily the leading man of Lampsacus, and that his daughter was . . . a woman of exceptional beauty, who was judged to be a woman of highest *integritas* and chastity (*summa integritas pudicitiaque*)" (Cic. *Verr.* 2. 1. 64);
- "At this time, meanwhile, Publius Sestius undertook to go to Caesar on my behalf, for the sake of my restoration [from exile]. What he did, and the degree of his success, have no bearing on the present trial. . . . But, still, you see the man's punctiliousness and *integritas* (*sedulitas atque integritas*)" (Cic. *Sest.* 71);
- "A panel of three men was established—Agrippa Menenius, Titus Cloelius Siculus, Marcus Aebutius Helva—for the purpose of founding a colony at Ardea; and these men avoided the [judicial] harassment [instigated by the tribunes] . . . by staying in the colony, which they had as a witness of their *integritas* and square dealing (*integritas iustitiaque*)" (Livy 4. 11. 7).

In such contexts, *integer* or *integritas* conveys the idea of ethical "wholeness" in a way that could be rendered in English, with suitable generality, as "upright" or "honest" ("uprightness" or "honesty"), whereas the accompanying term denotes a more specific virtue—"strictness," say, or "chastity" or "punctiliousness" or "justice." The idea of *integritas* in these places, the idea of "essential (ethical) wholeness," seems to stand in relation to the accompanying trait as, in fact, whole to part: the person so described is, on the whole, *integer* and, in particular, "strict" or "chaste" or whatever. In rhetorical terms, we could say that when we see a man described like this, as *vir integer et severus*, or a woman described as *summa integritate et pudicitia*, the presence of *integer* or *integritas* accomplishes two purposes at once: it signals that the other quality is the particular virtue most relevant to the discourse-situation—that the judge is strict, as judges in particular should be, or that the woman, while beautiful, is chaste, as women above all should be—and it suggests that that quality stands at the core of what the person essentially is. It is easy to find *integer* playing a similar role in many other settings that differ only formally: for example, when Cicero gives an obituary notice of Pompey as *integer et castus et gravis*; or when Horace famously declares the invulnerability of the man who is *integer* in respect of his way of life (as a whole) and innocent of crime (in particular: *integer vitae scelerisque purus*); or when Livy describes a segment of the Roman masses as *integer* and immediately glosses their "integrity" with an appositive phrase that specifies how that quality is expressed—through their loyalty to the "good men" (*boni*) who lead the community, say, or by their grateful memory of a man's past good deeds.[17]

That the idea of being *integer* should play the rhetorical role of a generic marker is not surprising or, for that matter, terribly revealing in itself. But it does suggest an interesting question: just what are the qualities that might be associated with it? To answer that question I surveyed all instances of the formula "vir integer et X" or "vir summa intergritate et X," and all other places where *integer* or *integritas* was closely associated with some ethical X, to see just what all the Xs would be. Such a survey, I supposed, would at least show the range of qualities that could be associated with the idea of essential ethical wholeness; at best, it would also show, cumulatively, what qualities were most closely and insistently associated with the idea when Roman authors had occasion to talk about it. Regarding this second possibility I frankly had very minimal expectations, because an earlier survey, in which I did not have this question squarely in mind, had left the impression that the qualities were all over the map—that just about any virtue could appear as the particular quality associated with the overall notion of being ethically "whole."

So much for trusting impressions; it turned out that I was quite wrong. The overwhelming majority of Xs (76 different Xs in all) allow themselves to be sorted into quite a small number of fields, as the following tabulation makes plain:[18]

- good faith: *fides* (14), *gratus* (2), *pius / -etas* (4) (*memor*)
- innocence: *innocens / -tia* (13), *simplex / -icitas* (3), *rectus* (2)
- justice: *severus / -itas* (5), *aequitas* (4), *iustus / -itia* (4) (*tristis*, in a judicial application)
- fixity (of resolve or conduct): *constans / -tia* (10), *gravis / -itas* (10)
- scrupulousness (esp. in respect of duty): *religio / -sus* (9), *diligens / -tia* (5), *industria* (2), *veritas* (2) (*sedulitas*)
- restraint (esp. of passions and appetites): *castus / -timonia* (10), *pudor* (7) / *pudicitia* (2), *continentia* (5), *modestus / -tia* (5), *frugalis / -itas* (4), *moderatus / -tio* (4), *verecundus / -dia* (4), *clementia* (3), (*bona*) *conscientia* (3), *quietus* (3), *temperantia* (3), *tristis* (3), *mansuetudo* (2) (*abstinentia, otiosus, timidus, pacatus*)
- goodness (of a generalized sort): *virtus* (12: non-martial, not "courage"), *bonus* (*optimus*) / *bonitas* (8), *mores probi* (*modesti*, vel sim.) (5)

- purity: *incorruptus* (5), *sanctus* / *-itas* (5), *sincerus* (5), *purus* (2), *sanus* / *-itas* (2) (*intemeratus, sine macula, sine crimine, sine fabula*)
- respect: *laus* (12), *probus* / *-atus* / *-itas* (7), *honos* / *honestus* (6), *auctoritas* (3), *dignitas* / *-atio* (3) (*amplus, splendidus*)

No doubt the sorting could be finetuned, and no doubt any such sorting would leave room for legitimate disagreement on this trait or that. But the general trends in the clustering of these traits seem clear.

The fact that a number of core Roman virtues are conspicuously absent from this clustering is one striking result of the survey. But let's set that absence to one side for the moment and consider first what sense can be made of the virtues that are present. Finding myself unexpectedly faced with these relatively few, reasonably distinct categories, I next asked myself if they could somehow be brought into a sensible relationship with one another. An answer is provided by the model represented in the accompanying figure 6.1.

According to this model, the foundation for *integritas* is provided by a well-defined set of personal behaviors or dispositions—restraint, fixity, scrupulousness—that are conducive to a well-defined set of social behaviors or dispositions—good faith, justice, innocence. The "personal" behaviors and dispositions, as I have labeled them, are (merely) "personal" in the sense that they are manifested primarily in elements of temperament or personal style, such as moderate appetites or an even temper, an inclination to circumspection or mildness or self-consistency, and the like: failures to display these qualities mostly cause damage to the self in the first instance (especially damage to the esteem in which the self is held), and most of them could be displayed by a person imprisoned in solitary confinement—indeed, such a person would almost certainly *have to* display these qualities, or put his sanity at risk. But he would not have the opportunity to display the "social" dispositions or behaviors—good faith or justice or even innocence—unless some other unfortunate happened to be tossed into the same cell.

Taken together, these personal and social behaviors and dispositions are constitutive of *integritas*: being ethically *integer* just means that you possess these dispositions and display these behaviors. Different behaviors and dispositions might be revealed in, or be explicitly relevant to, different situations, as we saw in the case of the strict judge or the chaste woman. But, whatever the situation, it seems that they all should be implied, insofar as there is a structural relation among the elements that causes them to be mutually entailing. Take away any one, and the others become insupportable, or at least improbable: without restraint one will not likely have fixity, or vice versa; without good faith one will not likely have justice, or vice versa; and without the personal qualities one will not likely have the social, or vice versa. In turn, possessing *integritas* generates two kinds of consequence, one personal, the other social: being *integer* allows you to think of yourself, and

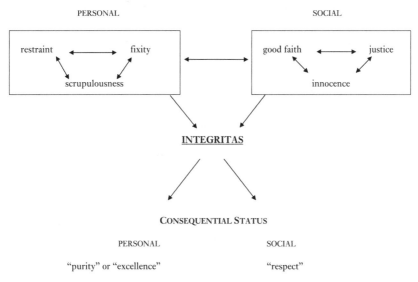

Figure 6.1. A Model of *Integritas*

to be thought of by others, as personally "good" or "pure" and so to have a claim on the "respect" of the community.

This model at least *looks* Roman in its implications—which, I stress, is the strongest claim I would make for it. I certainly do not suggest that the model shows how the Romans conceived these relations (we have no evidence that the Romans reflected on these relations at all); nor do I suggest that a Roman informant, if given to understand the model, would smite his forehead and say, "Yes, of course, *that's* the way it works." At most, I would be pleased if such a Roman would say, "Well, yes, I suppose that's one plausible way of looking at it." So let's take the model at the level of that modest claim and try to push it a bit.

The first thing that we can notice is the partiality of this *integritas*: though it is the virtue of "wholeness," it is far from being the whole of virtue. For one thing, it appears to be an entirely civilian virtue: from among the several hundred occasions where our texts show *integer* or *integritas* being used in an ethical sense, not a single one concerns the actions of Roman soldiers or their commanders. (This is perhaps the most obvious way in which *integritas* differs from another general ethical label, *virtus*.) In this respect, *integritas* aligns itself with the "civil" script of *pudor* (script 4), concerned to check discreditable "extension" of the self within the boundaries of the civil community: it is accordingly not surprising that the constitutive qualities of *integritas* seen earlier are precisely the qualities that, if consistently displayed, guarantee that you will never experience that form of *pudor*—or, for that matter, be the object of righteous *invidia*.[19]

Furthermore, even as a civilian virtue, *integritas* is rather limited: reasonableness, shrewdness, magnanimity, liberality, and benevolence are all qualities that the Romans commonly stressed when their speech took an ethicizing turn, yet these qualities appeared scarcely, or not at all, in my survey of the traits associated with *integritas*. That is not to say that reasonableness, shrewdness, magnanimity, liberality, or benevolence should be thought incompatible with *integritas*, but it would be very difficult to argue that they were thought necessary to constitute it. Possessing *integritas* by itself certainly did not bestow the good character implied by the cardinal virtues of Cicero's *On Appropriate Actions*, where "largeness of spirit" (*magnitudo animi*)—the most "resplendent" (*splendidissimum*) of the virtues—and "generosity" (*liberalitas*) play crucial roles.[20] In fact, it seems all in all an exceedingly quiet virtue, more defensive than assertive, more self-preserving than self-extending: its constitutive personal traits are rather the sort that keep you from performing acts thought to be ethically damaging than the sort that urge you to perform acts that are ethically expansive or enlarging.[21] In this respect, it seems a virtue rather different from our notion of "integrity." In this respect, too, *integritas* has about it an air of mistrust, of oneself no less than of others: an ethic that invests so much in restraint, fixity, and scrupulousness seems to fear a wild and treacherous caprice lurking not far beneath the surface.

Integritas therefore seems a minimal virtue—a threshold virtue, we might call it, or perhaps a foundational virtue: you can build upon it, by adding more assertive and positive virtues like courage or liberality, say, but you cannot dispense with it. Without it, we lapse into what Servius helpfully calls *huius vitae confusio*: treating the token that admits Aeneas to the Underworld, the golden bough, as a symbol of the path to virtue, he explains that the bough is represented as hidden in the forest because "in fact *virtus* and *integritas* are hidden amidst the confusion of this life and a multitude of vices."[22] Preserving *integritas* ensures that you remain ethically "unconfused," not confounded or adulterated, whole and self-contained, with your essential ethical components undiminished and in their proper structural relationship: we can think here, again, of an ethical counterpart to the great rivers that preserve their physical integrity, their volume and purity, in their course.

In fact, it is precisely as the virtue of self-containment that *integritas* appears in a famous and pivotal passage of Sallust's *War against Catiline*, where Caesar and Cato are compared and judged:

> Caesar was considered great in virtue of his kindnesses and generosity, Cato in virtue of the *integritas* of his life. The one was famous for his gentle and compassionate character, the other derived standing from

his sternness. Caesar achieved glory by acts of giving, support, and forgiveness, Cato by doling out nothing whatsoever. The wretched found the one a refuge, the wicked found the other a scourge; people praised the former's affability and the latter's resolve.[23]

Here all the traits attributed to Caesar are other-directed, radiating outward in acts of material and emotional generosity and magnanimity. All the contrasting traits of Cato are self-centered and self-contained, exercises of the will that keep the self at a safe distance from others: only Cato's sternness (*severitas*) and his standing as scourge of the wicked move outward to others, and then only as expressions of Cato's own righteousness. *Integritas*, it comes as no surprise to learn, is attributed elsewhere to no Roman more frequently than to Cato; it is no more surprising to learn that *integritas* is nowhere attributed to Caesar.[24]

We might pause for a moment now to consider the ground covered so far. We have seen some reason to believe that *integritas* can be thought of as an umbrella term for a set of personally and socially desirable traits, traits that constitute the "essentially whole" person. The traits contained in the set are recognizably Roman, especially in their concentration on restraint and good faith, but they are by no means the only traits that the Romans highly valued: they are very much pitched to the civilian style of life, and in fact ethical *integritas* is never remarked in connection with military endeavors. Furthermore, even within the civilian sphere, these traits seem a minimal set; the "wholeness" that they constitute seems a minimal wholeness that amounts to being "not defective." The *integer* person has a self whose basic moving parts are intact and in their proper relation—not diminished or confused—but that self, we could reasonably say, lacks something in vividness and warmth. It is certainly a self in an ethical state quite different from the one that the philosopher Xunzi was describing at much the same time in classical China, using the same metaphor of "wholeness" or "integrity" (*cheng*) to distinguish the "noble" from the "petty" man. Though concerned, like *integritas*, with the maintenance of a "constant character" and the performance of duty, *cheng* was not a minimal cluster of virtues that you were taken already to possess and that you then defended against loss or pollution; it was an all-inclusive state of virtue into which you tried to grow through self-cultivation and reflection. Though it conferred on the noble man the same sort of awesomeness and authority that Sallust ascribes to Cato, the condition inspired awe not least for the humaneness and beneficence that it embraced.[25]

To see what more can be said about *integritas*, let's consider its status as what I have called an "umbrella term." We certainly have ethical labels of this sort in English: to name just three, "goodness," "uprightness," or "honesty" each works in something like this way. "Honesty," for example, is quite a general term that embraces a number of more specific and concrete traits, like a concern for the truth and fair dealing (what an honest person can be relied on to respect), a degree of bravery (since the truth can be risky), and a certain capacity for absorbing disappointment (for while honest people will learn that not all others have this trait, that lesson should not diminish their own commitment); these specific traits can be conceived as complementary and mutually reinforcing in much the same way as the constitutive traits of *integritas*. But there is another interesting way in which the label "honesty" functions. It names one of those virtuous dispositions that chooses its characteristic actions *just because* those actions can be described in terms of itself: an honest person can choose (or refuse) to do X just because doing X can accurately be described as honest (or not)—just because it is (or is not) the sort of action that an honest person performs. ("Justice" is another label that behaves in this way, whereas "modesty" or "generosity" or even "courage" typically does not.)[26]

"Being honest" is, in other words, a disposition that not only urges its owner to act in a certain way but also does its urging in a certain way, by an appeal to self-consciousness: the disposition and its directives are prominent in their owner's self-awareness and self-conception. As I've already suggested, what we call "integrity" behaves in this way, too, as a disposition that shapes action under the impact of self-consciousness: "my sense of integrity in this case causes me to do X," a person might well reflect (in whatever form of words), "because in this case X is just what a person of integrity would do." And we know that the Romans conceived of ethical traits that they applied self-consciously and reflexively in much the same way. For example, being a *pudens* person—a person dispositionally inclined to experience *pudor*—meant that in any given transaction you could appeal to your sense of being such a person to determine how you would conduct yourself, the better to avoid seeing yourself being seen in a discreditable way: we have already seen Cicero handle the delicate chore of asking a big favor in just these reflexive terms.[27] Being an "honorable" (*honestus*) person—a person deserving of others' high regard (*honos*) and accordingly possessing a certain worthy rank and standing (*dignitas*)—is another example. Such a person can say, "Given that my *dignitas* is such, I should in this circumstance do X, because X is just what a person with such *dignitas* would do": in fact, we hear Cicero at one point explain in terms very much like these why he went into exile in 58 BCE, saying that it had always been his practice self-consciously "to gauge all [his] actions according to [his] *dignitas*," the rank and standing of which was held worthy.[28] For our present concerns, it is irrelevant that, in making this claim, Cicero was, as a matter of certain fact, vigorously improving on the way his actual behavior in 58 had appeared, not least to himself.[29] Or, rather, it is relevant only insofar as Cicero knew that the statement, if believed, would bring him credit: in the ideology of honorable behavior, saying that you had considered your position as a person with a certain *dignitas* was in itself an earnest token that you deserved the rank and standing of which you were held worthy.

At the same time, of course, mention of "credit" points to an important difference in orientation between the kind of reflection entailed in Cicero's claim and that entailed in your behavior as a "person of integrity." The honor-based reflection that Cicero refers to is aimed primarily at winning maximum credit for his performance from the spectators "out there" in his social world: *dignitas*—etymologically related as it is to thought of comely and fitting appearance (*decus*)—is first and foremost something that others ascribe to you, according to the way your behavior appears to them. As a "person of integrity," by contrast, you are not concerned in any decisive sense with the way your behavior appears to others, nor is "credit" what you are looking for, even from yourself, when you reflect on the way that the sort of person you are is tied to the behavior you should choose. Here, when choice is made under the impact of self-consciousness, the self of which you are conscious is not the creditable social actor whose performance is being judged "worthy" (or not) but the protagonist in your life's "true" narrative, which derives its "wholeness" from the coherence of your individual moral identity. Given these two quite different ways in which ethical traits can urge action by appeal to self-consciousness, we can turn to *integritas* and ask whether this trait acts on its possessor in either of these ways and whether, in particular, it exerts an influence in the manner of its modern descendant.

Let's spend the last few pages of this book, then, in considering how *integritas* is represented in action, as being somehow effective. It is obvious, first, that *integritas* is most often spoken of in terms of its impact on others: the passage from Sallust quoted earlier gives an example—"Cato [was considered great] in virtue of the *integritas* of his life"—where we learn more about the meaning of the virtue for Cato-watchers (it caused them to think him great) than we learn about its meaning for Cato himself. Other examples abound of a person's *integritas* having some effect on the opinion of others. For instance, Cicero writes to his brother in June of 58, encouraging Quintus to face any troubles that can be expected while he himself is in exile: "I trust," he says, "that your *integritas* and the citizens' affection for you and even pity for me will provide a measure of protection"—where it is assumed that Quintus's personal *integritas*, working in tandem with two emotions felt by the community at large (*amor* and *misericordia*), can achieve a political end, presumably because *integritas* can arouse a useful sentiment (like admiration), just as it provides a basis for a useful judgment (of innocence).[30] It is in a similar vein that Quintilian buoyantly remarks that "an upright character and the *integritas* of one's past life are always advantageous"—advantageous, that is, from the point of view of the defendant's advocate, because they create in the audience a presumption of innocence.[31] And Horace takes a similar line when he dismisses potential suspicions—*fuge suspicari*—by asserting that, when he praises a young woman's beauty, he does so only as an *integer* person of middle years: just the assertion of that state is expected to guarantee the virtue of his present intentions and behavior.[32]

Such examples are no more than expectable in terms of the model I suggested earlier. In effect, they start from the state of *integritas* and move down the schema toward the consequences of that state: Cicero assures Quintus that his *integritas* will bring him social "respect" (and, therefore, protection); Horace avoids the suspicion of being a dirty old man by asserting that he is *integer* and therefore, by implication, personally "pure." None of this, however, has much to do with the trait's internal orientation and its effectiveness in *motivating* its owner to behave in a certain way. Horace's claim to be *integer* is an assurance that he is now being sexually restrained, which is not quite the same thing as claiming that he is sexually restrained *because* he is *integer*; still less is it a claim that his sense of himself as *integer* would raise an obstacle to his being a dirty old man. Is *integritas* ever represented as being effective in that way? Are there instances in which we can find movement "up" the model as well as "down," with *integritas* conceived as *causing* behavior of a personally or socially appropriate sort? And, if there are such instances, is *integritas* ever conceived as causing behavior by appealing to the subject's self-conception as a normative reference-point, by making the subject reflect, "I ought to do X *just because* I am *integer*"?

The answer is a very heavily qualified "yes." *Integritas*, first, can be conceived as reinforcing its constitutive virtues, and not merely being constituted by them. Cicero, for example, in one of the long letters of advice he wrote to his brother as governor of Asia, approves the judicial strictness that Quintus has displayed, even at the cost of incurring the complaints and ill will of some of the locals: the sorts of decisions that you've made (he says), characterized as they are by an abundant strictness (*severitas*), could not easily be supported without the highest degree of *integritas*. Cicero's language, especially in the metaphor of "support" or "maintenance" (*sustinere*), makes plain that *integritas*—something that Quintus is evidently assumed already to possess— is conceived in this case as underwriting the virtue of *severitas*, providing it with a secure foundation.[33] More than that, Cicero also makes plain how *integritas* does its work by adding that Quintus should exercise the greatest *severitas* in his rulings "as long as it is not caused to waver by friendly influence (*gratia*) but remains fair." The foundation provided by *integritas* evidently includes qualities like resolve, consistency, and honesty, which do not allow Quintus's *serveritas* to be swayed by the *gratia* of this person as opposed to that; these qualities accordingly both give that *severitas* its firm place to stand and make it appear acceptable—by keeping it from appearing corruptible—in the eyes of those who witness its application.

Yet, it must be said that it is not at all common for *integritas* to be thought of and spoken of as Cicero apparently does here. More important, even this way of thinking or speaking plainly need not imply that *integritas* provides a basis for acting *reflectively*, with reference to itself as a normative principle. Cicero's remarks just quoted most straightforwardly imply that the virtue is thought to produce or reinforce certain behaviors as a matter of acquired character: on such a view, Quintus's general, habitual condition as an *integer* person will cause his judgments in any particular circumstance to be strict and scrupulous as a matter of course, without the self-conscious thought that his condition as *integer* demands a certain kind of response. On that view, then, *integritas* lacks much of the character and function that our notion of integrity importantly has today: defining an element of your self-conception and self-evaluation; creating a dispositional "sense of integrity" that yields the thought "My sense of integrity causes (or forbids) me to do X because X is (or is not) what a person of integrity would do"; and, by that thought, providing the impulse to behave in a certain way, as a sufficient motive arising from itself.

In fact, I know of only one instance where the notion of *integritas* is brought into play in a way that seems—and I stress "seems"—to entail the character of an inner, reflective imperative: that this instance concerns, yet again, the behavior of Cato might by this time seem inevitable. The occasion was Cato's return to Rome in 56 with the treasure of King Ptolemy of Cyprus; Plutarch tells the story this way (*Cat. min.* 39. 1–2, trans. Perrin):

> All the magistrates and priests, the whole senate, and a large part of the people went to the [Tiber] to meet him, so that both banks . . . were hidden from view, and his voyage up to the city had all the show and splendor of a triumph. Yet some thought it ungracious and stubborn (*skaion . . . kai authades*) that, although the consuls and praetors were at hand, he neither landed to greet them nor checked his course, but on a royal galley of six banks of oars swept past the bank where they stood, and did not stop until he had brought his fleet to anchor in the dock-yard.

Plutarch unfolds a gorgeous scene, graced (unintentionally) with a touch of farce, as we are led to picture the consuls, Cornelius Lentulus and Marcius Philippus, leading the crowds in waving their greetings to Cato—then slowly, gravely pivoting to wave goodbye as he sails resolutely on. ("Look—here comes Cato! Oops—there goes Cato!") Now consider the terms in which Velleius Paterculus casts this same incident when he comes to recount it in the second book of his history: yes, he grants, Cato's *integritas* was inexpressibly great and beyond all praise; yet, he could almost be convicted of *insolentia* for the way that he chose to demonstrate it on this occasion.[34] Here, if anywhere, *integritas* can be understood as a real "sense of integrity," Cato's sense of who he was, what character he sustained, and what that demanded of him in the circumstances: the thought is evidently that this quality caused him literally to continue on his appointed course—like some great "river" of ethical purity being borne upon the river Tiber—and to ignore the extraordinary reception mounted by the *senatus populusque Romanus* in a way that others could judge a symptom of self-will (*authadeia*, as Plutarch puts it) or an eccentric sort of arrogance (*insolentia*, in Velleius's terms). The referral of this behavior to *integritas* does not, of course, give us access to Cato's own thoughts but is Velleius's interpretation of a Cato who, by the time Velleius was writing, in the reign of Tiberius, already enjoyed near-legendary status as a figure of crusty, Stoicizing autonomy.[35] In any case, it does sound very like the Cato we think we know.

We can think of Roman "integrity," then, as comprising the bundle of dispositions and behaviors that anchored a person securely in the social world. These dispositions and behaviors were not technicolor traits tending toward large and vivid gestures; they included the quiet virtues of self-containment and self-control in personal comportment and understanding and meeting obligations in dealings with others. Despite being a bit colorless and lacking in panache—or, perhaps, precisely because it was a bit colorless and lacking in panache—this bundle of traits provided a stable social self that earned the respect of others, who could not feel threatened by it. In terms of the emotions that have been the subject of this book, we can say that a *homo integer* would certainly be an exemplar of *verecundia* and be dispositionally sensitive to the script of *pudor* that regulated behavior of a discreditably "self-extending" sort; such a person would therefore have little reason to feel *paenitentia* at acts of his own that were ethically unbecoming and, as already noted, could not deservedly be the object of *invidia* or *fastidium*. A community full of such people might even constitute a paradise—a somewhat bland paradise, perhaps, but paradise nonetheless—of the sort the Romans thought they once had.[36]

What Roman "integrity" appears largely to have lacked was the dimension of internal, reflective autonomy that is at integrity's core as we conceive it: the *homo integer* did not consult an authentic inner self as a source of normative principles, nor did he often find himself standing crosswise to all of society as a result of that consultation. Only Cato, as we perhaps saw, provides an exception. If that is so, then some added force is given to a remark (not unambiguous in any case) passed by Cicero in the exchange with which we began this epilogue, concerning his *supplicatio*: setting aside as impossible the thought that all or even many of us might be like Cato, Cicero says it was a "wonder" that even one Cato had emerged "in our civil community."[37] Indeed: for in the matter of *integritas*, as in not a few others, Cato would seem to have been not wholly Roman.

NOTES

Preface

1. The plainest allusion occurs at the top of p. 3 in the published version of the address, Kaster 1997.

Introduction

1. Respectively: Cic. *Rep.* 5. 1–2, Verg. *Aen.* 7. 203–4 (Latinus, on his people), Ov. *Fast.* 1. 249–51, Tac. *Ann.* 3. 26 (a similar theme is placed in Tiberius's mouth at *Ann.* 3. 54). Latin quotations not translated or closely paraphrased in the text are translated in the notes; unless otherwise indicated, all translations are my own. Abbreviations follow the format of the *Oxford Classical Dictionary* (3d edition) or, where *OCD*[3] gives no guidance, the *Oxford Latin Dictionary*.

2. For other forms of the folktale see, e.g., Sall. *Cat.* 6–13, Diod. Sic. 37. 3. 1–5, Barton 2001 (Part 1); bibliography on "golden age" myths is gathered at Woodman and Martin 1996, 240.

3. The Romans regarded each of the psychophysical states at the center of this study, together with some others that play a more occasional role (e.g., *taedium*), as a *perturbatio animi* ("upheaval of the mind") or *adfectus* ("affect"), the Latin terms that correspond most closely to Greek *pathos*. I use the English terms "emotion(al)" (most commonly) and "affect(ive)" (occasionally), not "passion(ate)," though I do not believe that a great deal rides on these choices.

4. On ancient pity, see Konstan 2001.

5. Val. Max. 2. 6. 8. Identification of Pompeius with the homonymous governor (cos. 14 CE) has sometimes been questioned, most recently by Wardle 1998, 1, on no good ground; the notion that he "may [have been] a humble unknown" (ibid.) is contradicted by the tenor and central details of Valerius's story.

6. For the custom, see Kaster 1995, 325–26 (on Suet. *Gramm.* 30. 6).

7. "Scorn" is in fact the choice in Hanson's Loeb Apuleius, cf. Vallette's "dédain." Other translators of Apuleius, when they do not fall back on some cognate ("fastidiousness," Taylor; "fastidio," Seroni), generally choose to convey the idea of a more or less vigorous refusal, without regard for its affective qualities: so "repulse" (Graves), "repulsion" (Lindsay), "rejection" (Butler), "[the

youth's] anger at being rejected" (Walsh), "rifiuto" (Carlesi), "Zurückweisung" (Helm).

8. For different approaches to this general question in different cultural contexts see, e.g., Ricks 1974, Harré and Finlay-Jones 1986, Heelas 1986, Lutz 1988, Miller 1993 (esp. 98–101, 175–201), Miller 1995, Miller 1997 (esp. 15–21, 143–78), and (for classical antiquity) Cairns 1993, Gill 1996, Barton 2001, Harris 2001, Konstan 2001, Cairns 2003b; for further references and valuable overviews, Mesquita and Frijda 1992, Shweder and Haidt 2000 (expanding and revising Shweder 1993). The essays collected in Braund and Gill 1997 offer valuable analyses of specific "passions in Roman thought and literature," though none quite addresses the issues raised here. For the outcome of the two tales of *fastidium*, see chapter 5 at n. 36 and n. 65, respectively.

9. Taking this as our premise, I generally avoid glossing Latin emotion terms as (e.g.) "roughly, shame" or "'shame,'" using some form of words or the scare-quotes to remind us that these equivalences are only approximate. Such markers soon become fantastically annoying, and the point can be borne in mind without them.

10. For the sources, see chapter 5 n. 5.

11. The article s. v. *fastidium* is structured as follows in *OLD*: "1 Aversion for food, distaste, lack of appetite, squeamishness. . . . 2 Aversion engendered by satiety, weariness. . . . 3 Repugnance, repulsion, disgust. . . . 4 a Haughtiness, pride. b disdain, scorn, contempt. . . . 5 A critical attitude, fastidiousness, niceness." Cf. the organization of the article in *TLL* 6: 314. 1 ff.: "I generatim: A praevalet notio aspernandi respuendi recusandi detrectandi: 1 i. q. *taedium* . . . 2 i. q. *satietas nimis* . . . 3 fere i. q. *detrectatio* . . . 4 i. q. *despectus* . . . B praevalet notio fastidiose, delicate, *eligendi, iudicandi* . . . C praevalet notio *fastus, arrogantiae, superbiae*" (the second segment of the article then categorizes *speciatim* some common elicitors of *fastidium*, such as odors, food, and so on). Both articles tend to define *fastidium* by identifying it with affective states—e.g., *taedium* (cf. chapter 5 n. 11), *superbia*— that would more precisely be counted among its causes or its antecedent and concomitant conditions.

12. You might test this proposition by matching your own understanding of English emotion-terms against the sorting of terms included in (and omitted from) Johnson-Laird and Oatley 1989, 107–22 ("A Corpus of 590 Emotional Words and Their Analyses . . ."). In the case of *fastidium* it is not difficult to find the lexica sorting the same usages rather differently: for example, while *OLD* tucks Livy 3. 1. 7 ("the abundant opportunity produced *fastidium*, as tends to happen, and so few sought to enrol that Volsci were added as settlers to fill up the number": "fecit statim, ut fit, fastidium copia adeoque pauci nomina dedere ut ad explendum numerum coloni Volsci adderentur") under the rubric "Aversion engendered by satiety," *TLL* places it under *detrectatio*, not *satietas*; and while *OLD* sees in Cic. *Phil.* 12. 20 ("I cannot look with equanimity upon so large a band of wicked and criminal enemies; and this is the result not of my *fastidium* but of my love for the commonwealth": "non possum animo aequo videre tot tam importunos, tam sceleratos hostis; nec id fit fastidio meo, sed caritate rei publicae") an instance of "repugnance, repulsion, disgust," *TLL* takes Cicero to be expressing *despectus*.

13. This fact constitutes not a criticism of the lexica—which are simply doing the job that lexica are supposed to do—but a reminder of their limitations: on this point cf. also chapter 4 at p. 86. *TLL* slightly softens the misleading impression through the implications of the phrase "praevalet notio . . ." in its main subheadings.

14. That emotions necessarily entail noncognitive "feelings"—the ineffable psychophysical effects we try to convey when we speak of the heart "sinking" (with disappointment or certain kinds of fear) or "swelling" (with pride or joy)—is a subject of current dispute: for argument that they do not, esp. in the case of nonconscious emotions, see Nussbaum 2001, 56–64. I set this interesting problem to one side and regularly speak below of "feelings" and "psychophysical effects," primarily because the Romans themselves standardly take it that such painful or pleasurable elements are an essential part of their emotions, as things consciously and transparently experienced: they would say, with Rousseau, "I cannot be deceived about what I have felt, nor about what my feelings have caused me to do" (*Confessions* Book 7, 1: 276 ed. Pléiade). See also n. 16.

15. An "occurrent" emotion is one experienced as actually occurring at the present moment, the state of being we mean to denote by saying "I'm really angry now" or "I'm so happy I could cry." For the distinction between occurrent emotion and emotional disposition, the latter attached to the same basic structure of thought but experienced differently, see chapter 1 n. 8.

16. I take it to be noncontroversial that the cognition in any such drama—e.g., my judgment that the large dog running toward me is intent not on play but on my throat—need not enter consciousness, so quickly can it occur (accelerated, perhaps, by past evaluations that leave me disposed to suspect the worst of large running dogs): it might then seem an "instinct" or "reflex," as much a product of the autonomic nervous system as the quickened pulse that soon follows. I also take it that the character and components of the response can vary widely and in several different dimensions: for example, two individuals at the same time (or the same individual at different times) might enact different fear-responses—whether in psychophysical effect or in behavior—when confronted with the same presentation; and while some emotions are closely associated with certain pragmatic action-tendencies (e.g., the "fight or flight" response of fear), others are more closely associated with expressive responses (e.g., the various gestures and attitudes associated with grief) than with any particular pragmatic response, and still others (e.g., wonder) are not closely associated with any particular pragmatic or expressive response at all.

17. Though none uses the language of "scripts," this is in effect the approach adopted—to quite different ends—by Gordon 1987 (a study in the philosophy of mind), Ortony, Clore, and Collins 1988 (a work of psychology that explicitly sets emotion-terms to one side in favor of attending to "emotion-types": see esp. p. 116), and Wierzbicka 1992, 135–79 (a study in cross-cultural semantics). On the nature of the scripts and the method of their construction, see further the introduction to chapter 2; and cf. Lakoff and Kövecses 1987, de Sousa 1987, 44–45, Shweder and Haidt 2000, 405–6, Russell and Lemay 2000, 496–97, Goldie 2002 (esp. 11–16).

18. The need to grant a complex relation between biology and culture in these matters is well stressed by Cairns 2003b, 14: "if it is proper for us to pay particular attention to the ways in which the construction of emotion varies from culture to culture, it is also necessary for us to accept that we cannot expect that variation to be free and unconstrained, [given] our nature as a physically embodied, social species." Beyond the work cited earlier in n. 8 and 17 and in n. 19, I have found the following to be especially helpful in understanding the "cognitive turn" and the current state of discussion more generally: Solomon 1973, Lyons 1980, Lazarus 1984, Taylor 1985, de Sousa 1987, Lazarus 1991, Ekman and Davidson 1994, Tomkins, 1995, Katz 1999, Elster 1999, Eich and Schooler 2000, Clore and Ortony 2000, Ledoux 2000, Roseman and Smith 2001. On the emotions in ancient psychology and philosophy, where the cognitive approach has its roots, see the important work of Frede 1986, Annas 1989, Brunschwig and Nussbaum 1993, Nussbaum 1994, Sihvola and Engberg-Pedersen 1998, Cooper 1999, Sorabji 2000, Graver 2002, Fortenbaugh 2003 (orig. 1975).

19. "Whole package deal": Shweder and Haidt 2000, 406 (= Shweder 1993, 425). The holistic approach to understanding emotion is well emphasized—if in differing, and occasionally conflicting, terms—by Damasio 1995 (esp. 127–64), Ben Ze'ev 2000 (esp. 49–78), Nussbaum 2001 (esp. Part I).

20. Cf. the use of "family resemblances" as a tool for explaining concepts (e.g., the concept "game") in Wittgenstein 1953 (*Familieähnlichkeiten* introduced specifically in I §67).

21. Cf. at chapter 2 n. 99.

22. Similarly Cairns 1993, 11–12, on parasitic or bleached uses of emotion-talk.

23. On the first point, see Miller 1993, 183–96, demonstrating how *Sir Gawain and the Green Knight* can clearly represent (by turns) what we would label embarrassment, humiliation, and shame, though no emotion-talk is used and though the text's Middle English lacked the lexical resources for distinguishing among them. Regarding the second point, we can note that the noun *indignatio* (for example) overlaps with an important corner of *invidia*, as the adjective *foedus* (for example) does with *fastidium*: though *indignatio* and *foedus* are not considered here, for reasons of space, their behavior is quite consistent with the terms that they shadow.

24. On Plin. *Ep.* 2. 9. 1–3, see chapter 2 at n. 80. The *pudor* that Pliny fears and the *pudor* of a defeated candidate in the Republic would have involved slightly different scripts, but the different scripts are themselves prominent in Roman emotion-talk from one end of our period to the other.

25. For the characterization, Harré and Finlay-Jones 1986, 221–22; on *acedia* in late antiquity, Toohey 1990, and cf. Toohey 2004, 132–57 (treating the state as a mental illness rather than an emotion).

26. Burton's *Anatomy of Melancholy* was published in 1632, "My Melancholy Baby" (lyrics by George Norton, music by Ernie Burnett) in 1912.

27. On this see the studies in the second half of Roller 2001.

28. See chapter 3 at n. 35. By contrast, even the strongly Stoicizing Seneca speaks of the categories of shame in thoroughly conventional ways, though not with-

out a certain occasional wryness (cf. chapter 1 at n. 25, on his *verecundia* at *Ep.* 87. 4–5).

Chapter 1

1. Gellius 1. 24. 4. For the motif of the "address to the wayfarer" in ancient epitaphs see, e.g., Lattimore 1942, 230–34.

2. Livy 2. 15. 5 "Vanquished by *verecundia*, the king said [to the Roman delegates], 'Since this is your firm resolve, I shall not dun you by seeking the same ends, time and again to no purpose, nor shall I deceive the Tarquinii by holding out hope of aid that I cannot provide. Whether their aim be war or peace, let them seek another place of exile, lest there be any obstacle to my peaceful relations with you'" ("rex verecundia victus 'quando id certum atque obstinatum est' inquit, 'neque ego obtundam saepius eadem nequiquam agendo, nec Tarquinios spe auxilii, quod nullum in me est, frustrabor. alium hinc, seu bello opus est seu quiete, exsilio quaerant locum, ne quid meam vobiscum pacem distineat'").

3. Livy 3. 70. 15; for the double-dative construction *aliquid* (*alicui*) *verecundiae esse* / "something is a cause of scruple (to someone)," see also Livy 3. 62. 9, 9. 26. 18, Val. Max. 2. 5. 5, 2. 7. 7, 9. 3(ext). pr., 9. 13. 2, Quint. *Inst.* 1. 3. 16.

4. Pliny *Ep.* 7. 16. 5 "I am on terms of most intimate affection with Calestrius Tiro, who is bound closely to me to me in affairs both public and private. We were in the service together, we were quaestors of the Emperor together. . . . [much detail of their reciprocal relations follows; then] I expect—no, I am confident—that I will easily prevail upon him to take a detour to see you. . . . There is no reason for you to worry that it will be tiresome for a man who would not think it out of the way to go clear around the world for my sake. So just put aside that excessive *verecundia* of yours and have thought for yourself. My bidding will be as pleasing to him as yours is to me" ("Calestrium Tironem familiarissime diligo et privatis mihi et publicis necessitudinibus implicitum. simul militavimus, simul quaestores Caesaris fuimus. . . . spero, immo confido facile me impetraturum, ex itinere deflectat ad te. . . . nihil est quod uerearis ne sit hoc illi molestum, cui orbem terrarum circumire non erit longum mea causa. proinde nimiam istam verecundiam pone, teque quid velis consule. illi tam iucundum quod ego, quam mihi quod tu iubes").

5. The concept of "face" relevant to this chapter is most familiar from the work of Erving Goffman, esp. 1963a and 1967, 5–45; cf. also esp. Oliensis 1998, 17–63, on issues of face management in Horace's *Sermones*. We can allow the concept to remain fairly simple for now, though it will be useful in the next chapter to add nuance by distinguishing "negative" face from "positive" face: see chapter 2 at n. 45.

6. The etymology is exploited or felt at, e.g., *Rhet. Her.* 2. 42 (= Cic. *Inv. rhet.* 1. 83), Cic. *Amic.* 83, Livy 2. 36. 3; for *verecundia* spoken of as an *adfectus*, see, e.g., Val. Max. 5. 7 (ext.). 1, Sen. *Dial.* 9. 2. 10, *Ep.* 11. 7, Quint. *Inst.* 12. 5. 3, [Quint.] *DMai.* 19. 11).

7. The strategic quality of *verecundia* is well brought out in Lossmann 1962, 69–106 (esp. 73–77), a study unhappily weakened by the false distinction it draws between *verecundia* (as "rational") and certain other emotions (as "irrational").

8. The emotions labeled by *pudor, invidia,* and *fastidium* all commonly admit dispositional senses, too; but, though in principle it is plainly possible to be "dispositionally *paenitens*"—to be inclined habitually to regret—it is a condition that, perhaps interestingly, the pre-Christian Romans did not speak of. On dispositional vs. occurrent forms of emotion—a distinction known in antiquity, too—see Cairns's helpful analysis (1993, 10–11, 397–98); the further distinction drawn there, between "first-order" and "second-order" dispositions (e.g., the difference between "being afraid of the dark"—when I am not actually in the dark and occurrently feeling fear— and "being timid"), though apt in theoretical terms, plays no role in my discussion, where references to "dispositional *verecundia*" (and the like) can typically be taken to refer to a second-order disposition.

9. Though not all ethical traits (e.g., being a just person) are dispositional forms of emotion, it seems true that all dispositional forms of emotion are ethical traits (certainly, as I write, I cannot think of an exception): this is so not just because they identify us as this or that sort of person but because through them some value is attached to that sort. Our very language of "positive" and "negative" emotions, though meant primarily to denote whether or not the experience of them is welcome, has a high correlation, connotatively, with the value we attach to the people who experience them dispositionally: we not only think dispositionally joyful people more pleasant company than the dispositionally irascible or fearful, we probably also think them better people, in the sense that they represent the sort of person we would choose to be, living the sort of life we would choose to live. (The fact that this can be said, in turn, suggests a handy way of distinguishing ethics from morals.) And, because, as has often been observed, "negative" emotions far outnumber the "positive," emotional dispositions have much more to do with vice than with virtue.

10. In return, we can expect to be paid the basic courtesy of "civil inatten-tion," an interaction in which "one gives to another enough visual notice to demon-strate that one appreciates that the other is present . . . , while . . . withdrawing one's attention from him so as to express that he does not constitute a target of special curiosity or design" (Goffman 1963a, 84).

11. Cicero *Off.* 1. 99 "Toward other people, then, we must show a certain re-spect, both for the best sort of people and for the rest. For to be careless of what each person thinks of oneself is a mark not just of an arrogant person but of one who is entirely wanton. In dealing considerately with people, moreover, there is a differ-ence between justice and *verecundia*: it is the role of justice not to violate people, of *verecundia* not to offend them; and in this latter regard the real meaning of 'befitting conduct' is particularly evident" ("adhibenda est igitur quaedam reverentia adver-sus homines et optimi cuiusque et reliquorum. nam neglegere quid de se quisque sentiat, non solum arrogantis est sed etiam omnino dissoluti. est autem quod differat in hominum ratione habenda inter iustitiam et verecundiam. iustitiae partes sunt non violare homines, verecundiae non offendere, in quo maxime vis perspicitur decori"). One might ask how Cicero's concern with avoiding offense, here and (as we will repeatedly see) elsewhere, coexists with his own boastfulness, which some contemporaries, and many since, have found offensive: for Cicero's own response, see chapter 2 at n. 93.

12. E.g., Plaut. *Trin.* 474–78 (a gluttonous character speaks) "By God, though he want it worth his life / I'll eat it up and gobble it down, both cheeks bulging, / and I'll make a point of snatching just what he fancies / and yield him not an inch. . . . / To be *verecundus* at the dinner table is unbecoming (*verecundari neminem apud mensam decet*)": the punchline, invoking the criterion of "decorum" to dismiss *verecundia*, nicely sets the ethical point on its head.

13. Cic. *De or.* 3. 165; cf. Cic. *Orat.* 81, *Opt. gen.* 4, *Fam.* 16. 17. 1; sim. Sen. *Ep.* 114. 1, Gell. *NA* 7. 15. 5, 17. 13. 9.

14. Cic. *Fam.* 5. 12. 8 (to Lucceius) "But if you do not grant me this [request, viz., that Lucceius write a monograph on Cicero's achievements], . . . I shall perhaps be forced to do what some people often criticize—write about myself. . . . But as I'm sure you're aware, there are drawback to doing this: people who write about themselves are bound to proceed with greater *verecundia* where praise is due and to pass by what deserves criticism ("et verecundius ipsi de sese scribant necesse est si quid est laudandum et praetereant si quid reprehendendum est")"; cf. Livy 37. 52. 6, Val. Max. 8. 12. 1, Plin. *Pan.* 91. 3, Tac. *Agr.* 8.3.

15. Porph. ad Hor. *Epod.* 1 pr. "It seems ill suited to Horace's *verecundia* that he calls himself Maecenas's 'friend' when he ought to say 'client'" ("non videtur verecundiae Horati convenire, ut amicum se Maecenatis dicat, cum clientem debeat dicere").

16. Cic. *Luc.* 127 "You lot talk about the size of the sun . . . as though you'd measured it with a yardstick, whereas I . . . say I do not rely on your measurement: can there be a doubt which of us is—to say the least—more *verecundus?*" ("solis autem magnitudinem . . . vos ergo . . . quasi decempeda permensi refertis; ego me mensurae vestrae nego credere: dubium est uter nostrum sit, leviter ut dicam, verecundior?"), cf. *Tusc.* 4. 47.

17. Invading opponents' space: Quint. *Inst.* 11. 3. 133. "Bending over backwards": Quint. *Inst.* 4. 1. 20, cf. Val. Max. 6. 5. pr., Vell. Pat. 2. 16. 2.

18. E.g., Plin. *Ep.* 5. 17. 3 (on a literary recital by Calpurnius Piso) "The substance of his recitation was learned and brilliant. . . . He made all this agreeable through his very pleasant way of speaking, while his speech was made agreeable by his *verecundia*: he blushed a great deal and wore a very anxious expression, traits that are an adornment to one giving a recitation. Indeed, in ways I can't quite explain, fear is more becoming in literary pursuits than confidence" ("recitabat . . . eruditam sane luculentamque materiam. . . . commendabat haec voce suavissima, vocem verecundia: multum sanguinis, multum sollicitudinis in ore, magna ornamenta recitantis. etenim nescio quo pacto magis in studiis homines timor quam fiducia decet"); cf. Hor. *Epod.* 17. 21, Livy 35. 16. 7, Ov. *Her.* 4. 72, *Met.* 1. 484, Petron. *Sat.* 132. Sen. *Ep.* 11, 87. 4, 12, Plin. *HN* 11. 225, 34, 140, Quint. *Inst.* 4. 2. 88, 11. 3. 78, *DMin.* 313. 1, Suet. *Dom.* 18. 2.

19. Cic. *Off.* 2. 15, cf. *Fin.* 4. 18, *Part. orat.* 79, *Rep.* 5. 6, *Amic.* 83.

20. Cic. *Tull.* 5 "What's to be done, then? Though the case calls for it, still . . . I do not customarily descend to abuse. Now, since my hand is forced, I shall speak, but still, if I chance to say anything [abusive], I shall do so with restraint and *verecundia*, and only with this end in view: that whereas Fabius could not regard me

as his enemy before, he now might recognize that I am a loyal and reliable friend to M. Tullius" ("quid ergo est? tametsi postulat causa, tamen . . . ad male dicendum non soleo descendere. nunc cum coactus dicam, si quid forte dicam, tamen id ipsum verecunde modiceque faciam, tantum ut, quoniam sibi me non esse inimicum potuit priore actione Fabius iudicare, nunc M. Tullio fidelem certumque amicum esse cognoscat"). How much of this prefatory ritual represents sentiment actually felt is unknowable and, fortunately, irrelevant to the argument, for which the only important point is that the ritual was demanded by, and credible in, its context; similar scruple appears, e.g., at *Planc.* 6, while his friend Torquatus's failure to exercise similar restraint when prosecuting P. Sulla gives Cicero a starting point for his defense (*Sull.* 2 ff., with Cicero's own show of restraint at ibid. 46).

21. Quint. *Inst.* 4. 2. 88; cf. also Quint. *DMin.* 313. 1, Livy 35. 16. 7.

22. On the various forms of "seeing" at work in the emotions of self-assessment, cf. the section "Regarding Others" in chapter 2.

23. For Quintilian see, e.g., nn. 3, 6, 17, 18, 21, 39; for Servius's alertness in detecting *verecundia* at work, esp. in settings of face-to-face speech and petition, see his comments at *Aen.* 1. 78, 237, 561, 737, 6. 66, 7. 229, 231, 8.76, 116, 515, 10. 34, 42, 11. 14, 347, 436.

24. Quint. *Inst.* 8. 3. 64–65.

25. Sen. *Ep.* 87. 4–5.

26. Miller 1993, 155. Tacit or express collaboration in face-maintenance is a central theme in the work of Goffman (see n. 5 and also Goffman 1959), extended in the work of, e.g., Brown and Levinson 1987.

27. The subject should repay examination, since *verecundia* (like *pudor*) is excluded from Moore's useful analysis of virtue-terms in Livy, on the ground that it "usually refer[s] to a temporary emotional state" (1989, 2 n. 2).

28. Livy 30. 31. 7–9: "As for myself, I both am mindful of human frailty and reckon well the power of fortune [sc. which can turn today's loser into tomorrow's winner] . . . ; however, just as I would acknowledge behaving arrogantly and violently if I spurned your . . . coming to sue for peace before I crossed over to Africa, so now, when I've drawn you, all resisting . . . , to Africa and we have nearly joined battle, I feel myself bound by no *verecundia* before you" ("quod ad me attinet, et humanae infirmitatis memini et vim fortunae reputo . . . ; ceterum quemadmodum superbe et violenter me faterer facere *si* priusquam in Africam traiecissem te . . . ipsum venientem ad pacem petendam aspernarer, sic nunc cum prope manu conserta restitantem . . . in Africam attraxerim nulla sum tibi verecundia obstrictus").

29. Livy 34. 2. 8: " . . . I would have said: 'What is this custom of dashing forth in public and laying siege to the streets, addessing yourselves to men who are not yours by blood or marriage? Could you not, each of you, have made that request of your own husbands at home? Or are you more winning in public than in private, and with other women's husbands more than with your own? . . . '" (" . . . dixissem: 'qui hic mos est in publicum procurrendi et obsidendi vias et viros alienos appellandi? istud ipsum suos quaeque domi rogare non potuistis? an blandiores in publico quam in privato et alienis quam uestris estis? . . . '").

30. For the *verecundia* of women (or its absence) in respect of public assemblies, see also Val. Max. 3. 8. 6, 8. 3. pr. Like Livy (on whom he amply draws) Valerius has a lively sense of *verecundia* in action: beyond the examples noted or discussed elsewhere in this chapter see, e.g., 2. 1. 9, 2. 3. 1, 4. 1. 4, 4. 5. 4, 5. 3. 26, 5. 4. 1, 5. 8. 3.

31. Cic. *Off.* 1. 127–29, concluding "Let us . . . follow nature and avoid everything that withdraws itself from the approval of eyes and ears. . . . Indeed, actors as a matter of custom adhere so strongly to old-school *verecundia* that none of them goes out on stage without undergarments; for they are worried lest they be seen in an offensive way should chance bring it about that certain parts of the body be exposed. According to our own custom, too, sons past puberty do not bathe with their parents, nor sons-in-law with their fathers-in-law. Let us maintain this sort of *verecundia*, then, especially since we have nature itself as our teacher and guide" ("nos . . . naturam sequamur et ab omni, quod abhorret ab oculorum auriumque approbatione, fugiamus. . . . scaenicorum quidem mos tantam habet vetere disciplina verecundiam, ut in scaenam sine subligaculo prodeat nemo; verentur enim, ne, si quo casu evenerit, ut corporis partes quaedam aperiantur, aspiciantur non decore. nostro quidem more cum parentibus puberes filii, cum soceris generi non lavantur. retinenda igitur est huius generis verecundia, praesertim natura ipsa magistra et duce").

32. Compare the Ovidian *magister*'s use of related sentiments in the protocols of "aversive conditioning" recommended at Ov. *Rem.* 411 ff.

33. Val. Max. 2. 1. 7 "Doesn't this sort of *verecundia* betweeen spouses [see at n. 41] appear consistent with that found in all other intimate relationships? To give just a very small token of its very great force, for some time it used to be the case that neither a father would bathe with a son past puberty nor a father-in-law with a son-in-law. Plainly, then, as much scruple properly was shown before kith and kin as before the immortal gods: for no more in relations bound by those sacred ties than in some sanctified place was it believed right to expose one's nakedness" ("huius modi inter coniuges verecundia: quid, inter ceteras necessitudines nonne apparet consentanea? nam ut minimo indicio maximam vim eius significem, aliquandiu nec pater cum filio pubere nec socer cum genero lavabatur. manifestum igitur est tantum religionis sanguini et adfinitati quantum ipsis dis inmortalibus tributum, quia inter ista tam sancta vincula non magis quam in aliquo sacrato loco nudare se fas esse credebatur").

34. The hortatory mode of Cicero's comments (*retinenda igitur est . . .*) and the past tenses in Valerius's (*aliquandiu . . . lavabatur . . . credebatur . . .*) suggest that both writers were addressing a propriety that they judged was slipping away, if not already gone. On nudity in bathing, see Yegül 1992, 34, Fagan 1999, 24–29: so far as I know, the latter's observation (214 n. 80) that "there have been, as yet, no serious studies of Roman attitudes toward pubic nudity" remains true.

35. *Dig.* 1. 12. 1. 8. As we shall see, only one text refers to slaves experiencing the related emotion of *pudor* (chapter 2 at n. 3), and that with reference to other slaves; they might in principle have been expected to feel *verecundia*, also, toward one another.

36. Soldierly *verecundia* figures at Livy 3. 62. 9 (where *pudor* immediately precedes), 28. 15. 9, 45. 37. 14, and Vell. Pat. 2. 55. 4. At Livy 7. 11. 6, soldiers experience *verecundia* in a context that is virtually domestic, when the city and the persons to whom they are bound by familial devotion (*pietas*) are right before their eyes ("The battle was waged not far from the Colline gate . . . within sight of their parents and wives and children: the considerations that greatly stir the spirit even when soldiers are away from home were then visibly present and fired them with *verecundia* and pity at the same time": "pugnatum haud procul porta Collina est . . . in conspectu parentum coniugumque ac liberorum; quae magna etiam absentibus hortamenta animi tum subiecta oculis simul verecundiâ misericordiâque militem accendebant"). Pliny *Ep.* 8. 14. 7 speaks of soldiers' lack of *verecundia*, and commanders' lack of "authority" (*auctoritas*), in a context that applies the language of civil relations to circumstances in which military discipline (*imperium*, *obsequium*) has broken down ("cum ducibus auctoritas nulla, nulla militibus verecundia, nusquam imperium nusquam obsequium, omnia soluta turbata atque etiam in contrarium versa . . . "): see following in text.

37. For Trajan's display of *verecundia* in various ways see *Pan.* 24. 2, 55. 4, 58. 2, 59. 2, 60. 4, 78. 4; since Pliny has Domitian particularly in mind as a contrasting character, it is worth comparing Mart. 8 pr. 8, on the *verecundia* of Domitian. Fronto's correspondence with princes makes clear that when an imperial personage invokes *verecundia* to extenuate an apparent discourtesy, he means *verecundia officii*, a lively awareness of and respect for the duties that are his burden: see *Ep. ad Verum* 2. 2. 1 with *Fer. Alsien.* 4. 2, *Ep. ad M. Caes.* 1. 2. 1. By contrast, it is symptomatic that Caligula valued his *inverecundia* above all, the feeling that there was no need for him to step back from asserting himself and his interests to the utmost (Suet. *Cal.* 29. 1).

38. See, e.g., Plaut. *Asin.* 833, Sen. *Controv.* 7. 7. 2, 3–4, 6, Quint. *DMin.* 330. 6, 9, 356. 1, [Quint.] *DMai.* 9. 2, Frontin. *Str.* 4. 1. 13, Gell. *NA* 2. 7. 13. A son's *verecundia* before his mother: Sen. *Controv.* 7. 4. 3; a daughter's before her father, *Dig.* 24. 3. 22. 6.

39. The father's attitude is as it should be, cf. Quint. *Inst.* 11. 1. 83 "That's the fervent prayer of all parents, that they have children more honorable than themselves" ("quod omnium sit votum parentum ut honestiores quam sint ipsi liberos habeant").

40. Livy 34. 2. 8 (see at n. 29), with 34. 1. 4–5 "No personal authority, no *verecundia*, no husband's command could keep the matrons at home, they laid siege to all the streets and entries to the forum, entreating the men as they made their way down" ("matronae nulla nec auctoritate nec verecundia nec imperio virorum contineri limine poterant, omnes vias urbis aditusque in forum obsidebant, viros descendentes ad forum orantes. . . ."); and cf. Val. Max. 2. 1. 5, 3. 8. 6, 8. 3. pr., *Dig.* 3. 1. 1. 5, 26. 10. 1. 7. This is the background against which the eulogy of the exceptional woman known as "Turia" must be read: see Hemelrijk 2004.

41. Val. Max. 2. 1. 6–7 (with the sequel quoted at n. 33). The goddess Viriplaca and her shrine are known only from this passage; on its place in the ideology of Roman marriage, see Treggiari 1991, 430.

42. For *verecundia* intersecting with female sexuality and modesty see, e.g., Enn. *Trag.* 181, Ov. *Am.* 1. 5. 7–8, *Met.* 1. 483–84, *Ib.* 477–80, Sen. *Controv.* 2. 7. 3, Plin. *HN* 35. 78, Quint. *DMin.* 259. 5, 270.27–28, 306. 4, 330. 5, 376. 5, Porph. ad Hor. *Carm.* 1. 9. 21–22. On *pudicitia* and concern for licit sexuality see Rousselle 1988, 78–92, Treggiari 1991, 105–7, 218–19 (quoting the encomium of *pudicitia* from Seneca's fragmentarily preserved tract "On marriage"), 236, Mueller 1998, Langlands 2000 (chap. 2).

43. *verecundia virginalis*: Cic. *Quinct.* 39 (applied mockingly to a man), Serv. ad *Ecl.* 10. 18, cf. id. ad *Aen.* 1 pr.

44. *verecundia* felt before: *aetas*, Livy 1. 3. 11, cf. 1. 6. 4, Val. Max. 4. 5 (ext). 2, Petron. *Sat.* 93. 4; the *maiestas* of magistrates, Livy 2. 36. 3, 9. 10. 7, 9. 26. 18, 9. 34. 23, 10. 24. 14, 24. 44. 10; literary authorities, Sen. *Dial.* 11. 2. 6; *maximi viri*, Val. Max. 9. 3 (ext). pr. (preparatory to reprobating their faults); the rich, Apul *Met.* 9. 35; the senate, Val. Max. 4. 5. 1 (an instance of literally knowing your place, in connection with seats in the theater); the gods, Val. Max. 4. 1. 10, Sen. *QNat.* 7. 30. 1.

45. For themes that variously pit the *dives* against the *pauper* see Sen. *Controv.* 2. 1, 5. 5, 8. 6, 10. 1, Quint. *DMin.* 259, 269, 271, 279, 301, 304, 305, 325, 332, 333, 337, 343, 345, 364, 370, 379.

46. See n. 37.

47. Cic. *Orat.* 238; the thought is echoed by Quintilian in the dedication of *Inst.*, 1. pr. 3 "Though . . . it was not so much confidence that I could provide the thing requested that prevailed upon me as *verecundia* at the thought of refusing . . ." ("quamvis . . . non tam me vinceret praestandi quod exigebatur fiducia quam negandi verecundia. . . .").

48. Cic. *Att.* 1. 17. 6–7.

49. For the issues of face involved in acknowledging a favor (if you are the recipient) or bringing it to the recipient's attention (if you are the benefactor) see, e.g., Sen. *Ben.* 2. 7. 3, 2. 10. 4, 5. 20. 7, 5. 21. 3, 7. 28. 3.

Chapter 2

1. On the role of shame and similar emotions in "alternative sanctions" and related issues of law and penology, see Kahan 1996, Kahan and Nussbaum 1996, Massaro 1999, Nussbaum 2004, and the exchange of views at Nussbaum 1999 and Kahan 1999. The literature on the modern "pathology" of shame is vast, and growing rapidly: by one survey, the number of articles on shame in journals of psychology increased nearly tenfold between 1975–79 and 1995–99: Haidt 2003, 853 table 45. 1. For different angles of attack, see, e.g., Piers and Singer 1953, Goffman 1963b, Morrison 1989, Lewis 1992, Gilbert and Andrews 1998 (esp. Part III), Tangney and Dearing 2002. My own understanding of shame and cognate emotions, ancient and modern, has been helped—more than the notes on specific points reflect—by the following especially: Herzfeld 1980, Epstein 1984, Taylor 1985, Gilmore 1987, Harré 1990, Cairns 1993, Williams 1993, Miller 1993, Stewart 1994, Geuss 2001.

2. On "shame and the social bond" see the helpful survey in Scheff 2000; Epstein 1984 and Barton 2001, 207–10, well observe the importance of shame as an emotion of "relatedness" and "presentness."

3. That *dignitas* and *existimatio* are prerequisites explains why slaves, who in the ideology of slavery have neither, do not experience *pudor* in our texts: I believe that Curt. 10. 2. 20 is the sole example of *pudor* being ascribed to slaves, and even then the ascription is made solely in respect of their dealings with other slaves.

4. The texts surveyed (just under 1800) comprise every occurrence of the noun *pudor*, the impersonal verb *pudet* (with the rare personal form *pudeo* and similarly rare compounds *subpud-*, *depud-*), and the derivative (quasi-participial) forms *pudens* ("characterized by a sensitivity to *pudor*," with its negation, *impudens/impudentia*) and *pudendus* ("that which ought to be the cause of *pudor*," with its "active" counterpart *pudibundus*, "in the throes of *pudor*"). Not included are the cognate but distinct concepts denoted by the terms *pudicus/pudicitia*, concerned exclusively with sexual behavior and dispositions ("chaste"/"chastity").

5. On the distinction between dispositional and occurrent forms of a given emotion (corresponding, for example, to the difference between being "irascible" and "angry" in common English usage), see chapter 1 n. 8.

6. Save in the case of *pudens* (with the negative *impudens/-tia*), which has only a dispositional sense, the Romans did not lexically distinguish dispositional from occurrent forms of the emotion with great rigor: the noun *pudor* and the verb *pudet* can each denote either state, and I will typically follow their practice by simply using *pudor* as the convenient label of the emotion. Note, however, as an empirical matter that the noun somewhat more often denotes the dispositional than the occurrent form, while the verb markedly more often denotes the occurrent than the dispositional form. Note also the use of *pudor* in a sense approaching "id quod me pudet" or "id quod tibi pudendum est" (something that is or ought to be a cause of occurrent *pudor*, that is, a *dedecus*/"disgrace"), which seems first to appear in Ovid: e.g., *Her.* 1. 95–96 "Irus egens pecorisque Melanthius actor edendi / ultimus accedunt in tua damna pudor," *Met.* 8. 157 "destinat hunc Minos thalamo removere pudorem [= the Minotaur]."

7. Just under 7 percent of "*pud-* contexts" are either too fragmentary to provide sufficient context or are too lacking in detail: the latter include (e.g.) mere catalogs of virtues or the many uses of *pudens* and *impudens* as highly general terms of praise or abuse (esp. in Plautus and Cicero). But though the "*pud-* talk" in such cases is highly general, other members of a catalog or other elements of the context often clearly hint which version of *pudor* is meant (typically, script 4): cf., e.g., Cic. *Rep.* 1. 2, *Fam.* 5. 16. 4, Sall. *Cat.* 16. 2, Hor. *Carm. Saec.* 57–58, Ov. *Met.* 1. 128–29, Sen. *Ag.* 112–13, *Dial.* 7. 26. 6.

8. Flor. 1. 22, sim. Sen. *Ep.* 108. 17, Quint. *Inst.* 2. 5. 3, [Quint.] *DMai.* 16. 2.

9. Plaut. *Epid.* 166–68. Still, as the phrases "when it's of no consequence" (*nil refert*) and "when it's useful" (*quom usus est*) show, the word play is based on the normative expectation that *pudor*, properly experienced, does some useful work.

10. Lucan 7. 617 ff. "It causes *pudor*, when the whole world is perishing, to have shed tears / over countless deaths and, in attending to the fates of individuals,

/ to ask whose innards the deadly wound / passed clean through, who trod on his vitals that had spilled on the ground, / who . . ." (and so on, and on: "inpendisse pudet lacrimas in funere mundi / mortibus innumeris ac singula fata sequentem / quaerere letiferum per cuius viscera volnus / exierit, quis fusa solo vitalia calcet, / ore quis adverso . . ."). Cf. also Petron. *Sat.* 119. 1. 45–46 (a dead-on parody of Lucan) and declamatory or quasi-declamatory contexts where sarcasm figures (Quint. *DMin.* 338. 14, sim. Stat. *Theb.* 8. 670, [Quint.] *DMai.* 1. 15) or where the speaker strains for paradox (see esp. Sen. *Dial.* 12. 16. 3, with [Quint.] *DMai.* 4. 5) or some other *outré* thought (*DMai.* 8. 6, 22). A few other turns of phrase that throw no useful light on ethics include Plin. *HN* 2. 247 ("a wicked piece of effrontery, but wrapped in so acute an argument that it would cause *pudor* not to believe it": ". . . inprobum ausum, verum ita subtili argumentatione conprehensum ut pudeat non credere," where the emotional force is mostly bleached away, as in Engl. "it would be a shame not to do X") and some—though not all—uses of the parenthetical expression "si (quis) pudor est" (~ "for heaven's sake!": e.g., [Quint.] *DMai.* 11. 11).

11. The Romans not only often associate dispositional *pudor* with a kind of fear but simply define it as such, see, e.g., Cic. *Rosc. Am.* 9, and n. 13. For an especially clear distinction between *inlicita* (things forbidden by external authority) and *pudenda*, see Plin. *Ep.* 5. 13. 9; for the contrast between *pudor* and the coercive *metus* created by legal sanction, force, and the like, see Apul. *Met.* 6. 4, with the passages collected at Kaster 1997, 4 n. 7.

12. These elements are too common to require documentation; for a vivid description of embodied *pudor*, see, e.g., Livy 9. 6. 9, and cf. Cic. *Dom.* 133 (addressed to his enemy P. Clodius): "To be sure, for all that you are a man of singular recklessness (*audacia*) and shamelessness (*impudentia*), your glance, your mien, your speech would nonetheless have been downcast, when [such distinguished men] had deterred you with their massively weighty words" ("Es tu quidem cum audacia tum impudentia singulari, sed tibi tamen oculi, vultus, verba cecidissent, cum te . . . verbis gravissimis proterruissent").

13. So the Latin translation by Gellius of a definition of Gk. *aischunê* offered by unnamed *philosophi*: 19. 6. 3 "For one can still ask why *pudor* causes blood to spread [sc. in a blush] whereas fear causes it to contract [sc. in pallor], when *pudor* is a kind of fear and is defined thus: 'fear of just criticism.' For that's the way philosophers define it: '*aischunê* is fear of just criticism'" ("adhuc enim quaeri potest, quam ob causam pudor sanguinem diffundat, timor contrahat, cum sit pudor species timoris atque ita definiatur: 'timor iustae reprehensionis.' Ita enim philosophi definiunt: *aischunê estin phobos dikaiou psogou*"). For the definition, see also at n. 121. The Stoic definition of *aidôs* attributed to Andronicus of Rhodes is similar (*Peri pathôn* 1. 6. 4 *aidôs . . . estin eulabeia orthou psogou*) but because the Stoics regarded *aidôs* as a "good passion" (*eupatheia*) characteristic of the sage's rational mind, "caution" (*eulabeia*) replaces the bad passion of "fear" (*phobos*): see Kamtekar 1998, 137–38.

14. In this respect, the Stoic definition of *aischunê* as a more generalized "fear of ill repute" (*SVF* 3.407–9 *phobos adoxias*; sim. Arist. *Eth. Nic.* 4. 9. [1128b11–12], on *aidôs*) corresponds better (though still not perfectly) to the Roman experience of

pudor than the definition quoted by Gellius. Unhappily, the definition of *pudor* that must have stood at Cic. *Tusc.* 4. 19 has fallen out of the text: see Graver 2002, 146.

15. In what follows I would have preferred to avoid using the ungainly labels "script 1," "script 2," and so on, but in many places the attempt would have inevitably resulted in some form of words even clumsier than the labels.

16. Quinctius in due course makes plain that he in fact holds the assembled citizens responsible (3. 67. 4 "For whom, in fact, did these most cowardly enemies show their contempt? For us, the consuls, or for you, the civilians? . . .": "quem tandem ignavissimi hostium contempsere? nos consules an vos Quirites? . . ."). His opening words, by which he takes the shame on himself, can thus be seen as a gambit in a speech that aims to shame *them* into action, but for the tactic to work—as it does, brilliantly (by speech's end Quinctius is universally regarded as Rome's singular champion, *unus maiestatis Romanae vindex*: 3. 69. 3)—it must first be found credible.

17. Country or place of birth: Mart. 4. 55. 8–10 and Apul. *Apol.* 24, in both of which *pudor* is in fact denied (perhaps then the sort of "*pud*-talk" remarked at n. 6). Aging or disease: Tac. *Ann.* 4. 57, Stat. *Theb.* 12. 237–38, Seren. Sammon. *Lib. Med.* 4. 43–45, [Quint.] *DMai.* 4. 11. Drooping breasts: Prop. 2. 15. 21–22 (focalized, of course, through the male speaker). Skin color: Plin. *HN* 6. 190 (on Ethiopian tribes) "Beyond [the Macrobii] are the Dochi, then the Gymnetes, who are always naked, then the Anderae, the Mattitae, the Mesaches; †hipdores† of black color smear their entire bodies with red dye" ("ultra eos Dochi, dein Gymnetes, semper nudi, mox Anderae, Mattitae, Mesaches; †hipdores† atri coloris tota corpora rubrica inlinunt") where for the corrupt *hipdores* Detlefsen conjectured a tribal name, *Hypsodores* (otherwise unattested), and Mayhoff (followed by Rackham) emended to *hi pudore* ("these, out of *pudor* at (their) black color . . ."). Snowden 1970, 320 n. 66, doubts the latter reading; if it is correct, Pliny is presumably projecting his own sensibilities onto the Africans. Such a move would be consistent with another habit in which Pliny indulges more often than any other Roman writer, that of projecting his own understanding of *pudor* onto animals: see *HN* 8. 12 (elephants), 8.160 (horses), 10. 44 (bird); the only animal to which other writers repeatedly ascribe the capacity for *pudor* is the lion (Mart. 1. 104. 19, Stat. *Silv.* 2. 5. 14–19, *Achil.* 1. 858–63). On emotional response to one's own physical appearance, see also Cic. *Cael.* 6, involving a witticism discussed at the start of chapter 3.

18. Cf. chapter 1 n. 5; the concept of "face" is further refined in the discussion of script 4, see at n. 45, where it is useful to distinguish "positive" and "negative" face. A Roman who was thought to have behaved shamefully could be asked, in tones of incredulity, "with what face" he came into the sight of others (Cic. *Verr.* 2. 4. 26 "in populi Romani quidem conspectum quo ore vos commisistis?," sim. *Vat.* 5, *Phil.* 2. 104, 7.21, Livy 26. 32. 4, 40. 27. 10); the answer could be that he had a "hard" or "iron face" (*os durum* or *ferreum*), one incapable of blushing (e.g., Ter. *Eun.* 806, Lucil. frag. 417 M., L. Crassus *ORF*² frag. 37, Catull. 42. 17, Cic. *Pis.* 63, Ov. *Am.* 1. 12. 24, *Ars am.* 3. 587, *Met.* 5. 451, 10. 241, *Pont.* 1. 1. 80, Sen. *Ben.* 7. 28. 3, *Dial.* 2. 17. 3, Quint. *Inst.* 6. 4. 11, Mart. 11. 27. 7, Suet. *Nero* 2. 2, cf. Cic. *Pis.* 53).

19. Sexually appraising glances: Suet. *Cal.* 36. 2, cf. also [Quint.] *DMai.* 18. 5 (a decent *matrona*'s concern for her face as such). For *contumelia* (or the like) ruffling *pudor*: e.g., Cic. *Verr.* 2. 3. 95, Ov. *Met.* 1. 755–61, Sen. *Dial.* 2. 15. 1 (sim. 2. 17. 3); cf. Cicero's advice to a young opponent in court, "not to bring charges against another at which you would blush were they falsely turned back upon you" (*Cael.* 7 "ea in alterum ne dicas quae, cum tibi falso responsa sint, erubescas"), and his comments on the limits to which his own forbearance can be pressed by personal attack before he feels he must "take account of [his] own *dignitas*" and retaliate (*Sull.* 46–47: Cicero makes plain that he grants more leeway than usual in this case because the attacker is both young and someone he counts as a friend). For the relation between *pudor* and *ira* see also n. 89.

20. E.g., Cic. *Har. resp.* 46, *Fam.* 5. 3. 1 (Metellus Nepos), Suet. *Tib.* 66. 1. This is of course compatible both with the Stoic view (e.g., Sen. *Ben.* 6.37.2) and with the more generally "philosophical" position sketched by Cicero for a man in exile: "wise men are upset by their own wrongdoing, not the wrongs done them by others" (*Fam.* 5. 17. 5 "homines sapientis . . . delicto suo, non aliorum iniuria, commoveri").

21. On "reflexive" honor, according to which "B's honor is ipso facto diminished or destroyed [by an insult from A] unless B responds with an appropriate counterattack," see Stewart 1994, 64, with, e.g., Miller 1993, 15–52. Neglect of the evidence for this *pudor*-script is the most important shortcoming of Kaster 1997 (see esp. at p. 6 and n. 11).

22. For the definition of "rape" in classical Roman law as *per vim stuprum inferre* / *per vim stuprare*, see *Dig.* 48. 5. 30. 9 and 48. 6. 3. 4, cf. 48. 6. 5. 2; on *stuprum* (sexual penetration of a disapproved sort, or committed in illicit circumstances), see Fantham 1991.

23. For the *rapta* as *vitiata*, see, e.g., Sen. *Controv.* 1. 5. 4, 7. 6. 5, 10, 7. 8. 4, 6, 8. 6, 9. 1. 11, Quint. *DMin.* 259, 262. 7, 270. 16, 18, 309; cf. the language of the law, in which *stuprum* = Gk. *phthora* (*Dig.* 48. 5. 6. 1). For the strain on dispositional *pudor* in this circumstance, see further at n. 84. On Ovid's rapes, see also Curran 1978 (for the shame of Ovidian *raptae*, pp. 223–24), Richlin 1992b, Johnson 1996–97 (who treats Callisto in particular, see following).

24. *Met.* 2. 447–52. Callisto again blushes and experiences *pudor* over her rape at *Fast.* 2. 153–92 (168 *erubuit*, 170 *pudet*).

25. Cf. *Met.* 2. 434–37 "Against him indeed, as much as a woman could / . . . against him indeed she struggles, but whom could a girl overcome, / or who could overcome Jupiter?" ("illa quidem contra, quantum modo femina posset / . . . illa quidem pugnat, sed quem superare puella, / quisve Iovem poterat?").

26. Cf. *Met.* 6.531–48 and 601–9, where Philomela, having been raped by her sister Procne's husband, twice refers to herself as her sister's illicit "rival" (*paelex*) in the throes of her shame.

27. *Rep.* 2. 46. On the rape of Lucretia, a far richer theme than I can pursue here, see especially Geldner 1977, Donaldson 1982, Joshel 1992, Moses 1993. That the sentiments surveyed here were not limited to rapes involving women is made

plain by (for example) Calp. *Decl.* 45, which in effect recasts the story of Verginia (cf. Livy 3.47. 1–48.6) in male dress: after killing his son, a *bellus adulescens*, rather than surrender him to the lust of a tyrant, a father declares "the person is dead but *pudor* lives on" (*perit homo sed pudor vivit*)—the boy would have been worse off stuprated than dead, because his sense of *pudor* (which we could also translate as "his honor") would have been destroyed.

28. Cf. Johnson 1996–97, 21, on "the core" of the rape-myths' "patriarchal version," stressing the enigma of responsibility in these tales: "Somehow, in some mysterious way, [the *rapta*] must have done something bad or what happened to her wouldn't have happened to her." A way into contemporary discussions of shame and rape is provided by Raine 1998.

29. Cf. Ov. *Tr.* 3. 1. 81–82, a nice conceit depicting the *pudor* of his "rejected" books.

30. On shaming rituals see more fully chapter 4 at p. 96.

31. *Apol.* 3. Cf. also esp. *Apol.* 6, and for (dispositional) *pudor* as a protective "garment," see Plaut. *Poen.* 304, SHA *Heliog.* 11. 4, and cf. Cairns 1996, Ferrari 2002, 72–86.

32. "Burden" (*pudorem onerare*): Livy 31. 15. 2, *Dig.* 3. 2. 20. pr. (cf. *pudorem urgere* at Stat. *Achil.* 2. 151, *aliquid pudori grave facere* at Curt. 8. 8. 9). "Bruise" (*pudorem suggilare*): *Dig.* 2. 4. 10. 12. "Prick" (*pudorem (per)stringere*): Quint. *DMin.* 342. 14, *Dig.* 47. 10. 1. 5. "Wound" (*pudorem laedere*): Ov. *Her.* 7. 97, *Met.* 7. 751, Sen. *Phaed.* 1189, *Dig.* 47. 10. 15. 27, in addition to Ov. *Met.* 2. 450 already cited. "Unburden" (*pudorem exonerare*): Serv. ad *Aen.* 11. 164. "Cleanse" (*pudorem purgare*): *Dig.* 3. 3. 25. pr. In a related metaphor, if you, as a decent person, respect my face, you are said to "spare my (sense of) *pudor*" (*pudori parcere*)—that is, refrain from doing it an *iniuria*: Ov. *Met.* 10. 411, Sen. *Controv.* exc. 4. 3. 1, *Suas.* 4. 5, Lucan 2. 518, Plin. *HN* 7. 77, *Dig.* 17. 1. 48. 1, 23. 2. 43. 1, 42. 5. 28. pr.

33. For similar *pudor*-scripts involving *cognati*, see, e.g., Ov. *Fast.* 6. 111–12, Sen. *Controv.* 7. 6. 11, Sen. *Clem.* 1. 9. 6 (if this alludes to plots against Augustus by his own family members, cf. Plin. *HN* 7. 149), *Apocol.* 10.1 (sim. [Sen.] *Oct.* 639–43), Quint. *DMin.* 298. 10, Stat. *Theb.* 3. 697–98. Similar thoughts structure the *pudor* in more fanciful settings as well, e.g., Ov. *Met.* 8. 157 (Minos vis-à-vis the Minotaur), V. Fl. 1. 44 (Sol vis-à-vis Aeetes); and cf. the strained thought at [Quint.] *DMai.* 18. 12, where having a son who deserves to be tortured by his father is the ultimate in *pudor*.

34. Ov. *Tr.* 4. 3. 48 ff. (wife), *Pont.* 2. 2. 105–6 (Messalinus), 4. 8. 13–16 (Suillius); cf. Quint. *Inst.* 11. 1. 83–84, for *pudor* experienced by the *domus* as a whole.

35. *Epist.* 1. 18. 76–77 (*incutiant aliena tibi peccata pudorem*). Similarly, e.g., Curt. 8. 4. 30, and for the metaphor *pudorem (alicui) incutere*, see also Sen. *Dial.* 5. 39.4. Note especially Cicero's remarks to his friend Fabius Gallus, acting on his behalf in the purchase of some sculpture, at *Fam.* 7. 23. 1 (trans. adapted from Shackleton Bailey) "Now please put yourself in my shoes: can you reconcile it with your *pudor* or mine to ask for credit in the first place, and in the second for more than a year's

credit?" ("fac, quaeso, qui ego sum esse te: estne aut tui pudoris aut nostri primum rogare de die, deinde plus annua postulare?"); and for the thought that your own *existimatio* is affected by the behavior of your agents, Cic. *QFr.* 1. 1. 12, 14.

36. Senator: Cic. *Phil.* 5. 4. Philosopher: Cic. *Leg.* 1. 49–50, sim. Sen. *Ep.* 97. 1, and cf. Plin. *Ep.* 2. 14. 12 (an advocate vis-à-vis other advocates), Fronto *Ep. ad Verum* 2. 1. 8 (a rhetorician vis-à-vis emperors who were poor speakers). Antony's partisans: Suet. *Nero* 3. 2; cf. Ov. *Met.* 13. 223–24 (Odysseus and the fleeing Greeks). Countrymen: e.g., Hor. *Carm.* 1. 35. 33–34, Lucan 9. 1059–61, and cf. Curt. 6. 6. 10 (a king vis-à-vis his crude subjects), Stat. *Theb.* 4. 345–49 (subjects vis-à-vis a shameful king). The "mane-fallen" lions in Statius's charming conceit at *Silv.* 2. 5. 14. ff. enact this script, too.

37. *Ep.* 8. 6. 17 (he assumes his correspondent is likewise disposed: "non dubito similiter adfici te. scio quam sit tibi vivus et ingenuus animus"); on the role of *fastidium* in this letter, see chapter 5 at n. 61. Very similarly, e.g., Ov. *Fast.* 5. 585–94 (on the Parthians's capture of Roman military standards), Sen. *Dial.* 11. 17. 4 (on the behavior of Caligula); cf. also Plin. *Pan.* 31. 6 (*pudor* of the Egyptians when the fecundity of their country fails).

38. Flor. 1. 22, Tac *Hist.* 2.61; see also Flor. 1. 5, Val. Max. 8. 5. 4, Tac. *Ann.* 11. 21, with similar gestures at Lucan 10. 47–48 and the Lucan-like churning at Petron. *Sat.* 119. 1. 14–27, 123. 1. 238–44; a variant on this narrative *pudor* will emerge under script 4.

39. Plin. *HN* 14. 123, 33. 49–50, 153, 34. 11; cf. Sen. *Ep.* 76. 4, registering *pudor* in respect of the human race as a whole (and his membership in it).

40. See Ortony, Clore, and Collins 1988, 77–79, on the concept of the "cognitive unit" relevant to emotions provoked by attributions of praise and blame (the quotation in the text is from p. 78).

41. Suet. *Aug.* 65. 2. Conversely, an *iniuria* done *to* a child concerns a father's *existimatio* and "pricks" his sense of *pudor* as much as it does the child's, if not more: *Dig.* 47. 10. 1. 1–5.

42. Philosopher's definition: see at n. 13. Consul: Livy 3. 67. 1, discussed under script 1. Compare L. Munatius Plancus's opening words in a letter to Cicero (*Fam.* 10. 21. 1): "I would feel *pudor* over my inconsistency were it not the result of another's fecklessness (*levitas*)." The same assumption is reflected, in similarly incidental ways, at (for example) Ov. *Met.* 3. 548 ff., Sen. *Controv.* 7. 7. 18 (with Serv. ad *Aen.* 2. 415), Curt. 8. 2. 12, Lucan 3. 148–49, Quint. *Inst.* 12. 5. 3, Mart. 4. 11

43. Cf., e.g., Ov. *Fast.* 6. 526 "it causes *pudor* to have committed a crime even in a frenzy" (*et furiis in scelus isse pudet*).

44. In an earlier version of this argument I used the metaphors "expansion" and "contraction" (instead of "extension" and "retraction")—until Margaret Graver pointed out that I had unconsciously adopted the metaphors that Stoicism applies to the effects of emotion on the mind, a coincidence that could distract or confuse readers familiar with the Stoic usage. I've therefore adopted the different terms, though I find them a bit less expressive: readers able to withstand the distraction or confusion should feel at liberty to think of "expansion" and "contraction," instead.

45. The distinction is drawn and developed most consequentially in Brown and Levinson 1987: for their definitions of the two forms of face, see esp. pp. 61–64 (the defintion of "negative" face offered here is closely adapted from p. 62).

46. The phenomenological basis of Jack Katz's perceptive and entertaining study of "road rage" ("Pissed Off in L.A.": Katz 1999, 18–86) could usefully be supplemented by analysis in terms of negative and positive face.

47. Pub. *Sent*. P. 41 "pudorem habere servitus quodammodo est."

48. Compare Cic. *Rosc. Am.* 149, on presenting oneself as an advocate when too young, with the very similar concern registered nearly two centuries later at Plin. *Ep.* 2. 14. 4 (cf. Quint. *DMin.* 279. 1, the *impudentia* of "playing the role of a man" prematurely—*nimium cito virum egisse*—by taking a wife). Cf. also Tac. *Hist.* 2. 22 (a general's *pudor* at an assault rashly begun) and 2. 53 (*pudor* before a man resolved on suicide).

49. Livy 34. 2. 10 "*pudor* kept married women within the bounds of what was theirs by right" (*sui iuris finibus matronas contineret pudor*), with Serv. ad *Aen.* 9. 479. Cf. Quint. *DMin.* 277. 9 for the implication that a wife's sleeping apart from her husband (unless pregnant) would be a cause for *pudor*, presumably as a species of what Quint. *DMin.* 327. 1 (in a different connection) calls "a certain willful freedom taken against her husband" (*aliqua adversus maritum licentia*); cf. also the *matronalis pudor* concerned with playing the proper role as a wife at Quint. *DMin.* 280. 16.

50. See esp. Curt. 8. 2. 12–13, depicting Alexander's elaborate *pudor* at his drunken murder of Clitus; also Prop. 4. 6. 51–52 (waging war without a *iusta causa*), Ov. *Fast.* 3. 281–82 (civil strife), Sen. *Med.* 900–901 (*pudor* setting a limit on revenge), and esp. Tac. *Hist.* 3. 34 (the general Antonius's *pudor flagitii*, the outrage in question being the destruction of Cremona). Cf. too the extravagant conceit of Val. Max. 3. 7. 10 (*fortuna* made to feel *pudor* at the savagery she unleashed against the virtuous Romans).

51. Mart. 3. 87. 1–4 "Rumor has it, Chionê, that you've never been fucked / and that there's nothing cleaner than your cunt. / Yet you cover that part when you bathe: wrong! / If you have any *pudor*, shift your panties to your face" ("Narrat te, Chione, rumor numquam esse fututam / atque nihil cunno purius esse tuo. / tecta tamen non hac, qua debes, parte lavaris: / si pudor est, transfer subligar in faciem"). On attitudes toward displays of nakedness, see chapter 1 at n. 31, 33; on typical male repugnance at female genitalia, cf. at n. 78 and esp. Richlin 1992a, 26–28, 67–69.

52. If directed at a free woman of respectable standing (as the addressee's name, Chionê, suggests she is not) the epigram would surely constitute an *iniuria*; in any case it aims to make the woman experience script-2 *pudor*. For a keen sense of the face issues at stake in vigorous exchanges between males, cf. Cic. *Cael.* 7–9, with *Fam.* 5. 1. 1 (Metellus Celer).

53. Cf. Flor. 2. 7 (a nice example of this same scruple set aside when the other party *deserves* to have his face paid little respect) and [Cic.] *Sal.* 14 (pursuing an aggressive line of questioning while failing to see that the same questions could be

asked still more damagingly of oneself). [Quint.] *DMai.* 3. 2–3 plays with this category in a typically "exquisite" way.

54. E.g., Ov. *Ars am.* 3. 803–4, *Rem.* 359–60, 407–8, *Fast.* 5. 531–32, Flor. 2. 8
(where the precautionary *pudet dicere* serves the same purpose as "honos auribus
habitus sit": Curt. 5. 1. 38, cf. Apul. *Apol.* 75).

55. See also Tac. *Ann.* 14. 55, where Nero speaks (with maximal disingenu-
ousness) of his *pudor* at the fact that Seneca has not grown as wealthy as he should
have from Nero's *caritas*; and cf. Plin. *Ep.* 8. 18. 7 (on making a will that fulfills all
officia as a product of *fides, pietas,* and *pudor,* with Quint. *DMin.* 325. 11), Quint.
Inst. 6. 4. 10 (proper respect for judicial procedure); the *pudor* of breaking a promise
in Serv. ad *Aen.* 11. 356.

56. E.g., Cic. *Prov. Cons.* 14, *Phil.* 2. 15, *Fam.* 5. 12. 1–3 (to Lucceius), Ov. *Tr.*
2. 1. 29–30, Quint. *Inst.* 12. 1. 12, Juv. 8. 83–84, *Dig.* 3. 2. 20. pr. (instigating a
calumnia); by the same token *pudor* demands that an advocate resign a *causa* he comes
to know is unjust (Quint. 12. 7. 6), for he otherwise risks "losing the value placed on
his own *pudor* in the cause of another's *impudentia*" (Cic. *Verr.* 2. 2. 192 "in alterius
impudentia sui pudoris existimationem amittere"). Extreme flattery (*adsentatio
immodica*) strains the *pudor* not only of the flatterer but of the flattered as well: Livy
31.15. 2.

57. See esp. Suet. *Otho* 9. 3 (vs. Val. Max. 9. 5 [ext.]. 1), and less dramatically
Rhet. Her. 4. 2 (cf. Hor. *Epist.* 2. 1. 79–82); cf. Persius 1. 83–84 (an advocate more
concerned with praise for style than effective defense), Mart. 1. 52, 12. 63 (on pla-
giarism), Plin. *Pan.* 60. 5 (reluctance to accept consulship that could be regarded as
claiming too much for oneself). The idea, in a radical form, is pursued at length in
[Quint.] *DMai.* 12 (esp. 14, 22–24), on cannibalism.

58. E.g., Quint. *Inst.* 9. 2. 76, 10. 1. 111. See also the very interesting remarks
on the *pudor* of judges at Quint. *Inst.* 11. 1. 76–78, with *DMin.* 266. 12 and Sen.
Controv. 1. 3. 5. Sen. *Ben.* 7. 28. 3 implies that failing to help another maintain his
positive face will cause him to lose his dispositional *pudor,* a thought that seems to
underlie Ov. *Met.* 10. 238–42, too.

59. E.g., Cic. *Verr.* 2. 4. 151 (sim. 2. 5. 5), *De or.* 1. 102 (sim. 2. 364). Adorning
oneself with false plumage (Phaed. *Fab.* 1. 3) is the characteristic shame of the intel-
lectual: Sen. *Suas.* 4. 5 (a declaimer), Plin. *HN* 7. 180 (a philosopher), Suet. *Gramm.*
30. 5 (an advocate), Quint. *Inst.* 2. 4. 29 (a rhetor) and esp. 10. 3. 19 (a master of
words at a loss for words).

60. Mart. 12. 94. 11 "omnia velle." See, e.g., Cic. *Verr.* 2. 5. 106, *Clu.* 26–27,
Sen. *Dial.* 9. 8. 6, Mart. 10. 78, 11. 49, Quint. *DMin.* 265. 1–2, Juv. 14. 177–78,
Tac. *Ann.* 4. 1. In the realm of script-4 *pudor* lying and greed are the core delicts for
men, as unchastity is for women.

61. Sex: e.g., Plaut. *Curc.* 57–58, Cic. *Phil.* 2. 61, Sen. *Phaed.* 96–98 (of
Theseus), Tac. *Ann.* 6. 1, Hyg. *Fab.* 148. 2. Luxury vel sim.: e.g., Suet. *Iul.* 47. 1
(slaves), Plin. *HN* 22. 118 (*deliciae*), Val. Max. 2. 5. 4 (drunkenness, cf. Plin. *HN*
14. 138), Sil. 11. 400–402.

62. On women's *pudor* tending to be identified with *pudicitia,* see Kaster 1997,

9–10; on women tending especially to *impatientia* in love, see Kaster 2002a, 139–40. A man's violation of *pudicitia* tends to be figured as effeminacy, and so as a discreditable "retraction" of the self (script 5) rather than discreditable "extension" (though see the unusual conception at Man. 5. 152–55): this is consistent with other ways in which "womanish" male behavior is regarded, see the discussion of script 5.

63. Livy 30. 12. 19, Curt. 10. 2. 10, Sen. *Ben.* 2. 7. 3.

64. In the case of *pudens* (*-ter*), this comes to not quite 90 percent (42/47) of the instances that can plausibly be assigned to a specific script, and in the case of *impudens* (*-ter*) / *impudentia*, an even more remarkable 97 percent (223/229): note that nearly two-thirds of the latter instances (140/223) are owed to Cicero, who is especially fond of this form of condemnation, and that nearly 20 percent (43/223) occur in Cic. *Verr.*, where the *impudentia* of Verres amounts to a controlling theme.

65. Cic. *Inv. rhet.* 2. 164 with *Fin.* 2. 73.

66. This script largely coincides with the values of the "good-contest culture" and the *virtus* of radical "manliness" evoked in Barton 2001 (esp. 34–87), though it will emerge that I interpret its place in Roman life somewhat differently.

67. Compare the *impudentia* of attacking those who cannot fight back (in a nonmilitary context), Plin. *HN* pr. 31, or the lack of generosity shown in failing to convey good news in a timely way to a friend, causing the latter to appear negligent in offering congratulations (Stat. *Silv.* 4. 8. 41–43). Cf. also Quint. *Inst.* 9. 3. 73, Plin. *HN* pr. 21.

68. Cic. *Fam.* 14. 3. 1–2 "culpa mea propria est. meum fuit officium vel legatione vitare periculum vel diligentia et copiis resistere vel cadere fortiter. hoc miserius, turpius, indignius nobis nihil fuit. qua re cum dolore conficiar, tum etiam pudore. pudet enim me uxori optimae, suavissimis liberis virtutem et diligentiam non praestitisse. nam mi ante oculos dies noctesque versatur squalor vester et maeror et infirmitas valetudinis tuae." This is perhaps the most complete and candid first-person expression of *pudor* outside imaginative literature (e.g., Dido), linking the feeling to a fault (*culpa*) fully acknowledged, clearly describing the failure that constitutes the *culpa*, and remarking the disgrace that attends the failure; on the connection of the sentiment to what we would call "remorse," see the discussion at the end of chapter 3, at n. 38. Cf. the basis of *pudor* at Caes. *BCiv.* 3. 20. 3 and Livy 22. 14. 4.

69. The civil and military dimensions are joined at Cic. *Fam.* 10. 23. 1 (Plancus), which expresses *pudor* at being vulnerable to criticism for prolonging war through passivity and lack of magnanimity (specifically, holding a grudge).

70. E.g., Livy 7. 15. 3, 44. 10. 4, cf. Caes. *BCiv.* 1. 67. 4. For *pudor* at being kept at bay by a weaker enemy, see Val. Max. 3. 2. 23.

71. E.g., Livy 3. 62. 8, Sall. *Iug.* 100. 5, Lucan 9. 884–87, V. Fl. 4. 653–55, Sil. 10. 260–64, Tac. *Hist.* 3. 17, with n. 96. For refusal to meet the sort of death that good men have met, see Cic. *Fam.* 6. 4. 4, and cf. *Att.* 14. 9. 2; for failure to measure up to the actions of better men, cf. also Cic. *Phil.* 10. 8.

72. Defeat: e.g., Cic. *Fin.* 5. 61, cf. Stat. *Theb.* 11. 154 ff., Plin. *Pan.* 69. 1, Tac. *Hist.* 4. 18, 5. 15. Pleasure: Frontin. *Str.* 2. 7. 9 (discussed in chapter 3, see at pp. 79–80). Competitions: e.g., Frontin. *Str.* 1. 11. 3 [= 4. 5. 11], V. Fl. 1. 172, Stat. *Theb.* 7.

435. Cf. Ov. *Fast.* 3. 65–66 (Romulus and Remus, learning of their lineage, are given "spirit" and stirred by *pudor* to perform worthy deeds), Verg. *Aen.* 9. 781–87, Ov. *Met.* 9. 31 (the *pudor* of backing down when you've "talked big").

73. "Childish": e.g., Livy 9. 11. 12 (engaging in "puerile" quibbles), Tib. 2. 1. 73–74 (of an old man declaring love at a mistress's threshold), Sen. *Ep.* 27. 2 (not having outgrown childish desires and plans, cf. *Ep.* 48. 5). Cf. Ter. *Hec.* 231, of an older (more mature) woman feuding with a younger person. "Servile": e.g., Cic. *Fam.* 15. 18. 1 "pudet enim servire" (under Caesar, cf. *Att.* 13. 15. 1), Ov. *Am.* 3. 11. 1–4, Curt. 6. 8. 8, Quint. *Inst.* 3. 8. 47 (cf. [Sen.] *Oct.* 93–93a, of Nero's receiving *imperium* through his mother's gift); for *pudor* entailed in cadging dinner invitations and other "parasitical" behavior, see, e.g., Mart. 2. 18, Quint. *DMin.* 298. 10 (*libertatem et ingenuum pudorem consumpsisti*), and cf. Mart. 6. 10, 11. 68 (the *pudor* of being deemed unworthy of having even small requests satisfied).

74. E.g., Curt. 8. 2. 28, on the *pudor* of valuing freedom less—i.e., being more servile—than a woman. See also, e.g., Sil. 13. 308–13 (entreaties for mercy figured as *femineum*), Tib. 1. 9. 29–30, Sen. *Controv.* 7. 8. 2 (the *pudor* of grovelling before a woman), Cic. *Tusc.* 2. 48 (of "irrational" behavior), [Tib.] (= "Lygdamus") 3. 2. 5–8 (confessing *impatientia* in love), or the conceit of Stat. *Achil.* 1. 271–72 (on the baby-hero's response to "soft"—unmasculine—treatment); the same thought is exploited to paradoxical ends at Sen. *Controv.* 10. 4. 16–17 (on degenerate, effeminate rich men said to feel *pudor* at being men). By contrast, a woman who behaves in a "mannish" way should incur the *pudor* of discreditable "self-extension," see at n. 49. On the cultural place of such talk in general, see, e.g., Edwards 1993, 63–97, Corbeill 1996, 128–73; on the relation between "servile" and "feminine" *patientia* in particular, see Kaster 2002a, 138–40.

75. Cf. Sen. *Controv.* 2. 7. 2, the *pudor* of being either so foolish or so complacent as to find nothing suspicious when a stranger installs one's wife as his heir.

76. This is the scruple that attaches to performing unbecoming physical labor: Verg. *G.* 1. 79–81, Tib. 1. 1. 29–32, Columella *Rust.* 10. 1. 1, Calp. Sic. 5. 39–42, with Ov. *Pont.* 1. 8. 45–46; cf. also Juv. 3. 168 f. (the *pudor* of eating from "common" dishware), 14. 185 (wearing the boots of a common farmer).

77. E.g., Catull. 6. 4–5, Ov. *Her.* 7. 167–68, *Ars am.* 3. 83–84, *Rem.* 709–10, *Fast.* 4. 176, Sen. *Ag.* 295, Serv. ad *Aen.* 4. 1, all concerned with having an unworthy lover (cf. Ov. *Fast.* 6. 574 *caelestem . . . homini concubuisse pudet*, with 579), and cf. also Cic. *Verr.* 2. 1. 32, *Phil.* 10. 22, Ov. *Ars am.* 2. 251–52, Sen. *Controv.* 10. 4. 8.

78. Ov. *Ars am.* 2. 719–22 "When you've found the places that a woman likes to have touched, / don't let *pudor* stand in the way of touching them. / You'll see her eyes sparkling with a tremulous light" ("cum loca reppereris, quae tangi femina gaudet, / non obstet, tangas quo minus illa, pudor. / aspicies oculos tremulo fulgore micantes, / ut sol a liquida saepe refulget aqua"): that genital massage is meant is suggested not just by the connection with *pudor* (touching, say, the nape of your lover's neck would not stir that emotion) but also by the signs of arousal noted in 721, which closely track Juvenal's description of masturbating schoolboys (7. 240–41 "it's no small task, with so many boys, / to keep a watch on their hands and on their eyes that quiver at climax":

"non est leue tot puerorum / observare manus oculosque in fine trementis"). Given the repugnance displayed by the Ovidian "teacher" toward female genitalia in *Rem.* (e.g., 405 ff.), the *pudor* here is presumably not fear of behavior that is discreditable because too forward or (still less) self-indulgent but fear of behavior that is demeaning (*cunnilingus* is commonly regarded in similar terms): cf. (*mutatis mutandis*) Seren. Samm. *Lib. Med.* 48. 899, on the *pudor* possibly felt at handling disgusting (yet healthful) matter. With the overtone of "disgust" in the last cf. Ov. *Pont.* 4. 3. 47–48 "Marius lay amid the filth and swampy reeds / and endured many things that must cause so great a man *pudor*" ("in caeno Marius iacuit cannaque palustri / pertulit et tanto multa *pudenda* viro") where the shame consists not in hiding (as a failure of courage, script 5) but in hiding in (ick!) a swamp. On the relation between "shame" and "disgust," see chapter 5 at nn. 28, 34.

79. "High-wire act": Kaster 1997, 11, and cf. Barton 2001, 197 ff. ("Part 3: On the Wire: The Experience of Shame in Ancient Rome").

80. *Ep.* 2. 9. 1–3 (trans. adapted from Radice). For the kind of patronage and the connection it entails, compare, e.g., Cic. *Fam.* 11. 16. 2–3 (to D. Brutus): "L. Lamia is seeking the praetorship. . . . [much detail about their relationship follows; then] Accordingly, my dear Brutus, please take it into your mind that *I* am seeking the praetorship (*quapropter persuade tibi, mi Brute, me petere praeturam*)."

81. By contrast, for example, were Pliny simply concerned that he would be seen to have exerted himself insufficiently, so that the loss could be attributed to his *inertia*, it would be a case of script-5 *pudor*.

82. *Fam.* 7. 3. 1 (to Marius) and 6. 6. 6 (to Caecina); cf. more briefly, on the same theme, *Fam.* 11. 27. 4 (to Matius) "There followed that crisis when my *pudor* or duty or fortune forced me to set out to Pompey" ("Secutum illud tempus est cum me ad Pompeium proficisci sive pudor meus coegit sive officium sive fortuna").

83. Hyg. *Astr.* 2. 13. 1. The same tale is told, and attributed to Euripides, at Eratosth. *Catast.* 13, without reference to the goddess's emotion or consequent action.

84. On rape and script 2, see at n. 23. It is in the nature of the case that the Roman rapist *should* experience occurrent *pudor* at his actions but seldom does: were he the sort to experience that feeling, his dispositional *pudor* would probably have restrained him from the actions to begin with.

85. Ovid, for example, plays with thoughts along just these lines in *Am.* 3. 7.

86. See at n. 41.

87. Cic. *Dom.* 101, cf. ibid. 142, referring to "the sight I must escape more urgently than death" (*conspectum morte magis vitandum fugiendumque esse*).

88. Similarly, e.g., Cic. *Verr.* 2. 3. 95, *Fam.* 5. 2. 9, 8. 12. 1 (Caelius), Sen. *Dial.* 5. 41. 3, Stat. *Silv.* 4. 8. 40–42, Quint. *Inst.* 9. 2. 72 and 12. 5. 3.

89. See, e.g., Livy 40. 27. 10, Val. Max. 3. 2. 23, Lucan 6. 153–55, Sil. 12. 455–56, Serv. ad *Aen.* 9. 789 On the links between anger and shame see, e.g., Cairns 1993, 383 ff., Wright 1997, 174, Harris 2001, 59–60, Cairns 2003b, 26–27.

90. Barton 2001, esp. 88–130, 281–83.

91. Pub. *Sent.* P. 41 "pudorem habere servitus quodammodo est."

92. Barton 2001, 1.

93. This is in essence Cicero's response to Clodius's criticism for "too boast-fully making declarations about myself" (*de me ipso gloriosius praedicare*) at *Dom*. 93–95 (sim. *Har. resp.* 17), and it is echoed by his admirer Quintilian at *Inst*. 11. 1. 17–18; it is ethically of a piece with his comments on the destruction of his house at *Dom*. 101, already discussed at n. 87. Allen 1954 collects much useful material for evalu-ating "Cicero's conceit."

94. The remarks here are drawn from Kaster 1997, 16–17.

95. *Audacia* and *audax* are among Cicero's most commonly used scare-terms: for their pairing with *impudentia / impudens* in the orations, see, e.g., *Rosc. Amer.* 96, 118, *Verr.* 2. 1. 1, 6, 36, 142, 2. 2. 134, 2. 3. 65, 83, 166, 169, 2. 4. 44, 84, 2. 5. 62, 106, *Caecin.* 1, 2, *Clu.* 26–27, *Flac.* 35, *Dom.* 116, 133, *Pis.* 66, *Phil.* 2. 4, 19, 3. 18, 6. 7. Wirszubski's (1961) reading of *audacia* against the specific backdrop of late Re-publican politics, and esp. his remarks on Milo and Caelius (1961, 15), converge with the more general argument here; see also Weische 1966, 28–33, 66–70, Achard 1981, 247–48.

96. For good "recklessness" aligned with "fortitude" and "virtue" see, e.g., Caes. *BGall.* 2. 26. 2, *BCiv.* 3. 26. 1, Livy 2. 10. 5–6, 2. 31. 6, 5. 16. 10, 25. 38. 11, 18 (cf. Serv. ad *Aen.* 8. 110 "Vergil uses the epithet *audax* whenever he wants to show courage without good fortune: accordingly he calls even Turnus *audax*": "audacem autem dicit ubique Vergilius quotiens vult ostendere virtutem sine fortuna: unde etiam Turnum audacem vocat," sim. ad *Aen.* 9. 3, Serv. Dan. ad *Aen.* 4. 615); and cf. n. 71.

97. And not just "you" who are my contemporary others, but also the others yet unborn, my posterity, whose patrimony I squander in the *luxuria* that is one of the chief stimulants of *pudor*-talk: to the moralizing Roman mind, satisfaction of the self in this form was not, ultimately, the acquisition of "more" but a path to destitution.

98. The theme of equality and its relation to *pudor* is explicit in, e.g., Livy 34. 4. 14 (a debate on sumptuary laws, cf. Tac. *Ann.* 3. 26) and is just below the surface in many, many other texts.

99. For *pudor* and the afflicted, see Sen. *Thy.* 925, and cf., e.g., Tac. *Ann.* 3. 54, implying that the utterly poor and the vastly rich are both, in different ways, removed from considerations of *pudor*; the thought that *aidôs* does not serve the needs of the poor appears already at Pl. *Charm.* 160E–161A. On the connection between the reckless (*audaces*) and the needy (*egentes*), see Wirszubski 1961, 17–18; after noting that "the earliest political *audax* whom we [meet] in the extant sources is Saturninus," he concludes his fine survey by suggesting "it is . . . likely that the derogatory term *audax*, which had always been a strong word of abuse [he cites Naevius com. 118 Ribb.], entered the vocabulary of Roman political life at the time when the struggles between the '*boni*' and the '*seditiosi*', ushered in by the Gracchi, became increasingly violent and bitter" (22). Perhaps, but it seems equally likely that *audax* was present in the vocabulary of Roman public life as long as there were Haves who wished to stigmatize the strivings of Have-Nots. That would take us back some time before the Gracchi.

100. Ov. *Ars am.* 1. 99–100 "Spectatum veniunt, veniunt spectentur ut ipsae:

/Ille locus casti damna pudoris habet." For dispositional *pudor* as a metaphorical garment that conceals our ethically naked selves, see n. 31.

101. On this formulation, see esp. the excellent discussion of Taylor 1985, 61–68.

102. A complete survey of the modes of "seeing" relevant to *pudor*, which this section does not claim to give, would also necessarily survey the full range of possible "audiences" and all the different reasons why their views must be taken to count, or not.

103. Plin. *HN* 36. 107–8 "He discovered a novel remedy, unheard of before or since: he crucified the bodies of those who had died [by suicide], so they could be seen by their fellow citizens and, at the same time, be torn by the beasts and birds. And so that peculiarly Roman (sense of) *pudor*, which has often salvaged desperate situations in battles, played a role then too, but on that occasion by blushing at the violence done after death, since it caused the living the same *pudor* they would feel when dead" ("novum, inexcogitatum ante posteaque remedium invenit ille rex, ut omnium ita defunctorum corpora figeret cruci spectanda civibus simul et feris volucribusque laceranda. quam ob rem pudor Romani nominis proprius, qui saepe res perditas servavit in proeliis, tunc quoque subvenit, sed illo tempore <v>i post vitam erubescens, cum puderet vivos, tamquam puditurum esset extinctos": the text is difficult, and I take Mayhoff's *vi post vitam erubescens* as the best alternative to the MSS' *inposuit iam erubescens* [dTh] or *in post vitam erubescens* [B]; in any case, the thought important to my point, that "puderet vivos, tamquam puditurum esset extinctos," is secure).

104. For the "*pudor* of the dead" as channeled through the living, see also esp. Gell. *NA* 15. 10. 2: an epidemic of virgin suicides at Miletus inspires a decree "that they all be carried naked in their funerals, with the same noose by which they had hanged themselves, [and] after the decree the maidens stopped committing suicide, deterred only by the *pudor* of so dishonorable a funeral" ("ut hae omnes nudae cum eodem laqueo, qui essent praevinctae, efferrentur. post id decretum virgines voluntariam mortem non petisse pudore solo deterritas tam inhonesti funeris"). See also Plin. *HN* 7. 77 (female corpses normally float face down, "as though nature were sparing their *pudor*"), and cf. Plin. *Ep.* 2. 5 and 5. 1, both concerned with testamentary matters that affect the *pudor* of the dead; and for similar "future projection" differently (and more rationally) deployed, cf. Cic. *Att.* 3. 23. 4 (sim. 13. 51. 1).

105. The formulation occurs at Barton 2001, 58.

106. See Cic. *Fin.* 2. 60, with *Fin.* 2. 73, *Leg.* 1. 49–50, Gell. *NA* 12. 11. 3.

107. E.g., Caes. *BCiv.* 2. 31. 7, Ov. *Am.* 1. 6. 59–60, *Met.* 10. 454, *Tr.* 3. 6. 31–32, Sen. *Thy.* 891, Sil. 2. 502–3, 9. 145–49, Tac. *Hist.* 4. 36, *Ann.* 14. 20.

108. E.g., Cic. *Fam.* 5. 12 (esp. 1–3), Ov. *Her.* 4. 10, *Met.* 9. 515–16, Quint. *Inst.* 5. 7. 1 (on giving oral vs. written testimony), Plin. *Ep.* 3. 20. 8 (on the secret vs. open ballot).

109. E.g., Plaut. *Epid.* 107–8, Catull. 6. 4–5 (sim. Prop. 2. 23. 28 [= 2. 24. 4]), Cic. *Fin.* 2. 77, Ov. *Am.* 3. 14. 16 ff., Sen. *Controv.* 7. 7. 18, Val. Max. 2. 5. 4 (on masks used to conceal drunkenness), Sen. *Ben.* 6. 38. 5, Stat. *Achil.* 1. 564–65, Plin.

Ep. 3. 9. 5 (with 9. 27. 2), Suet. *Tib.* 66. 1, Tac. *Ann.* 4. 1 (Sejanus's "mask" vs. his inner reality); for a variant on this thought—that being seen to have done wrong causes no *pudor* when those who see you have committed the same wrong—see Sen. *Ben.* 3. 16. 1–4, [Quint.] *DMai.* 12. 9 (cf. Tac. *Hist.* 3. 61 and *Ann.* 6. 44, where the delict of commanders undoes the *pudor* of the rank and file, and sim. *Ann.* 14. 14, on Nero's bad example undoing the *pudor* of others). Note also the related idea that once a secret delict is made public and occurrent shame has been experienced, dispositional *pudor* is lost: see esp. Ov. *Ars am.* 2. 555 ff., on the adultery of Mars and Venus.

110. The example, used by Max Scheler (1957, 79, along with the female patient or bather before a male physician or servant), is developed to good effect by Taylor 1985, 60–61.

111. E.g., Sen. *Ben.* 6. 37. 2, cf. Cic. *Fam.* 10. 21. 1 (Plancus).

112. See, e.g., Procris in Cephalus's narration at Ov. *Met.* 7. 741–44, with Ov. *Am.* 3. 6. 77–78, *Her.* 21. 47–48, *Met.* 1. 755–59, 9. 577–79, Sen. *Controv.* 7. 2. 1, V. Fl. 2. 470–71, Quint. *DMin.* 321. 2, Suet. *Tib.* 66. 1, Tac. *Ann.* 14. 49, *Dig.* 2. 4. 10. 12, and the marvelous vignette of Tisiphone and Pietas at Stat. *Theb.* 11. 482–96.

113. The reaction quoted in the text is Ovid's Cydippe, *Her.* 21. 111–13 "nomine coniugii dicto confusa pudore, / sensi me totis erubuisse genis, / luminaque in gremio veluti defixa tenebam": in the event she will have real cause to feel *pudor* for a different reason, see verse 242 with Kenney's fine note ad loc., drawing the connection with this earlier passage. Cf., e.g., the virgins' blush on the verge of marriage itself at Stat. *Theb.* 2. 230–34, where self-attention is compounded by their thoughts of the first sexual encounter—the *prima culpa*—soon to come.

114. For *pudor* linked to the "judgment" entailed in public speaking, see, e.g., Cic. *De or.* 1. 119–22, *Clu.* 51, Plin. *Ep.* 7. 17. 8–9, Quint. *Inst.* 10. 7. 16, and cf. Cic. *Sull.* 85; on settings of public speech as the crucible of male identity, see esp. Gleason 1995, Gunderson 2000. The *pudor* of being publicly praised (Cic. *Caecin.* 77) or the *pudor* of the *princeps civilis* (Plin. *Pan.* 2. 8, 24. 1, 73. 4) can be understood in similar terms.

115. Cic. *Flac.* 9–12 (the clause quoted in the text, "nostri mores ac disciplina plus valeret quam dolor ac simultas," stands in 11), with, e.g., Ter. *Phorm.* 281–84, Sen. *Ep.* 11. 4.

116. Silent requests: Cic. *Leg. Man.* 48 (cf. Sen. *Ben.* 6. 38. 5). Mezentius: Verg. *Aen.* 10. 846–71 (discussed in greater detail at the end of chapter 3), cf. Suet. *Otho* 9. 3 (Otho's compunction at bringing disaster to others). Literary exercise: Plin. *Ep.* 7. 9. 3. Cf. also Cic. *Pis.* 39 (being *pudens* = being *conscientia oppressus*), Ov. *Am.* 3. 11. 1–4 (sim. *Tr.* 3. 6. 29–30, reading *pudor* at the end of 30, as *adeo* in 31 suggests), Tib. 1. 9. 29–30 and 47–48 (present *pudor* caused by reflection on past deeds), Sulpicia (= [Tib.]) 3. 13. 1–2. Cf. also, e.g., Ov. *Met.* 7. 72 (the Dido-like Medea in soliloquy, cf. Juno at V. Fl. 3. 520), *Met.* 10. 368–72 (Myrrha's secret *pudor* and desire), *Tr.* 3. 1. 1–4 (the *pudor* of a solitary reader, alone with his *liber*), Val. Max. 5. 7 (ext.). 1 (Antiochus, out of *pudor*, conceals his secret passion for Stratonice almost to the point of death), Sen. *Dial.* 12. 2. 2 (the *animus* feeling *pudor* in respect of itself, sim.

12. 12. 4), Tac. *Ann.* 11. 25 (*pudor* the product of personal stock-taking, *de se consultare*), Gell. *NA* 5. 1. 3 (*pudor* and a cluster of other emotions experienced—wholly internally—while listening to a philosopher).

117. Philomela: Ov. *Met.* 6.537 (*paelex ego facta sororis*) with 603–6 (comforting refused). Legionaries: Tac. *Hist.* 4. 72. Varro: Val. Max. 4. 5. 2 (sim. Sil. 10. 630 ff.). Cf. also, e.g., Ovid's Lucretia at *Fast.* 2. 813–34, and Otho's reaction to being hailed as "Nero Otho" at Tac. *Hist.* 1. 78.

118. In saying, earlier, that this form of self-seeing "looks very much like" conscience, I intentionally sidestep a question—whether or not it actually *is* conscience—that I cannot fully pursue here. If it is a precondition of conscience that I have an autonomous and reliable standard of self-evaluation—independent of others' judgments of me and based on a coherent understanding of appropriate action achieved by reflection—then these cases very likely do not clear the bar, but that is probably to set the bar too high (for one thing, it would make conscience a near monopoly of philosophers). For compelling argument that the form of self-seeing implicated in the Stoic *aidôs* of Epictetus does clear that bar, see Kamtekar 1998, and cf. chapter 6 at n. 35. If conscience requires only that I be my own judge and "feel shame before myself," then the idea is expressly found already in the fifth cent. BCE, in Democritus (see Cairns 1993, 365–70), whose interest in "internalizing happiness" (Annas 1993, 362) is consistent with internalizing such judgments.

119. For the need to resist such stories, often cast in Whiggish terms of ethical "progress," see also chapter 3 at n. 5.

120. For the embodiment of *pudor* see n. 12; for *verecundia*, see, e.g., chapter 1 at n. 18.

121. Cicero speaks of "*verecundia*, which nature gave to human beings as a kind of fear of just reproof" (*Rep.* 5. 6 "verecundia, quam natura homini dedit quasi quendam vituperationis non iniustae timorem"); the phrase corresponds to the definition of *aischunê* at Gell. *NA* 19. 6. 3, quoted at n. 13.

122. Quint. *Inst.* 8. 3. 39 "Ego Romani *pudoris* more contentus . . . *verecundiam* silentio vindicabo" (the epithet *Romanus* is given point here by the common belief that the Greeks—and especially the Stoics and Cynics—had fewer compunctions in this regard: Cic. *Off.* 1. 127, Cels. *Med.* 6. 18. 1); Sen. *Ep.* 40. 13–14 "eo autem magis te deterreo ab isto morbo quod non potest tibi ista res contingere aliter quam si te *pudere* desierit. . . . non potest, inquam, tibi contingere res ista salva *verecundia*." Compare also, e.g., Val. Max. 5. 7. (ext.). 1, Sen. *Ep.* 83. 19, Plin. *HN* 11. 224, Quint. *Inst.* 1. 3. 16, 4. 5. 19–20; *Rhet. Her.* 4. 45 and Cic. *De or.* 3. 169, on metaphorical usage, speak of a *translatio pudens*, a notion expressed in terms of *verecundia* at Cic. *De or.* 3. 165, *Orat.* 81, *Opt. gen.* 4, sim. Sen. *Ep.* 114. 1, Gell. *NA* 7. 15. 5, 17. 13. 9.

123. Quint. *Inst.* 9. 3. 73; cf., e.g., Cic. *Verr.* 2. 4. 80 (sim. *Caecin.* 77, *De or.* 2. 3, *Rep.* 1. 67), Curt. 6. 2. 6, Sen. *Dial.* 9. 2. 10, Quint. *Inst.* 4. 5. 18–20, Tac. *Ann.* 1. 12.

124. On the distinctions among these three emotions, and their relation to the language used to denote them, Miller 1993 (esp. 175–201) is excellent.

125. The clause at *Rep.* 5. 6 quoted in n. 121 is followed immediately by the remark that "that great governor of commonwealths [sc. nature] strengthened this

[sc. *verecundia*] . . . and perfected it . . . so that *pudor*, no less than fear, would keep citizens from doing wrong" ("*hanc* [sc. *verecundiam*] ille rector rerum publicarum auxit . . . perfecitque . . . , ut *pudor* civis non minus a delictis arceret quam metus"); whereas at *Leg.* 1. 50 ("quid vero de modestia, quid de temperantia, quid de continentia, quid de verecundia pudore pudicitiaque dicemus?") the structure of the sentence implies both that *pudor*, *verecundia*, and *pudicitia* are distinct from one another and that they are felt to have more to do with one another than any one of them has to do with *modestia*, *temperantia*, and *continentia*. Cf. similarly Cic. *Fin.* 4. 18 "this animal alone [= the human being] is born with a share of *pudor* and *verecundia*" (*hoc solum animal natum est pudoris ac verecundiae particeps*), Sen. *Controv.* 7. 8. 10 "a young man naturally *verecundus* and of unsophosticated *pudor*" (*adulescens verecundus natura et rustici pudoris*), Gell. *NA* 14. 5. 3 "*pudor* and *verecundia* have me in their grip" (*me . . . pudor et verecundia tenet*), Apul. *Apol.* 3 "a spirit endowed with *pudor* and *verecundia*" (*pudens animus et verecundus*).

126. See chapter 1 at n. 36. Note Livy 3. 62. 8–9, a rare instance of *verecundia* in a script 5 context, where it provides welcome variation for the *pudor* just mentioned: "the two legions' cavalry . . . leap from their horses, fly to the head of their already-retreating forces, and simultaneously places themselves in the enemy's way and kindle their infantry's courage, at first by levelling the balance of the danger and then with *pudor*. For it was a matter of *verecundia* [for the infantry] that the cavalry were fighting [both on horse and on foot], whereas not even on foot was the infantry equal to the dismounted cavalry" ("equites duarum legionum . . . ex equis desiliunt cedentibusque iam suis provolant in primum, simulque et hosti se opponunt et aequato primum periculo, *pudore* deinde animos peditum accendunt. *verecundiae* erat equitem suo alienoque Marte pugnare, peditem ne ad pedes quidem degresso equiti parem esse").

127. Cic. *Fam.* 2. 6. 1 "Ego, si mea in te essent officia solum, Curio, tanta quanta magis a te ipso praedicari quam a me ponderari solent, verecundius a te, si quae magna res mihi petenda esset, contenderem. grave est enim homini pudenti petere aliquid magnum ab eo de quo se bene meritum putet." For the scruple involved, see sim. *Fam.* 4. 13. 6, and cf. Sen. *Ben.* 5. 20. 7.

128. Note that the point remains much the same if the *religio* in question is understood not as "a scruple having Jews as its object" (*OLD* s.v. 2) but as "a scruple felt by the Jews" (i.e., their "superstition," as *OLD* classifies the passage, s.v. 6b): in the latter case, Cicero denies that Pompey was restrained by any regard for Jewish beliefs, as opposed to Jewish persons. For other cases where *pudor* and *verecundia* are not simply fungible, consider Cic. *Sull.* 15 (sim. 77), *Font.* 28, *Caecin.* 104, *Mur.* 87, 90, and cf. Ascon. *Pis.* pp. 7–8 C.

Chapter 3

1. On the father's *magnitudo* overshadowing the son, Sen. *Controv.* 4. pr. 4 " . . . he left a son, Asinius Gallus, a great orator–were it not for the fact his father's greatness, as inevitably happens, caused him to be eclipsed, not advanced" (" . . . filium Asinium Gallum relinqueret, magnum oratorem, nisi illum, quod semper evenit,

magnitudo patris non produceret sed obrueret"); for Pollio's hostility to Cicero and his memory, Sen. *Suas.* 6. 15. For Claudius's "defense of Cicero against the books of Asinius Gallus" noted later in this paragraph, Suet. *Claud.* 41. 3.

2. Cic. *Cael.* 6 "id numquam tam acerbe feret M. Caelius ut eum paeniteat non deformem esse natum." Though the noun *paenitentia* is first attested in Livy, I generally use it, here and throughout, to denote the emotion, experience of which is expressed by the impersonal verb *paenitet.*

3. Asinius Gallus frag. 1 Mazzarino (= Gell. *NA* 17. 1. 6; Gellius does not expressly attribute these words to Gallus, but the context leaves no question of their source).

4. On agent-regret see Rorty 1980, Williams 1981, 20–39 (esp. 27 ff.); and on the role of regret in modern thought and literature more broadly, Landman 1993.

5. For the position described in this and the following paragraph, a straight line can be traced from Langen 1880, 247–49 (on *paenitet* = "Unzufriedenheit" in Plautus), through Eduard Fraenkel's influential remarks at Fraenkel 1957, 5 n. 6 (referring to *Serm.* 1. 6. 89, on which see at n. 22), to the baldly evolutionary sketch in Thome 2000, 43–46 ("Von Unzufriedenheit zur Reue"). The "afterthought" that leads to the "wish to undo" in cases of agent-regret is, of course, explicit in the Greek verbs that most closely correspond to *paenitet, metamelei* and *metanoēō,* on which see Thompson 1908.

6. Plaut. *Poen.* 283–84 [Anterastilis] "By Castor, when I look at our outfits, I experience *paenitentia* at how we're decked out" ("eu ecastor, quom ornatum aspicio nostrum ambarum, *paenitet / exornatae ut simus*"); cf. *Bacch.* 1181–82 [Nicobulus] "Your hospitality is enough, and more: / I experience not a bit of *paenitentia* at how I've been entertained" ("satis, satis iam vostrist convivi: / me nil *paenitet* ut sim acceptus"); *Stich.* 550–51 [Antipho] "'No, no,' that young man says, 'I'll give you two, if one's too few; / and if there's *paenitentia* felt at two,' he says, 'I'll add two more'" ("'immo duas dabo,' inquit ille adulescens 'una si parumst; / et *si duarum paenitebit*,' inquit 'addentur duae'"); *Trin.* 320–21 [Philto] "He's an upright fellow who feels *paenitentia* at how upright and worthy he is; / the person who's sufficiently pleased with himself is neither upright nor worthy" ("is probus est *quem paenitet quam probus sit et frugi bona; / qui ipsus sibi satis placet, nec probus est nec frugi bonae*"). Ter. *Phorm.* 172 [Phaedria] "That's the way we mostly all are by nature: we feel *paenitentia* at ourselves" ("ita plerique ingenio sumus omnes: *nostri nosmet paenitet*"); cf. *Hec.* 774–76 [Bacchis] "I must make sure Pamphilus gets his wife back; / and if I bring it off, I'll feel no *paenitentia* at the reputation [I'll get], to have been the only working girl to do what the others all avoid" ("Pamphilo me facere ut redeat uxor / oportet; quod si perficio *non paenitet me famae*, / solam fecisse id quod aliae meretrices facere fugitant").

7. So in different ways both *OLD* and *TLL* imply this sort of development: *OLD* s.v. *paeniteo* "1 To cause dissatisfaction, give reason for complaint or regret. . . . 2 To affect (a person) with regret (for an action, etc., for which he is responsible), cause to repent. . . . 3 To feel regret (for one's actions, etc.), think better (of). b (w. emphasis on consequent change of policy, etc.)"; s.v. *paenitentia* "regret for one's action, etc. b (in a weakened sense) change of mind or attitude."

TLL s. v. *paenitet* "i. q. *paenuriae* cuiusdam conscientia *afficit* aliquem dolore.
I potius cum respectu *quantitatis* non satisfacientis, sc. quae *parum*, non satis *habentem*
reddit. . . . **II** potius cum respectu *qualitatis* non satisfacientis, sc. quae reddit *non*
contentum, indignantem, aegre ferentem sim.: **A** -et alicuius *rei vel hominis* displicentis,
de quo non ratio est reddenda. . . . **B** -et alicuius *facti* non iam placentis vel *peccati*,
sc. de quo est *ratio reddenda* (sive sibi ipsi sive aliis, sc. sec. leges, mores, utilitates
sim.; spectat magis minusve ad mutationem animi vel sententiae . . .)" [Keudel, orig.
emph.]; s.v. *paenitentia* "fere i. q. *affectus paenitendi* (sc. sec. usum vocis *paenitet* illic
sub II descriptum) I usu communi [i.e., non Christiano]: **A** respicitur quod *per cul-*
pam nostram, nobis agentibus fit. . . . **1** *errores*, inconsiderate vel immoderate facta
sim. . . . **2** *scelera*, maleficia sim. . . . **B** respicitur quod potius *sine culpa* nostra, nobis
invitis fit (cf. *paenitet* sub IIA): **1** quod *displicet*, incommodat, sim. . . . **2** quod *amissum*
est, desideratur" [Korteweg, orig. emph.].

8. On the etymology see Ernout-Meillet 1959, 474, Walde 1965, 235.

9. Like the taxonomy of *pudor*, this taxonomy is also partial in omitting the finer
distinctions that could be drawn: for example, on the left side, between a state of
affairs generated by another person and one regarded as "natural" or otherwise just
given; or, on the right side, between a state of affairs that results—contrary to my
aims—from an action that in itself was "up to me" and a state of affairs that not only
results from an action that was "up to me" but is also the one I wished to bring about—
mistakenly, I now realize.

10. A sense of the performative dimension presumably underlies development
of the idiom *paenitentiam agere* / "to perform or enact *paenitentia*," attested first in
Valerius Maximus (1. 5 (ext.). 2, 3. 4. 2, 7. 2 (ext.). 1, 11) and thereafter common:
Sen. *Suas.* 6. 11, 7. 10, Curt. 8. 6. 23, Petron. *Sat.* 132. 12, Sen. *Dial.* 6. 20. 4, Plin.
Ep. 7. 10. 3, Quint. *Inst.* 9. 3. 12, *DMin.* 336. 4, Tac. *Dial.* 15. 2, Porph. ad Hor.
Carm. 1. 34. pr., *Dig.* 19. 2. 24. 4, 29. 2. 25. 14 (cf. *paenitentia acta* at *Dig.* 4. 4. 41.
pr., 17. 1. 27. 1, 47. 12. 3. 10).

11. See n. 6.

12. Kenney 1996, 110.

13. Zetzel 1999, 98. The Loeb edition's "I was scornful of our empire" is less
adequate still.

14. For thought expressly along just these lines cf. Plin. *HN* 7. 43 (on the causes
of miscarriage and abortion) "It causes pity and even *pudor* to ponder the fragile
origin of this proudest of animals [viz., the human being], seeing that the smell of
lamps being put out usually causes miscarriage. . . . You who rely on strength of body,
. . . whose thoughts are on dominion, who think yourself a god, swollen with your
success, you could have perished just like *that!*" ("miseret atque etiam pudet
aestimantem quam sit frivola animalium superbissimi origo, cum plerisque abortus
causa odor a lucernarum fiat extinctu. . . . tu qui corporis viribus fidis, . . . tu cuius
<i>mper<a>toria est mens, tu qui te deum credis aliquo successu tumens, tanti
perire potuisti!"). The pity here looks to humans' "fragile origins," the *pudor* to the
mindset of "this proudest of animals," whose false assumptions of grandeur are so
at odds with their precarious origin.

15. In fact, we can think of the gods here as experiencing not only ethically

oriented *paenitentia* at a state of affairs not up to them but also (implicitly) *pudor*, a version of script 3 ("*pudor* by association") discussed in the preceding chapter.

16. Plin. *HN* 35. 157. On the ethics of pottery vs. silver, cf. chapter 5 at n. 50.

17. Similar forms of *paenitentia*, aroused by circumstantial connections to discreditable persons, variously underlie Sall. *Iug.* 104. 5, Livy 9. 18. 10–15, 9. 34. 18, Tac. *Ann.* 11. 23, [Quint.] *DMai.* 9. 13. With the rhetoric of denial in Pliny's remarks, cf. n. 22.

18. For other express desires or attempts to "make someone sorry," see, e.g., Catull. 30. 11–12, Cic. *Clu.* 141, *Sest.* 60, *Fam.* 2. 9. 3, 3. 10. 1, Ov. *Her.* 14. 9–14, Apul. *Met.* 1. 12, 4. 30, 5. 30.

19. For the organization of the *TLL*'s entry on *paenitet*, see n. 7.

20. Cic. *Cat.* 4. 20 "But if at some point that band [sc. the Catilinarians], summoned up by some person's criminal madness, should gain the upper hand over your worthy standing and the commonwealth, I nonetheless shall never, conscript father, feel *paenitentia* at my deeds and policies. For truly, death, which they perhaps threaten, stands ready for all; no one has ever achieved distinction on the scale that you bestowed on me with your honorific decrees" ("quod si aliquando alicuius furore et scelere concitata manus ista plus valuerit quam vestra ac rei publicae dignitas, *me tamen meorum factorum atque consiliorum numquam, patres conscripti, paenitebit*. etenim mors, quam illi fortasse minitantur, omnibus est parata: vitae tantam laudem quanta uos me vestris decretis honestastis nemo est adsecutus. . . . ").

21. Cf. Cic. *Leg. agr.* 2. 26, *Flac.* 104, *Sest.* 95, *Mil.* 83, *Div.* 1. 27, *Fam.* 9. 5. 2 (sim. *Fam.* 7. 3. 1–2), *Att.* 13. 28. 2; cf. also Cic. *Fam.* 10. 23. 1 (Plancus), Livy 28. 39. 1 (sim. 10. 45. 5), Sen. *Dial.* 1. 3. 9, *Ben.* 4. 21. 6, 7. 26. 2, Quint. *DMin.* 270. 1, [Quint.] *DMai.* 3. 2, 16. 9 (sim. 7. 13).

22. This example, read against Plin. *HN* 35. 157 (n. 16), reminds us how close *utilitas* and *honestas* actually stand: both involve the same circumstance (one's connection with one's forebears), with the practical calculations of one's career foregrounded in Horace and embarrassment over one's uncouth ancestors active in the other; of course, neither type of consideration is completely insulated from the other.

23. Cf. Livy 4. 3. 13, 6. 37. 8–11, 7. 25. 1, 10. 7. 6 (plebeian magistrates), Sall. *Iug.* 85. 28 (Marius), Suet. *Vesp.* 1. 1 (ascendancy of the *gens Flavia*), Tac. *Ann.* 11. 24 (naturalization of men from Spain and Gaul). Note that Valerius, at least, covers the preference for mere utility with an ethicizing fig-leaf by making the outcome a result of Tarquinius's "outstanding excellences."

24. There is the related phenomenon whereby the same transaction can evoke different scripts of *pudor* or *invidia* or *fastidium* depending on the person through whose eyes the transaction is viewed (see chapter 2 at nn. 84–86, chapter 4 at n. 45, chapter 5 at n. 81). Though this phenomenon makes itself felt in *paenitentia*, too (e.g., Sen. *Ben.* 7. 26. 2, where the regret attaching to a defaulted debt will be differently constituted for the defaulter and the benefactor), it is—perhaps interestingly— much less common.

25. Plin. *Ep.* 1. 24. Note that our idiom "buyer's remorse" nicely illustrates the lexical fluidity of emotion-talk, since what is typically meant is not "remorse" at all: see the discussion at chapter's end.

26. See, e.g., Caes. *BGall.* 4. 5. 2–3, Cic. *Lig.* 30, *Acad.* 3. 2, Livy 6. 30. 2–4, Val. Max. 7. 2 (ext). 11, Plin. *Ep.* 1. 8. 8, Quint. *DMin.* 267. 1.

27. For hissing and other shaming rituals, see chapter 4 at pp. 96 ff. Caelius reports another hissing fit at *Fam.* 8. 11. 4, indicating that he included such incidents in the digest of urban news he periodically prepared for Cicero even though he thought them trivial (*ineptiae*); Cicero himself plainly tracked the way theater demonstrations reflected his own standing (*QFr.* 2. 15. 2).

28. Curt. 9. 7. 25–26: in the sentence introducing the anecdote—"often a sense of shame can muster less constancy than (awareness of) guilt" ("saepe minus est constantiae in rubore quam in culpa")—Curtius means that if you are in fact guilty but shameless (if you have a "hard face": chapter 2 n. 18), you can more easily maintain your own position (e.g., by ignoring others' discrediting looks) than if you are in fact innocent but have the strong sense of shame that makes you keenly sensitive to being viewed discreditably.

29. On the example of the artist's model, see chapter 2 at n. 110.

30. See at nn. 15–16, on Ov. *Her.* 7. 129–32 and Plin. *HN* 35. 157.

31. Tac. *Hist.* 3. 51 "nam proelio . . . Pompeianus miles fratrem suum, dein cognito facinore se ipsum interfecit, ut Sisenna memorat: tanto acrior apud maiores, sicut virtutibus gloria, ita flagitiis paenitentia fuit."

32. Livy 40. 56. 3 "Antigonum igitur [sc. Perseus] appellat, cui et palam facti parricidii gratia obnoxius erat, et nequa<quam> pudendum aut paenitendum eum regem Macedonibus propter recentem patrui Antigoni gloriam fore censebat." The disjunctive form of "or" (*aut*) that articulates the two emotion-terms does not indicate that the two sentiments are mutually exclusive but stresses the two most salient and distinct facets of them, the wounding self-assessment (*pudet*) and the urge to undo the damage (*paenitet*).

33. The following remarks on remorse, and its distinction from regret, owe most to Rawls 1971, 481; Taylor 1985, 85–107, Wuthnow 1997, Sarat 1999; on representations of remorse in classical Greece, see Cairns 1999.

34. The point is well stressed by Taylor 1985, 100–101.

35. See esp. Tert. *De paen.* 4.

36. Tert. *De paen.* 1, esp. 1. 4–5 "How irrationally they behave in experiencing *paenitentia* is made sufficiently clear by this one fact, that they experience it even in respect of their good deeds: they feel *paenitentia* for good faith, love, lack of duplicity, generosity, patience, and pity, in so far any of these meets with ingratitude, [and] they curse themselves for having done good" ("quam autem in paenitentiae actu inrationabiliter deversentur, vel uno isto satis erit expedire, cum illam etiam in bonis factis suis adhibent: paenitet fidei amoris simplicitatis liberalitatis patientiae misericordiae, prout quid in ingratiam cecidit, semetipsos execrantur quia benefecerint"); in *De beneficiis* Seneca several times touches upon just the sort of *paenitentia* to which Tertullian refers, see, e.g., 1. 1. 4, 4. 21. 6, 5. 1. 3, 6.29. 1, and esp. 7. 26. 2. Of course, emergence of a new, Christian conception of *paenitentia* did not displace the old but just augmented the repertoire: as Jim O'Donnell points out to me (personal communication), when Augustine takes pains to say that "God's *paenitentia* is not consequent on error"—for of course God makes no errors—his statement

reveals an assumption about what typically inspires the feeling that has nothing specifically Christian about it (*Contra adversarium legis et prophetarum* 1. 20. 40 "paenitentia dei non est post errorem"; Scripture makes God's *paenitentia* an issue, for
example, when second thoughts on the creation of humankind arise at Gen. 6. 7
"paenitet enim me fecisse eos").

37. Plin. *Ep.* 9. 21. 1–2 (trans. adapted from Radice). Cf. also Cic. *Tusc.* 4. 79,
Off. 1. 34, Ov. *Pont.* 1. 1. 59–60, Sen. *Controv.* 2. 3. 6, Val. Max. 5. 9. 4, Petron. *Sat.*
107. 4, Quint. *Inst.* 11. 1. 76, *DMin.* 267. 1, 297. 3, Tac. *Ann.* 1. 43, Apul. *Apol.* 94.

38. Cic. *Fam.* 14. 3. 2, quoted and characterized in Chapter 2 at n. 68 (the clause
translated in the text runs "nam mi ante oculos dies noctesque versatur squalor vester
et maeror et infirmitas valetudinis tuae").

39. Thought of this last wrong is more than an epic convention: cf., e.g., Cic.
Sull. 88, on a defendant's fear "lest he leave the blot of so great a crime upon his
family, lest this unhappy boy here be called the son of a conspirator and a criminal
and a traitor" ("ne exstinctor patriae . . . appelletur, ne hanc labem tanti sceleris
in familia relinquat, . . . ne . . . hic miser coniurati et conscelerati et proditoris filius
nominetur") and esp. *Att.* 3. 23. 5, the exiled Cicero's own regret that he is "leaving my poor little boy nothing but *invidia* and the disgrace of my name" ("meum
Ciceronem, cui nihil misello relinquo praeter invidiam et ignominiam nominis
mei").

40. Verg. *Aen.* 10. 870–71 "aestuat ingens / uno in corde pudor mixtoque
insania luctu." In Book 12 the description is repeated and extended (to include
love, courage, and frenzy), to convey Turnus's response to the shaming speech by
Saces, as he turns toward the final encounter with Aeneas: 666–68 "aestuat ingens
/ uno in corde pudor mixtoque insania luctu / et furiis agitatus amor et conscia
virtus."

Chapter 4

1. Cic. *Att.* 5. 19. 3 (trans. adapted from Shackleton Bailey).

2. Arist. *Rhet.* 2. 9 (1386b8–20) "Most nearly opposite to feeling pity (*to elëein*)
is what they call feeling *nemesis* (*to nemesân*); for feeling pain (*to lupeisthai*) at undeserved bad fortune (*anaxiai kakopragiai*) is in some sense opposite to, and derived
from the same character as, feeling pain (*to lupeisthai*) at undeserved good fortune
(*anaxiai eupragiai*). . . . But it might seem that *phthonos* too is opposite to feeling
pity (*to elëein*) in the same way, being close too and even the same as feeling *nemesis*
(*to nemesân*); but it is different. For while *phthonos* too [sc. like *nemesis*] is a pain that
disturbs the mind (*lupê tarachôdês*) and has good fortune (*eupragia*) as its object, it is
not [the good fortune] of an undeserving man (*anaxios*) but of one who is an equal
and like oneself (*isos kai homoios*)"; on the opposition of *phthonos* and *nemesis* see most
recently Konstan 2003. The standard Stoic definition of *phthonos* (*SVF* 3. 413–14,
416 "pain at another's goods [*allotria agatha*]") similarly stresses the "otherness" of
the goods; the one definition of *nemesis* to appear in a Stoic source (the list of *pathê*
attributed to Andronicus of Rhodes, *SVF* 3. 414 "pain at those who prosper

[*epairomenoi*] contrary to what is fitting [*to prosêkon*]") has "unfitting" as a criterion corresponding to Aristotle's "undeserving." At *Tusc.* 4. 16–17 (= *SVF* 3. 415) Cicero follows the Stoic line—"they say that *invidentia* [on the term, see n. 8] is distress experienced because of another's goods" ("invidentiam esse dicunt aegritudinem susceptam propter alterius res secundas")—but then stipulates that the goods in question not be a source of harm to the *invidens*: for someone who feels *dolor* at the goods of a person by whom he himself is harmed cannot rightly be said to *invidere* (". . . res secundas quae nihil noceant invidenti. nam si qui doleat eius rebus secundis a quo ipse laedatur, non recte dicatur invidere . . .": he gives as an example Agamemnon, who could not rightly be said to *invidere* Hector). Ignoring the glide from goods to person as the source of harm, we can see that the stipulation is neither Stoic nor Peripatetic in inspiration: I suggest that this is Cicero's attempt to acknowledge and deal with (largely by setting aside) the specifically Roman phenomenon of "righteous *invidia*," which necessarily had no counterpart in Greek philosophical discourse surrounding *phthonos*; see at n. 16. On Cicero's treatment of specific emotions in this segment of *Tusc.* 4 and its relation to earlier lists of emotions (Stoic vs. Aristotelian) see Graver 2002, 142–45, noting that "it is possible that Cicero has quietly altered some items in his Stoic source to adapt them to the Latin vocabulary of emotion" (144).

 3. On Cicero's use of Greek in the correspondence more generally see Swain 2002, 146–67.

 4. *OLD* invidia ~ae, *f.* [invidus + -ia]. **1** Ill will, spite, indignation; jealousy, envy. [~ *TLL* II, see n. 6]. . . . . **2** (particularly as affecting the object of the feeling) Odium dislike. . . . [~ *TLL* I.A] **3** (aroused against an opponent, as a way of contributing to his defeat). **b** the use of words or actions to arouse this feeling [~ *TLL* I.B].

 5. Jahn 1855 is the classic discussion of the "Evil Eye," and see now Rakoczy 1996.

 6. *TLL* 7. 2:199. 19–206. 14 s.v. *invidia* (K. Stiewe): **I. passive**: invidia ea, qua premimur ab aliis invidentibus: sive i. q. livor sive i. q. indignatio, offensio sim., quae notiones saepe seiungi non possunt **A.** in universum. . . . **B.** peculiariter, praecipue in sermone forensi et rhetorico: invidia petitur adversario sive dictis sive actionibus . . . . **II. active**: invidia ea, qua ipsi aliis invidemus: sive i. q. invidentia (quae notio sub hoc tit. praevalet) sive i. q. indignatio, offensio sim. (sc.in alios). For lexicographical approaches to the *invidia*-family, see also Stiewe 1959, Schaupp 1962, Weische 1966, 92–102, and the next note. On the distinction between "passive" and "active" *invidia*, see also n. 12.

 7. Both lexica have been influenced here by the excellent discussion of Wistrand 1946, to which I also owe much; the broad criticisms of Wistrand developed by Odelstierna 1949 are rightly rejected in *TLL* (indeed, Odelstierna offers a signal example of how the study of emotion-language, when conducted solely at the level of lexical "equivalents," can run badly off the rails). Yet, in suggesting that this adversarial sense arose as a specialized usage of forensic rhetoric and only then percolated through other domains of Roman life and discourse, Wistrand seems to have got the direction of influence just the wrong way around.

8. See Cic. *Tusc.* 3. 20 "If the sage could be liable to distress, then he could be liable to pity, he could be liable to *invidentia*. I didn't say *invidia*, which exists when one is 'looked against' [passive voice]; however, we can rightly derive the term *invidentia* from 'looking against' [active voice], so as to avoid the ambiguous term *invidia*" ("si sapiens in aegritudinem incidere posset, posset etiam in misericordiam, posset in invidentiam. non dixi invidiam, quae tum est cum invidetur; ab invidendo autem invidentia recte dici potest, ut effugiamus ambiguum nomen invidiae"), sim. 4. 16; and cf. *TLL* 7. 2:190. 39–191. 15 s.v. *invidentia*.

9. Presumably the *Thesaurus* means something like this when it says "livor sive . . . indignatio, offensio sim., quae notiones saepe seiungi non possunt."

10. For the *dolor* or *aegritudo* caused by another's advantage or success (*commoda, res secundae*), see, e.g., Cic. *De or.* 2. 209, *Tusc.* 3. 20, 4. 16–17, sim. Ov. *Met.* 2. 780–82, Sen. *Dial.* 6. 19. 6, 11. 9. 3–9.

11. The possibility of "righteous *invidia*" most clearly distinguishes the emotion from Greek thought on *phthonos*: see n. 2, on the unexpected turn that Cicero takes at *Tusc.* 4. 16–17.

12. This fact largely explains the distinction between "active" and "passive" *invidia* noted in antiquity and reproduced in modern lexica (nn. 5 and 7): the "passive" *invidia* to which I am subjected by others (unjustly, of course!) is primarily the *invidia* of scripts 1 and 2; the "active" *invidia* that I feel toward others (with perfect justification, of course!) is primarily the *invidia* of scripts 3 and 4.

13. On both Claggart and Iago see recently Epstein 2003, 47–50. On the envy of mere differential status, with no moral content, see Rawls 1971, 533–34, and Taylor 1988.

14. Ov. *Met.* 2. 780–81 "videt ingratos intabescitque videndo / successus hominum," 791 "quacumque ingreditur, florentia proterit arva." These are symptoms of script-1 thoughts and feelings; but when Invidia poisons Aglauros, it is to make her act out a version of script 2, causing her to feel pain specifically at her sister Herse's goods because they are her sister's: 802–6 "and lest her woes arise from causes diffused over too broad a range, / she sets her sister and her sister's happy / marriage before her eyes . . . / and magnifies it all; galled by this Cecrops' / daughter is gnawed by a distress unseen" ("neve mali causae spatium per latius errent, / germanam ante oculos fortunatumque sororis / coniugium . . . ponit /cunctaque magna facit; quibus inritata dolore / Cecropis occulto mordetur"). Note that at no point in her poisoning by Invidia does Aglauros imply that she wants Herse's goods for herself, much less that the goods ought "rightly" be her own: it is simply the sight of the other's happiness that makes her want to die (812 "saepe mori voluit, ne quicquam tale videret").

15. *Invidia virtutis*: e.g., *Rhet. Her.* 4. 36, Cic. *Cat.* 1. 28–29, *Balb.* 15–16, 18, *Rab. Post.* 48, *Phil.* 8. 29–31, Sall. *Cat.* 3. 2, 37. 3, *Iug.* 10. 2, [Sall.] *Ad Caes.* 2. 8. 7, 2. 13. 7, [Q. Cic.] *Comment. Pet.* 39–40, Hor. *Serm.* 2. 3. 13, *Carm.* 3. 24. 31–32, 4. 8. 24, *Epist.* 2. 1. 12, Nepos *Timol.* 1. 5, *Hann.* 1. 2, Livy 2. 7. 4–8, 6. 11. 3, 8. 31. 2–3, 35. 43. 1, 38. 49. 5, Prop. 3. 1. 21, Phaed. 3. 9, 5 pr. 9, Sen. *Dial.* 7. 19. 2, 8. 8. 2, *Ep.* 74. 4, 79. 13, 87. 34, Mart. 5. 10. 3, Quint. *Inst.* 3. 1. 21, 6. pr. 10, 12. 11. 7, [Quint.] *DMai.* 3. 18, Pliny *Ep.* 1. 8. 6, *Pan.* 14. 5, Tac. *Agr.* 1. 1, *Dial.* 23. 6, *Ann.* 2. 71, Fronto *Princ.*

Hist. 2. 4. *invidia* strikes the "peaks": e.g., Lucr. 5. 1131, Livy 8. 31. 7, 45. 35. 2–9, Ov. *Met.* 2. 792, Vell. Pat. 1. 9. 6, 2. 13. 3, 2. 40. 5, 2. 48. 6, Lucan 1. 70, cf. Cic. *Verr.* 2. 3. 98, Val. Max. 6. 9 (ext.). 5, 8. 1 (damn.). 1, Sen. *Ep.* 94. 73, [Quint.] *DMai.* 13. 2, with Cic. *Att.* 7. 3. 5 cited at chapter 6 n. 3. These scripts of *invidia*-as-*livor* are most relevant to the iconography of *phthonos / invidia* discussed in the excellent survey of Dunbabin and Dickie 1983, and to the species of the emotion on which Barton 1993, 107–75, focuses.

16. Cf. n. 2, on the criteria "undeserving" (*anaxios*) and "contrary to what is fitting" (*para to prosêkon*) in (respectively) the Peripatetic and Stoic conceptions of *nemesis*, and the way in which Cicero acknowledges the double nature of *invidia* at *Tusc.* 4. 17. The present treatment of script 3, especially, improves on the analysis presented in Kaster 2002b and 2003.

17. We could also distinguish scripts 3 and 4 by saying that the former always concerns a violation of distributive justice that is explicitly self-referential, whereas the latter is neither (explicitly) self-referential nor as limited in the kinds of "right" it invokes: see, e.g., Cic. *Inv. rhet.* 1. 22 (~ *Rhet. Her.* 1. 8) on arousing *invidia* against others "if their strength, power, wealth, family relations are put forward for consideration and their use is arrogant and insufferable, so that they might appear to rely more on these [resources] than on [the merits of] their case" ("si vis eorum, potentia, divitiae, cognatio proferentur atque eorum usus arrogans et intolerabilis, ut his rebus magis videantur quam causae suae confidere," sim. Quint. *Inst.* 4. 1. 14 and 6. 1. 14); for a textbook example of arousing just this sort of *invidia*, see Cic. *Flac.* 13, sim. *Mur.* 59–60.

18. On the distinctions among such notions, see, e.g., Rawls 1971, 530–34, with the response in Nozick 1974, 239 n.

19. To take another example: our "jealousy"—in the sense of my begrudging you a good that I have (e.g., my wife) and do not want you to gain because it would cease to be mine—would be a proleptic version of script 3 (my *dolor* at the anticipation of your enjoying a good that I regard as rightfully mine). Note that though this form of the sentiment appears to correspond to the "*phthonos* of the gods" of archaic Greece (see at n. 40), it only rarely appears as Latin *invidia* in any connection.

20. Redfield 1975, 113–19, Cairns 1993, 51–54, Williams 1993, 80–81, cf. Cairns 2003b, 33–38.

21. Williams 1993, 80.

22. Redfield 1975, 116, 117.

23. The present discussion can accordingly be read as a partial correction of the claim made in Kaster 1997, 14 n. 33: "Latin can of course express all the sentiments that *nemesis* comprises, but it has no single term that both embraces them all and forms a reflexive pair with *pudor*: *invidia* perhaps comes closest in semantic range, but it is of far broader application, and its uses have no particular association with *pudor* or *impudentia*."

24. Suet. *Gramm.* 30. 3–5 = Kaster 1995, 37. The anecdote of the botched suit, discussed later, is probably derived from Sen. *Controv.* 7 pr. 6 f. (cf. also Quint. *Inst.* 9. 2. 95).

25. On the technicality see Kaster 1995, 322.

26. Pers. 1. 83–84 "Do you feel no *pudor* at all that you can't ward off danger from [your client's] gray head / without wanting to hear a lukewarm 'nicely done'?" (*"nilne pudet* capiti non posse pericula cano / pellere quin tepidum hoc optes audire "decenter?"").

27. Cato *Agr.* pr. 1–4. On the text, reading *est<o>* at the outset, see most recently Courtney 1999, 50.

28. Cicero *Cat.* 1. 22 "Yet if, struck through by terror at my words, you shall be persuaded to go into exile, I see how great a storm of *invidia* (*tempestas invidiae*) looms over me, if not immediately, when memory of your crimes is still fresh, then for the future"; cf. *Cat.* 1. 28–29, 2. 3, 15, 3. 3, 28–29, *Sull.* 9, 33, *Dom.* 44, *Har. resp.* 61, *Pis.* 72, *Mil.* 82, *Phil.* 3. 18, *Leg.* 3. 26, sim. Sall. *Cat.* 22. 3, 43. 1, Suet. *Jul.* 14. 1.

29. Verg. *Aen.* 10. 846–52, quoted at chapter 3 p. 82.

30. Cf. *Aen.* 11. 539–540, on the Mezentius-like figure of Metabus, father of Camilla, "driven from his realm on account of *invidia* and [i.e., at] his arrogant violence" (*pulsus ob invidiam regno virisque superbas*). Note that Servius gets the nuance more or less right in commenting on the latter case ("DRIVEN ON ACCOUNT OF *INVIDIA* At his cruelty, that is; for there follows the line [586] 'nor would he have surrendered in his ferocity'": "PVLSVS OB INVIDIAM scilicet crudelitatis; nam sequitur 'neque ipse manus feritate dedisset'"). But in the case of Mezentius—whose attack of conscience Servius doggedly refuses to recognize—he says "DRIVEN ON ACCOUNT OF *INVIDIA* He [the poet] says this in extenuation, lest he appear to have been expelled justly" ("PVLSVS OB INVIDIAM excusat, ne merito expulsus esse videatur"), evidently understanding a form of *invidia* corresponding to script 1 or script 2: Servius supposes that the phrase *ob invidiam* is meant to remove the ethical burden from the object of *invidia* and place it by implication on the *invidentes*, who (on this view) behaved unjustly.

31. Mart. 3. 21 "proscriptum famulus servavit fronte notatus. / Non fuit haec domini vita, sed invidia"; cf. Val. Max. 6. 8. 7 (on the escape of Antius Restio, the presumed model for Martial's poem) "[The slave] himself, scarce more than a shadow bearing the imprint of his punishments, judged that salvation was the finest compensation for the man who had punished him so severely, and though it would have been enough, and more than enough, to let his anger go, he even added an act of kindness" ("ipse [sc. servus], nihil aliud quam umbra et imago suppliciorum suorum, maximum esse emolumentum eius a quo tam graviter punitus erat salutem iudicavit, cumque abunde foret iram remittere, adiecit etiam caritatem").

32. On *pudor* and the various ways of "seeing yourself being seen," see chapter 2.

33. Tac. *Ann.* 2. 37–38 is a vivid shaming duel: in seeking a subvention from Tiberius before the full senate, the impoverished senator Hortensius says that he does not aim to put Tiberius on the spot and arouse *invidia* against him (*nec ad invidiam ista sed conciliandae misericordiae refero*), while Tiberius in his reply makes plain that he believes Hortensius intended to do exactly that (. . . *non enim preces sunt istud, sed efflagitatio* . . .), and he returns the favor by referring to Hortensius's "slothfulness" (*ignavia*).

34. Drawing attention to this idiom was a great merit of Wistrand 1946.

35. On the creation of *invidia* in the late Republican *contio*, Pina Polo 1996, 94–126, Morstein-Marx 2004, 237–39, 271–72.

36. The aim of the performance is to "wring a blush from the bitch's iron-hard face" (16–17 *ruborem / ferreo canis exprimamus ore*): on the *os ferreum*, see chapter 2 at n. 18. Cf. Cicero writing in jest to his brother, "Your writing tablets [sc. used for a short note] abusively demanded this letter from me" (*QFr.* 2. 10. 1 *epistulam hanc convicio efflagitarunt codicilli tui*), and the *flagitatio* imagined as shaming a plagiarist at Mart. 1. 52. 8–9 "If you shout this out three or four times, / you'll impose *pudor* on the thief" (*inpones plagiario pudorem*). Usener 1901 is the classic discussion of this form of "folk-justice"; see also Nippel 1995, 39–42, and Lintott 1999, 6–10.

37. Cic. *Fam.* 8. 2. 1 (Caelius), discussed in chapter 3 at n. 27.

38. Creating *invidia* against the gods: in connection with death and mourning, see [Ov.] *Epic. Drusi* 187–90, Ov. *Met.* 4. 543–48, Val. Max. 2. 6. 7, Lucan 2. 28–36, [Sen.] *Herc. Oet.* 1857–62, *Dial.* 6. 17. 7 ("freeing" the gods from *invidia*, in connection with the varied fortune of raising children), Stat. *Silv.* 5. 3. 69–70 (~ 5. 5. 78), *Theb.* 3. 195–98, 9. 722–23, [Quint.] *DMai.* 8. 14, 10. 9; for a failure to protect one's city or holy precincts, see Porph. ad Hor. *Carm.* 1. 2. 35–36, Serv. ad *Aen.* 2. 326, Serv. Dan. ad *Aen.* 2. 365, 2. 602 (Venus "purging" the *invidia* against her), 3. 3; for failures to keep a "bargain," see Juv. 15. 122–23, cf. Ov. *Met.* 7. 603–5, Serv. Dan. ad *Aen.* 4. 204 (on Iarbas); for assorted other "injustices," see Ov. *Am.* 3. 3. 17–18 (*di* generalized), 3. 6. 21–22 (a river in flood), *Rem.* 17–20 (Cupid), *Pont.* 3. 3. 23–28 (Cupid), 3. 6. 15–16 (Augustus, whom Ovid "defends"), Sil. 6. 396–402. For one god creating *invidia* against another, see Ovid *Met.* 5. 512–15 (Ceres before Jupiter, on behalf of Proserpina), Stat. *Theb.* 7. 193–94 (with the preceding speech of Bacchus), Serv. Dan. ad *Aen.* 1. 230, Serv. ad *Aen.* 5. 782, 10. 20 (and passim in this speech). For a god "swayed" by anticipated *invidia*, see Mart. 1. 12 (Fortuna), 7. 47 (Dis), but see also 9. 86 (since even the gods cannot save their favorites from death, they do not merit *invidia*—that is, they do not enjoy the requisite advantage), Stat. *Silv.* 3. 5. 40–42.

39. [Ov.] *Epic. Drusi* 187–90, cf. also the brilliant shaming of personified Nature at Stat. *Silv.* 5. 5. 13 ff., on the death of a foster child the poet had raised as his own.

40. See, e.g., Walcot 1978, 46–49, Lloyd-Jones 1983, 69–70, Bulman 1992, 32–34 (differently Rakoczy 1996, 247–70); Cairns 2003a, 249–50, on the "politics" of divine *phthonos*, complements the points made here.

41. Livy 5. 21. 15 (cf. 5. 27. 12) ~ Val. Max. 1. 5. 2, Livy 30. 30. 30 (Hannibal), Curt. 6. 2. 18–19 (Alexander), 8. 5. 20, 10. 5. 9–11, Sen. *Ep.* 73. 16 (denied), Sil. 7. 57–61, 15. 510–12, Quint. *Inst.* 6 pr. 10.

42. That is, script 1 or script 2 *invidia*, comparable to (Lat.) *livor* or (Gk.) *baskania*: the gods at (e.g.) *Carm. Epigr.* 54. 2–3 (aet. Sull.), Prop. 1. 12. 7–9, Vell. Pat. 1. 10. 4, Lucan 4. 243–45, 9. 64–66, Sil. 4. 397–400, 12. 236–38, 14. 580–84, V. Fl. 2. 375–77, 3. 306–8, Florus 1. 7 (divine *invidia* of this sort is denied at Ov. *Am.* 3. 10. 5–6, Val. Max. 2. 6. 7, Sen. *Ben.* 2. 28. 1–29. 6, Tac. *Germ.* 33. 1); *fatum* or

fata at (e.g.) Ov. *Pont.* 2. 8. 57–60, Sen. *Apoc.* 3. 2, Lucan 1. 70–72, Phaed. 5. 6, Plin. *HN* 35. 92 (sim. 35. 156), Mart. 9. 76. 6–8, 10. 53, 12. 14. 7–8, Stat. *Theb.* 10. 384–85, *Silv.* 2. 1. 120–22, [Quint.] *DMai.* 8. 10. Cf. the abstract *invidia* or personified *Invidia* at Sall. *Iug.* 55. 3, Hor. *Serm.* 2. 1. 74–78, Curt. 4. 5. 1–3, Sen. *Dial.* 6. 13. 3, Stat. *Silv.* 2. 1. 121–22, 2. 6. 68–70, 4. 8. 15–17, 5. 1. 137–38, *Achil.* 1. 143–46, Mart. 5. 6. 3–5, Sil. 17. 187–89, Apul. *Met.* 4. 14, 4. 34, 7. 6 (and the formula "absit Invidia / invidia (verbo)" at Livy 9. 19. 15, 28. 39. 11, 36. 7. 7, Curt. 10. 2. 24, 10. 9. 6). More generally, *invidia Fortunae* (the commonplace quality of the thought is suggested by the prevalence of rhetorical / declamatory texts and texts strongly influenced by declamation): *Rhet. Her.* 4. 44 (in an example), Catull. 64. 169–70, Sall. *Cat.* 58. 21 (speech of Catiline), Verg. *Aen.* 11. 42–44 (cf. Serv. ad *Aen.* 9. 212), Man. 4. 564–65, Lucan 1. 82–84, 4. 503–4, Sen. *Her. F.* 524–25, *Dial.* 6. 16. 6, Plin. *HN* 28. 39, 37. 3, V. Fl. 2. 473–74, Flor. 2. 13, Juv. 15. 93–96, Calp. *Decl.* 42, [Quint.] *DMai.* 6. 8.

43. For Cicero on himself, see *Verr.* 2. 5. 181–82, *Leg. agr.* 2. 103, *Mur.* 17, *Sull.* 23–25 (where Cicero gets much mileage from a patrician opponent's taunting of him as a "foreigner"), *Fam.* 1. 7. 7–8 (sim. [Q. Cic.] *Comment. Petit.* 13), and note *Att.* 4. 5. 2, on the *invidia* felt toward him by Optimate leaders for (among other reasons) owning a villa that had once belonged to the noble Catulus. On other *novi homines*, *Clu.* 69, *Balb.* 18, *Planc.* 60, *Phil.* 9. 4. Cf., on Marius, Sall. *Iug.* 85. 18, Livy *Perioch.* 68, [Quint.] *DMai.* 3. 18; sim. Livy 9. 46. 1–10 (Cn. Flavius Cn. filius scriba), Val. Max. 3. 4. 2 (Tarquinius Priscus), Nep. *Eum.* 7. 1–2.

44. On the "audacity" of striving have-nots stigmatized as "shameful" for disturbing the status quo, see chapter 2 at n. 99.

45. On the place of focalization in appreciating the interplay of the emotions' scripts, see also chapter 2 at nn. 84–86 and chapter 5 at n. 81.

46. So Pliny at *HN* 28. 17: "quid? non et legum ipsarum in duodecim tabulis verba sunt: 'QVI FRVGES EXCANTASSIT,'" cf. Sen. *QNat.* 4. 7 (*XII Tab.* 8. 8a, *FIRA²* 1:55).

47. Weische 1966, 92–102, discusses the relation between *invidia* and *diabolê*.

48. Val. Max. 5. 1. 10 "So too, when Caesar heard of Cato's death, he said that he felt *invidia* for Cato's glory and Cato had felt *invidia* for his own, and he kept Cato's estate intact for his children. And by God, saving Cato [through his clemency] would have been no small part of Caesar's achievements" ("Catonis quoque morte Caesar audita et se illius gloriae invidere et illum suae invidisse dixit patrimoniumque eius liberis ipsius incolume servavit. et hercule divinorum Caesaris operum non parva pars Catonis salus fuisset"). Bloomer 1992, 211–12, contrasts Valerius's report with those in Plutarch (*Cat. min.* 72. 2 = *Caes.* 54. 1) and Cassius Dio (43. 12. 1: cf. n. 50) and rightly notes how this version "slant[s] the episode to Caesar's favor." On Valerius's Caesar more generally, see Wardle 1997.

49. Cf. Val. Max. 4. 2. 4, taking Cicero's coerced "reconciliation" with his enemy Gabinius as evidence of the former's pure *humanitas*. Margaret Graver suggests to me an alternative way to read Caesar's *invidia* as it was understood by Valerius: his Caesar, "being a noble soul, also acknowledges that Cato's death is courageous and

hence glorious. His *invidia* of this victory carries a double meaning, doubly credit-able to himself: he envies Cato his strength of character—making the best of a bad job for himself by at least aspiring to moral excellence—and he also displays his own characteristic magnanimity by wishing that Cato had not gained this bitter *gloria* but had remained alive." Though this richer reading seems to me inconsistent with the way Valerius's mind works, readers who construct a more interesting Valerius could well prefer it; otherwise, it offers a fourth way to understand the *invidia* at issue, through its reception by a reader more perceptive than our source.

50. Cf. Cassius Dio's version, "Caesar said that he was angry (*orgizesthai*) with [Cato] because he *ephthonēse* (had felt *phthonos* for ~ begrudged) Caesar the glory of having spared him"; similarly the direct quote reported by Plutarch, "O Cato, I feel *phthonos* for you at your death, for indeed you felt *phthonos* for me at (the prospect of) my saving you."

Chapter 5

1. In what follows I treat together the noun *fastidium* and its derivatives, the verb *fastidire*, 'to feel or express *fastidium*," and the adj. (adv.) *fastidiosus* (*-e*), "char-acterized by a feeling or expression of *fastidium*" (adv. "in a manner characterized by . . ."); in some instances, the adj. can be read dispositionally ("prone to feeling or expressing . . .": e.g., Plaut. *Mil.* 1233, *Rhet. Her.* 4. 32, Cic. *Brut.* 207, *Rep.* 1. 66–67, Columella *Rust.* 8. 8. 6, Sen. *Ep.* 47. 17, 77. 6), but there seemed no gain in dis-tinguishing these instances from the occurrent usages. Plural forms of the noun (nom.-acc., dat.-abl.) appear to denote something on the order of "feelings of *fas-tidium*." Two-thirds of the plural forms occur in verse, a phenomenon no doubt encouraged by the fact that nom.-acc. pl. *fastidia* (with the gen. sing. form *fastidi*) is the only form of the word readily used in a well-formed hexameter line: the other pl. forms cannot be used at all; the sing. forms in *-ium*, *-ii*, *-io* can be used only if the last syllable is elided before a light syllable with initial short vowel, a form of elision that is vanishingly rare when the elided syllable is itself preceded, as in this case, by a light syllable.

2. In fact, it would be possible to construct a more elaborate taxonomy of *fastidium*-scripts, tracing more specific forms of the response in specific circumstances (such subtypes are implied in some of the analyses that follow); but I judged that entities need not be multiplied beyond necessity, and in this case the distinction most important for the arguments I will make is the one between the two basic forms of *fastidium* I am about to describe. Note too that, whereas the most important dis-tinction in our other taxonomies is based on some aspect of the emotion's cogni-tive content (whether or not a given state of affairs is "up to me," in the case of *pudor* and *paenitentia*; whether or not a judgment of "right" is entailed, in the case of *invidia*), the distinction most important for *fastidium* is based both on the con-tent of the judgment (whether the *fastidium*-inducing entity is absolutely or rela-tively repellent) and on the nature of the judging (whether it is experienced as "reflexive" or "deliberative").

3. I stress that throughout this discussion I am concerned only with the ways in which the relevant experiences are represented: terms like "reflexive" or "autonomic" refer to the modes expressed or implied in the texts, not to my own understanding of the processes involved. I take it as obvious that even emotional reactions I myself might represent as "reflexive"—say, disgust at the thought of eating a cockroach—arise from learned, culture-dependent evaluations; cf. also Introduction n. 16.

4. Because there are well over 400 texts in which the Romans speak of *fastidium*, any attempt to give an exhaustive survey of the evidence would (even if space allowed) produce in readers the sort of *fastidium* typically associated with satiety and *taedium* (see at n. 11).

5. *Fastidium* for food in animals: Cato *Agr.* 103. 1, Varro *Rust.* 2. 5. 15, 3. 7. 6, 3. 9. 21, Columella *Rust.* 6. 6. 1, 6. 8. 1, 2, 6. 34. 1, Plin. *HN* 8. 52, 8. 101, 25. 91, 29. 38, 100; in humans: Cels. *Med.* 2. 3. 3, 2. 4. 4, 2. 7. 35, 2. 8. 5, 23, 3. 6. 11, 4. 14. 1, 4. 22. 3, 4. 23. 3, 6. 6. 17, 7. 3. 1, 7. 26. 5h–i, 8. 4. 12, Columella *Rust.* 10. 1. 1 (178–82), Plin. *HN* 19. 127, 20. 34, 21. 157, 22. 109, 155, 23. 8, 10, 54, 161, 26. 41, 27. 48, 29. 79, 32. 43, 64, cf. Sen. *Ep.* 2. 4, [Quint.] *DMai.* 5. 15. Conditioning: see Columella *Rust.* 8. 5. 23, cf. Plin. *HN* 14. 99.

6. Varro *Rust.* 2. 7. 8 "If there is *fastidium* at mounting, they grind the middle of a squill with water to about the thickness of honey, and then they put it in contact with the seasonal discharge of a mare's genitals and apply [it], from that part of the mare, to the horse's nostrils" ("si fastidium saliendi est, scillae medium conterunt cum aqua ad mellis crassitudinem: tum ea re naturam equae, cum menses ferunt, tangunt; contra ab locis equae nares equi tangunt").

7. Plin. *HN* 8. 188 "arieti naturale agnas fastidire, senectam ovium consectar<i>." Compare the *fastidium* of doves (*columbae*) for filthy coops: Columella *Rust.* 8. 8. 6 "The place . . . should be promptly swept out and cleaned. For the cleaner it is, the happier the bird is seen to be (*tanto laetior avis conspicitur*), and so disposed to *fastidium* is it (*tam fastidiosa est*) that it often conceives a deep dislike for its home and leaves it, if given the opportunity to fly away." As often, the animal is treated anthropomorphically (cf. "happier," *laetior*): the birds' *fastidium* is presumably conceived as comparable to a human's finding repugnant a dwelling filled with excrement (cf. on defecation at the end of this section).

8. Mart. 3. 76. 1–3 "arrigis ad vetulas, fastidis, Basse, puellas / . . . Hic, rogo, non furor est, non haec est mentula demens?"

9. Plin. *HN* 7. 41 "On the tenth day from conception these are the symptoms that a human being has begun to develop: headaches, dizziness and darkening of vision, *fastidium* for food, an upwelling from the stomach (*fastidium in cibis, redundatio stomachi*)." Vergil has the *fastidium* of pregnancy in mind when he tries to coax a smile from the baby of *Eclogue* 4: "Begin to recognize your mother with a smile, little boy, / (ten months have brought your mother long feelings of *fastidium*)" (60–61 "incipe, parve puer, risu cognoscere matrem / (matri longa decem tulerunt fastidia menses)"), to which Serv. Dan. ad loc. adds, "because pregnant women usually suffer feelings of *fastidium* (*fastidia pati*)."

10. Ov. *Pont.* 1. 10. 14 "stabit et in stomacho pondus inerte diu."

11. Hor. *Epist.* 1. 10. 10 "utque sacerdotis fugitivus liba recuso," with Porph. ad loc.: "*Fastidium* for constant [residence in the] city grips me, he says, and I pine for my beloved countryside, just as a priest's fugitive slave who has been accustomed to eat the sacrificial cakes . . . so deeply misses and praises bread because of his enduring *fastidium* at the offerings." This form of aversion-reaction aligns *fastidium* with *taedium*: as an affective discomfort caused by being at the limit of what is physically or psychologically endurable, produced by prolonged or intense exposure to a thing (person, state of affairs) and experienced as some combination of weariness, boredom, or annoyance, *taedium* is often among the constitutive elements of *fastidium*, standing in relation to the ultimate "turning away" as cause to effect. See n. 83, on Ov. *Rem.* 537–42, and cf., e.g., Sen. *Controv.* 10 pr. 1, Sen. *Dial.* 9. 2. 15–3. 1, Quint. *Inst.* 1. 12. 5; on the possible etymological link between *taedium* and *fastidium*, see n. 76.

12. Force-feeding: Varro *Rust.* 3. 9. 21 "Some people stuff them with wheat bread ground up in water, adding in some good, nicely scented wine, and in this way make them fat and tender within twenty days. If they feel *fastidium* from being stuffed with too much food (*si in farciendo nimio cibo fastidiunt*) . . ." (with remedy following), sim. Columella *Rust.* 8. 7. 4–5. *Fastidium* induced by monotony of diet: Columella *Rust.* 7. 3. 20, 8. 10. 4.

13. Cf. the separate subheading devoted to *satietas* at *TLL* s. v. *fastidium*, 6: 314. 12–29. For interesting observations on the role that surfeit plays in our contemporary experience of "disgust," see Miller 1997, 120–27.

14. Cic. *De or.* 3. 98 "difficile enim dictu est, quaenam causa sit, cur ea, quae maxime sensus nostros impellunt voluptate et specie prima acerrime commovent, ab eis celerrime fastidio quodam et satietate abalienemur," cf. ibid. 100, Sen. *Ben.* 7. 2. 2, Plin. *HN* 12. 81.

15. [Quint.] *DMai.* 17. 14 "ex nimia prosperitatis continuatione fastidium."

16. Cic. *Mur.* 21, Suet. *Tib.* 10. 1 (". . . so that by avoiding the *fastidum* aroused by his constant presence he might preserve and even increase his authority by his absence": ". . . ut vitato assiduitatis fastidio auctoritatem absentia tueretur atque etiam augeret"). Along the same lines cf. the declaimer who remarks—with what justice readers can decide for themselves—"*fastidium* is the fate of marriage" ([Quint.] *DMai.* 18. 5 *fastidium fatum est coniugii*).

17. Familiarity: Plin. *HN* pr. 14 (cf. ibid. 15, the difficulty of giving "charm to things subject to *fastidium*," *fastiditis gratiam*). Lists: Plin. *HN* 3. 28 (cf. Serv. ad *G.* 4. 336, on the names of sea-nymphs). Excess information: Plin. *HN* 10. 79, cf. Plin. *Ep.* 2. 5. 4 (seeking advice on revising a speech that he fears is too long), Porph. ad Hor. *Epist.* 1. 20. 7–8 (explaining that a recital must be abbreviated on account of the *fastidium* of the audience, *fastidio poscent<u>m*).

18. Variety of lessons: Quint. *Inst.* 1. 12. 5 "ideo et stilus lectione requiescit et ipsius lectionis taedium vicibus levatur. . . . mutatione recreabitur sicut in cibis, quorum diversitate reficitur stomachus et pluribus minore fastidio alitur." Monotonous habits: Quint. *Inst.* 9. 1. 21 (monotony and *satietas*), 9. 3. 3 (the *fastidium* pro-

duced by *sermo* shaped in the same way every day); sim. *Rhet. Her.* 4. 32 (with n. 14, on the quickly cloying effect of *voluptas*), Cic. *De or.* 3. 193, Tac. *Dial.* 19. 5.

19. I borrow the phrase from a chapter title in Miller 1997. The following few paragraphs only skim the surface of the Roman sense of the noisome and the ways it is constituted.

20. Plin. *HN* 17. 231 (olives), 24. 3 (sweets), 28. 256 (potion); cf. Columella's assurance that bread made of millet can be ingested without *fastidium* if it is eaten before it cools (*Rust.* 2. 9. 19).

21. Plin. *HN* 28. 164 (asses' urine), 12. 91 (wood), 25. 79 (euphorbea).

22. I have found only one text that seems to associate *fastidium* with sounds perceived as repugnant per se: a declaimer's account of Phalaris, "who shut people up in his bronze bulls and set a fire under them so that they would bellow, being incapable of speech. Oh what a wretch, given to *fastidium* in his cruelty: he didn't want to hear [them speak], though he wanted to torture [them]" (Sen. *Controv.* 5. 8. 1 [exc.] "qui inclusos aeneis tauris homines subiectis urebat ignibus, ut mugitum ederent, verba non possent. o hominem in sua crudelitate fastidiosum, qui, cum vellet torquere, tamen nolebat audire!"; the *fastidium* associated with monotonous sound effects in oratory, n. 18, is a different matter). Cf. the remarks of Miller 1997, 82–85, on the small role played by hearing in our construction of disgust today. In noting the absence of "touch-*fastidium*" I am thinking of the response to touching nonhuman objects, e.g., the sorts of slippery, slimy, squishy, or wriggly things that elicit aversion in the average North American today; for *fastidium* produced by contact with certain persons, see at n. 30, on Ov. *Ars am.* 2. 323–24, and n. 85, on Sen. *Clem.* 2. 6. 2.

23. Hor. *Serm.* 2. 4. 78–80 "magna movet stomacho fastidia, seu puer / unctis tractavit calicem manibus, dum furta ligurrit, / sive gravis veteri creterrae limus adhaesit." The second elicitor mentioned straightforwardly concerns the link between visual image and anticipated nosiome ingestion. I take it that the first elicitor has mainly to do with the trace of *greasy* hands, independent of the fact that the hands were those of a slave—mainly, but perhaps not exclusively: see at n. 85, and cf. the reaction of the elder Pliny's highly anthropomorphized elephants, who "hate" mice above all other animals and so experience *fastidium* if they see that a mouse has touched the food in their stalls (*HN* 8. 29).

24. Mart. 13. 17. 1–2 "Ne tibi pallentes moveant fastidia caules, / Nitrata viridis brassica fiat aqua."

25. Cf. the sight-*fastidium* of the gourmand described by Seneca, who has "the serving stand heaped high with birds' breasts (for seeing the whole birds is a cause of *fastidium*)" (*Ep.* 78. 24 "in repositorio . . . pectora avium (totas enim videre fastidium est) congesta ponentur").

26. Plin. *HN* 30. 90 "lacerta viridis cum condimentis, quae fastidium abstergeant, ablatis pedibus ac capite." On the metaphor of *abstergere*, see at n. 44.

27. The same considerations seem to be at work in the directions Pliny gives for the medicinal use of the tortoise at *HN* 32. 118 ("when the feet and head have been cut off and the internal organs removed, the rest of the flesh can be so seasoned as to be edible this side of *fastidium*": "decisis pedibus, capite, cauda et

intestinis exemptis, reliqua carne ita condita, ut citra fastidium sumi possit") and of frogs at *HN* 32. 80 ("individual frogs are boiled down in measures of vinegar, so that one's teeth can be rinsed and the juice kept in the mouth. Should *fastidium* be an obstacle, Sallustius Dionysius used to suspend the frogs by their hind legs, so that the slime from their mouths would drip down into the boiling vinegar— that's from several frogs; to stronger stomachs he gave the frogs to be chewed": "decocuntur et ranae singulae in aceti heminis, ut dentes ita colluantur continea- turque in ore sucus. si fastidium obstaret, suspendebat pedibus posterioribus eas Sallustius Dionysius, ut ex ore virus deflueret in acetum fervens, idque e pluribus ranis; fortioribus stomachis . . . mandendas dabat"). Cf. the seasonings (*blandimenta*) that supposedly would allow the legatee to consume the testator's flesh at Petron. *Sat.* 141. 8, and at n. 33.

28. Cf. the remark at *HN* 29. 140, introducing the discussion of beetles that leads to the passage quoted in the text: "this animal too is among the things that ought to arouse *pudor*, but out of wonder at its nature and at the scrupulous atten- tion of my predecessors, the whole topic should be set forth in this passage" ("hoc quoque animal *inter pudenda est*, sed propter admirationem naturae priscorumque curae totum in hoc loco explicandum"); cf. Seren. Sammon. *Lib. Med.* 48. 899–90, also mingling concern for *pudor* with medicinal bedbugs. On the "*pudor* of decent narration" represented here, see chapter 2 at n. 38, and on the ethical dimension of per se *fastidium*, see n. 33.

29. And if we say "all of the above," what exactly do we mean? Short of actual sensory hallucination, human beings do not smell imagined smells or touch imag- ined touches in the same way that they see imagined sights or hear imagined sounds: the character or style of the imagined repugnance therefore varies from sense to sense.

30. Touch—specifically, ministering to the sick with one's own hands—seems to be the cause of *fastidium* at Ov. *Ars am.* 2. 323–34 (advice to the lover when his be- loved falls ill) "nor let feelings of *fastidium* at the cranky disease come over you, / but let your own hands do what she herself will allow" ("nec tibi morosi veniant fastidia morbi, / perque tuas fiant, quae sinet ipsa, manus"), though the phrase *morosi . . . morbi* might rather (or also) indict the invalid's crankiness as repellent. Old age is apparently the cause of per se *fastidium* at Juv. 10. 201–2 ("so grievous to his wife and children and himself / that he would arouse feelings of *fastidium* in the legacy-hunter Cossus": "usque adeo gravis uxori natisque sibique, / ut captatori moveat fastidia Cosso"; cf. Porph. ad Hor. *Carm.* 3. 14. 25, 4. 13. 1), as is "filth" at [Quint.] *DMai.* 14. 7 ("cui non licet excludere debilitates, fastidire sordes," of a prostitute who cannot afford to refuse infirm clients or feel *fastidium* at dirty ones), though the sense offended is not specified.

31. Respectively, Plaut. *Men.* 166–69; Plin. *HN* 12. 81; Sen. *Ep.* 95. 25; Hor. *Epod.* 12. 1–16, esp. 4–11.

32. Petron. *Sat.* 141. 2, 6–7. In its inspired misanthropy, the stipulation bears comparison with Guy Grand's offer in Terry Southern's *Magic Christian* ([1959] 20–27): on a busy Chicago street corner, passers-by can reap a fortune in cash, if only they will pluck it, one $100 note at a time, from a heated vat of cattle blood, urine, and feces (they do); cf., in turn, Petron. *Sat.* 43. 1, on the person "prepared to

pluck a penny from a dungheap with his teeth." For the *fastidium* of cannibalism, see also Ov. *Ib.* 427–28, [Quint.] *DMai.* 12. 2 (evoking a person who "makes a face full of *fastidium*" because his fellow citizens were compelled by famine to commit cannibalism).

33. Val. Max. 9. 13. 2. The link is found in Plutarch's version of the story, too (*Pomp.* 10. 4), in which Carbo asks leave to empty his bowels only after he sees the sword drawn for his execution.

34. With the last sentence in Valerius's account compare Plin. *HN* 29. 61 and 29. 140, quoted at n. 28, with reference to the "*pudor* of decent narration" remarked in chapter 2.

35. For defecation and *fastidium* see also Sen. *Ep.* 70. 20, discussed at pp. 125–26. On the link between ethics and disgust in contemporary thought see Miller 1997, 179–205, Nussbaum 1999 and 2004, Kolnai 2004 (esp. 62–72, 81–86).

36. See Introduction at pp. 5–6.

37. Apul. *Met.* 10. 7 "se vocasset indignatus fastidio novercae iuvenis, . . . ulciscens iniuriam filii eius mandaverit necem. . . ."

38. Cf., conversely, Juv. 10. 323–29, invoking Phaedra and Hippolytus: having made her offer of illicit sexual intercourse (*stuprum*), Phaedra became the object of Hippolytus's *fastidium*, which arose from his morally serious way of life (*grave propositum*); having borne this *fastidium*, Phaedra herself then felt shame (*erubuit, pudor*), anger (*excanduit*), and hostility (*odio*). On the progression from *fastidium* to *odium*, see immediately following; on the relation between shame and anger, chapter 2 at n. 89.

39. Both taboos, of course, are subject to scripts of *pudor*: the coward is expected to enact one form (script 5), the empty self-promoter another (script 4).

40. Quint. *Inst.* 11. 1. 15 "in primis igitur omnis sui vitiosa iactatio est, eloquentiae tamen in oratore praecipue, adfertque audientibus non fastidium modo sed plerumque etiam odium." For the relation between *fastidium* and *odium*, cf. Porph. ad Hor. *Epist.* 2. 1. 22 "[The phrase *fastidit et odit* is an instance of] amplification; for *odit* is more [forceful vel sim.] than *fastidit*" (*auxesis; plus enim odit quam fastidit*: Brink, on the same passage, quotes Quintilian and translates "not only tedium but often disgust," which I believe misses both *fastidium* and *odium*), and n. 38 (on Juv. 10. 323–29); on conceit (*adrogantia*) at one's eloquence arousing *odium*, see Cic. *Div. Caec.* 36. For the expectation that boasting would arouse *fastidium* in the sense relevant here, cf. Livy 38. 50. 11–12; for boasting (*gloriari*) as the object of *fastidium* see Sen. *Controv.* 4 pr. 2.

41. Quint. *Inst.* 11. 1. 16 "habet enim mens nostra natura sublime quiddam et erectum et inpatiens superioris. . . . at qui se supra modum extollit, premere ac despicere creditur nec tam se maiorem quam minores ceteros facere." The remark makes plain why we should diagnose the *fastidium* here as reflexive, for it is taken to proceed from our very "nature." A deliberative and ranking response, by contrast, would imply that there are some ways of being treated with contempt that you would actually find attractive.

42. Ov. *Pont.* 1. 10. 7, Hor. *Serm.* 2. 4. 78, Petron. *Sat.* 141. 6, Plin. *HN* 32. 43, 80 (associating *fastidium* with indigestion, *cruditas*: cf. Columella *Rust.* 6. 6. 1, Plin. *HN* 26. 41, 27. 48, 29. 79, 32. 43, Porph. ad Hor. *Serm.* 2. 2. 44).

43. Petron. *Sat.* 141. 8 (*operi modo oculos . . .*), cf. Cic. *Fam.* 2. 16. 2 ("nosti enim non modo stomachi mei . . . sed etiam oculorum . . . fastidium").

44. *Fastidium (-ia) movere,* Ov. *Pont.* 1. 10. 7, Hor. *Serm.* 2. 4. 78, Quint. *Inst.* 2. 4. 29, Mart. 13. 17. 1, Juv. 10. 202; *fastidium de-(abs-)tergere,* Columella *Rust.* 8. 10. 5, Plin. *HN* 20. 34, 26. 41, 27. 48, 30. 90: compare the physicality of the metaphors applied to *pudor,* chapter 2 n. 32. "Befall" or "oppress": Plin. *HN* 32. 43 (*fastidium . . . incidat*), Cels. *Med.* 3. 6. 11 (*fastidio urgetur*). Cf. also the physicality of *fastidium* implied by idioms like *fastidium detrahere* (Plin. *HN* 22. 155), *fastidium auferre* (23. 10), *fastidia discutere* (23. 54), *fastidium abigere* (23. 161).

45. I speak of "objects" and "consuming" advisedly, though the referents include "people": the choice is borne out, at least metaphorically, by the evidence to come.

46. Gell. *NA* 15. 8. 2 (birds); Hor. *Serm.* 1. 2. 114–18 (delicacies, but touching as well on all three basic drives, for food, drink, and sex, "When your throat's burning with thirst, you don't demand golden / cups, do you? When you're famished, you don't feel *fastidium* for anything except / peacock and turbot, do you? When your balls are swelling and / there's a slave girl or boy on whom you could fall / straightway, you don't prefer to have them burst, do you?": "num, tibi cum faucis urit sitis, aurea quaeris / pocula? num esuriens fastidis omnia praeter / pavonem rhombumque? tument tibi cum inguina, num, si / ancilla aut verna est praesto puer, impetus in quem / continuo fiat, malis tentigine rumpi?"); *Serm.* 2. 6. 86–87 (town mouse).

47. Juv. 11. 79–81 ". . . holuscula, quae nunc / squalidus in magna fastidit conpede fossor, / qui meminit calidae sapiat quid volva popinae." Cf. the *fastidium* felt by Horace's bailiff toward his master's farm (*Epist.* 1. 14. 1–2): as we subsequently learn, this judgment, too, is informed by a memory of urban pleasures (25–27 "the corner tavern's not at hand / to provide you wine, nor the working-girl-*cum*-flute-player at whose / braying you prance and thump your weight upon the ground": "nec vicina subest vinum praebere taberna / quae possit tibi, nec meretrix tibicina, cuius / ad strepitum salias terrae gravis"); since we also learn that the same man hankered for the country when he was in the city (14), we are to understand that his *fastidium* is that of the man who perpetually measures what he has by the standard of what he thinks he is missing.

48. See, e.g., *Ep.* 110. 12, 119. 15, 123. 2, and at nn. 92–93. After Seneca, who is the undisputed maestro of the emotion in this form, Horace is the author who most often revisits themes of deliberative, ranking *fastidium*—perhaps because, as a freedman's son, he had so often been the object of it himself?

49. A commander less concerned to make his own righteousness the transaction's focus would have done what Pompey did when the king of Iberia sent him a gold couch, table, and throne: refuse to use them himself but convey them to the treasury at Rome (Plut. *Pomp.* 36. 7).

50. The framing of the tale, contrasting the ascetic hero of old with the *fastidium* of lower-class types "today," is identical to that of Juv. 11. 79–81 at n. 47. Compare also the jeremiad of Plin. *HN* 33. 152, and for the ethics of pottery vs. silver, cf. the "regret" denied by Pliny at *HN* 35. 157 (discussed in chapter 3 at n. 16).

51. Cic. *Att.* 2. 1. 1 "quem [sc. librum] tibi ego non essem ausus mittere nisi eum lente ac fastidiose probavissem"; such *fastidium* would be acceptable from intimates as well, cf. the rather labored joke at Plin. *Ep.* 7. 12. 3.

52. Cic. *Brut.* 247 "Gaius Memmius, the son of Lucius, the compleat literary scholar—but in Greek, and of course given to *fastidium* where Latin literature is concerned" ("C. Memmius L. f. perfectus litteris sed Graecis, fastidiosus sane Latinarum"). In principle, one could presumably find *litterae Latinae* repellent per se, but the juxtaposition with *litterae Graecae* shows the standard to which judgment is referred in this case; the concern recurs in other works by Cicero from the same period (*Opt. gen.* 12, 18, *Fin.* 1. 4–5, 10).

53. Plin. *HN* 29. 28 "These points must be made . . . against the senseless opinions of some people who reckon that nothing is useful unless it is expensive. Nor indeed would I doubt that the creatures which will be my subject will inspire *fastidium* in some people—but Vergil had no such feeling in mentioning ants and weevils [*G.* 1. 186] (he didn't have to mention them) . . . , nor did Homer, when he described a naughty house-fly amid the battles of the gods [*Il.* 17. 570], nor did nature in producing such creatures, though she produced human beings too. So let each person set a value on the causes and effects that things have, not on the things themselves" ("haec fuerint dicenda . . . contra attonitas quorundam persuasiones, qui prodesse nisi pretiosa non putant. neque enim dubitaverim aliquis fastidio futura quae dicentur animalia, at non V<e>rgilio fuit nominare formicas nulla necessitate et curculiones . . . , non Homero inter proelia deorum inprobitatem muscae describere, non naturae gignere ista, cum gignat hominem. proinde causas quisque et effectus, non res aestimet"): the concern with ranking judgment is made explicit by *pretiosa . . . putant* and *aestimet.*

54. Cf. Suet. *Aug.* 86. 2 (the emperor's *fastidium* for the novel affectations of Maecenas and the archaism of Tiberius), Sen. *Ep.* 58. 1, 6, Quint. *Inst.* 8. 3. 23 (*fastidium* in respect of word-choice).

55. Plin. *Ep.* 6. 17. 1–5 (trans. adapted from Radice).

56. Their affect was thus a type of script-2 *invidia*, displeasure at the other's good because it is the other's and not your own. Cf. the elder Seneca's characterization of the rhetor Albucius Silus, who "listen[ed] with *fastidium* to those for whom he could feel *invidia*" (*Controv.* 10. 1. 13 *fastidiosus auditor eorum quibus invidere poterat*).

57. So *Rhet. Her.* 4. 52, which offers a veritable catalog of what the elite Roman male mind regarded as the worst faults: "[The rhetorical figure known as] 'concentration' involves bringing together in one place elements scattered throughout the case as a whole, so that the speech is weightier or sharper or more accusatory, like this: 'Is there *any* vice that this terrible man lacks? . . . He has betrayed his

own chastity and set traps for that of others; he is lustful and unrestrained, coarse, and arrogant; he shows no devotion to his parents, no gratitude toward his friends, and only hostility toward his kin; he is defiant toward his superiors, *fastidiosus* toward equals and peers, and cruel toward his inferiors; in short, he is insufferable to all'" ("frequentatio est, cum res tota causa dispersae coguntur in unum locum, quo gravior aut acrior aut criminosior oratio sit, hoc pacto: 'a quo tandem abest iste vitio? . . . Suae pudicitiae proditor est, insidiator alienae; cupidus intemperans, petulans superbus; impius in parentes, ingratus in amicos, infestus cognatis; in superiores contumax, in aequos et pares fastidiosus, in inferiores crudelis; denique in omnis intolerabilis'").

58. Sen. *Dial.* 5. 32. 1 "Aliud in alio nos deterreat: quibusdam timeamus irasci, quibusdam vereamur, quibusdam fastidiamus. Magnam rem sine dubio fecerimus, si servulum infelicem in ergastulum miserimus!"

59. The distinctive self-concern of deliberative *fastidium* is discussed later in the chapter. Common *fastidium* toward slaves is implied, though deprecated, by Val. Max. 3. 3 (ext.). 7 (affirming that virtue is *non fastidioso aditu*, admitting even a slave), sim. Sen. *Ep.* 47. 17 (against the *fastidiosi* who would forbid geniality toward slaves).

60. Cynthia Damon (personal communication) nicely compares the attitude toward "military" *liberti* expressed or implied at Tac. *Hist.* 1. 76. 3 and 3. 12. 3.

61. On the form of *pudor* that Pliny expresses in this emotionally charged letter, see chapter 2 at n. 37.

62. Contrast Pallas's attitude with the proper attitude toward such things that Pliny praises in Trajan, who by deigning to accept lesser honors made plain that he did not reject the greatest honors out of arrogance (*superbia*) and *fastidium* (*Pan.* 55. 4 ". . . ut adpareat non superbia et fastidio te amplissimos honores repudiare, qui minores non dedigneris"). Indeed, Pallas managed to behave not only like a wicked freedman, in getting above himself, but also like a wicked emperor, since his *fastidium* for the honors implied a *fastidium* for the senate that bestowed them: cf. Plin. *Pan.* 24. 5 immediately following in text.

63. On *verecundia* as the emotion guiding behavior in situations marked either by hierarchy or equality, see chapter 1 at nn. 44, 47–48; on the *verecundia* of the *princeps civilis* in particular, see chapter 1 at n. 37.

64. Sen. *Dial.* 2. 18. 2 "Good gods, that a man should hear this, that an emperor should say it, and that license should have reached the point where an emperor would retail his adultery and his *fastidium* to [the woman's] husband, let alone to a consular and a friend!" ("di boni, hoc virum audire, principem scire, et usque eo licentiam pervenisse ut, non dico consulari, non dico amico, sed tantum marito princeps et adulterium suum narret et fastidium!").

65. See Introduction at n. 5.

66. Note the importance of the whole context in judging which process is at issue. Were the lady represented as saying only "because you did not feel *fastidium* at (the thought of) watching me die," we might reasonably treat the episode as an ambiguous case (cf. n. 77), for the text could also mean that Pompeius would be expected to feel an absolute and reflexive revulsion at the prospect of watching her die. But, because being a *hortator vitae* could not plausibly be thought to arouse such

revulsion, and because the narrative as a whole so strongly emphasizes both the lady's concern with status and Pompeius's virtue—and so, by implication, his *intentional* acts—the deliberative-ranking orientation of the thought is plain.

67. Gifts: Sen. *Ben.* 1. 11. 1, 2. 15. 3, 2. 24. 2. Cases at the bar: Quint. *Inst.* 12. 9. 7, and cf. Cic. *Brut.* 207 "Antonius, who was most sought after [as an advocate], was ready when it came to taking cases on; Crassus showed greater *fastidium*, but still he took them on" ("Antonius, qui maxume expetebatur, facilis in causis recipiendis erat; fastidiosior Crassus, sed tamen recipiebat").

68. Curt. 5. 5. 11–12 "Those who rely heavily on the pity of their own [friends and family] fail to recognize how quickly tears [of pity] dry. No one reliably esteems the person for whom he feels *fastidium*: for misfortune is given to complaint, good fortune to arrogance. Thus each person is weighing his own lot when he ponders another's" (" . . . nam qui multum in suorum misericordia ponunt, ignorant, quam celeriter lacrimae inarescant. Nemo fideliter diligit, quem fastidit: nam et calamitas querula est et superba felicitas. Ita suam quisque fortunam in consilio habet, cum de aliena deliberat").

69. Sen. *Ep.* 66. 25 "[If you would esteem the rich or robust man more than the poor or frail one], then given two equally good men you will esteem the one who is well-oiled and perfumed more than the one who is dirty and scruffy; and then you will reach the point where you will esteem the one who is sound and hale in all his limbs more than one who is lame or blind in one eye; and little by little your *fastidium* will reach such a pitch that—given two men who are equally righteous and wise—you will prefer the one with a nice head of curly hair" ("aut si hoc est, magis diliges ex duobus aeque bonis viris nitidum et unctum quam pulverulentum et horrentem; deinde hoc usque pervenies ut magis diligas integrum omnibus membris et inlaesum quam debilem aut luscum; paulatim fastidium tuum illo usque procedet ut ex duobus aeque iustis ac prudentibus comatum et crispulum malis").

70. Cf. Plaut. *Mil.* 1233–35 (Acroteleutium speaks) "That's the fear that makes me wither—because he's given to *fastidium*—/ lest his gaze change his judgment, when he looks at me, / and his own demanding taste reject me at first sight" ("ergo iste metus me macerat, quod ille fastidiosust, / ne oculi eius sententiam mutent, ubi viderit me, / atque eius elegantia meam extemplo speciem spernat").

71. Verg. *Ecl.* 2. 14–19 "Wasn't it better to put up with Amaryllis's pouty snits / and her feelings of haughty *fastidium*? Wasn't it better to put up with Menalcas, / for all he's swarthy while you're snow white? / Oh pretty boy, don't bank too much on complexion: / white privet-blossoms fall neglected, the dark whortleberry gets picked. / I am held in contempt by you, Alexis, and you don't even ask who I am" ("nonne fuit satius tristis Amaryllidis iras / atque superba pati fastidia? nonne Menalcan, / quamvis ille niger, quamvis tu candidus esses? / o formose puer, nimium ne crede colori: / alba ligustra cadunt, uaccinia nigra leguntur. / despectus tibi sum, nec qui sim quaeris, Alexi" (with the reassurance, in the final verse, "You'll find another Alexis, if this one regards you with *fastidium*": 71 "invenies alium, si te hic fastidit, Alexin"). Cf. Tib. 1. 8. 67–70, Ov. *Rem.* 305, 537–42 (discussed in section III), and Porph. ad Hor. *Carm.* 1. 19. 7, 2. 12. 25–26, *Serm.* 1. 2. 105–6. For this kind of *fastidium* in erotic contexts the term *fastus* (cf. n. 76) is preferred, particu-

larly by poets, who doubtless found it metrically more tractable than *fastidium*: first attested at Catull. 55. 14 and especially favored by Propertius (11 instances), it is attested in prose first in the mid-first century CE (Petron. *Sat.* 96. 7, cf. 131. 2–3, Sen. *QNat.* 3. 18. 2–3) and only very rarely thereafter.

72. In 97 I accept *quam super Oenones faciem mirarer? in orbe* as a stopgap for the corrupt text (*quas super Oenonem facies mutarer in orbem*) offered by Stephanus Corallus's edition of 1477, our only witness for *Her.* 16. 39–144; the general sense is anyway clear. *Sed* at the beginning of 99 resumes the narrative interrupted at 89 *interea sero.* . . .

73. For use of *soror* and *frater* as euphemisms for "sexual partner," see *OLD* s. vv. 1d and 3b, respectively.

74. Quint. *Inst.* 11. 3. 80–81 "naribus labrisque non fere quicquam decenter ostendimus, tametsi derisus contemptus fastidium significari solet."

75. Porph. ad Hor. *Serm* 1. 6. 5 "quod vulgo dicunt: 'denasas' [desanas *codd.*], id est, per fastidium quoddam derides." *denasas* (attested at Plaut. *Curc.* 604–5 in the rather different sense "de-nose," used of biting someone's nose off) seems preferable to the MSS's unknown and unintelligible *desanas*.

76. An "absolute and deliberative" reaction (a considered judgment that a person or thing causes *fastidium* per se) is in principle possible, though I have found no obvious cases represented in our texts; a "ranking and reflexive" reaction seems more difficult to conceive. In either case, possible instances of such responses would probably better be analyzed in terms of the "piggy-back" *fastidium*-reactions discussed later. That the range of *fastidium*-reactions is constituted, and limited, as I have described would be consistent with the derivation *fastidium* < *fasti-tidium* (= *fastus* + *taedium*: so *OLD* s. v., after Walde 1965, 1: 460, Ernout and Meillet 1959, 219; differently *TLL* 6: 313. 55–60): if that etymology is correct, *fastidium* would by origin bundle together the deliberative ranking typical of *fastus* (cf. n. 71) and the absolute and autonomic response typical of *taedium* (cf. n. 11). I am grateful to my colleague Joshua Katz for helping me be more respectful of this etymology than I once was.

77. Plin. *HN* 21. 97; cf. the anthropomorphized trees at *HN* 16. 134, some of which fail to flourish when transplanted out of *fastidium* for the new location, whereas others fail out of sheer bloody-mindedness (*contumacia*). The following passages seem to me capable of being read with equal plausibility either way, or as instances of one or another type of ambiguity considered later: Cic. *Pis.* 68, Anon. *Lydia* 134–40, Sen. *Controv.* 2. 1. 21, 2. 5. 5, Sen. *Ben.* 6. 16. 4, *Dial.* 9. 2. 4–5, 12. 7. 10, Plin. *HN* 3. 28, 16. 134–35, 21. 97, Mart. 2. 61, Suet. *Tib.* 49. 1, [Quint.] *DMai.* 8. 6, Serv. ad *G.* 4. 519.

78. For the principle that distinct scripts of a given emotion can be experienced simultaneously, see chapter 2 at pp. 48 ff., chapter 3 at pp. 75 ff., chapter 4 at p. 91.

79. Cf. Suet. *Vesp.* 23 (= Cass. Dio 65. 14. 5), on another smelly source of income: "when his son Titus reproached him for thinking up a way to derive income from urine, [Vespasian] took a coin from the first payment and held it up to his son's nose, asking whether he was offended by the odor; and when Titus said he wasn't, Vespasian said, 'And yet, it's from piss'" ("reprehendenti filio Tito, quod etiam urinae

vectigal commentus esset, pecuniam ex prima pensione admovit ad nares, sciscitans num odore offenderetur; et illo negante: 'atquin,' inquit, 'e lotio est'").

80. If the stench of tanning is taken to be the *cause* of its low social standing relative to soldiering, this would be a case of "piggy-back" ambiguity: see later discussion. For other possible examples of overdetermined *fastidium*, cf. Quint. *DMin.* 306. 18, Apul *Met.* 8. 23.

81. On focalization in cases of *pudor, paenitentia*, and *invidia*, see (respectively) chapter 2 at nn. 84–86, chapter 3 at n. 24, and chapter 4 at n. 85.

82. Quint. *Inst.* 9. 4. 116 "optime . . . de illa iudicant aures, quae plena sentiunt et parum expleta desiderant, . . . et stabilia probant, clauda deprendunt, redundantia ac nimia fastidiunt. ideoque docti rationem componendi intellegunt, etiam indocti voluptatem." Jaap Wisse reminds me that Cicero makes an analogous distinction at *De or.* 3. 100: "gaudy flaws are recognized not only by the judgment of the ears but even more by the judgment of the mind" ("non aurium solum, sed animi iudicio etiam magis infucata vitia noscuntur").

83. As often, the satiety-response finds *taedium* (539) associated with *fastidium* as cause to effect: see n. 11.

84. See n. 71, on the *fastidium* of Verg. *Ecl.* 2; and for the sort of focalization at issue here cf. Mart. 5. 44, on the parasite Dento: lines 1–7 concern the parasite's implied *fastidium* for the speaker's table, which (though once energetically sought) he now ranks lower than another, richer one, whereas lines 8–11, in which Dento is figured as a dog, evoke the (presumably) reflexive *fastidium* that the new host will feel once he recognizes Dento for the sort of creature he is (". . . et maior rapuit canem culina. / iam te, sed cito, cognitum et relictum / cum fastidierit popina dives, / antiquae venies ad ossa cenae"). The levels of narrative complexity add interest to the focalization of *fastidium* at Apul. *Met.* 4. 7 and 5. 28.

85. *Clem.* 1. 21. 4 and 2. 6. 2, respectively; cf., e.g., Curt. 8. 3. 5–6. For the general principle stated in the first sentence of *Clem.* 1. 21. 4, cf. *Dial.* 5. 32. 1 at n. 58.

86. Orwell 1958, 143 (original emphasis).

87. For other likely examples of this piggy-back form, cf. Val. Max. 6. 9. 6, Sen. *Ep.* 58. 32.

88. Varro *Rust.* 3. 9. 18 "gallinae Africanae sunt grandes, variae, gibberae, quas meleagridas appellant Graeci. haec novissimae in triclinium cenantium [*Keil*: genanium *codd.*] introierunt e culina propter fastidium hominum. veneunt propter paenuriam magno."

89. Varro *Rust.* 3. 3. 9–10 ~ Columella *Rust.* 8. 16. 3–4 (concluding that Marcius's oath "had the effect of making many a man's gullet more refined, and taught palates that had become learned and cultivated to feel *fastidium* for the wolf-fish, save one that the Tiber's current had worn out," noting at the end the one variety that was highly valued: "hoc igitur periurium multorum subtiliorem fecit gulam, doctaque et erudita palata fastidire docuit fluvialem lupum, nisi quem Tiberis adverso torrente defetigasset").

90. On this invective, considered from other points of view, see Barton 1993, 114–22, and Edwards 1993, 173–206.

91. Gell. *NA* 6. 16. 6 ". . . repertas esse non per usum vitae necessarium, sed per luxum animi parata atque facilia fastidientis per inprobam satietatis lasciviam."

92. Sen. *Ep.* 90. 18 "nature was not so cruel as to give all other creatures a ready source of livelihood, while leaving human beings unable to live without so many artifices. . . . *We* have made everything difficult for ourselves out of *fastidium* for the things that are ready to hand (*nos omnia nobis difficilia facilium fastidio fecimus*). Our dwellings, the things we use to clothe and care for our bodies, our food, and the things that now have become a big deal [to obtain] were right there in front of us, free and easy to get."

93. Sen. *Ep.* 114. 10 "cum adsuevit animus fastidire quae ex more sunt et illi pro sordidis solita sunt. . . ." On *fastidium* vs. the "natural" cf. also *Ep.* 110. 12, 119. 15, 123. 2, and on Hor. *Serm.* 2. 2. 14–16 at n. 48.

94. Sen. *Dial.* 9. 2. 15 "this [flaw] has driven some men to death, because the aims they set themselves changed and came round again to what they were before and left no room for novelty: life and the world itself came to be objects of *fastidium* for them, there occurred the thought redolent of rotting delicacies: 'how long the same old thing (*quousque eadem*)?'"; cf. ibid. 13. For the tag *quousque eadem?* see also *Ep.* 24. 26, developing a similar theme, and for the image of monotonous "revolution" see *Ep.* 77. 6; cf. *Ep.* 28. 5 and already at Lucr. 3. 1050–75, where similar lessons are presented in terms of the *taedium* characteristic of satiety-reactions.

95. Tac. *Ann.* 11. 26 "iam Messalina facilitate adulteriorum in fastidium versa ad incognitas libidines profluebat."

96. Tac. *Ann.* 11. 36 "ne Trauli quidem Montani equitis Romani defensio recepta est. is modesta iuventa, sed corpore insigni, accitus ultro noctemque intra unam a Messalina proturbatus erat, paribus lasciviis ad cupidinem et fastidia."

97. Sen. *Controv.* 2. 1. 13 (trans. Winterbottom), from a theme in which a rich man, having disowned his three biological sons, attempts to adopt a poor man's son and is opposed by the would-be adoptee. Papirius, a follower of the philosopher Quintus Sextius and a teacher of the younger Seneca, was born ca. 35 BCE. For the building mania of the wealthy as a symptom of weird or unhealthy *fastidium*, cf. also Quint. *DMin.* 337. 13.

98. For other texts that can be read in the same terms, see Columella *Rust.* 12 pr. 9 (on the *fastidium* of effete *matronae* for homespun garments), Sen. *Dial.* 5. 35. 5 (*fastidium* for things that meet one's eyes at home and abroad), Plin. *HN* 19. 137 (on sprout cabbages, the *luxuria* of Apicius, and the chastisement of Tiberius), 33. 152 (on the *fastidium* of women who use silver bidets).

99. On second-order volition and its role in defining a person see Frankfurt 1971, Taylor 1985, 111–12.

100. The phrase is Seneca's, from his diatribe on the sort of people who trade day for night in cultivating a nocturnal way of life, *Ep.* 122. 18: "Still, the chief cause of this disease (*morbus*), it seems to me, is a *fastidium* for the shared way of life (*vitae communis fastidium*). Just as they seek to distinguish themselves from all the rest in their dress, in the refinement of their meals, in the elegance of their carriages, so they want to be set apart even in their ordering of the clock."

101. The instances of "perverse" ambiguity discussed in section III are not

exceptions to this rule, since they involve the per se reactions of the denatured rich, who are by definition not "normal." For other instances where per se *fastidium* is both negatively valued and a trait of persons otherwise deemed "crazy" or depraved, see Sen. *Controv.* 2. 1. 21, 2. 5. 5, 5. 8. 1 (exc.), Mart. 3. 76, Apul. *Met.* 4. 7.

102. Cases in which deliberative, ranking *fastidium* has a positive coloration mostly involve circumstances where status is not seriously at stake (in *fastidium* toward one's own or a friend's writings, see at n. 51; in *fastidium* toward a slave, see at n. 59), or where a "Callimachean" aversion for common poetic inspiration is meant (Hor. *Epist.* 1. 3. 11), or where the exception proves the rule, since the *fastidium* is felt toward external goods that *should* be spurned (Sen. *Controv.* 4 pr. 2, Curt. 4. 1. 16–18, Sen. *Dial.* 1. 6. 5, Tac. *Dial.* 8. 4). The only truly interesting exception is Cicero's characterization of Marcus Pupius Piso Frugi's "honorable and free *fastidium*" at *Brut.* 236 (*ingenuum liberumque fastidium*).

103. Matthew Roller helpfully supplements this thought (personal communication): "this normative state is itself focalized by the status of the subject. So when Juvenal (for example) complains that his superiors are not pretending to be his peers, those superiors would take the view that they are simply maintaining an appropriate hierarchy in the face of inferiors who are pretending to be better than they are. Both views represent the norm . . . , but thanks to the asymmetry of that norm, it leads to social conflict when maintained simultaneously by parties of different status." For a similar point made plain by the focalization of *invidia*, see chapter 4 at p. 101.

104. On this aspect of *invidia* see chapter 4 at n. 12.

105. So the analysis of boasting at Quint. *Inst.* 11. 1. 16, quoted at n. 41.

Chapter 6

1. The exchange underlying this and the next paragraph is preserved at Cic. *Fam.* 15. 5 (Cato)—an exercise in "humbug" (Shackleton Bailey 1972, 124)—and 15. 6 (Cicero); these were preceded by Cicero's long account of his military activities, in which he requested Cato's support and justified the request (15. 4, esp. 11–14). Caelius's letter to Cicero of September 51 (*Fam.* 8. 5. 1) first moots the goal of a triumph; Caelius recounts the lobbying for the *supplicatio* in a letter of April 50 (*Fam.* 8. 11). On Cicero's military ventures see the balanced view of Mitchell 1991, 226–31 (esp. 228); on the correspondence with Cato, see also Wistrand 1979, 3–40, taking a more favorable view of Cato than I can persuade myself to adopt.

2. Equanimity: *Fam.* 2. 15. 1 (to Caelius) and more elaborately *Att.* 7. 1. 7–8 (characterizing Cato's letter as "most agreeable," *iucundissimas litteras*); given the resentment that boils over in the letter about to be quoted, this can plausibly be seen as Cicero's attempt to put the best face on the matter, both for his own sake and for the sake of Atticus, who was Cato's friend (his request—"Forgive me" / *ignosce*— in the next letter is not merely a polite formula). Cicero knew that his resentments over insults, though suppressed, were likely to erupt under provocation: see *Fam.* 1. 9. 20 (on his feeling for the triumvir Crassus).

3. Cic. *Att.* 7. 2. 7 "Cato . . . qui quidem in me turpiter fuit malevolus: dedit integritatis iustitiae clementiae fidei mihi testimonium, quod non quaerebam; quod postulabam negavit. itaque Caesar iis litteris quibus mihi gratulatur et omnia pollicetur quo modo exsultat Catonis in me ingratissimi iniuria! at hic idem Bibulo dierum xx. ignosce mihi, non possum haec ferre nec feram" (Shackleton Bailey, ad loc., is probably correct that the characterization *Catonis . . . ingratissimi* reflects Caesar's phrasing). The length of Bibulus's *supplicatio* pointedly, even mockingly, equated his honor with that won by Caesar in Gaul four years earlier (*BGall.* 4. 38), when Cato had attacked Caesar in the debate over the honor (Plut. *Caes.* 22. 3, *Cat. min.* 51. 1). The "exultant" emotion ascribed to Caesar in *Att.* 7. 2. 7, as already in 7. 1. 7 (*gratulans mihi Caesar de supplicatione triumphat de sententia Catonis*), is a form of gloating, the satisfaction derived from seeing your judgment confirmed—in this case, because your enemy (Cato) has shown himself to be as bad as you think he is—not satisfaction derived from seeing another's (Cicero's) misfortunes (*Schadenfreude* = Gk. *epichairekakia*, cf. *SVF* 3. 400–402; Latin here was as lexically challenged as English, managing nothing more precise than "ill-wishing": Cic. *Tusc.* 4. 20 *malevolentia* as "the pleasure derived from another's misfortune with no advantage to oneself"). Cicero was still irate at what he termed Cato's *invidia* when he wrote to Atticus about two weeks later (7. 3. 5): "By honoring [Bibulus] Cato made plain as day that he feels *invidia* only for those whose prestige is already supreme, or nearly so" ("quem cum ornavit Cato, declaravit iis se solis invidere quibus nihil aut non multum ad dignitatem posset accedere"); this is accordingly the form of *invidia* that "strikes the peaks," see chapter 4 at n. 15.

4. Being denied the *supplicatio* once it was requested would have been an enormous disgrace—all but unprecedented, Cicero claimed, when gloating over his enemy Gabinius's rebuff five years earlier (*Prov. cons.* 14–16, *QFr.* 2. 8. 1, cf. *Pis.* 45)—and Cato cannot have been unaware of that fact. On the connection of this sort of *iniuria* with *pudor*, see chapter 2 at n. 19 and following.

5. Displaying *integritas* is a recurrent theme in the first long letter of advice that Cicero had written, not quite a decade earlier, when his brother governed Asia: *QFr.* 1. 1. 8, 12, 18, 20, 37, 45; cf., e.g., *Sest.* 13 and n. 33, on *QFr.* 1. 1. 19–20.

6. On the contemporary concept of "integrity" sketched here, as it bears on the present discussion, Taylor 1985, McFall 1987, and Halfon 1989 are especially helpful. Beebe 1992 offers a psychological (specifically, Jungian) perspective; Carter 1996, a political-religious protreptic. Though used as an ethical term in English as early as the mid-sixteenth century (*OED*), primarily as a synonym of "innocence" or "honesty," the label appears to have acquired its more inclusive force—associated with interiority, autonomy, and reflection—only later. I have been unable to find a history of the modern concept, which seems a story worth telling; it is sure to be related closely to the stories told in (e.g.) Trilling 1972, Nehamas 1985, Schneewind 1997, and Williams 2002, 172–205.

7. This brief account leaves aside, as not essential to the account of *integritas* I want to give, other questions that our notion of integrity raises, concerning the sort of self that it implies (as opposed, for example, to the sort of self implied by utili-

tarianism) and the basis for thinking it a virtue (given that it is all too obviously possible to serve, reflectively and consistently, principles that are daft or destructive or both: cf. chapter 2 in Halfon 1989). For a clear and concise orientation to such questions, see Diamond 2001.

8. It is perhaps curious that though the term "integrity" has become fully naturalized in English, there is no adjectival form that corresponds straightforwardly to *integer*: English idiom certainly does not describe a "person of integrity" as an "integral" or "integrated person," though "integrated personality" (or the like) is a term of art in some areas of academic and clinical psychology.

9. *Integer intactusque* in Livy 5. 38. 7, 10.14. 20, 10. 27. 9, 10. 36. 3; cf. Curt. 5. 6. 5, Sil. 10. 63–64, Sic. Fl. *De condic. agr.* p. 108. 17 Thulin.

10. *Integer et incorruptus*, e.g., Cic. *Font.* 3, *Nat. D.* 2. 71, Gell. *NA* 7. 5. 8; . . . *et inlibatus*, e.g., Sen. *Dial.* 2. 6. 7, Plin. *Pan.* 25. 1, Fronto *Ep. ad M. Caes.* 1. 2. 2; . . . *et inviolatus*, e.g., Cic. *Verr.* 2. 4. 130, Livy 6. 3. 10, Quint. *DMin.* 275. 5.

11. *Piper integer* in Apicius: 2. 4. 1, 2. 5. 3, 3. 20. 2, 4. 2. 13–14, 6. 8. 13, 7. 7. 1, 8. 7. 1, 8. 7. 14, 9. 4. 2. The *cibi integri* of flat-fish: Columella *Rust.* 8. 17. 11.

12. Respectively, Quint. *Inst.* 8. pr. 19 (*sanguis*), Hor. *Carm.* 1. 26. 6 (*fons*), Columella *Rust.* 12. 20. 7 (*vinum*); cf. Hor. *Serm.* 2. 4. 54, Columella *Rust.* 12. 51. 3 (*sapor*).

13. Plaut. *Truc.* 821 (*filiam meam . . . integram*), Ter. *Hec.* 150 (*integram* [sc. *virginem*]), Catull. 61. 36 (*integrae virgines*, cf. 34. 2 *puellae et pueri integri*), Hor. *Carm.* 3. 4. 70–71 (*integrae . . . Dianae*), sim. Sen. *Controv.* 1. 2. 20, Stat. *Theb.* 7. 366.

14. *Vires integrae et recentes*, or the like (vs. "wearied" or "wounded": *fessi, defatigati, saucii*): e.g., Caes. *BGall.* 3. 4. 2–3, 7. 48. 4, *BCiv.* 3. 94. 2, Anon. *BAfr.* 78. 6, *BAlex.* 26. 2, Livy 26. 45. 6, Frontin. *Str.* 2. 1. 2, Tac. *Hist.* 3. 50, Flor. 1. 36, Gell. *NA* 17. 12. 3.

15. The articles on *integer* and *integritas* in *TLL* use the categories *quantitas* and *qualitas* to get at much the same distinction suggested here, between change-by-subtraction / detriment and change-by-addition / adulteration: *TLL* 7. 1. 2073–79, 2084–87 (Kuhlmann).

16. Pompon. *Chor.* 2. 79 "The Rhône rises not far from the sources of the Ister [= lower Danube] and the Rhine; then after being received by Lake Geneva it maintains its course, passing *integer* through the middle of the lake and emerging with its volume undiminished" ("Rhodanus non longe ab Histri Rhenique fontibus surgit: dein Lemanno lacu acceptus tenet impetum, seque per medium *integer* agens quantus venit egreditur"); Sen. *Ep.* 104. 15 "The Tigris vanishes from sight and then, having followed its course through places unseen, is restored with its size *integra*" ("Tigris eripitur ex oculis et acto per occulta cursu *integrae* magnitudinis redditur"), cf. *Dial.* 6. 17. 3 "having slipped beneath the earth, the river [remains] *integrum* beneath so many seas, saved from mingling with water of lesser quality" (of the spring Arethusa: "inlapsum terris flumen *integrum* subter tot maria et a confusione peioris undae servatum"); Tac. *Hist.* 5. 6 "the Jordan is not received by the open ocean but flows *integer* through one lake, then another, and is captured by a third" ("nec Iordanes pelago accipitur, sed unum atque alterum lacum *integer* perfluit, tertio retinetur").

17. Cic. *Att.* 11. 6. 5 "I cannot but feel pain at [Pompey's] misfortune; for I knew in him a person *integer* and pious and substantial" ("non possum eius casum non dolere; hominem enim integrum et castum et gravem cognovi"); Hor. *Carm.* 1. 22. 1–2 "A person *integer* in his way of life and free of crime / does not need [weapons for his protection]" (*integer vitae scelerisque purus / non eget Mauris iaculis. . . .* , with Ancona 2002); Liv. 9. 46. 13 "From that time the civil community was split in two: one side was maintained by the *integer* populace, which favored and paid its respects to good men, the other by a faction active in the forum" ("ex eo tempore in duas partes discessit civitas; aliud integer populus, fautor et cultor bonorum, aliud forensis factio tenebat. . . ."), 39. 50. 5 "On the following day the *integra* masses, mindful of his former services to the civil community, judged that he ought to be spared, whereas the authors of the rebellion . . . resolved upon his death" ("postero die multitudo quidem integra, memor pristinorum eius in civitatem meritorum, parcendum . . . censebant, defectionis auctores . . . ad necem eius consentiebant").

18. Numbers in parentheses indicate the number of times the particular trait appears; words in parentheses are traits that appear only once.

19. You might, however, be the target of *invidia virtutis*: chapter 4 n. 15. On "civil" *pudor* see chapter 2 at p. 54; on "righteous *invidia*," chapter 4 at pp. 92–96.

20. On *magnitudo animi*, Cic. *Off.* 1. 61–92; on *liberalitas*, *Off.* 1. 42–60 (as the "positive" counterpart of *iustitia*), 2. 52–85. Ethical *integritas* keeps company with *magnitudo animi* only at Cic. *Sest.* 60, where both are attributed to Cato, and with *liberalitas* only at Cic. *Amic.* 19, in a list of the virtues of "good men": "let us reckon that the label 'good men' ought to be applied to those who so conduct themselves that their loyalty, *integritas*, fairness, and generosity win approval, who are without passionate desire, lust, and recklessness, and who display great consistency in their behavior" ("qui ita se gerunt, . . . ut eorum probetur fides, integritas, aequitas, liberalitas, nec sit in eis ulla cupiditas, libido, audacia, sintque magna constantia, . . . hos viros bonos . . . appellandos putemus").

21. On creditable and discreditable "extension" and "retraction" of the self and their relation to *pudor*, see chapter 2 at p. 54.

22. Serv. ad *Aen.* 6. 136 "ergo per ramum virtutes dicit esse sectandas, qui est 'y' litterae imitatio: quem ideo in silvis dicit latere, quia re vera in huius vitae confusione et maiore parte vitiorum virtus et integritas latet."

23. Sall. *Cat.* 54. 2 "Caesar beneficiis ac munificentia magnus habebatur, integritate vitae Cato. ille mansuetudine et misericordia clarus factus, huic severitas dignitatem addiderat. Caesar dando sublevando ignoscundo, Cato nihil largiundo gloriam adeptus est. in altero miseris perfugium erat, in altero malis pernicies. illius facilitas, huius constantia laudabatur."

24. For Cato, beyond the passage of Velleius discussed at n. 34, cf. Cic. *Mur.* 3, *Sest.* 60, *Att.*1. 18. 7, Anon. B*Afr.* 88. 5. With Caesar's traits stressed by Sallust cf., e.g., the small panegyric offered at Cic. *Rab. Post.* 42–44. On Sallust's Cato, reaching by a different route a conclusion similar to that found at the end of this chapter, see also McDonnell 2003, 256–58.

25. Nylan 2003, esp. 116–24 (the description of the "presence" of the man of *cheng*, p. 118, reminds one of nothing so much as Artistotle's "great-spirited man," *megalopsuchos*, at *Eth. Nic.* 4. 3 [1125a 12–16]). My warm thanks to Michael Nylan for discussing with me the similarities and differences between the Chinese and Roman notions.

26. My approach here is shaped by Williams 1985, 1–21 (esp. p. 10), and Long 1996, 156–78, and has benefited more generally from the discussion of "right action" in Hursthouse 1999, 25–42. On being "courageous," in this regard, note the opinion of one authoritative observer that "the most courageous men are generally unconscious of possessing the quality" (William Tecumseh Sherman, quoted in Miller 2000, 43).

27. See *Fam.* 2. 6. 1, quoted and discussed at chapter 2 n. 127.

28. Cic. *Sest.* 48 "cum omnia semper ad dignitatem rettulissem . . . ," cf. ibid. 87 (on Milo) "he gave the most scrupulous thought to the course of action worthy of the commonwealth and of himself, to who he was, to the goals he ought have, and to the compensation he owed his ancestors" ("quid re publica, quid se dignum esset, quis ipse esset, quid sperare, quid maioribus suis reddere deberet, diligentissime cogitabat").

29. This is the same behavior that we have seen Cicero decry as stupid, spineless, and shameful in a letter written much closer to the event, *Fam.* 14. 3. 1–2, already quoted twice in the preceding chapters (chapter 2 at n. 68, chapter 3 at n. 38).

30. Cic. *QFr.* 1. 3. 5 "nunc . . . erige te et confirma, si qua subeunda dimicatio erit. spero . . . tibi et integritatem tuam et amorem in te civitatis et aliquid etiam misericordiam nostri praesidi laturum." Returning to Rome from his governorship of Asia, Quintus was being threatened with prosecution for extortion, the specific conflict (*dimicatio*) to which Cicero refers.

31. Quint. *Inst.* 7. 2. 33 "probi vero mores et ante actae vitae integritas numquam non plurimum profuerint"; cf. *Rhet. Her.* 2. 5, Cic. *Inv. rhet.* 2. 36–37.

32. Hor. *Carm.* 2. 4. 21–24 "bracchia et voltum teretesque suras / integer laudo—fuge suspicari—/ cuius octavum trepidavit aetas / claudere lustrum."

33. Cic. *QFr.* 1. 1. 19–20 "This set of principles and practices can maintain the strictness in rendering judgment that you've applied in those cases from which— I'm not at all sorry to see—we've incurred some grudges. . . . These and all the other very strict measures you've established in your province there are the sort we could not maintain without [displaying] the utmost *integritas*. Accordingly, let the utmost strictness inform your behavior as judge, as long as it is not caused to waver by friendly influence but remains fair" ("haec institutio atque haec disciplina potest sustinere in rebus statuendis et decernendis eam severitatem qua tu in iis rebus usus es ex quibus non nullas simultates cum magna mea laetitia susceptas habemus. . . . haec et cetera plena severitatis quae statuisti in ista provincia non facile sine summa integritate sustineremus. qua re sit summa in iure dicendo severitas, dum modo ea ne varietur gratia sed conservetur aequabilis").

34. Vell. Pat. 2. 45. 5 "Cato brought back to Rome a greater sum of money than had long been expected. And whereas it is unthinkable [i.e., unthinkably presumptuous] that his *integritas* be praised, he could almost be convicted of arrogance, be-

cause when he came up the Tiber with his fleet—though the consuls and the senate and the whole civil community had poured forth to meet him—he did not disembark until he reached the place where the money was supposed to be deposited" ("pecuniam longe sperata maiorem Cato Romam retulit. cuius integritatem laudari nefas est, insolentia paene argui potest quod una cum consulibus ac senatu effusa civitate obviam cum per Tiberim subiret navibus, non ante is egressus est quam ad eum locum peruenit ubi erat exponenda pecunia"). Though Velleius plainly intends to acknowledge Cato's *integritas* as laudable (*integritatem laudari* and *insolentia argui* are contrasting ideas in antithetical clauses), the transmitted text puts the idea rather oddly (lit. "it is unspeakable that [his] *integritas* be praised"): if that is sound, the thought must run along the lines indicated in my text, viz., praising Cato's *integritas* is "unspeakable" because it is presumptuous for a lesser man like the narrator to do so—Cato and his *integritas* are beyond all praise. This is the line taken by Woodman 1983, 70, seeing here an instance of the "inexpressibility *topos*"; yet this seems a particularly strained instance of the commonplace, and one understands the impulse behind Aldus's "cuius integritatem <non> laudari nefas est."

35. The form of Stoic self-scrutiny implicated in Epictetus's conception of *aidôs* produces what we would recognize as reflective integrity, but without the strongly individualistic sense of our concept: see the important discussions of Kamtekar 1998 and Long 2002, 205–30. On the philosophical discourse of "being (true to) yourself," from Panaetius to Plutarch, see Gill 1994: the idea of living a "unified life," essential to our concept of integrity, has an important place in this story, but, as Gill compellingly shows, that unity is conceived as the product of being true to one's nature as a rational animal, not to an inner self—private, unique, autonomous—that is taken to be the real self.

36. On the folktale of virtue unconstrained by law or coercion: Introduction at n. 1.

37. Cic. *Fam.* 15. 6. 1 "et si non modo omnes verum etiam multi Catones essent in civitate nostra, in qua unum exstitisse mirabile est, quem ego currum aut quam lauream cum tua laudatione conferrem?"

BIBLIOGRAPHY

Achard, Guy. 1981. *Pratique rhétorique et idéologie politique dans les discours "Optimates" de Cicéron.* Mnemosyne Supplement 68. Leiden: E. J. Brill.

Allen, Walter, Jr. 1954. Cicero's Conceit. *Transactions of the American Philological Association* 85: 121–44.

Ancona, Ronnie. 2002. The Untouched Self: Sapphic and Catullan Muses in Horace, *Odes* 1. 22. In *Cultivating the Muse: Struggles for Power and Inspiration in Classical Literature,* ed. Efrossini Spentzou and Don Fowler, pp. 161–86. Oxford: Oxford University Press.

Annas, Julia. 1989. Epicurean Emotions. *GRBS* 30: 145–64.

———. 1993. Response. In *Images and Ideologies: Self-Definition in the Hellenistic World,* ed. Anthony Bulloch et al., pp. 354–68 Berkeley: University of California Press.

Barton, Carlin A. 1993. *The Sorrows of the Ancient Romans.* Princeton: Princeton University Press.

———. 2001. *Roman Honor: The Fire in the Bones.* Berkeley: University of California Press.

Beebe, John. 1992. *Integrity in Depth.* College Station, TX: Texas A&M University Press.

Ben Ze'ev, Aharon. 2000. *The Subtlety of Emotions.* Cambridge, MA: MIT Press.

Bloomer, W. Martin. 1992. *Valerius Maximus and the Rhetoric of the New Nobility.* Chapel Hill: University of North Carolina Press.

Braund, Susanna Morton, and Christopher Gill, eds. 1997. *The Passions in Roman Thought and Literature.* Cambridge: Cambridge University Press.

———, and Glenn Most, eds. 2003. *Ancient Anger: Perspectives from Homer to Galen.* Yale Classical Studies volume 32. Cambridge: Cambridge University Press.

Brown, Penelope, and Stephen C. Levinson. 1987. *Politeness: Some Universals in Language Usage.* Studies in Interactional Sociolinguistics 4. Cambridge: Cambridge University Press.

Brunschwig, Jacques, and Martha C. Nussbaum, eds. 1993. *Passions & Perceptions: Studies in Hellenistic Philosophy of Mind.* Cambridge: Cambridge University Press.

Bulman, Patricia. 1992. *Phthonos in Pindar.* University of California Classical Studies, vol. 35. Berkeley: University of California Press.

Cairns, Douglas L. 1993. *AIDŌS: The Psychology and Ethics of Honour and Shame in Ancient Greek Literature.* Oxford: Oxford University Press.

———. 1996. Off With Her AIΔΩΣ: Herodotus 1. 8. 3–4. *Classical Quarterly* 46: 78–83.

———. 1999. Representations of Remorse and Reparation in Classical Greece. In *Remorse and Reparation*, ed. Murray Cox, pp. 171–78. London: Jessica Kingsley Publishers.

———. 2003a. The Politics of Envy: Envy and Equality in Ancient Greece. In *Envy, Spite, and Jealousy: The Rivalrous Emotions in Ancient Greece*, ed. David Konstan and Keith Rutter, pp. 233–52. Edinburgh Leventis Studies 2. Edinburgh: University of Edinburgh Press.

———. 2003b. Ethics, Ethology, Terminology: Iliadic Anger and the Cross-Cultural Study of Emotion. In *Ancient Anger: Perspectives from Homer to Galen*, ed. Susanna Morton Braund and Glenn Most, pp. 11–49. Yale Classical Studies volume 32. Cambridge: Cambridge University Press.

Carter, Stephen L. 1996. *Integrity*. New York: Basic Books.

Clore, Gerald L., and Ortony, Andrew. 2000. Cognition in Emotion: Always, Sometimes, or Never? In *Cognitive Neuroscience of Emotion*, ed. Richard D. Lane and Lynn Nadel, pp. 24–61. Oxford: Oxford University Press.

Cooper, John. 1999. *Reason and Emotion: Essays on Ancient Moral Psychology and Ethical Theory*. Princeton: Princeton University Press.

Corbeill, Anthony. 1996. *Controlling Laughter: Political Humor in the Late Roman Republic*. Princeton: Princeton University Press.

Courtney, Edward. 1999. *Archaic Latin Prose*. American Philological Association: American Classical Studies 42. Atlanta: Scholars Press.

Curran, Leo C. 1978. Rape and Rape Victims in the *Metamorphoses*. *Arethusa* 11: 213–41.

Damasio, Antonio R. 1995. *Descartes' Error: Emotion, Reason, and the Human Brain*. New York: Avon Books.

de Sousa, Ronald. 1987. *The Rationality of Emotion*. Cambridge, MA: MIT Press.

Diamond, Cora. 2001. Integrity. In *Encyclopedia of Ethics*, ed. Lawrence C. Becker and Charlotte B. Becker, 2: 863–66. New York: Routledge.

Donaldson, Ian. 1982. *The Rapes of Lucretia: A Myth and Its Transformations*. Oxford: Oxford University Press.

Dunbabin, Katherine M. D., and Matthew W. Dickie. 1983. Invidia Rumpantur Pectora: The Iconography of Phthonos/Invidia in Graeco-Roman Art. *Jahrbuch für Antike und Christentum* 26: 7–37.

Edwards, Catherine. 1993. *The Politics of Immorality in Ancient Rome*. Cambridge: Cambridge University Press.

Eich, Eric, and Jonathan W. Schooler. 2000. Cognition/Emotion Interactions. In *Cognition and Emotion*, ed. Eric Eich et al., pp. 3–29. Oxford: Oxford University Press.

Ekman, Paul, and Richard J. Davidson, eds. 1994. *The Nature of Emotions: Fundamental Questions*. Oxford: Oxford University Press.

Elster, Jon. 1999. *Alchemies of the Mind: Rationality and the Emotions.* Cambridge: Cambridge University Press.

Epstein, Arnold L. 1984. *The Experience of Shame in Melanesia: An Essay in the Anthropology of Affect.* Occasional paper (Royal Anthropological Institute of Great Britain and Ireland) no. 40. London: Royal Anthropological Institute of Great Britain and Ireland.

Epstein, Joseph. 2003. *Envy.* New York: Oxford University Press.

Ernout, Alfred, and Antoince Meillet. 1959. *Dictionnaire étymologique de la langue latine: Histoire des mots.* 4th edition. Paris: C. Klincksieck.

Fagan, Garrett G. 1999. *Bathing in Public in the Roman World.* Ann Arbor: University of Michigan Press.

Fantham, Elaine. 1991. Stuprum: Public Attitudes and Penalties for Sexual Offences in Republican Rome. *Échos du Monde Classique* 35: 267–91.

Ferrari, Gloria. 2002. *Figures of Speech: Men and Maidens in Ancient Greece.* Chicago: University of Chicago Press.

Fortenbaugh, William W. 2003. *Aristotle on Emotion: A Contribution to Philosophical Psychology, Rhetoric, Poetics, Politics, and Ethics.* 2nd edition. London: Duckworth.

Fraenkel, Eduard. 1957. *Horace.* Oxford: Oxford University Press.

Frankfurt, Harry. 1971. Freedom of the Will and the Concept of a Person. *Journal of Philosophy* 68: 5–20.

Frede, Michael. 1986. The Stoic Doctrine of the Affections of the Soul. In *The Norms of Nature: Studies in Hellenistic Ethics,* ed. Malcolm Schofield and Gisela Striker, pp. 93–110. Cambridge: Cambridge University Press.

Geldner, Harald N. 1977. *Lucretia und Verginia. Studien zur Virtus der Frau in der römischen und griechischen Literatur.* Mainz (s.n.).

Geuss, Raymond. 2001. *Public Goods, Private Goods.* Princeton: Princeton University Press.

Gilbert, Paul, and Bernice Andrew, eds. 1998. *Shame: Interpersonal Behavior, Psychopathology, and Culture.* Oxford: Oxford University Press.

Gill, Christopher. 1994. Peace of Mind and Being Yourself: Panaetius to Plutarch. *Aufstieg und Niedergand der römischen Welt* II 36.7: 4599–4640.

———. 1996. Ancient Passions: Theories and Cultural Styles. In *The Literary Portrayal of Passion Through the Ages: An Interdisciplinary View,* ed. Keith Cameron, pp. 1–10. Lewiston-Queenston-Lampeter: Edwin Mellen Press.

Gilmore, David Denny. 1987. Introduction: The Shame of Dishonor. In *Honor and Shame and the Unity of the Mediterranean,* ed. David Denny Gilmore, pp. 2–21. Special Publication of the American Anthropological Association, no. 22. Washington, DC: American Anthropological Association.

Gleason, Maud. 1995. *Making Men: Sophists and Self-Presentation in Ancient Rome.* Princeton: Princeton University Press.

Goffman, Erving. 1959. *The Presentation of Self in Everyday Life.* New York: Doubleday.

———. 1963a. *Behavior in Public Places: Notes on the Social Organization of Gatherings.* New York: Free Press.

———. 1963b. *Stigma: Notes on the Management of Spoiled Identity*. New York: Simon and Schuster.

———. 1967. *Interaction Ritual: Essays on Face-to-Face Behavior*. New York: Pantheon Books.

Goldie, Peter. 2002. *The Emotions: A Philosophical Exploration*. Oxford: Oxford University Press.

Gordon, Robert M. 1987. *The Structure of Emotions: Investigations in Cognitive Philosophy*. Cambridge: Cambridge University Press.

Graver, Margaret, ed. 2002. *Cicero on the Emotions: "Tusculan Disputations" 3 and 4*. Chicago: University of Chicago Press.

Gunderson, Erik. 2000. *Staging Masculinity: The Rhetoric of Performance in the Roman World*. Ann Arbor: University of Michigan Press.

Haidt, Jonathan. 2003. The Moral Emotions. In *Handbook of Affective Sciences*, ed. Richard J. Davidson, Richard J., Klaus R. Scherer, and H. Hill Goldsmith, pp. 852–70. Oxford: Oxford University Press.

Halfon, Mark S. 1989. *Integrity: A Philosophical Inquiry*. Philadelphia: Temple University Press.

Harré, Rom. 1990. Embarrassment: A Conceptual Analysis. In *Shyness and Embarrassment*, ed. W. Ray Crozier, pp. 188–204. Cambridge: Cambridge University Press.

———, and Robert Finlay-Jones. 1986. Emotion Talk across Times. In *The Social Construction of Emotions*, ed. Rom Harré, pp. 220–33. Oxford: Oxford University Press.

Harris, William V. 2001. *Restraining Rage: The Ideology of Anger Control in Classical Antquity*. Cambridge, MA: Harvard University Press.

Heelas, Paul. 1986. Emotion Talk across Cultures. In *The Social Construction of Emotions*, ed. Rom Harré, pp. 234–66. Oxford: Oxford University Press.

Hemelrijk, Emily A. 2004. Masculinity and Femininity in the *Laudatio Turiae*. *Classical Quarterly* 54: 185-97.

Herzfeld, Michael. 1980. Honour and Shame: Problems in the Comparative Analysis of Moral Systems. *Man* 15: 339–51.

Hursthouse, Rosalind. 1999. *On Virtue Ethics*. Oxford: Oxford University Press.

Jahn, Otto. 1855. Über den Aberglauben des bösen Blicks bei den Alten. *Berichte über die Verhandlungen der königlich sächsischen Gesselschaft der Wissenschaften zu Leipzig*, philologisch-historische Classe 7: 28–110.

Johnson, Walter R. 1996–97. The Rapes of Callisto. *Classical Journal* 92: 9–24.

Johnson-Laird, P. N., and Keith Oatley. 1989. The Language of Emotions: An Analysis of a Semantic Field. *Cognition and Emotion* 3. 2: 81–123.

Joshel, Sandra R. 1992. The Body Female and the Body Politic: Livy's Lucretia and Verginia. In *Pornography and Representation in Greece and Rome*, ed. Amy Richlin, pp. 112–30. Oxford: Oxford University Press.

Kahan, Dan. 1996. What Do Alternative Sanctions Mean? *University of Chicago Law Review* 63: 591–653.

———. 1999. The Progressive Appropriation of Disgust. In *The Passions of Law*, ed. Susan A. Bandes, pp. 63–79. New York: New York University Press.

————, and Martha Nussbaum. 1996. Two Conceptions of Emotion in Criminal Law. *Columbia Law Review* 96: 269–374.

Kamtekar, Rachana. 1998. AIΔΩΣ in Epictetus. *Classical Philology* 93: 136–60.

Kaster, Robert A., ed. 1995. *Suetonius: "De grammaticis et rhetoribus."* Oxford: Oxford University Press.

————. 1997. The Shame of the Romans. *Transactions of the American Philological Association* 127: 1–19.

————. 2001. The Dynamics of *Fastidium* and the Ideology of Disgust. *Transactions of the American Philological Association* 113: 143–89.

————. 2002a. The Taxonomy of Patience, or When is *patientia* not a Virtue? *Classical Philology* 97: 131–42.

————. 2002b. *Invidia* and the End of *Georgics* 1. *Phoenix* 56: 275–95.

————. 2003. *Invidia, nemesis, phthonos*, and the Roman Emotional Economy. In *Envy, Spite, and Jealousy: The Rivalrous Emotions in Ancient Greece*, ed. David Konstan and Keith Rutter, pp. 253–76. Edinburgh Leventis Studies 2. Edinburgh: University of Edinburgh Press.

Katz, Jack. 1999. *How Emotions Work*. Chicago: University of Chicago Press.

Kenney, E. J., ed. 1996. *Ovid: "Heroides" XVI–XXI*. Cambridge: Cambridge University Press.

Kolnai, Aurel. 2004. *On Disgust*. Edited and with an introduction by Barry Smith and Carolyn Korsmeyer. Chicago: Open Court.

Konstan, David. 2001. *Pity Transformed*. London: Duckworth.

————. 2003. *Nemesis* and *Phthonos*. In *Gestures: Essays in Ancient History, Literature, and Philosophy Presented to Alan J. Boegehold*, ed. G. W. Bakewell and J. P. Sickinger, pp. 74–87. Oxford: Oxbow Books.

Lakoff, George, and Zoltan Kövecses. 1987. The Cognitive Model of Anger Inherent in American English. In *Cultural Models in Language and Thought*, ed. Dorothy Holland and Naomi Quinn, pp. 195–221. Cambridge: Cambridge University Press.

Landman, Janet. 1993. *Regret: The Persistence of the Possible*. Oxford: Oxford University Press.

Langen, Peter. 1880. *Beiträge zur Kritik und Erklärung des Plautus*. Leipzig: Teubner.

Langlands, Rebecca. 2000. Gender and Exemplarity in Valerius Maximus. DPhil. diss., University of Cambridge.

Lattimore, Richmond. 1942. *Themes in Greek and Latin Epitaphs*. Urbana: University of Illinois Press.

Lazarus, Richard S. 1984. On the Primacy of Cognition. *American Psychologist* 39: 124–29.

————. 1991. *Emotion and Adaptation*. Oxford: Oxford University Press.

Ledoux, Joseph. 2000. Cognitive-Emotional Interactions: Listen to the Brain. In *Cognitive Neuroscience of Emotion*, ed. Richard D. Lane and Lynn Nadel, pp. 129–55. Oxford: Oxford University Press.

Lewis, Michael. 1992. *Shame: The Exposed Self*. New York: Free Press.

Lintott, Andrew. 1999. *Violence in Republican Rome*. 2nd edition. Oxford: Oxford University Press.

Lloyd-Jones, Hugh. 1983. *The Justice of Zeus*. Revised edition. Berkeley: University of California Press.

Long, Anthony A. 1996. *Stoic Studies*. Cambridge: Cambridge University Press.

————. 2002. *Epictetus*. Oxford: Oxford University Press.

Lossmann, Friederich. 1962. *Cicero und Caesar im Jahre 54: Studien zur Theorie und Praxis der römischen Freundschaft*. Hermes Einzelschriften 17. Wiesbaden: F. Steiner.

Lutz, Cora. 1988. *Unnatural Emotions: Everyday Sentiments on a Micronesian Atoll and Their Challenge to Western Theory*. Chicago: University of Chicago Press.

Lyons, William E. 1980. *Emotion*. Cambridge: Cambridge University Press.

Massaro, Toni M. 1999. Show (Some) Emotions. In *The Passions of Law*, ed. Susan A. Bandes, pp. 80–120. New York: New York University Press.

McDonnell, Myles. 2003. Roman Men and Greek Virtue. In *Andreia: Studies in Manliness and Courage in Classical Antiquity*, ed. Ralph M. Rosen and Ineke Sluiter, pp. 235–61. Mnemosyne Supplement 238. Leiden: E. J. Brill.

McFall, Lynne. 1987. Integrity. *Ethics* 98: 5–20.

Mesquita, Batja, and Nico H. Frijda. 1992. Cultural Variations in Emotions: A Review. *Psychological Bulletin* 112: 179–204.

Miller, William Ian. 1993. *Humiliation: And Other Essays on Honor, Social Discomfort, and Violence*. Ithaca: Cornell University Press.

————. 1995. Deep Inner Lives, Individualism, and People of Honour. *History of Political Thought* 16: 190–207.

————. 1997. *The Anatomy of Disgust*. Cambridge, MA: Harvard University Press.

————. 2000. *The Mystery of Courage*. Cambridge, MA: Harvard University Press.

Mitchell, Thomas N. 1991. *Cicero: The Senior Statesman*. New Haven: Yale University Press.

Moore, Timothy. 1989. *Artistry and Ideology: Livy's Vocabulary of Virtue*. Beiträge zur klassichen Philologie 192. Frankfurt am Main: Athenäum.

Morrison, Andrew P. 1989. *Shame: The Underside of Narcissism*. Hillsdale, NJ: Analytic Press.

Morstein-Marx, Robert. 2004. *Mass Oratory and Political Power in the Late Roman Republic*. Cambridge: Cambridge University Press.

Moses, Diana C. 1993. Livy's Lucretia and the Validity of Coerced Consent in Roman law. In *Consent and Coercion to Sex and Marriage in Ancient and Medieval Societies*, ed. Angeliki E. Laiou, pp. 39–81. Washington, D C: Dumbarton Oaks.

Mueller, Hans-Friedrich Otto. 1998. "Vita," "pudicitia," "libertas": Juno, Gender, and Religious Politics in Valerius Maximus. *Transactions of the American Philological Association* 128: 221–263.

Nehamas, Alexander. 1985. *Nietzsche: Life as Literature*. Cambridge, MA: Harvard University Press.

Nippel, Wilfried. 1995. *Public Order in Ancient Rome*. Cambridge: Cambridge University Press.

Nozick, Robert. 1974. *Anarchy, State, and Utopia*. New York: Basic Books.

Nussbaum, Martha C. 1994. *The Therapy of Desire: Theory and Practice in Hellenistic Ethics*. Princeton: Princeton University Press.

————. 1999. "Secret Sewers of Vice": Disgust, Bodies, and the Law. In *The Passions of Law*, ed. Susan A. Bandes, pp. 19–62. New York: New York University Press.

————. 2001. *Upheavals of Thought: The Intelligence of Emotions*. Cambridge: Cambridge University Press.

————. 2004. *Hiding from Humanity: Disgust, Shame, and the Law*. Princeton: Princeton University Press.

Nylan, Michael. 2003. On the Politics of Pleasure. *Asia Minor* 26: 73–124.

Odelstierna, Ingrid. 1949. *Invidia, Invidiosus, and Invidiam facere: A Semantic Investigation*. Uppsala Universitets Årskrifft 1949: 10. Uppsala: Lundequistska Bokhandeln.

Oliensis, Ellen. 1998. *Horace and the Rhetoric of Authority*. Cambridge: Cambridge University Press.

Ortony, Andrew, Gerald L. Clore, and Allan Collins. 1988. *The Cognitive Structure of Emotions*. Cambridge: Cambridge University Press.

Orwell, George. 1958. *The Road to Wigan Pier*. New York: Harcourt Brace.

Piers, Gerhart, and Milton B. Singer. 1953. *Shame and Guilt: A Psychoanalytic and a Cultural Study*. American Lecture Series no. 171. Springfield, IL: Thomas Press.

Pina Polo, Francisco. 1996. *Contra arma verbis: Der Redner vor dem Volk in der späten römischen Republik*. Heidelberger althistorische Beiträge und epigraphische Studien, 22. Stuttgart: Franz Steiner.

Raine, Nancy Venable. 1998. *After Silence: Rape and My Journey Back*. New York: Crown.

Rakoczy, Thomas. 1996. *Böser Blick, Macht des Auges und Neid der Götter: Eine Untersuchung zur Kraft des Blickes in der griechischen Literatur*. Tübingen: Narr.

Rawls, John. 1971. *A Theory of Justice*. Cambridge, MA: Harvard University Press.

Redfield, James R. 1975. *Nature and Culture in the "Iliad": The Tragedy of Hector*. Chicago: University of Chicago Press.

Richlin, Amy. 1992a. *The Garden of Priapus: Sexuality and Aggression in Roman Humor*. Revised edition. Oxford: Oxford University Press.

Richlin, Amy. 1992b. Reading Ovid's Rapes. In *Pornography and Representation in Greece and Rome*, ed. Amy Richlin, pp. 158–79. Oxford: Oxford University Press.

Ricks, Christopher. 1974. *Keats and Embarrassment*. Oxford: Oxford University Press.

Roller, Matthew. 2001. *Constructing Autocracy: Aristocrats and Emperors in Julio-Claudian Rome*. Princeton: Princeton University Press.

Rorty, Amélie Oksenberg. 1980. Agent Regret. In *Explaining Emotions*, ed. Amélie Oksenberg Rorty, pp. 489–506. Berkeley: University of California Press.

Rosaldo, Maria Z. 1984. Toward an Anthropology of Self and Feeling. In *Culture Theory: Issues on Mind, Self, and Emotion*, ed. Richard A. Shweder and Robert A. LeVine, pp. 137–157. Cambridge: Cambridge University Press.

Roseman, Ira J., and Craig A. Smith. 2001. Appraisal Theory: Overview, Assumptions, Varieties, Controversies. In *Appraisal Processes in Emotion: Theory, Methods, Research*, ed. Klaus R. Scherer, Angela Schorr, and Tom Johnstone, pp. 3–19. Oxford: Oxford University Press.

Rousselle, Aline. 1988. *Porneia: On Desire and the Body in Antiquity*, trans. Felicia Pheasant. Oxford: Basil Blackwell.

Russell, James A., and Ghyslaine Lemay. 2000. Emotion Concepts. In *Handbook of Emotions*, ed. Michael Lewis and Jeannette M. Haviland-Jones, pp. 491–503. 2nd edition. New York: Guilford.

Sarat, Austin. 1999. Remorse, Responsibility, and Criminal Punishment: An Analysis of Popular Culture. In *The Passions of Law*, ed. Susan A. Bandes, pp. 168–90. New York: New York University Press.

Schaupp, Manfred. 1962. Invidia: Eine Begriffsuntersuchung. Diss. Universty of Freiburg.

Scheff, Thomas J. 2000. Shame and the Social Bond: A Sociological Theory. *Sociological Theory* 18: 84–98.

Scheler, Max. 1957. Über Scham und Schamgefühle. In *Schriften aus dem Nachlass: Zur Ethik und Bekenntnisslehre*, 1: 65–154. Bern: Francke.

Schneewind, Joseph. 1997. *The Invention of Autonomy: A History of Modern Moral Philosophy*. Cambridge: Cambridge University Press.

Shackleton Bailey, David Roy. 1972. *Cicero*. New York: Scribner

Shweder, Richard A. 1993. The Cultural Psychology of the Emotions. In *Handbook of Emotions*, ed. Michael Lewis and Jeannette M. Haviland, pp. 17–31. New York: Guilford.

———, and Jonathan Haidt. 2000. The Cultural Psychology of the Emotions: Ancient and New. In *Handbook of Emotions*, ed. Michael Lewis and Jeannette M. Haviland-Jones, pp. 397–414. 2nd edition. New York: Guilford.

Sihvola, Juha, and Troels Engberg-Pedersen, eds. 1998. *The Emotions in Hellenistic Philosophy*. Dordrecht: Kluwer Academic.

Snowden, Frank M., Jr. 1970. *Black in Antiquity*. Cambridge, MA: Harvard University Press.

Solomon, Robert C. 1973. Emotions and Choice. *Review of Metaphysics* 27: 20–41.

Sorabji, Richard. 2000. *Emotion and Peace of Mind: From Stoic Agitation to Christian Temptation*. Oxford: Oxford University Press.

Southern, Terry. 1959. *The Magic Christian*. New York: Random House.

Stewart, Frank Henderson. 1994. *Honor*. Chicago: University of Chicago Press.

Stiewe, Klaus 1959. Beiträge aus der Thesaurus-Arbeit XI: invidia, invideo. *Museum Helveticum* 16: 162–71.

Swain, Simon. 2002. Bilingualism in Cicero? The Evidence of Code-Switching. In *Bilingualism in Ancient Society: Language Contact and the Written Word*, ed. J. N. Adams, Mark Janse, and Simon Swain, pp. 128–67. Oxford: Oxford University Press.

Tangney, June P., and Ronda L. Dearing. 2002. *Shame and Guilt*. New York: Guilford.

Taylor, Gabriele. 1985. *Pride, Shame, and Guilt: Emotions of Self-Assessment*. Oxford: Oxford University Press.

———. 1988. Envy and Jealousy. *Midwest Studies in Philosophy* 13: 233–49.

Thome, Gabrielle. 2000. *Zentrale Wertvorstellungen der Römer I*. Bamberg: C. C. Buchners Verlag.

Thompson, Effie Freeman. 1908. *ΜΕΤΑΝΟΕΩ and ΜΕΤΑΜΕΛΕΙ in Greek Literature until 100 A.D.* Chicago: University of Chicago Press.

Tomkins, Silvan S. 1995. *Exploring Affect: The Selected Writings of Silvan S. Tomkins.* Ed. E. Virginia Demos. Cambridge: Cambridge University Press.

Toohey, Peter. 1990. *Acedia* in Late Classical Antiquity. *Illinois Classical Studies* 15: 339–52.

———. 2004. *Melancholy, Love, and Time: Boundaries of the Self in Ancient Literature.* Ann Arbor: University of Michigan Press.

Treggiari, Susan. 1991. *Roman Marriage: Iusti Coniuges from the Time of Cicero to the Time of Ulpian.* Oxford: Oxford University Press.

Trilling, Lionel. 1972. *Sincerity and Authenticity.* Cambridge, MA: Harvard University Press.

Usener, Hermann. 1901. Italisches Volksjustiz. *Rheinisches Museum* 56: 1–28.

Walcot, Peter. 1978. *Envy and the Greeks: A Study of Human Behaviour.* Warminster: Aris & Philips.

Walde, Alois. 1965. *Lateinisches etymologisches Wörterbuch.* 4th edition, by J. B. Hofmann, 2 vols. Heidelberg: C. Winter.

Wardle, D. 1997. "The Sainted Julius": Valerius Maximus and the Dictator. *Classical Philology.* 92: 323-45.

———, ed. 1998. *Valerius Maximus: "Memorable Deeds and Sayings" Book I.* Oxford: Oxford University Press.

Weische, Alfons. 1966. *Studien zur politischen Sprache der römischen Republik.* Orbis Antiquus 24. Münster: Aschendorff.

Wierzbicka, Anna. 1992. *Semantics, Culture, and Cognition: Universal Human Concepts in Culture-Specific Configurations.* New York: Oxford University Press.

Williams, Bernard. 1981. *Moral Luck.* Cambridge: Cambridge University Press.

———. 1985. *Ethics and the Limits of Philosophy.* Cambridge: Cambridge University Press.

———. 1993. *Shame and Necessity.* Berkeley: University of California Press.

———. 2002. *Truth and Truthfulness.* Princeton: Princeton University Press.

Wirszubski, Chaim. 1961. *Audaces*: A Study in Political Phraseology. *Journal of Roman Studies* 51: 12–22.

Wistrand, Erik. 1946. Invidia: Ein semasiologischer Beitrag. *Eranos* 44: 355–69.

Wistrand, Magnus. 1979. *Cicero Imperator: Studies in Cicero's Correspondence 51–47 B.C.* Studia Graeca et Latina Gothobburgensia 41. Göteborg: Acta Universitatis Gothoburgensis.

Wittgenstein, Ludwig. 1953. *Philosophical Investigations.* Oxford: Basil Blackwell.

Woodman, Anthony J., ed. 1983. *Velleius Paterculus: The Caesarian and Augustan Narrative* (2. 41–93). Cambridge: Cambridge University Press.

———, and Richard Martin, eds. 1996. *The "Annals" of Tacitus: Book 3.* Cambridge: Cambridge University Press.

Wright, M. R. 1997. *Ferox virtus*: Anger in Virgil's *Aeneid.* In *The Passions in Roman Thought and Literature,* ed. Susanna Morton Braund and Christopher Gill, pp. 169–84. Cambridge: Cambridge University Press.

Wuthnow, Robert. 1997. Repentance in Criminal Proceedure. In *Repentance: A Comparative Perspective*, ed. Amitai Etzioni and David Carney, pp. 171–86. Lanham, MD: Rowman & Littlefield.

Yegül, Fikret. 1992. *Baths and Bathing in Classical Antiquity*. New York and Cambridge, MA: Harvard University Press.

Zetzel, James E. G., ed. 1999. *Cicero: "On the Commonwealth" and "On the Laws."* Cambridge: Cambridge University Press.

INDEX OF SUBJECTS AND PERSONS

Persons are listed as they are named in the text; if a Roman's *nomen gentilicium* is used in the text, that is the name used for the listing: thus, e.g., "Antius Restio" vs. "Atticus, (Titus Pomponius)." Other elements of nomenclature or indications of identity are for the most part added only to avoid ambiguity or uncertainty: e.g., "Paris (prince of Troy)." Ancient authors are listed in the "Index of Ancient Authors and Works," by the forms of their names most commonly used in English: e.g., "Cicero," "Horace."